My best wishes
always for your
well-being,
Floyd.
And every encourage-
ment in your
ministry -

Ben

PHILOSOPHIES OF LIFE OF THE ANCIENT GREEKS AND ISRAELITES

Philosophies of Life of the Ancient Greeks and Israelites

(An analysis of their parallels)

BEN KIMPEL

PHILOSOPHICAL LIBRARY
New York

Overseas distributor: George Prior Ltd.
37-41 Bedford Row, London WC1R 4JH, England

Library of Congress Catalog Card No. 80-81697
ISBN 8022-2371-0

MANUFACTURED IN THE UNITED STATES OF AMERICA

In memory of my parents

Foreword

The thinking man has always been concerned about the nature of human life; and, in a very real sense, this has been the role of the philosopher-poet: to examine and analyze the quality of life.

Two great cultures have contributed greatly to western civilization, Israel and Greece. Certainly, Matthew Arnold, the eminent Victorian writer, recognized this in his essay *Hebraism and Hellenism*. But all too often scholars have viewed the philosophies of the ancient Greeks and Israelites as two separate and discrete unities, having little in common with each other.

Now Dr. Ben Kimpel presents in a short but provocative volume the concept that there are definite parallels between these two remarkable cultures. Dr. Kimpel draws on his excellent insight into the philosophy, the religion and the literature of both these ancient cultures and presents the reader with their concepts about the nature of life.

This is an important book. It is more than a scholarly thesis written by a respected academician, more than a philosophic dissertation developed by a man who has spent a good portion of his life in this area, more than a literary monograph—although it doubtless has the elements of all three. It is rather a book that will force both the educated layman as well as the committed scholar to rethink of his preconceived theories concerning the two cultures that may well be the cornerstones of western civilization.

The philosopher stated that the unexamined life is not worth living. Professor Kimpel has written a book that examines life and its various aspects as seen by the great minds of two prominent ancient cultures. And as such this book addresses itself to all ages and to all men.

DAGOBERT D. RUNES

Contents

x

Preface

This book is an analysis of similarities in ideas about the nature of human life as they are expressed in the literatures of two ancient cultures which have influenced western civilization. These literatures show striking parallels both in religious and moral considerations.

Acknowledging such parallelism implies giving up a long defended prejudice of the philosophical uniqueness of the Greeks. Although their merit may well be the systematic character with which they organized their reflecting, there is no comparable uniqueness in the profundity of their ideas about human life and its problems. Acknowledging such parallelism likewise implies that the reflecting which is expressed in the ancient writings of priests and prophets among the Israelites will not be attributed to a special disclosure to them, which is religiously interpreted as a revelation to one people to the exclusion of others.

Since basic problems of human life are similar, it is understandable that there should be similarities in reflecting about human life, irrespective of geographical or historical differences of cultures. Taking account of such similarities or parallelism in reflecting on the nature of human life increases one's admiration for the human mind which is not restricted to geographical or ethnic limitations, but transcends them.

In so far as the prophets and priests among the ancient Israelites affirmed thoughts about human life which are also affirmed in the literature of ancient Greece, one has evidence for a "timeless" character of profound reflecting that transcends the idiosyncracies of cultures, and admits one into a "world" of thought which increases his esteem for serious reflecting. This study attempts to point out the freedom of which the human mind is capable in being liberated from ideas which are as dated as the whims and fads that emerge for a brief time in localities, only to be displaced by others which are no more profound. Taking account of thoughts which are of a different order from such dated ideas is one way to be admitted into a

time-transcending order, whose benefit for serious human life has no equiv
alent. This study has attempted to make available such a benefit for any
one who is willing to rethink thoughts about human life as they have bee
affirmed in these two ancient cultures.

The similarity or parallelism of reflecting on the nature and problem
of human life expressed in the ancient literatures of the Israelites an
Greeks supports the premise that such ideas are so fundamental to seriou
reflecting on human life that they constitute a moral and religious philos
ophy which is as cogent today as it was for those in antiquity.

The Old Testament and apocryphal writings record ideas of a reflectiv
Semitic people who trace their origin from Jacob, a grandson of Abrahan
whose name "Jacob" was changed to "Israel", and so the term "Israelite'
as it is used in this study, refers to this people. Although several transla
tions of the Old Testament and apocrypha have been consulted, the trans
lation which is used in this book, with few exceptions, is THE NEW ENG
LISH BIBLE WITH THE APOCRYPHA, which is published by Oxford
University Press.

"Greek" likewise is a general term for denoting a culture or a civiliza
tion whose earliest known literary records are *The Odyssey* and *The Iliad*
attributed to Homer. Many ideas affirmed in these epics are also affirmed
in writings attributed to Hesiod and Theognis, but since this study is in
terested only in these ideas, it does not presume to consider scholarly prob
lems of their authorship or their probable dates. Since this is not a history
of Greece, one part of which Herodotus claims to record, it takes accoun
only of his ideas about human life as they express his reflecting about
human history.

His reflecting about the nature and problems of human life, as well a
comparable reflecting by the earlier poets, are denoted by the general term
"philosophy", since as reflective ideas, they are as "philosophical" as are
the ideas of the early Milesians, Pythagoreans, and Eleatics. Such a tradi
tion of reflecting continues in more systematic form, although not in
greater profundity of thought, in the writings of later Greek philosophers

A principal literary source for Greek ideas about human life and its
many problems is, of course, the great dramatists, Aeschylus, Sophocles
and Euripides, whose masterpieces are used in this study as sources for re
flective considerations about human life, without also presuming to consider
specifically literary problems which are outside its scope. Such scholarly
problems are considered in the commentaries to the various translations
which have been used. These include the Loeb Classical Library, published
by Harvard University Press; THE COMPLETE GREEK DRAMA

dited by Whitney J. Oates and Eugene O'Neill, Jr.; and THE COM-
PLETE GREEK TRAGEDIES, edited by David Greene and Richmond
Lattimore.

Heraclitus declared that "Men who love wisdom must enquire into very
many things." (Fragment 49) Among these "many things" which can contribute to such a wisdom are the literatures of the two ancient civilizations
which are considered in this study.

BEN KIMPEL

North Bennington
Vermont

Acknowledgments

Permissions to quote from the following copyright books are gratefully acknowledged:

THE NEW ENGLISH BIBLE, copyright: The Delegates of the Oxford University Press and the Syndics of the Cambridge University Press, 1961, 1970.

THE OLD TESTAMENT, volumes I and II, Revised Standard Version of the Bible, Thomas Nelson and Sons, New York, 1952.
Permission from the National Council of the Churches of Christ in the U.S.A. (References in the text indicated by an asterisk.)

THE ILIAD OF HOMER, translated by Richmond Lattimore, The University of Chicago Press, Chicago, 1951.

THE ILIAD, translated by E. V. Rieu, Penguin Classics, 1950. Copyright: The Estate of E. V. Rieu, 1950.

THE ODYSSEY, translated by E. V. Rieu, Penguin Classics, 1946.

THE ODYSSEY OF HOMER, translated by Richmond Lattimore, Harper and Row, New York, 1967.

THE COMPLETE GREEK TRAGEDIES, volumes I, II, III, IV, edited by David Grene and Richmond Lattimore, The University of Chicago Press, Chicago, reprints respectively: 1960, 1960, 1960, 1959.

THE COMPLETE GREEK DRAMA, edited by W. J. Oates and Eugene O'Neill, Jr., Random House, New York, 1938.
Permission from Oxford University Press to quote from F. M. Stawell's translation of *Iphigenia in Aulis* and from Gilbert Murray's translation of *The Trojan Women*.

PHILOSOPHIES OF LIFE OF THE ANCIENT GREEKS AND ISRAELITES

I

The Tragic Nature of Human Life

1. *Both the early Israelites and ancient Greeks affirm a sobering*
view of human life

The Old Testament patriarch Job refers to human life as "a hard service". He compares it to the life of "a slave who longs" for the relief of
shade after laboring throughout the day. And then he adds that even after
such a struggle for livelihood, men's nights are "troubled" with the "misery" of disturbing dreams. (7:1-3)

After Job reflected about a life of suffering, he wondered if he had the
strength to endure it, and he asked: "Is my strength the strength of
stone?" (6:12) Aware of his limited capacities to alter life's difficulties,
he asked the second question: "How shall I find help within myself?" His
answer to this question is: "In truth, I have no help in me." (vs. 13) His
realization of the limits of what he could do to help himself is, therefore,
affirmed as a premise of his philosophy of life: "Man is born to trouble."

This sobering analysis of life, consisting of "months of futility" and
"troubled nights", culminates in Job's cursing the day that he was born.
(3:1, 2)

Although his reflecting on the tragic character of life seems to be on
the borderline of disbelieving in the providence of a god, he, nevertheless,
prays that God would pity him enough to end his life: "Cut me off! For
that would bring me relief." (6:9, 10)

If one should be surprised that Job's attitude toward life is affirmed in a
scripture whose purpose is to declare the providence of a god, he would be
even more surprised to read the Old Testament book of *Ecclesiastes*, at-

3

tributed to "the son of David" and characterized as "The Words of the Preacher". (1:1) The point of view about human life which it affirms could be regarded as the primary premise of an outright philosophical nihilism. It declares that the "brief span" of human life is "empty existence" and "there is nothing good for a man to do" other than grasp at the fleeting moments of transient experiences. (7:15)

If one is distressed by the points of view expressed in the books of *Job* and *Ecclesiastes,* he will be bewildered as well as distressed when reading the book of *Jeremiah!* Notwithstanding Jeremiah's faith in the providence of God, he asks: "Why did I come forth" into a life which consists only of "sorrow". (20:18) And the full impact of this question, asked by one of the greatest of the Old Testament prophets, is readily realized in reading Oriana Fallaci's reference to this question as "that dreadful blasphemy".[1]

A bewildering experience in reading the Old Testament as an affirmation of religious faith is confronting these irreverent protests against the unfairness or injustice for having been born. One is, therefore, almost stunned that a scripture attributed to an inspiration by a god includes Job's curse of the day he was born and Jeremiah's declaration: "A curse on the day when I was born!" (20:14)

One, however, would not be so bewildered if he were to read the same assertions in philosophical writings which do not claim to be expressions of religious faith. But that writings which are revered as inspired should affirm a disbelief in the worth of life itself seems to be a basic contradiction of religious life in the providence of a god. Yet, if one respects the honesty of such reflecting, in spite of its tragic character, he moves from bewilderment to esteem for the integrity itself of such reflecting.

Reflecting of this type is declared by Isaiah: "I have labored in vain; I have spent my strength for nothing and vanity." (49:4) What is sobering about this statement is that it declares a conclusion occurring in the life of a prophet who devoted himself to what he trusted as affirming true prophecy. Such an undercutting of faith by doubt, even though momentary, should however not be disparaged as incompatible with trust in the justice of a god because it is a mode of human life consisting of a struggle through which even the most devout must go to establish a faith, strengthened by the struggle itself. Such struggle, therefore, is not floundering in "vanity". It is rather transcending the vanity of assuming that what is most important in life could come about without struggle. Often included in such a struggle, however, is an inclination to want to be free from the struggle itself, irrespective of the gains that come only through such struggle.

4

This is the type of indecisive commitment recorded in the book of *Jonah*. Jonah tried to run away from an obligation which he clearly understood he ought to respect, and the biblical account of the penalty for his attempt to run away is the graphic narrative of the sun beating down on him "till he grew faint". "Then he prayed for death and said, 'I should be better dead than alive.'" (4:8)

This statement of Jonah is not a disparagement of the worth of life. It is rather an acknowledgment of the justice for being oppressed when he tried to deny an obligation which he could not rightly dismiss. There is, therefore, a world of difference in the curses upon life uttered by Job or Jeremiah, and Jonah's admission that he "should be better dead than alive". This is Jonah's realization of the moral penalty brought upon himself for trying to shirk an obligation which he acknowledged was his duty.

Only some of the many records of men's reflecting on the perplexing problems of human life have been incorporated into institutionally approved collections or canons. Many writings whose value may equal if not surpass such canonical collections constitute noncanonical records. One such writing is *Second Esdras*, the author of which retired into a solitary country to devote himself to uninterrupted reflecting. Yet, after days of reflecting, he remained troubled by the fact that perplexing questions still were not resolved. It thus was as if his dedicated thinking accomplished nothing of all that he had hoped it would accomplish. His attempt to think through problems about "the ways of the Most High" left him "weary" and "utterly exhausted". (12:5) In this respect, of course, he differed in no way from Job.

As if anticipating Descartes, the author of *Second Esdras* is bewildered by the fact that men have the "power of thought" to reflect, and yet "are tortured by it". (7:64) His reference to men's discouragement in attempting to resolve their questions may indeed be overstated as "torture". Yet, there are many who have devoted their life to thinking and have concluded that they have only clarified the nature of their questions, without in any way achieving an understanding of the realities about whose nature they questioned.

An individual who is serious about the extent of men's moral responsibilities cannot help being distressed by the fact that the scope of moral responsibilities includes neither the occasion for life's beginning nor the time of its ending, as the philosophical author of this apocryphal writing points out: "Without your consent you came here, and unwillingly you go away." Thus the scope of life within which men's moral decisions can be made does not include two occurrences which, nevertheless, are of utmost moral significance to them. In other words, it is only after one is born and before he dies that he has the opportunity to make choices which come within the range of his moral responsibility. What is also sobering for this reflective person is that even the length of time during which a human being is intellectually mature enough to make moral choices is short: "Only a brief span of life is given you." (8:5, 6)

This fact is sobering enough. But it is even more sobering to reflect on the conditions which further restrict opportunities for genuine choice. Before an individual has reached an age of maturity in which he can exercise morally responsible choice, his capacity to do so is decreased by the very contexts in which he lives. He unconsciously absorbs the biases and prejudices of others which impair or "corrupt" his own so-called "freedom". In light of the conditioning of his thinking and his nature by the thinking and natures of others, he is not "morally free", but rather is in bondage to the prejudices of all who influence his life. This fact troubled the reflective author of this writing, attributed to "the prophet Ezra". He declares: "A man corrupted by the corrupt world can never know the way of the incorruptible." (4:11) This tragic fact, of course, is true, and the admonitions, therefore, of Scripture itself that men should prepare themselves diligently to know "the will of God", in order to conform to His commandments, are thus confronted by this disturbing fact.

This author anticipates a doctrine basic to the canonical writings of St. Paul when he declares that "every man alive is burdened and defiled with wickedness", and therefore is "a sinner through and through". (7:68, 69) St. Paul's emphasis upon the universal depravity of human life became fundamental in the thought of St. Augustine, and through him, it became basic to Luther's analysis of the tragic plight of human life which is totally dependent upon Jesus Christ for salvation from its own evil nature.

There is, of course, no such christology in *Second Esdras*. What constitutes the most tragic aspect of human life for its author is that men cannot "explain" or understand the "world of wickedness and suffering". His despair about life thus arises from his characteristically Greek way of thinking that the human being's essential nature is his capacity to think, and it is this rational capacity which cannot resolve the very problems of which men themselves become reflectively aware. He declares that it would, therefore, have been "Better never to have come into existence than to be born into a world of wickedness and suffering which we cannot *explain*!" (4:12, 13)

6

Another basis for his sense of life's tragic character is its inevitable end. And what intensifies his sense of its tragic nature is that men are reflectively aware of the fact that they must die. He declares: "We are doomed to die and we know it," and this brings about a "sorrow for mankind". (7; 65) From this point of view, the brevity of life as such is not the cause for sorrow so much as is the reflective anticipation of its inescapable brevity. He is sobered by his awareness that death cannot indefinitely be deferred by anything that men can do. Rethinking his analysis of the human plight enables one to understand something of the nature of the Gospel as St. Paul interprets it that Jesus Christ can do for men what they cannot do for themselves. But without this faith which St. Paul affirms, the author of *Second Esdras* disparages the status of human life in contrast to the more enviable status of nonreflective animals. He declares: "How much better their lot than ours", and the reason for this envy of their nature is that they do not project reflecting into a future. According to him, it is such projecting of thought about a destiny of human life which troubles the human being and causes one of his intensest sorrows. He believes that if men could live without anxiety about a future, they would be spared from the oppressive uncertainty of their destiny. This way of thinking, therefore, parallels the Greek philosopher Epicurus's way of thinking since he also maintained that if men did not believe there was a future beyond this present life, they could enjoy this life more than they do when they do not restrict their thought to the span of this life alone. Thus for the author of *Second Esdras* it is not only the fear of a future punishment which constitutes a blight upon men's happiness, but it is also an anxiety about the uncertainty itself of a future beyond death. In his statement about the more desirable nature of animal life, he points out that animals "have no knowledge of torment or salvation after death". (vs. 66)

Another indication of this author's philosophical daring is his questioning of the Creator's scheme to have made man with the inclination to do wrong, when such acting constitutes the basis itself for a condemnation by his own creator. This way of thinking may certainly seem irreverent to those whose religious faith outweighs their need to reflect. Yet, insofar as a religious interpretation attributes men's capacities for reflecting to a divine creator, it gives the Creator credit for this ability for "irreverent" questioning. But what constitutes such so-called "irreverence" when reflecting is honest is not a philosophical question, since philosophy is reflecting without self-imposed limits.

Although the author of *Second Esdras* raises questions which were not raised in the canonical books already cited, he, nevertheless, comes to the tragic conclusion which is very much the same as theirs. He asks: "For what good does it do us all to live in misery now." (7:47)

This philosophical author's way of thinking is furthermore affirmed when he reflects about the validity of rationality itself. As a skeptical philosopher would do, he questions the validity of reasoning, and he concludes that if "the mind of man" is no more than "a product of the dust", such as Scripture proposes in its account of creation, "Far better then if the very dust had never been created, and so had never produced man's mind!" (7:63)

It would hardly be possible for a reflective person to entertain a more devastating idea since he would be using his capacity to think to disparage the capacity itself. This recoil of reflecting upon itself certainly reminds one of the wisdom of the Greeks who maintained that going beyond limits is evil! Using one's capacity to reflect to depreciate the capacity itself, however, is other than a strictly philosophical procedure. It is a basic immorality: it denies that there is moral dignity in devoting one's life to serious reflecting even though some of it may be painful and bewildering.

In light of the disparagement of the human being's chief merit, which is his reflecting, it is no great surprise that the writings of *Second Esdras* were not included in the biblical canon formulated by a religious institution. It is also understandable that *Ecclesiasticus* was likewise not included in this canon, since it declares that "When you are born, you are born to a curse, and when you die, a curse is your lot". (41:9) Thinking this way about the tragic character of human life accounts for its author's proposal, which is identical with Solon's: "Call no man happy before he dies." (11:27)

The tragic character of human history, with its endlessly recurring wars, certainly cannot be ignored by anyone who seriously thinks. Yet, a mere reminder that wars recur to cancel men's achievements is so devastating to encouragement that it is understandable that writings such as *Ecclesiasticus* (also known as "The Wisdom of Jesus Son of Siarch"), were not included in a canon whose purpose is to reinforce faith in the providence of God. In light of this principle, it is also understandable that *First Maccabees* is not included in the Canon, since it includes the sobering question asked by Mattathias, the father of Judas Maccabeus, after he saw "the sacrilegious acts committed in Judaea and Jerusalem": "Oh! Why was I born to see this, the crushing of my people, the ruin of the holy city?" (2:7) Even though Mattathias was a priest, his faith in the

8

ustice of Providence was put to a stern test when he took account of the oppressive rule of Antiochus IV of Syria, whose disrespect for the religion of the Israelites was expressed in his intolerant attempt to Hellenize their culture.

Although the terms "Hellenic" and "Greek" were used only after an earlier use of "Attic" or "Achean", the term "Greek" may, nevertheless, be used to refer to the historical background out of which the history of Athenian culture emerged. If this terminology is understood, it may then be said that there is a parallel in the Greek sense of the tragic nature of human life and in the Old Testament writings, as well as in the Apocrypha, which retains the reflecting of priests and prophets of ancient Judah and Israel, referred to in this writing as "Israelites".

Just as the dates for the earliest writings included in the Old Testament canon and Apocrypha are uncertain or unknown, so likewise are the dates for the earliest of the great Greek epics, the *Iliad* and *Odyssey,* traditionally ascribed to Homer. The problems of dates and authorship can be discussed only by specialists, but in this study of the parallelism of concepts of two cultures, Greek and Hebrew, it is sufficient to point out similarities in the uncertainty of dates and authorship of the earliest literature of both of these peoples. If the author (or authors) of the two great epics of the Greeks is regarded either as early as the twelfth century B.C., or as late as the eighth century, these dates then are comparable to the dates assigned to the earliest Old Testament sources, transmitted orally for centuries before being reduced to written form.[2]

What is significant for this study is that the two great epics in the history of the Greeks affirm points of view which in basic respects are similar to and even identical with points of view affirmed in both the Old Testament and in the apocryphal writings of the Israelites. Even though the early literature of Greece has no general term for "religion", its point of view about the nature of human life in relation to a reality transcendent of it is a basic characteristic also of the religious literature of the Israelites.[3]

These epics, attributed to Homer, affirm a fundamentally religious philosophy of human history since they declare on many occasions in the narrative of human events that men are under the judgment of gods. Whatever the particular theology about such deities may be, it is secondary to the fact that these earliest expressions of Greek literature affirm the same basic conviction as the earliest literature of the Israelites. It is that men are not the ultimate determiners of their destiny. They are subordinate rather to a reality transcendent of human life which includes

within its authority or its sovereignty, the final or the ultimate determination of men's destiny.

No one, therefore, could read these early epics without being impressed
by their philosophy of history, which affirms some version of a theology
even though this theology has no similarity to a consistent monotheism.
It is rather as polytheistic as are the cultures which bordered on the
kingdoms of Judah and Israel, and which threatened the monotheistic
philosophy of history affirmed by the principal leaders of the Israelites.

Both epics, whether the product of one author or of more than one,
affirm interpretations of gods who control human destiny and who regard
human beings as pathetic. As Rieu points out: "They take men seriously
and regard them as miserable".[4] The eighth book of the *Iliad* interprets
the goddess Here as "sorry for men when she saw their plight." Scully
maintains that "the *Iliad* is the most realistic statement ever made of
the helplessness of the individual before the facts of force, and the noblest
statement as well, since it recognizes that all men, native or foreign, Greek
or Trojan, suffer the same".[5]

This generalization might also be regarded as a premise in the philosophy of human life affirmed in the Old Testament and in the writings in
the Apocrypha.

The ancient literatures of both Greeks and Israelites are accounts of
the tragic nature of human beings who make choices which bring upon
them the misfortunes from which they suffer. As Lattimore points out,
"the Iliad is a story of people."[6] The same may be said of the Old
Testament and of the Apocrypha. These ancient writings express the
consequences of decisions made by men which are always under the final
sovereignty of a reality transcendent of them as the ultimate determiner
of their destiny.

If "religion" is defined as all that men do to relate themselves to "the
power or powers which they conceive as having ultimate control over their
interests and destinies", then the basic orientation of the two ancient
epics is as genuinely religious as are the writings in the Bible.[7]

If both the terms "religion" and "theology" are used with some latitude,
it is understandable why Rieu should refer to the author of the epics as
the "first theologian" whom "the Greeks accepted" and "the creator of
the Olympian religion".[8] Scully also points out that the Greeks regarded
Homer "as their first great religious teacher and his poetry as the bible
of their civilization".[9]

If the term "theology" denotes discourse about the nature of god or
gods, then the Greek interpretation of an ultimate determiner of human

estiny cannot be restricted to a theology. It is prior to any philosophy
f history in terms of a deity or deities. Its basic premise is that there
s a determiner of human history which is other than a god. It is Fate
r Destiny. But the conviction that there is a reality transcendent of
nen and of human history is basic to the earliest literature of the Greeks
n the Epics, and it is also basic to their first historian, Herodotus,
.nd basic likewise to the three greatest of their tragic dramatists, Aeschylus,
;ophocles, and Euripides.

Underlying all of this serious Greek literature is a conviction which is
.ffirmed in the sixth book of the *Iliad* when Helen predicts that her
[rojan husband, Paris, "one day will suffer" for the outrage of disregard-
ng the sacred character of hospitality which her Spartan husband, Men-
:laus, had extended to him. In spite of whatever is censurable in the be-
aavior of Helen, the *Iliad* at least points out that she was oppressed by
aer conscience for the wrong she had done, not only in her infidelity to
Menelaus, but also for the evil of the Trojan War. Reflecting on the evils
'or which she had been responsible, she confides to the Trojan Prince
Hector that she was unworthy to live, and expressed the wish that she
had been destroyed on the day of her birth: "Ah how I wish that on
:he very day when my mother bore me . . . the waves had overwhelmed
ne before all this could happen."[10]

Her acknowledgment that it would have been better if she had never
)een born or had been destroyed at birth affirms a parallel to the profoundest tragic character of human life affirmed in ancient Hebrew liter-
.ture. The same judgment upon the tragic nature of human life is affirmed
by Theognis, the sixth century B.C. elegaic poet of Megara, extant fragments of whose writings include the tragic admission that "Never to have
been born at all would be the best thing for mortals. . . . Or, once born,
to hasten quickly through the gates of Hades, and lie down heaped over
with earth."[11]

The same sense of the tragic nature of human life was affirmed in the
following century by the great dramatist Sophocles, whose chorus in
Oedipus at Colonus declares that anyone "who craves excess of days",
thereby wanting more than "the common span of life", would have to be
regarded as inferior in reflective maturity. This disparagement of anyone
not sufficiently sobered by life's suffering to be satisfied with the "normal"
span of life could not have offended the thousands of Greeks who attended
the theaters. If Sophocles' disparagement had offended them by running
counter to their own reflective sobriety about life, it is unlikely that he
would have been awarded the first prize among Greek dramatists as many

11

as eighteen or twenty times. His chorus which characterizes the "grievous load" and the "weary road" of human life speaks for more than himself. He affirms a basic Greek view that "come it slow or fast" the "doom of fate doth all await". And rather than affirming the wish that such doom might be deferred and the duration of life extended, he affirms that death is the "deliverer which freeth all at last". What would be regarded as oppressive in cultures not prepared to acknowledge the sober character of human life must have been regarded by the thousands of Greeks who attended his plays as a sound appraisal of the serious nature of human life. Hence they were not offended by the chorus which affirms that "Not to be born at all is best", but it is even better after one is born "with least delay to trace the backward way".[12]

Euripides' view about the tragic nature of human life is in every respect the same as the views of Aeschylus and Sophocles. And the fact that he was awarded the first prize several times in dramatic contests may be construed as evidence that the views which the characters in his plays affirm were not outside the scope of what the spectators regarded as credible and even as defensible expressions of a philosophy about human life. The nurse in his *Hippolytus* laments "the ills of mortal men" augmented by "the cruel diseases they endure", and then generalizes about the tragic character of human life by saying that "Man's whole life is full of anguish" and there is "no respite from his woes".[13] In addition to the sobering awareness that life has more than its fair share of "bitter pain", man is also made clearly aware that he knows nothing of what awaits him after the end of his life of "affliction". "There speak no voices from the tomb" is a view which no reflective Greek could challenge.[14] Fewer, of course, would agree with the outright cynicism affirmed by the Nurse when she continues to disparage the limited range of man's knowledge by declaring: "We drift on fable's shadowy stream." Or as another translation affirms: "Trusting to fables we drift at random."[15]

This sobering philosophy of the tragic character of human life cannot be attributed to any purely personal failure in the life of Euripides. His philosophy is not merely "defeatism".[16] It is rather a reaffirmation of the philosophy of Solon which persisted in the reflective life of the Greeks from the sixth century after which Solon's intelligence earned for him the tribute of being one of the "Seven Wise Men of Greece". Andromache in Euripides' play by the same name declares the same generalization attributed to Solon: "Never mayst thou call any mortal blest." Another translation affirms: " 'Tis never right to call a son of man happy, till thou hast seen his end."[17]

2. Both early Israelites and ancient Greeks stress the limits with which human beings are confronted in controlling their own well-being

A reflective individual is aware of limits both in his abilities and also in his knowledge. He is aware of the restricted nature of his intelligence and his resources when confronted with many occurrences in life over which he does not have final control. He, therefore, does not need to be reminded by *Job* that he cannot "bind the cluster of the Pleiades or loose Orion's belt."

Anyone who realizes that there is much which he cannot do is also aware that there is much which he can do. He, therefore, is likewise not impressed with the argument of *Job* that man cannot "proclaim the rules that govern the heavens". (38:31-33) These limits are so obvious that no sensible individual would be inclined to protest what Job regards as evidence for the limited nature of a human being's capacities.

On the other hand, anyone would agree with *Job* that human beings do not even "comprehend the expanses of the earth" to say nothing about being unable to "guide Aldebaran and its train". But on the basis of enumerating all that the human being cannot do—most of which isn't very cogent—Job declares that the human being is "only a handful of clay". A less disparaging translation is that man was "formed from a piece of clay".[18]

Although Job reaffirms the picturesque account in *Genesis* of man's origin from the materials of earth, he goes far beyond the estimate of Genesis about man's nature when he compares a human being to "straw before the wind, and like chaff that the storm-wind carries away." (21: 18) This estimate of man's instability and incompetency would seem excessively depreciatory even of most animals who brave adversities of weather in their efforts to survive. But Job's underlying purpose for this disparagement of human self-sufficiency is obvious. It is his way of arguing that men do not determine either all of the events which occur in their life or the outcome of their life. His insistence upon what is beyond men's control is his way of affirming a religious interpretation of human life. According to his argument, human beings are limited and so are not the final determiners of their destiny. Men's inability to control handicaps produced by weather, to control many diseases, to prevent the inevitable decrease of their physical strength as they age, are only some of the many aspects of reality which no sensible person would deny as limits with which men are confronted. All that Job declares about the limits of human capacities is, therefore, a way to support his religious

13

premise that men are related to realities which are not within their final control. Hence he argues that a human being "deceives himself" when he trusts in his own self-sufficiency and places a "high rank" upon himself (15:31) What he affirms in stressing the limits of human capacities thus is for the purpose of stressing a human being's confrontation with realities other than himself which set limits to what he can do, and so set limits to what he can sensibly presume to be.

Isaiah even outdoes Job in reminding men that they are not the ultimate reality, but rather are subordinate to it in its final sovereignty over their lives. Hence his philosophy of history is summed up in declaring that "nations are like a drop from a bucket". This comparison also is for the religious purpose of arguing that whereas nations emerge for a time in the course of history, they also disappear. And after centuries, their significance in the total span of human life is the same as a single drop after it has fallen from a bucket. In a tragic sense, the history of a people or a country in relation to the centuries of human struggle is something of the character of "the dust on the scale". (40:15)* The scale continues to exist after dust collected on its surface does not. This can be swept off its surface as a civilization can be swept from the surface of the earth by some vast catastrophe. Isaiah's purpose in arguing in this manner is to stress the limits with which men are confronted in their relation to occurrences over which they do not have final control. His argumentative reason for affirming that the earth's inhabitants "are like grasshoppers" is stressing that their duration is brief in contrast to the Eternal whose sovereignty envelops the earth, and whose status in contrast to the nature of human beings is as one enthroned "on the vaulted roof of earth".

What is significant in this figure of a final determinant of human destiny transcendent of earth itself is not the dated cosmology of concentric circles at the center of which is earth. What is significant is the religious philosophy of human history. Human history according to Isaiah is under the final sovereignty of an eternal reality which reduces "the inhabitants of the height" or of the most "lofty city" to the lowest level of impotence. Before this reality, even the most "fortified city" is not capable of determining its own future. Isaiah thus affirms the sense of a destiny which is not within human control when he declares: "He has brought low the inhabitants of the height, the lofty city." (26:5) The poignant sense of the brevity of what is mightiest among men's achievements is summed up in his comment that even "the fortified city is left solitary" and her history ends in God's "brushing her away".[19]

Almost identically the same view of the limits of human beings is af-

14

firmed in the early centuries of Greece. As has been pointed out, Homer repeatedly stresses "the helplessness of the individual before the facts of force".[20] One such example in the *Odyssey* is the discourse of Odysseus with Amphinomous when he asks him to "listen carefully" while he points out that "Of all creatures that breathe and creep about on Mother Earth, there is none so helpless as a man". He supports this sobering disparagement of mankind by saying that men do not even think that there are difficult ordeals in their future so long as they have not already encountered them: "As long as heaven leaves man in prosperity and health, he never thinks hard times are on their way."[21] In other words, the range of a man's thinking is limited to whatever comes his way as he wishes it to come. But when there are changes in his fortune, he learns little from such tragic occurrences, being oriented only to thinking of what is favorable to himself. This is basically a moral weakness since it is a deficiency of character to forget lessons that should be retained for their value in enlightening one of the precarious nature of his well-being and of the unpredictable aspects of his life which can so quickly cancel his good fortune.

Homer's religious philosophy of history is affirmed by Odysseus when he declares that "the blessed gods bring misfortune" even though it does not fit into the hopeful expectation of human beings who anticipate only what is favourable, as if this were an established certainty. Being intellectually unprepared to accept the inevitable reverses in life, a human being is thus dislocated by shock when his good fortune terminates. But as Homer emphasizes, good fortune is not the consistent scheme of any human life. According to him, no one is exempt from sorrow, suffering, and the gravest of reverses. Since these occur so universally in human life, Homer infers that they are included in divine intentions that such is the nature of all life other than the "blessed gods" themselves. In this analysis both of the precarious nature of human fortune and the character-weakness of the human being in failing to learn that such is the inescapable nature of life, Homer established himself as the first great moralist among the ancient predecessors of the later Athenian moralists. The Stoics of Athens might well have traced their sensible moral principles to Homer's wisdom and courage to recognize that suffering is integral to human life, and therefore it is moral wisdom both to acknowledge it as inevitable and to accept life on these stern terms. Although they give credit to Socrates for this philosophy, it actually was affirmed by Homer centuries before Socrates.

If one accepts a ninth century date for Homer, then another very influential individual in the history of ancient Greece might well be looked upon as four centuries later in Herodotus, esteemed as the "Father of His-

15

tory". His history of the Greco-Persian wars from 500 to 479 is as much a religious philosophy of history as are the epics attributed to Homer. And his comments upon the men who influenced the history of the world which he discusses are also as much genuine moral philosophy as are the Epics If philosophy is serious thinking about aspects of human life and reality which confront an individual with problems sufficient to challenge him to think as seriously as he can about them, then the beginning of Greek philosophy is long before the Ionian school. It begins with Homer and Hesiod. And an eminently worthy member of this tradition is also Herodotus.

The primary premise in what may be looked upon as Herodotus' moral philosophy is that "there was no mortal (before Xerxes) nor ever would be, to whom at birth some admixture of misfortune was not allotted".[22] Anyone with maturity of character would, therefore, take this universal fact into account in preparing himself for such inevitable reverses and such inescapable disappointments. The moral benefit of accepting this fundamental premise about life is that it enables a human being to cultivate a capacity to understand what life actually is. He thereby acquires the benefit of enlightened life which is not an inherited equipment with which anyone begins the struggle to cope with the reverses of life. It is rather a supremely important achievement because it saves one from being tossed about by events over which he has no control when he has not prepared himself in time to be fortified for their occurrence. Herodotus' comments on the disaster of Xerxes—notwithstanding the vast armaments and the hundreds of thousands of soldiers with whom he invaded Greece—are in the form of a philosophy about the nature of human life. He declares that "the invader of Hellas was no god, but a mortal man". He would, therefore have shown the intelligence of moral maturity had he taken into account the high likelihood that his invasion would collide with occurrences over which he had no control, such as the storms which destroyed hundreds of his ships and thousands of his men. On the other hand, he showed his essential immaturity of character when, confronted by reverses at the Hellespont, he ordered the violent waves to be beaten for not respecting his wishes and his plans. In spite of his ability to dominate men and nations, he was a fool in his failure to acknowledge the limits of his capacities to control and determine adversities which thwarted his plans. As Herodotus points out, "being but mortal" he was not morally prepared to be "disappointed of his hope".[23]

In addition to Herodotus' unmistakable qualifications as a moral philosopher, he is equally admirable for the consistency with which he interreted occurrences from the premise of a divine determinant in human history. He declares that "It is not we (the Greeks) that have won this victory (over Xerxes and his forces), but the gods and the heroes".[24] The addition of "the heroes" in Herodotus' acknowledgment of the forces which accounted for the victory of the Greeks is not a weakening of his religious interpretation since the character of heroes, from his point of view, is also a reality other than the nature of ordinary nonheroic human beings. It is as transcendent of common men as are the gods, since the heroism of the few towers over the weakness of the many as certainly as deities are other than occurrences in human history.

Herodotus interprets the defeat of the Persians as an expression of a divine wisdom which "deemed Asia and Europe too great a realm for one man to rule, and that a wicked man and an impious; one that dealt alike with temples and homes, and burnt and overthrew the images of the gods".[25] This analysis is as definitely a theology as any affirmation in the Bible. It affirms the same fundamental religious belief as the writings of the Prophets in the Old Testament who also were convinced that human history is not finally determined by what men plan to do. It is determined by a reality whose jurisdiction over men is just, such as men's practices are not.

Herodotus' religious philosophy of history affirms the conviction that there are limits beyond which men cannot go in desecrating the sacred. From his point of view, the grounds surrounding a temple are not merely conventional bounds, whose designation as "holy" is merely abritrary. He believes that the function of the temple as the place for the indwelling of a divine reality confers sacredness or holiness upon whatever is associated with it. Hence the justice for the defeat of the impious Persian for whom temples were merely buildings constructed by men.

As a religious person, Herodotus believed that the purpose for which men constructed temples determined the nature of the temples. This way of interpreting the function of temples expresses a religious philosophy both of men's worship of the Divine and also men's subordination to the Divine. According to Herodotus, the final judgment upon men who transgress the limits established by the temenos or sacred temple-ground is not men's doing. It is done to men by a reality other than men. This belief is the fundamental religious orientation with which Herodotus wrote his account of human history.

Included in his religious version of history is also a moral philosophy that men bring upon themselves suffering and misfortune which they could avoid were they to understand and respect the limits which they cannot transgress without penalty. This same basic conviction, which is both re-

17

ligiously and morally profound, is fundamental to the versions of human life in the dramas of the great tragedians of the sixth and fifth centuries B.C.

Aeschylus, as Homer and Hesiod before him, was convinced that men's disregard for what it would be wise for them to do accounts for their suffering and their sorrows. Men's limitless ambitions bring about wars, which, as Aeschylus points out, "stain the ground". The King of Argos in *The Suppliant Maidens* comments on the "sea of ruin, fathomless and impassable" brought about by the wrongdoing of men. And by virtue of their wickedness, "nowhere is there a haven from distress".[26] The "affliction (which) wandereth impartially abroad and alighteth upon all in turn" is affirmed by Prometheus in *Prometheus Bound*.[27] This is brought about by men's folly and madness.

Aeschylus does not maintain that human beings are driven by vindictive forces transcendent of themselves to commit outrages against other human beings and sacrileges against the gods. Such offenses are committed by men themselves and they could be averted by what men also could do. But men cannot control the justice with which their wrongdoing is punished. This is the working of a reality over which they have no control and under whose sovereignty they suffer for their failures to overcome their weaknesses of character.

Euripides' indictment of human beings for their responsibility to bring about their own misfortunes affirms in every respect the moral philosophy and the philosophy of history basic to the dramas of Aeschylus. He declares the same fact of tragic human history that "There is not a man alive that hath wholly escaped misfortune's taint".[28] He does not consistently trace the cause for such misfortune to a source other than human beings. By virtue of their own follies, men bring upon themselves their most tragic misfortunes. They fail to use their intelligence for an effective directing of their actions to bring about their well-being. The Chorus in *Ion* declares: "How numberless the ills to mortal man, and various in their form."[29] But underlining all of these misfortunes, with their inevitable suffering, is the folly of human beings whose madness they themselves could have controlled had they disciplined themselves and thereby made a fundamental difference in their characters.

Acting which expresses character can be altered only as character is cultivated, and the cultivation of character is the responsibility of a human being. The tragic suffering, therefore, which is brought about in human life as the concomitant of human folly is the inevitable penalty for men's moral failures to do other than what they most often do. The inevitability of this sequence is not men's making. It is rather judgment upon what they do, and this judgment is not within their control. What is within their control is the cultivation of character, which when cultivated in time, could alter what would otherwise be men's tragic destiny. This is a type of destiny which is not initiated by any reality transcendent of men themselves, since it is brought about by what men themselves fail to do. Their failure is their responsibility when they could have learned in time to do other than what entails their misfortune and their suffering. Suffering from moral failure is a stern relationship which is not within men's province after men themselves act in ways which entail their inevitable misfortune.

Because moral negligence is universal, human suffering from moral failure is likewise universal. Hence the chorus in Euripides' *Hippolytus* affirms this tragic generalization of human life when it declares: "I dare not name of mortals any man happy."[30] Man's life and so his well-being are contingent not only upon what he himself does, but also upon what others do whose acting makes a fundamental difference in his life.

The impairment of one person's happiness by the acting of another indeed seems unjust and unfair. But it is a fact, and this fact itself constitues the ground for a moral challenge. The challenge is that no one has the right to be negligent in doing less than he could do to discipline himself and so to control his acting which adversely affects the life of anyone else. This challenge might well be regarded as a universal moral imperative. If it were respected, the nature of human life would be other than what it is. If men were respectful of their obligations to control themselves by intelligence and discipline so that they would not handicap the life of another and bring about suffering and sorrow for another, the tragic character of human life would come within human control. If there were such moral determining of human relations, human life would not be "born to suffering", such as Electra declares.

What Euripides affirms about human life, "full of tears", is a judgment upon human wrongdoing.[31] Wrongdoing entails suffering. The relation between the wrong of which men are capable, and for which they are responsible, is inescapably related to the suffering brought about by such wrongdoing. The inescapable relation has the inevitability which is a property of the Greek notion of Fate. But Fate, as a factor other than human life, expresses the Greeks' awareness that the penalty entailed in what men do that is wrong is a judgment upon men which they cannot avert except by cultivating a character which enables them to act without doing evil either to themselves or to others. When the nurse declares to Phaedra in *Hippolytus* that "suffering for mortals is nature's iron law", she states Euripides' philosophy of the inescapable correlation between suffering and its antecedent of human wrongdoing.[32]

The foregoing interpretation of Euripides' philosophy of history, as affirmed by characters in his tragic dramas, may seem inconsistent with what he has Hecuba, Queen of Troy, say when she declares: "Lo, I have seen the open hand of God; and in it nothing, nothing, save the rod of mine affliction." But this same statement also continues with a qualification when it mentions "the eternal hate, beyond all lands, chosen and lifted great for Troy". This explanation for the affliction of herself, her royal family, and the people of her kingdom, does not include a reference to a divine reality. It refers only to the enemies of Troy who have laid siege to it and its people. Her disparagement of the futility of "prayer and incense and bulls' blood on the altars" is, therefore, not so much her disbelief in the efficacy of religious practices directed to a divine reality as it is her disbelief that such practices can alter the hatred of the rulers of Argos who led a military expedition against Troy, and enlisted the support of all other rulers whom they could persuade to join them. Thus in this single declaration by the Queen in *The Trojan Women*, Euripides attributes the inevitability of the suffering of one people to the hate of other people who are their enemies.[33] This much sound philosophy of history can readily be extracted from the mythological aspects of the drama, such as a divine parentage for Helen, whose escape from Sparta to Ilium provides a colorful appeal for the story, such as a sobering moral philosophy could not do. Although the drama is not for the purpose of moral instruction, it certainly conveys it. The moral philosophy and the philosophy of history with which Euripides conceives the structure of his dramas are fundamental to their tragic character. Apart from these, they would be on the level of mere story telling and amusement. Their function, from the point of view of Euripides, is serious instruction: it is a confrontation of human life with the sobering aspects of it which no sensible individual can discount as incidental. Moral failures of men are basic to the tragic character of human history.

The tragic nature of human history is the inevitability of the consequences of men's moral failures. This correlation between human wrongdoing and the penalty which human beings suffer for it is other than human acting. As such, it is transcendent both of what men do and of what they neglect to acknowledge. It is thus judgment upon their moral deficiencies.

The chorus in *Heracles* affirms Euripides' sobering awareness of the universal plight of human beings who suffer from human wrongdoing: "With grief and many a bitter tear we go our way, robbed of all we prized most learly."[34] Another translation of this last line of this tragic play may be looked upon as summing up Euripides' philosophy of human history: "With mourning and weeping sore do we pass away."[35] The tragedy of human life is loving what is subject to destruction by the wickedness and cruelty of human beings.

3. Early Israelites and ancient Greeks alike correlate excessive good fortune with a threat of misfortune

A distrust of good fortune is affirmed again and again by both the early Israelites and the ancient Greeks. They stress the uncertainty of what most people regard as good fortune. Job declares that a man may be both rich and poor within the course of a single day: "He goes to bed rich, but will do so no more; he opens his eyes, and his wealth is gone." (27:19) The same uncertainty which overshadows men's wealth casts a comparable gloom upon the insecurity of their political and social achievements: "For a moment they rise to the heights, but are soon gone." (24:24) This sobering sense of the uncertainty of whatever men esteem as worth their struggle to achieve is summed up by Job in a condensed philosophy of human history: "Men die in a moment, in the middle of the night" and "the mighty vanish though no hand is laid on them." (34:20)

Reflecting on the uncertainty of retaining things for which human beings struggle is as ancient as the earliest origins of the Israelites. It is basic to the *Psalms*. The Psalmist declares what many would also say when they seriously reflect: "The riches" for which men strive "are no more than vapour" and man himself is "only a puff of wind". (39:5, 6) This comparison of the insubstantial nature of wind and human life is used by the Psalmist to appraise not only the strivings of men, but even their thoughts, which he says are "but a puff of wind". (94:11)

This disparagement, of course, is not from the perspective merely of men's achievements. It is rather a contrast of the transiency of men's achievements with a reality other than human beings which is not subject to the same uncertainty as the goods in which men invest their trust. The Psalmist's repeated comparison of human life to the nature of wind thus has its basis in a religious metaphysic whose primary premise is that there is an eternal reality which is not subject to change, such as is everything other than it. It is in contrast to this eternal reality, therefore, that the Psalmist points out that "mortal men . . . pass by like a wind and never return". (78:39) According to the criterion of duration, men have the same transient status as every living thing on earth. "Men are like oxen,"

21

says the Psalmist, "whose life cannot last." (49:20) And of course, the life of men cannot last beyond highly restricted limits on a principle which Aristotle likewise is sensible enough to acknowledge: "Everything that eats must die." This generalization made by Aristotle, therefore, is no more disparaging of the nature of human beings in comparison with non-human forms of life than is the Psalmist's. It is merely a generalization about the comparative brevity of human life in contrast to a reality other than transient life. The ninetieth psalm attributed to "A Prayer of Moses" acknowledges that "our years die away like a murmur". Another translation is that "our years come to an end like a sigh". (90:9) This is not cynical or even despondent. It is merely understanding that there is no sensible way to ignore the brevity of human life./

Whatever Isaiah affirms about the uncertain duration of men's accomplishments could also be included in the discourse of Job, since both affirm the same sobering version of the inability of men to control the accidents which threaten their transient achievements. Isaiah declares: "The pride of men shall be brought low" when the things to which they cling, with the mistaken notion that they can permanently possess them, slip from their grasp. (2:17) He declares that even "the wisdom of their wise men shall vanish". (29:14)

Isaiah interprets the uncertain aspects of human life from the point of view of a theistic philosophy of history. According to this way of interpreting human history, human beings are under the scrutiny of God, and therefore it is God who pronounces judgment upon men by taking from them what they grasp as if it were secure. Such tenacious grasping, according to Isaiah, expresses the human delusion which mistakes ephemeral goods for security. Isaiah declares that God's judgment "reduces the great to nothing" and is not deflected even by the most mighty of the earth's powerful, since even "earth's princes" are reduced to "less than nothing". Under such judgment, men "wither away" and their achievements are reduced to the status of "chaff". (40:23-24)

Jeremiah's sobering commentary on human life and its achievements is as well known as are the reflectings of Job, and a knowledge of the history of Israel enables one to understand the factual basis for his reflecting. He predicted the destruction of Jerusalem on the basis of observable tendencies which his contemporaries refused to acknowledge. His prediction of its destruction was affirmed when its people were still impressed with its glory, such as its imposing "palaces". Although he too was aware of how "delightful and lovely" the great city was, he also was aware of the penalty for its practices and its policies. These he regarded as the grounds for its inability to survive, notwithstanding its power and its preëminence as a city of importance, wealth, and influence.

Jeremiah saw his predictions confirmed, and, therefore, in retrospect spoke about "How solitary lies the city, once so full of people! . . . once queen among provinces". His lament that "Joy has fled from our hearts, and our dances are turned to mourning" is a commentary on what took place which confirmed his awareness of what was inevitable on the basis of people's presumption that their future was secure notwithstanding their follies.[36] Most of his contemporaries were not morally courageous enough to take account of what was taking place as evidence for anticipating what most likely will subsequently take place. This is the principle of prophecy, the foundations for it are neither sulphur fumes exuding from the earth nor glass globes which fortune-tellers manipulate to their advantage. The foundations for genuine prophecy, such as Jeremiah's, are courageous observations of what has taken place as a consequence of what has previously taken place. And it is on the basis of this knowledge that what is highly likely to occur in a future is foretold. Such foresight is possible for anyone who is both sufficiently aware of what has been and is also courageous enough to take account of what is therefore likely to be repeated. After the destruction of Jerusalem "in the days of her affliction and bitterness", everyone recalled, as the Prophet points out, "all the precious things that were hers from days of old".[37] But the penalty for not having sufficient intelligence to see the relation between unsound practice and the tragic penalty for it is what Jeremiah refers to as being "hurled down from heaven to earth".[38] In other words, what once was "the glory of Israel" remained only a memory.

All that Jeremiah affirms both in the Old Testament book entitled *Jeremiah* and also in *Lamentations* is based upon a philosophy of history identical with Isaiah's. Their philosophy of history is based upon a belief in a reality transcendent of human beings which passes judgment upon their folly for not doing what they might have done had they taken full advantage of their abilities to remember what had previously taken place as a means to understand what might again take place. Such moral accountability for their failure is based upon the assumption that there is a lawful, and so a predictable, relation of events. The Old Testament prophets interpret this lawful relation as one expression of God's final sovereignty over human beings. Hence the unsoundness of men's presumption that by what they themselves do in building their "fortified towns" they will be assured security. Such mistaken security is an antecedent to the "rubble" of their ineffectual schemes. This philosophy of history is summed up by

23

Isaiah in declaring "thou hast turned cities into heaps of ruin, and fortified towns into rubble." (25:2) The correlation between mistaken human notions about means for establishing security and the tragic consequences of such mistaken beliefs is interpreted by Isaiah as an expression of God's determining the course of events in human history. He declares: "The Lord has thrown down the high defences of your walls . . . and brought them down to the dust." (25:12)

Jeremiah's *Lamentations* points out the same tragic phenomenon of the rapid convertibility of human fortunes: "Those who were brought up in purple lie on ash heaps." (4:5) This generalization can, of course, be supported by almost countless instances in which the mightiest of rulers have been disposed of as if they were nothing. Hence the translation of this same passage in the *New English Bible* makes this tragic change in human fortunes all the more graphic: "Those nurtured in purple now grovel on dunghills."

The apocryphal writing *Ecclesiasticus* points out the same radical character with which human achievements and human ambitions are treated as if totally ineffectual for securing what is capable of justifying them: "Many kings have been reduced to sitting on the ground." (11:5)

Ezekiel saw the similarity of the mighty among human beings and stately trees which are cut down. He declares that as men "bring low the tall tree" so the highest among mankind are brought low. (17:24)

Zechariah likewise points out the unsound confidence with which men fortify themselves against the inroads of misfortune, pointing out that even the tallest ramparts do not provide security. He spoke specifically of the power and wealth of Phoenician Tyre as only pseudo-security: "Tyre has built herself a rampart, and heaped up silver like dust, and gold like the dirt of the streets. But lo, the Lord will strip her of her possessions." (9:3, 4) This stern judgment upon the insecurity of human possessions under the gloss of wealth and power is one of the sobering aspects of human history which becomes evident in the histories of country after country. Tyre for the Ancients was a symbol of maritime power and wealth, but it was also a symbol for the inevitable judgment upon the folly of human presumption that wealth and achievements are themselves guarantees of security.

The one predictable certainty under which human history takes place is that whatever accomplishments are not morally entitled to endure will not endure. This is judgment upon men, but it is not men's judgment upon themselves. It is a confrontation which they cannot escape, notwithstanding the fortifications and the possessions they amass under the mistaken

24

notion that such things can yield a dependable security. Discrediting their mistaken assumptions about security is moral judgment upon whatever men assume has a merit which it does not actually have. This explanation by the Old Testament prophets for an inescapable moral judgment internal to whatever is not morally worthy of enduring is essentially other than a principle or a premise within a moral philosophy. It is rather a basic premise of a religious philosophy of history such as is affirmed by Zechariah when he declares that Tyre's destiny will be determined not by its ramparts and its wealth but by the judgment of God: "The Lord will strip her of her possessions." (9:4) This judgment is upon her unworthiness to endure upon foundations which express her mistaken notions of what is worth enduring.

The folly of believing that any military might is capable of offering men real security is affirmed time and time again in the reflecting of the Prophets among the Israelites, whether or not their philosophies of history are included in the canon of the Old Testament. The author of *First Maccabees* points out how Ptolemy of Egypt entered Antioch "where he assumed the crown of Asia", and in his confidence in his military capacities, "wore two crowns, that of Egypt and that of Asia". (11:13) This historian of the Israelites then points out the brevity with which this military triumph was enjoyed since only two days after another military triumph against Alexander, Ptolemy died, and "his garrisons in the fortresses were killed by the inhabitants". (11:18, 19) On the basis of the endlessly repeated tragedies of war, the author of this writing declares the sound principle which might be a primary premise in formulating a philosophy of history: "Today (a man) may be high in honour, but tomorrow . . . all his schemes come to nothing." (2:63, 64) This is not an expression of cynicism, because this religious interpreter of history reflects upon history with a confidence that what men do is not the final fact. The final fact in human history is that men's acts come under judgment, and are destroyed by the weight of their own folly.

No more graphic account of this basic principle underlying a philosophy of history can be found than is given in another apocryphal book entitled *Judith*, which narrates the reigns of several of the most powerful rulers of antiquity, whose fortunes were the same. It describes how the Assyrian Nebuchadnezzar laid seize to Ecbatana, the capitol of the ruler of the Medes. The capitol had been fortified with every available means such as "a wall built of hewn stones which were four and a half feet thick and nine feet long". The wall was "a hundred and five feet high and seventy-five feet thick". "At the city gates" towers were constructed "a hundred and fifty feet high with foundations ninety feet thick." The gates themselves were "a hundred and five feet high and sixty feet wide to allow his army to march out in full force with his infantry in formation". (1: 2-4) This account of the fortifications constructed by Arphaxad, the king of the Medes, gives one some idea of the extent to which men expend their material resources and their energies to create what they presume will give them security. But the delusion of this way of thinking is pointed out by the author of this book. He says that when Nebuchadnezzar "reached Ecbatana, he captured its towers, looted its bazaars, and turned its splendour to abject ruin. He caught Arphaxad in the mountains of Ragau, speared him through, and so made an end of him." (1:15, 16)

The sobering disparagement made by Israelite writers upon the most impressive of human achievements, and especially upon all that men do to secure for themselves what is after all only a pseudo-security, is well supported by this account of the final ineffectiveness of even the most extraordinary of human accomplishments to effect what is presumed to be security, whereas such security is not within the scope of such achievements alone.

Herodotus offers another account which supports the Israelites' philosophy of history that men's plans and their most brilliant accomplishments are not exempt from a judgment which discredits their unsound presumptions. He describes the scheme of defense planned for Babylon, which he says "was planned like no other city" of which he had knowledge. "Round it runs first a fosse deep and wide and full of water, and then a wall of fifty royal cubits' thickness (85 feet) and two hundred cubits' height." (341 feet) "There are a hundred gates in the circle of the wall, all of bronze, with posts and lintels of the same."[39] He then characterizes "these walls (as) the city's outer armour", and points out that "within them there is another encircling wall, well nigh as strong as the other, but narrower", and "In the midmost of one division of the city stands the royal palace, surrounded by a high and strong wall."[40] After this description of what the Babylonians did to secure themselves against defeat, Herodotus narrates how "Cyrus . . . marched . . . against Babylon", and after lowering the channel of the Euphrates until he could cross it, captured Babylon.[41] What took place in the defeat of the Babylonians is the same type of occurrence which supports Old Testament philosophy of history as a record of men's pathetic attempts to create for themselves a defense against the inroads of a misfortune brought about by their mistaken presumption that they had discovered a principle for devising an enduring security.

The tragic destiny of Babylon, with its massive means for securing what had been trusted as a way to establish its security, did not end with Cyrus. It ended rather with Darius. Herodotus points out that Babylon, in spite of its incredible walls for defense, was taken again by Darius, but this time, after "having mastered the Babylonians", he "destroyed their walls and reft away all their gates, neither of which things Cyrus had done at the first taking of Babylon".[42]

A survey of just a fraction of human history is sufficient to help one realize that the philosophy of the transiency of human life and human achievement is not a distorted version, but instead, is indisputably accurate. It is a fact, as the apocryphal book *Ecclesiasticus* points out, "today's king is tomorrow's corpse". (10:10) Although this pronouncement is applicable to people other than kings, a part of its significance, as it is affirmed, is the reminder of the incapability of even the mightiest of men to escape the same inevitable end as the lowliest of men must also face. Nothing within the scope of men's power can indefinitely extend their security or their life. Everyone, therefore, irrespective of his status in relation to other human beings, shares the same eventual end of life, as this author of *Ecclesiasticus* affirms: "All men are dust and ashes" in contrast to what is capable of enduring. (17:32)

This commentary both upon what men are and also upon what they do runs throughout the Bible. It is a metaphysical contrast between two orders of reality, such as St. Paul affirms in his address to the Corinthian congregation: "Things that are seen are transient"; only things invisible are eternal."[43] The influential role of Plato's philosophy in the history of Christianity rests upon this same metaphysic of distinguishing a changeless and eternal reality from realities whose nature is transient.

If one were to have the courage to accept this distinction and to recognize without protest that his nature is included in the order of the transient, he would be spared the folly of trying to ignore it or to deny it. It is simply a fact, as the author of *Ecclesiasticus* affirms: "Man's body wears out like a garment." (14:17) The same inevitable occurrence takes place with all that human beings achieve, even through their most devoted work: "All man's works decay and vanish, and the workman follows them." (vs. 19) In a sense, this is sobering, but it is oppressively sobering only when one vainly wishes it were otherwise. Hence, no one who reflects on the nature of human life can ignore the sound sense of the Stoic: insofar as man accepts the nature of whatever is, he is freed from the futile struggle to deny it or to escape it. His freedom then is from folly based on ignorance. And his liberty is living without the curse of fear that fact will contest his fraudulent make-believe.

A folly from which men suffer stern judgment is letting the vanity of a fake notion about life dominate the way they orient themselves to life itself. This is pointed out by the author of *Ecclesiasticus*: "Vain hopes delude the senseless, and dreams give wings to a fool's fancy." (34:1) This is one of the most remarkable generalizations in serious writing. Almost any combination of these terms would carry the load of a profound philosophy about human life. The nature of a "fool's fancy" consists of "vain hopes". The role of such hopes in his life is that they constitute his "senseless" nature. And a nature whose essential character is so "deluded" attempts the futile effort to determine his life by "dreams" and not by reality. When my boat comes in. Lottery

This version of "dreams" and "hope" is the derogatory sense with which such modes of human life can be distorted to the detriment of human well-being. The stern commentary about this type of misdirected life is "like clutching a shadow, or chasing the wind". (vs. 2) This analysis of human life as contingent upon much that a human being in moments of fancy might wish were other than they are, is, nevertheless, the basis upon which an enlightened moral philosophy may be affirmed. As this writer points out, it is morally effective intelligence "In time of plenty to remember the time of famine". In so doing, an individual has leverage over adversity, and the converse of this sound suggestion for preparing for what is unexpected and unwanted is that "in days of wealth" to be aware of the confrontation with possible "poverty and need". These eminently sensible suggestions of what might equip an individual to be prepared for adversities rests upon the realization of the unpredictable character of specific occurrences with which human life is confronted.

The fact that "Between dawn and dusk times may alter" is not one of the givens which admit of men's altering. (18:26) But what a sensible individual can do is accept the fact and refuse to admit into his thinking the vanity of wishing that he somehow would be exempt from this stern character of life. A sensible individual who does not put his trust in his own wishful thinking is not confronted with a challenge to his folly of trying to ignore what cannot intelligently be ignored. The practical proposal made by the author of *Ecclesiasticus* is that an effective safeguard against the shock of dislocation is cultivating the moral capacity to recognize one's nature. His counsel is "The greater you are, the humbler you must be". So stated, this is moral counsel, and this moral counsel in turn is coupled in the same verse with the assurance that "the Lord will show you favour". (3:18)

Another proposal given by the author of *Ecclesiasticus* for reducing and

28

even eliminating human discouragement about the brevity and uncertainty of the duration of one's life is taking account of his contribution to another life which will follow his. This moral challenge is affirmed in pointing out the parallel of the cycle of nature in which the scope of human life is included: "In the thick foliage of a growing tree one crop of leaves falls and another grows instead." (14:18) Thus by extending the range of one's reflecting beyond the brevity of his own life to the more inclusive cycle of life in which one span of life is succeeded by another, an individual, with the benefit of such an enlightened character, gains encouragement by thinking of his role in benefitting the life of another who will live after him. This philosophy of human history thus is based upon a perspective which is not confined to oneself, but is expanded into a greater scope. This difference alone in perspective entails a fundamental difference in an individual's attitude to the otherwise tragic fact that "Man's body wears out like a garment; for the ancient sentence stands, You shall die." (vs. 17, 18)

The same type of reflecting on the brevity of an individual's life in a more inclusive cycle of life and death, death and life, is affirmed in the Iliad: "As is the generation of leaves, so is that of humanity. The wind scatters the leaves on the ground, but the live timber burgeons with leaves again in the season of spring returning. So one generation of men will grow while another dies."[44] Only from the restricted perspective of an individual's own span of life is this interpretation discouraging. But from the enlarged perspective of an inclusive cycle of life in which one is included as an occurrence in an unending sequence, this reflecting on human life is not discouraging. It is, on the other hand, a challenge to devote one's life to giving others the benefit of what he has learned and what he achieved during his lifetime. This different point of view about the relation of one's life to others makes a world of difference in one's own life. The "world", as it were, in which he lives and against which he otherwise would complain for allotting so restricted a span of life to him as an individual becomes a different "world".

The cycle of growth and decay, of life and death, of every individual living being about which the Iliad comments is regarded by Herodotus as evidence for the wisdom of a divine ordering of the earth. It is one of the many aspects of reality which Herodotus regards as supporting his religious interpretation of human history that "there are many clear proofs of the divine ordering of things". The constancy of recurrence of the cycle of growth and decay is, from this point of view, evidence for justice in the providence with which the cycle occurs in the sense that a termination of life of one individual gives an opportunity for another. If there were not such limits within which each living being enjoys a span of life, the opportunity so allotted would be restricted to a relatively few.

The notion of any indefinite or unlimited extension is offensive to a reflective Greek, and so on the basis of his attitude alone toward the unthinkability of an infinite extension, it is understandable that Herodotus, as a religious person, should construe the brevity of individual life in the cycle of life and death as evidence for a wisdom transcendent of the greed with which individual human beings cling to whatever augments their own advantage. According to Herodotus, a cycle in which there are limits to what men can do, including also limits to the length of their lives, prevents human tendencies from trespassing without limit upon their lives. This way of thinking is affirmed in the frequently repeated Greek declaration that "the greater the man, the greater the misfortune".[45] As this is commonly construed, it is regarded as an expression of the Greek sense of basic injustice in what occurs to blight the continued opportunities once achieved by individuals who enjoy rare and extraordinary blessings. But another way of thinking about this same generalization is that this conforms to the Greek metaphysic of limit as a condition for whatever is esteemed as good. The Pythagorean list of opposites includes "limit" with "good" in contrast to "unlimited" with "evil". In finding some basis for defending the so-called "justice" for the termination of extraordinary achievement in its negation, one therefore must take account of the fundamental metaphysic of the Greek. Herodotus attributes to "Croesus the Lydian" his philosophical understanding of this metaphysic when he declares: "I must first teach you this: men's fortunes are on a wheel, which in its turning suffers not the same man to prosper for ever."[46] With this way of thinking, one sees the fairness of limits to the prosperity of one or a few when others are not capable of competing with them for a share of such benefits. It is, therefore, as if there were some underlying justice in the sequence of natural events, even in the cycle of growth and decay of leaves to which both the reflective author of *Ecclesiasticus* and Homer refer.

Herodotus' philosophy of history reaffirms a willing acceptance of the same universal imposition of limits upon human life as evidence for the wisdom or providence of a universal ordering which surpasses what most human beings can respect when blinded by a greed with which they cling to what they have acquired, and protest against the limits set upon the length of life. Herodotus accepts the fact of the imposition of limits, without protesting against its inequity. From his point of view, it is one of the principles of existence, a clear understanding of which constitutes a lev-

30

:rage against a frequently experienced embitterment that "human prosperity never continues in one stay".[47]

According to Herodotus, indefinitely extended prosperity would go counter to the over-all principle of limit as a condition for reasonable existing, since an imposition of limit is a condition for existing itself, as this is formulated in Plato's *Timaeus*. In maintaining this, Plato therefore does not introduce a thought peculiar to himself. He merely formulates it as a metaphysical principle. Herodotus is not a metaphysician, such as Plato is. But his philosophy of history is based upon a metaphysic as this is affirmed in the philosophy of the Pythagoreans and as it is given a more systematic formulation by Plato.

Aeschylus likewise is not a metaphysician, but his reflecting, as this is affirmed in his dramas, is unmistakably metaphysical. When the Chorus in *Agamemnon* reminds the spectators of the play that "Glory in excess is fraught with peril," it is accompanied by the reminder that " 'tis the lofty peak that is smitten by heaven's thunderbolt".[48] In pointing out this parallelism in human life and in a world other than human life, Aeschylus affirms a metaphysic that there are limits to the extent to which anything can go without being checked or having a limit set upon it as consistent with an over-all tendency in reality. So analyzed, this metaphysic is as basic to his dramas as this metaphysic is basic to the history narrated by Herodotus.

The consistency with which Aeschylus interprets reality from this metaphysical premise is illustrated in his interpretation even of the gods of Olympus. One universal principle applies to them as it applies to human beings and to every element of the world. Although these deities differ from men in many respects, there is one respect in which they do not differ: they too are confronted with limits, and so they even suffer the reverses to their ambitions just as men suffer. In protesting against the adversity which he suffers at the hands of Zeus, Prometheus consoles himself by declaring, "Let him hold his power for his little day—since not for long shall he bear sway over the gods".[49] This might seem irreverent if it were thought about without a knowledge of Greek mythology and so of the mythological accounts of the struggles among the gods, interpreted with the traits of human beings. It is in light of this mythology that Aeschylus has Prometheus recall how Zeus demoted his own father Cronos from ultimate sovereignty, and therefore cannot expect that he himself will be exempt from the same cycle of rising to power and losing power, or having an achievement to which he cannot indefinitely cling.

This mythology of the Greeks is as profoundly metaphysical in its pic-

31

torial way of interpreting deities as Plato's nonmythological philosophy i
in interpreting ultimate principles of existence. A metaphysic of limit i
thus basic to Prometheus' question: "Have I not seen two sovereigns cas
out from these heights?" It is on the basis of a metaphysic of limit whicl
imposes a terminus to whatever takes place that Prometheus predicts th
end also of the reign of Zeus: "A third, the present Lord, I shall live t
see cast out in ruin most shameful and most swift."[50]

Just as the gods of Olympus are transcendent of men, so the ultimat
principle of limit is transcendent of the gods themselves. It is, therefore
from this perspective that a reflective Greek interprets human life, and i
is from this perspective that he interprets the gods of Olympus, as well a
occurrences in nature which are under their sovereignty.

Sophocles likewise thinks within the strictures of the Greek perspectiv
that there is no indefinite or unlimited extension either in the physica
world or as the general nature of nonphysical events which occur withi
the order of nature. A notion that there is an unlimited extension is a
intolerable from his point of view as it is unthinkable from Aristotle'
point of view. And in this respect, Aristotle reaffirms the metaphysic of hi
teacher Plato, who in turn reaffirmed the metaphysic of Parmenides, whon
he esteemed as his "intellectual father". The graphic version of reality as
sphere, which Parmenides proposed, becomes Aristotle's notion of the con
centric circles internal to which is the totality of whatever is. The outer
most is the Primum Mobile, which in the discourse of theistic religion ha
been referred to as "God". The very pattern of the sphere affirms th
notion of cycle. Whatever is extended, turns upon itself. What takes plac
within human life likewise conforms to this principle. The principle tha
there can be no indefinite or unlimited extension of any magnitude be
comes the principle with which Sophocles interprets human life: "Earth'
might decays, the might of men decays." So stated, this is not a cynica
disparagement of what takes place. It is rather consistent with the natur
of whatever is subject to change. But when Sophocles has Oedipus, em
bittered by the reverses in his life, declare, "Honour grows cold, dishonoui
flourishes, there is no constancy 'twixt friend and friend, or city and city,'
he also affirms an aspect of what takes place within human life.[51] That thi
tragic misfortune between human beings should occur, however, is not
necessary. It does not follow with the necessity of "growing old". Although
every aspect of human life is subject to the limits of duration, it is, never
theless, capable of orienting itself to a changeless reality, and so is capable
of benefitting by this wisdom even during the brief span of human life.

What is esteemed as human "honor" is incapable of indefinite duration, by virtue of being human. Although this seems tragic from the point of view of reflecting that the opposite of honor should set temporal limits to honor, this would be discouraging, even to the extent of cynicism, if one were not to think of another aspect of this cycle other than its duration. The fact that honor is contributed by some human beings to the record of human history is not cancelled by the emergence of its moral opposite. A fact is not cancelled by other facts.

Sophocles also took account of another aspect of human life which averts the conclusion of cynicism when he considered the human ability to predict occurrences as men's leverage over them. Although human achievements, such as "success", are not indefinitely extended for any human being, still a human being can have the intellectual advantage of anticipating its relative brevity. This constitutes a moral advantage provided it is influential in conditioning his way of reacting to the inevitable termination of what he should like to continue to possess or enjoy. Deianira in Sophocles' *Trachiniae* admits that "one who thinks on change and chance must dread lest . . . success be prelude to a fall".[52] The fear that this may occur is an understandable human response, and it expresses a realistic awareness of what occurs. But if one were to be convinced of the validity of the philosophical generalization of limit with which every event is confronted, he would also have the advantage of the philosophical Stoic. He would anticipate a termination of his good fortune, not with protest, but with acceptance. This obviously would not take place in the life of anyone apart from stern discipline, and it would be no less sad for him who has cultivated such discipline than it would be to the one who had not. But he would differ in his leverage over such sadness. The sadness of the disciplined would have limits such as the sadness of the undisciplined would not. This is the severity of moral judgment for moral deficiency. If one were to prepare himself for what is inescapable in the terminating of good fortune or happiness, he would spare himself a suffering from which others are not exempt, and it is this essentially Stoical point of view which Sophocles affirms when Philoctetes points out that "Seeing upon how slippery a place fortune for mortals and misfortune stand," it is wise for "the man that lives at ease" to "look for rocks ahead, and when he prospers most, watch lest he suffer shipwreck unawares".[53]

What is so sensible about this counsel is that being aware of the limits to which everything in life is subject, one can fortify himself against shock and embitterment by anticipating the ending of good fortune even before it comes about. This is not morbidity, provided one is sensible to enjoy his good fortune when it is possible for him to have it, and to relinquish it without prolonged protest when it passes from him. This likewise is not a Pollyanna point of view. It is the morality which was respected by every Greek who esteemed the good sense of Zeno as well as by the Romans who listened to the teaching of Epictetus with envy that they too could believe this to the point of acting in conformity to its sensible scheme.

Another of Sophocles' characters, Hyllus, affirms the same sort of sensible view about the unpredictability of the length of time that one can enjoy a good to which he might wish with all his heart that he could indefinitely cling, but which in his wiser moments of reflecting, he understands is not possible: "What is yet to be none knows."[54] Admitting this cannot be looked upon as cynical. It is a fact. It is, therefore, sound sense also to acknowledge that "if any man counts on the morrow, or on morrows more he reckons rashly". Disappointing as this limitation upon the prospects for continued well-being may be, one is sensible to understand and accept the fact that he is not omniscient. What he can claim to know with certainty is what has taken place during the course of a day, and then if there is no foreseeable reason for questioning its continuity in a following day may with reasonable presumption anticipate its continuing in the coming day. It is this prosaic but sensible counsel which Hyllus continued to give: "Morrow is there none, until to-day its course has safely run."[55]

As almost every statement that anyone can make can be construed in more than one way, so this statement surely can be. It can be regarded as affirming a defeatist sense of human impotence in the face of the unpredictable. But it may also be interpreted differently as affirming a reasonable basis on which a reasoned anticipation of a future may be made.

Remembering the wisdom of Solon, Sophocles acknowledged in the words of Deianira that "There is an old-world saying current still, 'Of no man canst thou judge the destiny to call it good or evil, till he die'."[56] At first glance, this seems stern and even cruel that there should be such limits set upon the scope of man's knowledge of a future. But even a momentary reflecting on one's own response makes him aware that no man is omniscient. He knows past occurrences as he cannot know future occurrences. He may, of course, venture predictions upon what is highly likely in a future, but such prediction cannot be mistaken for knowledge. Since there is an unpredictable number of unforeseeable events in the future of every human being, one is sensible to acknowledge this limitation of the scope of his knowledge. Admitting it and accepting it as what is incapable of being sensibly denied, an individual does not presume to transcend the inescapable limits of his knowledge when he tries, with inevitable failure, to divine a future. Such knowledge is not within the range of human for-

34

une. Denying that it is, is not equivalent to misfortune, except to an individual who obstinately refuses to acknowledge and to accept the limits of human knowledge of occurrences which have not yet taken place. In the discourse of contemporary empirical philosophy, this fact would be affirmed as the impossibility of affirming any empirical proposition with absolute certainty. By definition, an empirical judgment is one which may reasonably be affirmed only with a degree of probability, although this degree may approximate logical certainty, it cannot *in principle* be assumed as certainty.

Among the extant plays of the three great dramatists, those of Euripides seem to be most preoccupied with the aspect of uncertainty in human life, and Euripides offers more explanations for such uncertainty than do the other tragedians. As both of the others, he too respected Solon's counsel that "none should envy him who seems to thrive, until they see his death". A reason which he offers for this is simply the fact that "fortune's moods last but a day".[57] But he may also have been thinking of the metaphysic of Heraclitus when he declared "naught continueth at one stay". Since human life occurs within the wider context of a world of essential flux or change, it would follow that " 'Tis man's lot" that there should be no enduring good fortune.[58] A human being, such as Hecuba, may be Queen of Troy the very day before which she became the slave of Agamemnon. Hence Euripides' comment: "From a palace dragged to face a life of slavery."[59]

In light of this rapid shift of human fortune, he affirms only one aspect of the metaphysic of Heraclitus. Whereas Heraclitus maintains that there is a changeless logos transcendent of the world of flux, Euripides based his tragedies on the factor of change. In affirming that "the chances of the years dance like an idiot in the wind", he takes account only of one type of reality in the metaphysical dualism of Heraclitus.[60] And it is by virtue of his preoccupation with the flux of events which influence the life of human beings that he disparages a human being for his stupidity to assume that good fortune or prosperity, enjoyed one day, will continue until another day: "A fool is he, who, in prosperity secure rejoices."[61]

And yet Euripides is clearly aware that it is the common tendency of human beings to think only of the moment during which they enjoy prosperity, and so they do not think of the likelihood of its ending. He explains this tendency to be so preoccupied with good fortune, though only momentary, as an expression of men's vanity: "O vain is man who glorieth in his joy and hath no fears."[62] Such vanity is men's presumption that their good fortune is due only to their own exceptional aptitudes, and for

35

this reason they take no account of another explanation for a good fortune which may have come their way. They are so self-satisfied that their good fortune is a consequence only of their superiority to those less fortunate that they cannot conceive of it ending, since such ending would discredit their vain presumption that it was they alone who were responsible for their prospering as others do not. In this sense, they would not condescend to think of their advantages as "good fortune". From the perspective of their vanity, it would not be "fortune's" gift to them. It would be their achievement, and so they would maintain that "This world of man tossed to and fro by waves of contradiction and strange vicissitudes" applies to others but not to them.[63]

Euripides, however, was not satisfied merely to take account of men's attitude toward good fortune so long as it lasted for them. He attempted to explain it. One of the several explanations he offered is the Greek metaphysic that a "balance" must be maintained as a condition even for existing. According to this metaphysical principle, the rapidity with which good fortune passes into its opposite is for the necessity of maintaining a balance. Although acknowledging to Hecuba "how sad thy lot, as sad as once 'twas blest", she also is told that her tragedy is in accordance with the necessity of preserving a balance: "setting this in the balance to outweigh thy former bliss".[64]

One explanation offered in turn to account for maintaining such balance is theological. Hecuba is told: "Some god is now destroying thee." Another explanation is that it is the working of "fate", and this explanation is also proposed in *Iphigeneia in Taurica*: "Fate draws us ever on to the unknown," and since such determination by fate is incapable of being known, "none foreseeth ill".[65] According to the explanation in terms of Fate, human beings are not responsible for their failure to avert the misfortunes which displace their good fortune. But if this were the case, there would be no basically tragic nature of misfortune since it would not be brought about by men's failure to do what they might have done. Only one aspect of dramatic tragedy is that there is a factor over which a human being does not have full control. But another factor is his failure to do what he might have done. There would, therefore, be no tragic character in human life if men were merely passive pawns in a world without moral options. For dramatic reasons, if for no other, Euripides explains the determining of human events by a god. This explanation is consistent with the tragic character of human life since men can relate themselves in favorable ways to a god, just as they can be negligent in so doing. Thus their misfortune is something for which they are indirectly responsible, alhough it is explained as directly brought about by a god. But actually it was a human being's negligence to do what he ought to have done in relation to the god which accounts for his suffering by the action of the god. In one sense, therefore, "the god changed his good fortune".[66] But in another sense, it was man himself who was responsible for this change.

There is no such division of responsibility for misfortune according to another explanation which Euripides offers in *Orestes*: the reason that "Great prosperity abideth not amongst mankind" is that "some power divine, shaking it to and fro like the sail of swift galley, plunges it deep in the waves of grievous affliction".[67] This explanation if pressed without qualification by a man's responsibility would be incompatible with dramatic tragedy itself, since a human being must in some sense be responsible for his misfortune. Preserving this responsibility, therefore, is essential to the very structure of dramatic tragedy. It consequently is not enough to end an explanation for misfortune by attributing it to "the malice of heaven".[68] There must be a human responsibility for the malice, otherwise "affliction's death-ravening tide" is not dramatically tragic. Hence a metaphysic compatible with such literary requirements is essential, and Euripides was aware of this. After acknowledging that "Nought is there man may trust, nor high repute, nor present weal—for it may turn to woe," he proposes the explanation he had given before: "All things the Gods confound, hurl this way and that, turmoiling all." Then he introduces a remarkable twist which saves its dramatic tragic character and also proposes an explanation for the genesis of religion: ". . . that we, foreknowing nought, may worship them."[69] According to this explanation, man can be respectful of the gods, and by so doing they could avert the displeasure of the gods and thereby be spared a punishment imposed by them. It is this shift to men's responsibility for their misfortune and suffering which thus saves the explanation of misfortune as compatible with dramatic tragedy. But in addition to its literary merit, it is also a remarkable anticipation of Frazer's explanation for the genesis of religion. According to Frazer, the aleatory occurrences in human life are intolerable for men. Hence they devise means either of magic or religion to enable them to act in ways which they believe are effective in enabling them to control the otherwise unpredictable, and thus prevent its handicap to their life.

Euripides offers still another explanation for the fact that men by their own efforts cannot preserve or entirely control what they may regard as their own possessions. This religious explanation is the same which is proposed by Socrates. "Riches make no settled home, but are as transient as the day" because "man indeed hath no possessions of his own; we do bu have a stewardship of the gods' property; and when they will, they tak it back again."[70] Socrates taught this religious view, and this is the reaso he gave that man is not permitted to take his own life. He maintaine that man's life is a property of the gods.[71]

4. *Misfortune may give rise to cynicism*

There are limits to the human capacity to suffer without becoming em bittered to the extent of cynicism. The fact of this relation is thus on instance of the Pythagorean principle that a decrease of limit is itself th increase of evil. This inverse relation holds between the blight of huma well-being by misfortune and the additional handicap to its well-being b the emergence of cynicism. Although this relationship is illustrated with fa greater frequency in ancient Greek literature than in the writings of th early Israelites, it at least is basic to one mode of Job and to one mod of the author of *Ecclesiastes,* as well as to the author of the apocrypha writing of *Ecclesiasticus.*

After Job took account of the "hard service on earth" which blights th well-being of so many human beings, he thought of their life as a futil struggle. He likewise spoke of the "months of futility" which were also hi "portion". (7:3) Entertaining the notion of the futility of life is indee significant for Job since he is commonly esteemed as an example of humai life which, in spite of its misfortune, retains its faith in the providence an justice of God. But what is especially significant in this instance of hi comment on the futility of his life is the threadline separation under som circumstances between living with faith and losing faith.

. A total loss of faith in the worth of life itself is outright cynicism. Thi comes about when adversities in life go beyond the limits of an individual' endurance. Preserving faith in the worth of life is a struggle. And unde some circumstances, the struggle ends in a defeat of the strongest will t preserve confidence in the worth of life.

Questioning the worth of one's own life under conditions of its adversi ties is very different, however, from questioning the worth of human life itself. This extension of doubt is the negation of faith which might other wise save an individual from cynicism. Such cynicism, however, is reachec in *Ecclesiastes* when its author declares that "Good men and sinner fare alike". This is a cynical negation of the moral differences in human beings even though they all alike must die. This is the type of cynicism which Plato forbade to be uttered in the ideal Republic, the basic faith of which

38

vas the indisputable worth of moral goodness, notwithstanding every adversity or misfortune. The author of *Ecclesiastes* seems to argue that because all men die, irrespective of the differences in their moral merit, there therefore is no respect in reality itself for moral difference in human life. He declares: "This is what is wrong in all that is done here under the sun." So stated, his cynicism is not only toward the injustice of human beings who do not respect the difference between moral right and moral wrong. It is rather a denial that there is any aspect of reality itself which supports the moral effort of some human beings to respect a just way of acting as their supreme obligation. There thus is no cynicism which can surpass the bitterness which maintains that "one and the same fate befalls every man". (9:3) If anyone were to despair of the moral justification for the effort to discipline his life in order that his character might determine the quality of his acting, it is understandable that he should find no moral reason for living.

A preference for the termination of life because the struggle to live is too difficult to justify the effort to live is of a very different character. Under some circumstances, it may be morally justified to prefer death to continuing to live. When this preference is based upon a serious reflecting of which is the better, the preference is itself the achievement of character. And no character is achieved without the faith that there are fundamental differences between what is worth effort and what is not worth effort.

There likewise is a radical difference between regarding what many people do as futile, and coming to the conclusion that what everyone does is futile. The latter point of view is a cynicism about moral differences in human effort. It is this type of cynicism which is affirmed in a passage in the *Iliad*: "A man dies still if he has done nothing, as one who has done much."[72] The fact that both die is indisputable. What is morally important, however, is what each did before he died. If it were to be believed that there is no difference in what they did, so that the records of their lives are the same irrespective of their conduct, then of course this would be total cynicism about what constitutes the moral worth for living. Just as Socrates maintains that "the unexamined life is not worth living," so he would also maintain that there is a fundamental difference in the worth of living if one lives for the purpose of seriously reflecting on life or lives without such purpose or without any purpose whatever.

One of the sobering aspects of human life is that many people achieve advantages without being morally entitled to do so. And conversely, the lives of many upright and honest human beings end in misfortune. The apocryphal writing *Ecclesiasticus* points this out when its author declares

39

that "Many kings have been reduced to sitting on the ground". This radical change in their status is often without relation to their moral merit as kings. Such adversities are simply part of human history. And it is also a fact, as this writer points out, that "a mere nobody has worn the crown".[7] Both of these occurrences occasion moral protest as being unfair and unjust. Yet, the record of human history is saturated with examples of such unfairness and injustice. Acknowledging this fact is not a cynicism. It is simply realistic reporting of what takes place. It is the same sort of reporting which was done by Aristophanes in *The Knights* when he declares that one man may "reign until a filthier scoundrel than he arises".[7] This is a discouraging and disappointing aspect of human history. But it is not a basis for a thoroughgoing cynicism about human life. It is rather an indictment of a type of human life whose status in a society is without relation to his moral merit.

Even Aeschylus' contempt for the rule by Zeus who, "with new-fangled laws wieldeth arbitrary sway," is not a cynicism either about gods or about the difference between the merits of their rule.[75] Prometheus' complaint that "Zeus is harsh and keepeth justice in his own hands" is simply an indictment of the capricious rule of a "tyrant" usurping rule in a heaven as conceived in Greek mythology.[76]

The term "cynicism" is often misused to express an individual's displeasure for another's enumeration of unpleasant aspects of life, such as the increasing handicaps which attend aging. It would be used in this sense if one were to classify as "cynical" the account of life given in the Chorus in Sophocles' *Oedipus at Colonus* when it narrates that as "youth passes . . . troubles on troubles follow, toils on toils, pain, pain". For many human beings this is a factual statement entirely apart from its use to argue anything about the joyless character of life as human beings age. It would, therefore, be a misuse of this term to speak of this enumeration as an expression of a "cynicism" about life, although it is a sobering aspect of human life that there is "Envy, sedition, strife". Added to this sobering nature of life is that in spite of men's heroism there is "carnage and war" in which heroes are destroyed. Sophocles declares that all of these negations of well-being "make up the tale of life". In spite of the pathos that life is so blighted, this generalization about "the tale of life" is not a cynicism. And it likewise is not a cynicism to acknowledge that "Last comes the worst and most abhorred stage of unregarded age, joyless, companionless and slow. Of woes the crowning woe."[77] This long enumeration of handicaps to well-being, ending with an account of the plight of many who age alone, abandoned by others who are indifferent to them, is simply an accu-

rate commentary on the nature of life for many. If, however, a generalization were added to this commentary that nothing had occurred during the
lifetime of such individuals to be worthy of their suffering, the generalization would then be a cynicism. It would be a disparagement of the justification for the struggle and the suffering which many endure. But insofar
as there is some aspect of life other than the struggle which redeems it,
then its struggle is not futile. It is only the belief that there is nothing to
redeem the struggle and the suffering which constitutes a cynicism about
the significance of life.

On the other hand, a very different characterization of human life is
given in Sophocles' play *Electra* when Electra declares: "Life to me were
misery and death a boon."[78] As stated, this might well be regarded as a
cynicism in its disparagement of life, without taking account of a single
factor which redeems it. Unqualified suffering would be total evil, and its
termination by death would indeed be "a boon". An equally unredeemed
despair is affirmed by Chrysothemis, the sister of Electra, when she declares: "Mere death were easy, but to crave for death, and be denied that
last boon—there's the sting".[79]

If only such total negation of good in life were considered, a generalization about the worth of life on such terms would understandably be a cynicism about the worth of life. But if there were something to redeem the
suffering, the disparagement, stern though it might be, would not be a
cynicism.

Sophocles and Solon were both aware of the tragic aspects of human
life. Both knew many examples of meritorious life crushed by men without
scruples. On the basis of their knowledge, it is understandable that both
should counsel that it is wise to "wait to see life's ending ere thou count
one mortal blest; wait till free from pain and sorrow he has gained his
final rest".[80] Their counsel expresses their long acquaintance with injustices committed by the cruelest of men against those most worthy to be
held in esteem. The existence of human beings who merit gratitude of
others, even though they do not receive it, cannot be thought of as a
cynicism about human life as such. The fact that there are some who are
more entitled to live than others constitutes a basis for an esteem for what
can be achieved in human life notwithstanding all that may negate it.

The threadline which often separates reflecting about the sobering character of human life and a cynical disparagement of the moral justification
for life itself is illustrated in Euripides' *Orestes*. Electra's declaration, "O
human nature, what a grievous curse thou are in this world!" surely justi-
fies a classification of "cynicism" about human nature. According to this

41

declaration, human life would be an unqualified evil, and as such, ther
would be no worth internal to it to redeem it and so to justify it. Bu
Electra adds the qualification to such cynicism when she declares: "Wha
salvation, too, to those who have a goodly heritage therein!"[81] Since bot
of these declarations are included in one comment about "human nature
it seems to affirm a contradiction. Such an apparent contradiction woul
have been avoided in her commentary on life, however, had she indicte
only most of human nature as a "grievous curse". Then the part of huma
nature not included in this "curse" would be those whose moral role is
responsibility to make up for the moral deficiency of the greater numbe
of human beings.

On the other hand, an unqualified cynicism about human effort is af
firmed by the Nurse in Euripides' *Hippolytus* when she declares: "W
waste our toil to no purpose."[82] If this were the case, and there actuall
were nothing beneficial brought about by all that some human beings dc
then this disparagement of human effort would certainly be an outrigh
cynicism about the justification for expending effort when it is only futile
Anyone, therefore, who maintains, as the Nurse in this play does, tha
"We toil and spend our strength for naught" declares an unqualifie
cynicism.[83]

One may be cynical about the worth of an aspect of human life withou
also being cynical about life itself. A cynical disparagement of the truth
character of religious faith, for example, is affirmed by the herald o
Agamemnon in Euripides' *Hecuba* when he sees the Queen of Troy re
duced to total poverty after sharing the rule in her wealthy kingdom
"Great Zeus! what can I say," asks the Herald, "that thine eye is ove
man? or that we hold this false opinion all to no purpose, thinking ther
is any race of gods, when it is chance that rules the mortal sphere?"[8]
This is an unequivocal cynicism about a religious belief whose truth h
doubts because so much which occurs in human life collides with what i
affirmed in such faith. The particular instance of a cynicism, as is affirme
by the herald, is a disparagement of a particular religious faith. It is
depreciation only of the aspect of a religion which maintains that there is
providence whose role is watchful of human beings so that they do no
suffer misfortune. There is no evidence internal to human history to sup
port this type of interpretation of Providence or deity. There are, how
ever, other interpretations of Providence or deity which merit respect an
are justifiably revered for their truth-character.

If it were believed that there are no religious interpretations whic
merit respect for their truth, such belief would certainly be outright cyni

ism about religion. Such a cynical attitude is affirmed by the Nurse in
uripides' *Hippolytus*, when reflecting on religious beliefs, she declares
trusting to fables we drift at random". She comes to this attitude toward
eligious beliefs after contrasting her estimate of "Man's whole life (as)
ull of anguish" with a religious assurance that there is something "to
ove beyond this life". She sees no evidence to support this assurance
nd declares: "Night's dark pall doth wrap it round."[85] Her type of cyni-
ism thus is based upon a disparity between what is assured by a religion
nd what an individual critical of it believes because of negative evidence
hich he regards as discrediting such assurance. This is, therefore, a
ighly restricted type of cynicism. Rather than even being so classified, it
ould be more defensible to look upon it as an instance of critical reflect-
1g which prevents life from being engulfed in ignorance and therefore
rasting its opportunities to discover truth by clinging instead to "fables"
nd thereby "drift(ing) at random".

Some of the characters in Euripides' plays express a type of despair
nd cynicism which became widespread in Greece after the many years of
varfare during which there were "sudden shifts in fortune". As Frederick
Grant points out, "A city or a citizen, wealthy and at peace today, might
omorrow be impoverished or sold into slavery."[86] Under conditions such
s this, there is every understandable reason for disbelief of the truth of a
eligious assurance that there is a providence protecting men against such
vils which are brought about by men. A providence which supports a man
rho devotes his life to doing good cannot also be presumed to perform the
ole of preventing other men from doing evil. The cynicism, therefore, to-
vard religion is often for the indefensible claims made by a particular
eligion. It is toward such claims that disparagement is appropriately di-
ected. But such a critical appraisal of unsound doctrines introduced into a
eligion should not be mistaken for a cynical disparagement of religion as
an orientation of human life to a reality transcendent of human life, which
oy virtue of its different nature from human life, can bestow upon it what
auman resources cannot do.

There is often an indistinct or ambiguous borderline between despair
and cynicism, except for the clarity of a definition which distinguishes
hem. There likewise is a parallel ambiguity in interpretations of the rela-
ion of human life to a deity or divine reality transcendent of human life.
This is illustrated in the claim which Prometheus made of the benefits he
oestowed upon human beings. He declares: "I caused mortals no longer
:o foresee their doom" of cheerless death. So stated, this is a benefit for
vhich human beings ought to be grateful to Prometheus. But two lines

further in Aeschylus' play, Prometheus declares: "I caused blind hope to dwell within their breasts."[87] Thus the two claims constitute an ambiguity about the benefit of hope itself in human life. If a hope is "blind" in the sense that there is no support for it in reality, it can hardly be regarded as worthy of a morally courageous life. Hopes for which there can be no confirmation in reality are deceptive, even though for the time that they are maintained they may give a specious sense of benefit. But regarding such a deceptive hope as actually beneficial rests upon a cynical disparagement of a human being's failure to have character sufficient to accept reality without grasping at a fraudulent hope to support his mistaken interpretation of reality. The assumption furthermore that reality is devoid of genuine benefits for morally courageous human beings is also outright cynicism about the nature of reality.

From the point of view of any morally honest human being, the disparity between what is hoped for and a reality which cannot justify such hope is not a blessing. It is rather a "curse", as the Theban Herald in Euripides' play *The Suppliants* regards it. He declares: "Hope is man's curse." But the type of hope of which he speaks is one which in the nature of reality is incapable of being confirmed. As such, it is "delusive". Living by delusions is repellent to an individual who wants to devote his life to reducing the burden of ignorance which includes deceptive ideas about reality. As the Herald points out, a delusive assumption that one's own country will be the victor in a war accounts for the rashness of wanting such a war. If, on the other hand, there were a clear and sensible awareness of the perils of every war, men would not be so eager to bring about a war. He declares: "If death had been before their own eyes when they were giving their votes, Hellas would ne'er have rushed to her doom in mad desire for battle."[88] This is an expression of sensible reflecting on the tragic disparity between a hope for victory which presses human beings to a venture in war and the stern nature of war which discredits such a hope. This is not a cynicism about hope, but rather about a type of human life which destroys itself by acting upon a "blind hope" or one which is "delusive".[89]

Living without hope for what can be achieved in the future would be bondage to a present. Hence a life without hope would indeed justify a cynicism toward such a life. But a human ability to distinguish between a hope which sustains a life of constructive activities and a "delusive hope" which misdirects a life is the difference between respect for human abilities and a cynicism toward human weakness. The author of *Ecclesiasticus*

44

therefore soundly points out that it is "vain hopes (which) delude the senseless". (34:1)

A clear distinction between a hope which is vain because deceptive or delusive and a hope which is sound, and so capable of directing human efforts into constructive behavior, is itself a tribute to human character. And no human being who respects the moral benefits of character would want to live without such a capacity to make so clear a distinction. In light of the ability of some human beings to be aware of the radical difference between unsound and sound hopes, one is surprised that Jeremiah should accuse the god of the Israelites of unfairness for permitting men to "hope for better days" when such hopes are not confirmed. As Jeremiah states his complaint, he affirms a cynicism about faith in a god for creating men with a capacity to have deceptive hopes. He confronts the god whom he regards as the Creator with the question which implies this twofold basis for genuine cynicism: "Why hast thou wounded us, and there is no remedy; why let us hope for better days, and we find nothing good, for a time of healing, and all is disaster?" (14:19)

If, on the other hand, Jeremiah had maintained that human beings are morally responsible for what they believe as the basis for what they do, he would not have attributed the mode of deceptive hope in human life to a god's responsibility. Thus the twofold cynicism which Jeremiah affirms in his question directed to the god of the Israelites derived from attributing responsibility to a god for what men are actually responsible. Had he regarded human beings morally responsible for their interpretations of a god, he would not have attributed responsibility to the god of the Israelites for what is a responsibility of human beings.

5. *Both early Israelites and ancient Greeks maintain that men are responsible for much of the misery in their lives*

No clearer statement could be made of human responsibility for much of human suffering than is affirmed in the *Odyssey* when Homer represents Zeus declaring to the Immortals: "What a lamentable thing it is that men should blame the gods and regard *us* the source of their troubles when it is their own wickedness that brings them sufferings worse than any which Destiny allots them."[90] This accusation of human beings for bringing about much of their own misfortune is Homer's courageous criticism of the popular belief that the principal cause for human misery is not human beings, but is realities other than them.

Although Homer believes that there are realities transcendent of human

45

beings upon whom at least some of men's well-being is contingent, he also believes that many of the ills of human life for which men accuse gods are derived from men's failure to do what they could do to avert handicaps to their well-being. Lattimore's translation stresses unequivocally the moral responsibility of men when he interprets this statement of Homer to affirm that it is the human being's "own recklessness (which) win sorrow beyond what is given".[91] This translation is significant for two reasons. One is that men are not responsible for all of the handicaps to their well-being. There is in other words a "given" over which men have no final control. This is consistent with Homer's basic philosophy of human history that men's destinies are in part determined by divine realities. But over and above the so-called "given" are occasions in which men could do more to bring about their well-being than they do. It is under these particular circumstances that they are "reckless" of their welfare when they are negligent in doing what they could do if they were to take advantage of their resources and their capacities, limited though they may be. Rieu's translation in terms of men's "wickedness which brings them sufferings" is not as unqualified an accusation of men's moral neglect as is the analysis of their "recklessness". Since there is a "wickedness" of which much religious literature speaks which is man's essential nature, and in this sense is not something for which he is directly responsible, Rieu's translation does not affirm the same philosophy of human responsibility for human misery as does Lattimore's translation.

The human responsibility for human injustice is stressed in Rieu's translation of Homer's account of the generous intervention by Meleager on behalf of the Aetolians, when "at the dictates of his own conscience," he "saved the Aetolians from disaster".[92] Yet, in return for his morally motivated willingness to "save" them, "they gave him none of the splendid gifts they had offered" to give him for his help. In this incident in the *Iliad*, if defensibly attributed to Homer, Homer points out not only the ingratitude of which human beings are capable to disappoint one who does his part to offer others help when they are in need. He also points out the capacity of human beings to break promises, and in so doing disrespect their word. Such disregard for a promise or an agreement is thus a type of moral deficiency in human life which destroys the moral foundation for integrity in human relations.

Herodotus is no less clear than is Homer that most human beings could do more for their own well-being than they often do. He does not believe that all men are capable of the moral capacity to bring about moral benefits for themselves or for others. But he is confident that there are at least

46

some human beings who bring about benefits for human life which would not otherwise come into being. He declares: "Great successes are not won save by great risks."[93] In maintaining this, he thereby rejects more than one popular belief among his contemporaries. One such belief is that Fate determines all that takes place in human life. Another belief he thus challenges is that what is not determined by Fate is determined by gods, when they themselves are not under the final control of Fate. Herodotus, on the other hand, maintains that there is a latitude within reality over which men themselves have the final control. Such control, however, is not guaranteed or assured them. Men risk defeat in undertaking to bring about what they aim to achieve. But they also may gain by their initiative, and it is on the basis of the probability that they may accomplish what they set their minds and energies to accomplish that they stake this wager. What is remarkable about the point of view maintained by Herodotus is that it anticipates Pascal's analysis of the wager which men make on faith. By virtue of such a wager, men accomplish what could not otherwise come about. Such wager demonstrates not only men's courage to undertake what is not assured of achievement. It also demonstrates their willingness to hazard a venture which is precarious. And they affirm their willingness with a clear realization that there is a high likelihood of not achieving the end for which they commit themselves. When such a risk entails their life, one can appreciate the cost with which some of these wagers are made by courageous human beings.

Herodotus does not underestimate the risk entailed in some of the ventures on which some human beings wager their very life. He asks "how shall one that is but man know where there is security?" as a basis, in other words, to give him some evidence of the likelihood of success in his venture. And he answers his own question when he declares: "It is, I think, impossible." Yet, in spite of the almost total unpredictability of success in a wager, some men nevertheless make such wagers. And what is remarkable about Herodotus' explanation for the initiative taken by some against every odd of unsuccess is the clarity with which he points out the moral determinant of such a wager. He declares: "It is they, then, who have the will to act that do oftenest take account of all chances." Their wager, in other words, is not a rashness of plunging into a venture without first considering what is entailed in their own responsibility for its accomplishment. Pinpointing the final determinant as men's *will* to do what they are not compelled to do is the clearest possible anticipation of the most penetrating analyses in subsequent moral philosophies, culminating in the clarity of analysis in the *Nicomachean Ethics*.

47

Herodotus was thoroughly acquainted with the obstacles that human beings place upon others who have a moral courage to do what they themselves do not have either the courage or the intelligence to do. After acknowledging that "all Hellas glorified" Themistocles "for the wisest man by far of the Greeks" he was also aware of the Athenians' change of attitude toward this statesman and general when they ostracized him by virtue of an accused complicity in the treason of Pausanias.[94] If the accusation were justified by what Themistocles actually did, then the deficiency of his character would illustrate Herodotus' clear awareness of the grave moral limitations even of the most outstanding among men. But if he were not guilty of the accusation, his willingness to ally himself with the Persian Artaxerxes, the enemy of the Greeks, would confirm his capacity for disloyalty to his own country. "The brief and brilliant pre-eminence of Athens in Hellas" began and also ended with two invasions of Greece by the Persians.[95] Hence Themistocles' willingness to accept a pension from the Persian ruler confronts one with a sobering realization of what human beings can do that is morally reprehensible.

The character of Themistocles thus offers a contrast to the character of Aristides, an Athenian statesman and general who was a contemporary of Themistocles. He also was ostracized by the Athenians for proposing a military policy which differed from Themistocles. But when Themistocles policy was approved by the Athenians, Aristides loyally supported his rival in the Salamis campaign, and gave his support to the Athenian cause notwithstanding their ostracism of him. He thus illustrates the fact that men's character is the final determinant of what men do, and such characters differ. The bewildering aspect of human life, as Aristotle points out, is that there must be character to bring about praiseworthy acting, and yet it is only by such acting that character itself is cultivated.

This relation between morally determined acting by character and the cultivation of character itself by such acting is also clearly pointed out by Euripides in *Hippolytus*. Phaedra declares: "By teaching and experience we learn the right but neglect it in practice."[96] Thus even though an individual may have practiced conduct and thereby acquired the discipline which makes conduct possible, yet such capacity for conduct does not always determine praiseworthy acting.

It is this ambivalence in human life which includes a basis both for a sobering regret of human failure or deficiency as well as an admiration for what a human being can achieve through a discipline of character. Conduct is the result of character determining activity. Yet such character includes a latitude of acting. One type of which is praiseworthy and another type of which is censurable. Hence internal to one human being is a twofold capacity. Acting which is determined by the capacity for conforming to an acquired standard of character is admirable and therefore praiseworthy. But a failure to do what otherwise might be done is a basis for censuring the same person who otherwise might have merited praise. Euripides, according to A. S. Way's translation of the same passage, gives a twofold explanation for deficiency of character in determining conduct: Some human beings are morally deficient in their acting "from sloth, and some preferring pleasure in the stead of duty".[97]

Euripides is a profound moral philosopher because he is a penetrating analyst of human nature. No moral philosophy, of course, would be worth its salt if it did not rest on a sound and penetrating understanding of human capacities and human tendencies. In what Theseus says to his son Hippolytus, Euripides points out the grave limits with which human beings are confronted in depending upon the acting of others which is not determined by a predictable character. He says: "Man needs should have some certain test set up to try his friends, some touchstone of their hearts, to know each friend whether he be true or false." This is as sobering an analysis of the frailty of the human being as one can conceive. Even among those whom one cherishes as friends are some who are not worthy of being trusted. Of course this analysis of the frailty of human character is best known in the New Testament's accounts of Peter's denial that he even knew Jesus and in the betrayal of Jesus by Judas. No one, therefore, who is acquainted with the New Testament could think that Euripides was needlessly uncharitable in the account he takes of the uncertain loyalty of which some are capable even in relation to others who trust them as friends and so depend upon their fidelity. In light of the inability of the human being who trusts another to be assured that his trust is justified, Euripides suggests that "All men should have two voices, one the voice of honesty, expediency's the other, so would honesty confute its knavish opposite, and then we would not be deceived".[98]

Euripides' commentary on human nature points out that men's knowledge is not only limited about the nature of gods, of which there is much complaint both in Greek literature and in the Bible. Men's knowledge is also limited about other human beings, and even about those with whom they most frequently associate and in close relation to whom they may live. This is therefore a sobering commentary on the human failure to be what is helpful for human beings when it is within the scope of human ability to be helpful.

Euripides states another profound insight into the human struggle to seek encouragement in a human being's relation to other human being. It is in the same play, *Hippolytus*, that the Chorus affirms: "The thought I have about the gods, whenso they come into my mind, do much to soothe its grief, but though I cherish secret hopes of some great guiding will, yet am I at fault when I survey the fate and doings of the sons of men".[99]

What is remarkable in this analysis is taking account of a twofold type of moral deficiency. One is the character weakness of others which causes a grief in those who trust them without justification. The other is the character weakness or deficiency of not being sufficiently critical in one's own estimates of the character of others. If one were adequately critical so that he would not be mistaken in misdirecting his trust, he would spare himself a "grief". He then would not need to seek solace in his "secret hopes of some great guiding will" upon whose trustworthiness he may depend without disappointment. In a sense, therefore, the suffering which is brought about in human life by the untrustworthiness of human beings could in some degree be averted or diminished by a more consistent exercise of critical intelligence of which human beings are also capable. Whether the deficiency is in intelligence or in character, the failure to do what a human being might otherwise have done is a human failure. As such, whatever sorrow or suffering it brings about is due to human deficiency, and not to any intervention in human life by a reality other than human life, whether interpreted as a deity or as impersonal Fate.

One of the strongest indictments against the human failure to do as much as it should do to bring about well-being is affirmed by Aristophanes in *The Birds*. The Leader of the Chorus narrates one of the most poignant commentaries on the plight of human beings at the mercy of other human beings: "Weak mortals, chained to the earth, creatures of clay as frail as the foliage of the woods, you unfortunate race, whose life is but darkness, as unreal as a shadow, the illusion of a dream."[100]

What is remarkable in this analysis of human life at the mercy of other human beings is Aristophanes' characterization of the context in which human beings live. This is identical with Plato's as it is affirmed in the seventh book of the *Republic*. But there is also a very significant difference in Plato's and Aristophanes' versions of the status of human life. According to Plato, some human beings are not confined to "darkness" and do not live by "the illusion of a dream". They are the human beings who by stern discipline of their mentality acquire an understanding of reality and so have developed the dialectical ability to distinguish the Real from the unreal, Truth from falsehood, and therefore they do not ive as "weak mortals, chained to the earth". Plato thus expresses his confidence in what human life could achieve through its capacity to distinguish differences in value of which most others are incapable. Aristophanes, on the other hand, does not think in terms of normative human life, but only in terms of human life with which most people are acquainted. Such human beings are understandably characterized as "weak mortals . . . creatures of clay".

The characterization of human beings as "creatures of clay" seems as if it were quoted from the Bible. The parallelism, therefore, of philosophical anthropology is remarkable. A widespread notion is that Greek thought goes to an unqualified excess in its confidence in what human nature is and what it is capable of doing. Although it is optimistic about what human beings can do, it is also realistically sobering in its awareness of the limitations which are internal to human nature. And, of course, the writings of the ancient Israelites are no less clear about handicaps which human beings themselves impose upon human life.

Job points out to the friends with whom he talks that men may be killed in the use of language which gives the impression of their wisdom, and yet such skill may be totally without bearing upon their capacity to be understanding of the plight of another who, as Job himself, suffers misfortune. Job, therefore asks: "What do the arguments of wise men prove?" He points out that there is no doubting of the human ability to use language, but there certainly is much evidence to doubt the human ability to be sympathetically respectful of "a man past hope" or of "an orphan".[101] Linguistic aptitude is often assumed to be a mark of intelligence that is consistent with an equal achievement of character. But notwithstanding this assumption which is widespread, it is, according to Job, mistaken nonetheless. He accuses his friends of their failure to be critical of this intellectual aptitude which often has no relation whatever to character. He confronts them with the accusation that notwithstanding the intelligence which men exhibit in their use of words, such skilled use may gloss over moral depravity. Skilled though one may be with language, he might also be depraved enough to "cast lots over the fatherless and bargain over (a) friend".[102]

Job's analysis of the moral handicaps which human beings can impose upon other human beings in spite of their many skills is not peculiar to him in the Old Testament. A comparably stern commentary upon the level of which human life is capable is stated in one of the proverbs which declares that a human being is capable of being "A sluggard (who) plunges his hand in the dish but is too lazy to lift it to his mouth".

(26:15) This is a commentary about what some human beings are capabl of becoming through disregarding their aptitudes for cultivating characte They are defeated by the sheer inertia of their inability to take th initiative to become a human being who is even capable of trying. Thi is the tragic dilemma which is the converse of the dilemma of whic Aristotle speaks when he points out that character is cultivated by act of character. The converse is that an inability to do what is essential t character negates even the feeblest initiative to start the cultivation c character. Both relations, the one pointed out by Aristotle and the on pointed out in *Proverbs*, confronts an individual with a problem that i beyond reconciling with what is fair in human life. The fact that ther are individuals without the help either of a context to supplement thei weakness or without a human help to reinforce their weakness to becom what they otherwise might be points to a tragic waste of human lif Such human beings are cast off as if life itself were an impersonal strugg in which only those who have already gained a foothold are given a opportunity to take a second step.

Jeremiah is no less stern in his appraisal of human nature than i either *Job* or the reflecting preserved in *Proverbs*. He addresses himsel to "foolish and senseless people, who have eyes and see nothing, ears an hear nothing". (5:21) Those to whom he addresses this stern rebuke hav capacities to see and to hear, but who do not use their capacities. Thu his commentary about their lethargy is an indictment of the moral weak ness of human beings who do not use capacities they have. The use o eyes for the achievement of what can be learned through sight is a mora challenge. The use of ears to hear what can be heard by the developmen of such native capacities is another moral challenge. These challenges ar moral obligations. Anyone equipped with such capacities ought to us them to their maximum for the enrichment of his own life. And with thi moral accomplishment, he would be prepared to enrich the lives of other by what he does in relation to them. But the failure to do anything o moral worth with native endowments is a moral indictment of an individua who so fails.

Those human beings, on the other hand, who are deprived of the op portunity even to use their capacities for the beneficial advantage of th enrichment of their life are, of course, not included in such censureship It is only those who could do what they fail to do are morally censurable What is significant in this particular analysis is that a human deficiency is itself a cause for human misery.

In spite of Jeremiah's frequent religious explanations for human mis fortune as brought about God's acting, he also takes account of the humar responsibility for human misery, and he does so without referring to God's acting. This is evident in his accusation of human beings for their wrongdoing when he declares: "Your wrongdoing has upset nature's order, and your sins have kept from you her kindly gifts."(vs.25) This is pointing out an unqualified human responsibility for an impoverishment of human well-being.

It is on the basis of this clear-cut and thoroughly moral analysis of a source for human suffering and misery that Jeremiah proposes the essential type of solution for such suffering and the means by which such misery can be diminished. His proposal does not mention what human beings can do to enlist a divine help to lessen their misery. It is rather a direct confrontation of human beings with what they themselves ought to do because they are capable of such acting. He declares: "Mend your ways and your doings, deal fairly with one another, do not oppress the alien, the orphan, and the widow, shed no innocent blood . . . do not run after others gods to your own ruin."(7:5) The obligations of which Jeremiah thus reminds men are their moral responsibilities. By respecting such responsibilities of which they are capable, they themselves could reduce the misery to which great numbers of human beings are subject.

It therefore must be acknowledged that although Jeremiah does emphasize men's dependence upon the providence of God, he also offers an analysis of means by which human well-being could be increased by what human beings themselves are able to do for the benefit of others, and so for the enrichment of human life. If men "truly execute justice one with another", there would be no injustice from which human beings suffer. "If (human beings) do not oppress the alien, the fatherless or the widow, or shed innocent blood" there would be none of these evils to handicap the achievement of well-being in human life.[103] Jeremiah's version of what human life could be is not a theoretical or fantastic utopia. It is what could be if human beings with their abilities and their resources were to do what they actually could do. If this were done, then every human being would be spared encountering what the author of *Ecclesiastes* characterizes as "the wicked deeds done here under the sun."(4:3) Such deeds are human beings' deficiency in respecting their moral obligation to use their capacities and their resources of the earth available to them for the enrichment of human life.

6. *The greatest degree of human misery is caused by war, for which human beings are solely responsible*

A considerable part of the histories of Israelites and Greeks is about

53

warfare. The fourteenth chapter of *First Kings* points out that there was "continual fighting" between Rehoboam, King of Judah, in the early part of the tenth century B.C., and Jeroboam, who revolted under his rule which succeeded in dividing the Hebrews into two kingdoms.(14:30) Thus the history of the Israelites begins in warfare internal to the twelve Hebrew tribes. The result of this was the formation of the Kingdom of Israel and the Kingdom of Judah. Hence when the author of *Second Maccabees,* seven centuries later, refers to the "evils brought about by his wars" when Antiochus Epiphanes destroyed Jewish temples in Syria and declared Judaism illegal, he actually sums up centuries of tragic Hebrew history. (10:10) Irrespective of the occasions for the wars throughout these several centuries, the tragedy of war itself as a method used by human beings cannot be overestimated. Notwithstanding results which may be regarded as necessary for the preservation of a people or for the preservation of its liberty or its religion, it still remains tragic that such a means is employed by human beings to achieve an end which may seem to justify it.

If the Epics record any actual historical events, then Homer's version of early Greek history stresses the same "tragic futility" of war as is stressed by the historians of the Israelites.[104] Just as the history of warfare in which Israelites engaged for centuries is recorded in the Old Testament, so the wars in which the Greeks struggled against the Persians is recorded by Herodotus. One can get some estimate of this tragedy from the description which Herodotus gives of the massive equipment and the hundreds of thousands of men with whom Xerxes invaded Greece. He points out: "If the forces of sea and land be added together, their total sum will be two millions, three hundred and seventeen thousand, six hundred and ten."[105] He then points out that in addition to the men equipped to fight "the service-train that followed them . . . was five millions, two hundred and eighty-three thousand, two hundred and twenty."[106] Even though these figures are not accurate, it is significant to take account of the massive numbers of people used by Xerxes to carry out his own desires. In the battle of Thermopylae "as many as twenty thousand" were killed and most were "buried in digged trenches . . . covered with leaves and heaped earth, that the men of the fleet might not see them".[107] The destruction of this number of men in the armies of Xerxes alone is sobering and it would be a sufficient basis for the most pessimistic and cynical philosophy of history when such occurrences are repeated more times than are even recorded. It is the tragedy of cancelling human life as if it were

no account and as if each human being so destroyed had no moral right
to live. This sobering sense of massive tragedy is vastly intensified when
Herodotus records the "panic" which totally disorganized the Persian
forces so that "the Greeks (were) able to make ... a slaughter of the two
hundred and sixty thousand that remained after Artabazus had fled with
his forty thousand, scarce three thousand were left alive".[108]

The purpose for citing the few accounts given by Herodotus is merely
to indicate the impersonal way in which hundreds of thousands of human
lives can be destroyed as if they were without significance except as means
to carry on warfare. Yet, more than human lives are destroyed in warfare.
Everything to which they had previously devoted their lives is likewise
cancelled as if it were of no essential worth except to demonstrate the
destructive capacities of an enemy. This is illustrated by Herodotus' account of the ruthless destruction of Athens by the Persian general
Mardonius who "burnt Athens, and utterly overthrew and demolished
whatever wall or house or temple was left standing".[109] Such destruction
of cities built by the industry of human beings is recorded in records of
war as it were primarily of statistical importance to indicate the superiority
of an enemy's equipment to destroy a people who is not equally equipped
to defend their homes and their cities.

Herodotus not only points out the tragic destruction of human beings
and cities in war, but he also takes account of equally tragic manifestations
of the low moral level of which some human beings are capable when they
become traitors to their own people. It was, for example, the traitor
Epialtes who, "thinking so to receive a great reward from Xerxes, ... told
him of the path leading over the mountain to Thermopylae; whereby he
was the undoing of the Greeks who had been left there".[110] Thus the
relatively few soldiers under Leonidas were destroyed by the perfidity of
one human being. That the courage and heroism of men should be ineffective against the treachery of a single human scoundrel is one aspect of
the tragedy of war in which the merit of character is often of no consequence in the outcome of military encounters.

Not only single individuals are capable of being traitors, but entire
communities are equally capable of treachery under the direction of leaders
without scruples. Herodotus narrates how "the whole Phocis" was overrun
and destroyed by the Persians who had been given the help of "the
Thessalians". By virtue of the Thessalians' support of the Persians, the
Persians were able to destroy "all that came within their power ... setting
fire to towns and temples".[111] Another commentary which Herodotus makes
on the disloyalty of which human beings are capable is that "Seven

55

nations (which) inhabit the Peloponnese . . . sat apart from the war"
which the rest of Greek city-states were struggling to preserve themselv
against the Persians. Herodotus adds: "By so doing they took the pa
of the enemy."[112]

Entirely apart from any moral consideration of the evil of war as
method by which human beings assume they can resolve problems, the
is the moral consideration of what human beings do within the trag
prosecution of a war. While some give their lives on the principle
defending their homes, others betray such gallant men. The perfidity
some human beings indicates something of the low level of which som
human beings are capable, in contrast to the heroism of which others a
capable. Thus one aspect of the tragedy of warfare is that it provides a
occasion for the most reprehensible aspect of human nature to appear
if it were more effective in human history than heroism and gallant sacr
fice. What constitutes the most sobering aspect of this tragedy in turn
that it provides a basis for a cynical disparagement of the merits
heroism as an expression of the sacrifice which some human being
willingly make in order to do what they regard as their moral obligatio
to their country. In addition to its countless other evils, war provides f
doubting the worth of a supremely praiseworthy aspect of human li
which is a heroism that does not flinch at the sacrifice of its own life. Thu
Croesus, as narrated by Herodotus, affirmed the sensible philosophy of hi
tory, when after his defeat by Cyrus, he declared: "No man is so foolis
as to desire war more than peace: for in peace sons bury their father
but in war fathers bury their sons."[113] Herodotus sums up the tragi
character of war in citing a "Cadmean victory" in which brothers kille
each other.[114] Any reflecting of the nature of such a "victory" is itself
sobering philosophy of history.

The great dramatists of Greece affirm philosophies of the tragic natur
of war, as Aeschylus does in *The Persians* when Atossa, the mother c
Xerxes, declares: "All the youth of the land is now utterly destroyed.
The absurdity of the occasion of the Persian invasion of Greece in whic
the youth of Persia were destroyed is made clear in what she say
about her son: "Impetuous Xerxes, unpeopling the whole surface of th
continent."[115]

The tragic nature of the battle of Salamis, for example, is portraye
by means of Aeschylus' literary skill such as it could not be done by th
factual narrative of Herodotus. He describes the battle in which "the se
was . . . strewn . . . with wrecks and slaughtered men . . . groans and shriek
together filled the open sea until the face of sable night hid the scene

And then he declares that "there never perished in a single day so great a multitude of men".[116]

Aeschylus likewise describes the tragic results of the warfare entailed in the struggle for the throne of Thebes when the bodies of the slain soldiers from Argos were forbidden burial. The king of Argos, making appeal on behalf of the mothers, children, and wives of the unburied soldiers declares: "It is a sea of ruin, fathomless and impassable . . . and nowhere is there a haven from distress."[117] What is profoundly significant in the philosophy implied in Aeschylus' portrayal of this tragic circumstance is the moral right of the women to appeal for the burial of the men whom they love. But pressing for such permission to be granted by the ruler of Thebes would entail additional fighting. Thus Aeschylus points out how the use of military means to gain an end which is morally right may well intensify the tragic evils from which human beings already suffer from war. He points this out in the address of the King of Argos to the suppliant women. He first acknowledges the rightness of their appeal: "The pollution thou namest is beyond all range of speech." Then he points out to them: "Yet if I take my stand before the walls and try the issue of battle with . . . your kinsmen, how will the cost not mount to a cruel price—men's blood to stain the ground for women's sake?"[118]

Aeschylus declares in *Suppliant Maidens* one of the most profound of philosophies about the moral tragedy of war when he takes account of the fact that there often are moral issues which prompt human beings to believe that war is a justified means to resolve them. Yet, taking account of the consequences of such a means in terms of the disregard for other moral considerations is an analysis of the ambivalent character of many, maybe of most, moral issues in human life. This disturbing fact of the ambivalence of moral issues which constitutes the basis both for defending warfare and also for censuring it is pointed out by Aeschylus when the King of Argos declares: "There is no issue without grievous hurt."[119] Acknowledging this fact is itself a critical philosophy of the moral tragedy of war, since there are moral reasons for justifying that human beings do all they can to curb its moral injustice. But there also are moral considerations of which account must be taken when the moral consequences of some of these means are considered. Pointing out this dilemma which is entailed in the moral ambivalence of war is a mark of the philosophical profundity of Aeschylus. In fact, there is nothing either in Plato or Aristotle about the moral issue of warfare which equals this profound reflecting of Aeschylus.

Sophocles points out a sobering fact of human psychology which explains

57

the failure of human beings to take account of the consequences of wh
they do to achieve what seems to them at the time to justify their actir
The wife of Ajax declares: "Men of mean judgment know not the go
thing they have and hold till they have squandered it."[120] This pathe
handicap of human nature which accounts for the intensifying of hum
misery is a deficiency for which moral responsibility can be assigned on
in relatively few instances of human acting. Most human beings are n
capable of projecting in reflecting or in imagination unfavorable cons
quences of acting for which they are impulsively prompted. The trag
character of human life can in great part be attributed to this deficien
of human beings' ability to determine their acting by a realization
what will be entailed in it.

Euripides contributes to the profundity of the dramatists' philosopl
of the tragedy of warfare in *The Trojan Women*. Gilbert Murray declar
that "European literature can boast a no more potent document on tl
theme" of "the cruelty, folly, and futility of war" than is affirmed in tl
drama.[121] A consequence of the suffering entailed in warfare is point
out by Euripides which is not equally stressed by the other Gre
dramatists. It is the total cancellation by many human beings of all ho
for any redemption from the misery of war. This includes giving up i
hope offered in a religion which otherwise might give encouragement
human beings defeated by every other attempt to find escape from tl
heavy weight of their burden of suffering.

Euripedes declares: "When a still city lieth in the hold of desolatio
all God's spirit there is sick and turns from worship."[122] This loss
possible consolation is illustrated in the despondency of the Queen
defeated Troy, who expresses the total abandonment of trust in any he
proposed in a religious faith. She declares: "Ye Gods . . . Alas! Why c:
on things so weak for aid?" But the desolate poverty of all other mea:
of help available in the extremity of such need is thereupon also admitt
by the Queen: "Yet there is something that doth seek, crying for Go
when one of us hath woe."[123]

This analysis of the total helplessness of a human being, brought abo
by the ravages of war, is a fact of which account must be taken in estima
ing the tragic character of this aspect of history. Under circumstances
an absolute destruction of everything that is cherished, it is expecting t
much of a human being to regain a buoyancy to start a struggle ov
again. After being pulverized to the extreme of a negation of every avai
able and imaginable good, it is, therefore, nothing less than sheer herois
of some human beings to reaffirm a courage to try again to find somethi

n life to justify its efforts. When anyone has taken account of the extent o which the demolition of every human good is entailed for many who ;uffer in war, there is then a foundation in his reflecting for understanding he Theban Herald's affirmation: "How much better peace is for mankind han war—peace, the Muses' chiefest friend, the foe of sorrow, whose oy is in glad throngs of children, and its delight in prosperity. These are he blessings we cast away and wickedly embark on war."[124]

Aristophanes points out the alternative with which human beings are onfronted for their failure to cultivate the determination to pursue the methods of peace: "Our cities will soon be but empty husks."[125] Although he specific occasion for this prediction was the Peloponnesian War, it is ts timeless character which is so impressive. Moral conditions for averting he tragedy of destruction through warfare are even more monumental in heir struggle than the energies expended in warfare itself. These condi- ions are nothing less than those stipulated in the Fourth Gospel in the onversation of Jesus with Nicodemus: "Unless one is born anew"—the meaning of which is obvious.(3:5) Unless there is so radical a revision in ne's nature that his impulses to anger, hate, revenge, are dominated by . control which is acquired only through the most persistent of moral liscipline, there is no reasonable basis to anticipate anything in human istory other than a repetition of the tragedies with which mankind has uffered through the centuries, the tragic character of which was antici- ated in the biblical story of the brothers Cain and Abel.

. *Human beings put themselves into moral bondage*

Greek mythology affirms in many graphic ways men's reflecting upon uman misery. Many accounts circulated in mythology about Chiron who uffered from an incurable wound, from the pain of which he could not nd release. What is attributed to this figure in mythology is thus a rojection of what many people regard as the nature of human life. For any, the duration of life is a prolonged endurance of suffering. In ythology, some of the causes for human suffering were attributed to uman beings themselves, and it is, therefore, this analysis which comes vithin the general scope of Greek reflecting on moral responsibility.

The background of the moral philosophies of the celebrated Athenian chools consists of centuries of reflecting on human problems. A primary ifference in the moral philosophy of popular mythology and such academic hilosophies is the systematic character with which the reflecting of the tter is formulated.

Odysseus declares to Alcinous, King of the Phaeacians, that there is "nothing in the world . . . so incontinent as a man's cursed appetite". If this same affirmation were stated as the premise of reflecting on the tragic character of human life, brought about by one aspect of human life itself it would be the basis for a moral philosophy. Notwithstanding the fact that Homer does not expand this generalization about human life to the extent of a systematic moral philosophy, it nevertheless has the philosophical significance of the primary premises in major Athenian moral philosophies formulated centuries after Homer.

Homer points out the fact that one type of bondage in which human beings lose their moral freedom is brought about by their failure to control their inclinations and desires. Uncontrolled impulses, undirected inclinations, and uncriticized desires constitute what Homer refers to as "accursed appetite". He explains the derivation of one type of moral bondage from the vitality with which such an appetitive aspect of a human being's nature "calls for attention so loudly that he is bound to obey it". Its coercive nature is the basis for a moral bondage when there is too little capacity of character to pass judgment upon it as a reflective means by which it is subjected to control. The pathos of human helplessness brought about by virtue of such deficiency of character is pointed out by Homer when Odysseus admits that although his "heart is sick with grief, yet (his) hunger insists that (he) shall eat and drink".[126] The dictate of hunger as one of the bodily appetites thus presses a human being to do what he himself regards as disrespectful to himself during a period of his sorrow. The ambivalence, therefore, of being pressed by one drive within the total nature of an individual's life to displace his own respect for himself for his failure to do what he himself recognizes he ought to do is the tragic nature of bondage to an appetite. What is tragic about a coercive hunger is that it usurps the total life of a human being which also includes sensitivities to be mindful of a respect that under such coercive pressure is disregarded.

When, however, Odysseus admits that "it makes me forget all I have suffered," it seems as if such an appetitive drive were a blessing. But when he continues to admit that it "forces (him) to take (his) fill," he points out the moral cost he has to pay for what might seem to be beneficial in enabling him to forget his sorrow. His sorrow, nevertheless, persists. And in addition to the heavy heart it continues to oppress, an individual suffers from censorship of himself for giving in to the coercive demand of a single aspect of his nature which he cannot approve as justified to usurp sorrow for a privation in his life which is far more acute than any delay in eating could possibly be.

It is the self-analysis which takes place in Odysseus' reflecting that indicates the extraordinary profundity of Homer's capacity as a moral philosopher. This single analysis includes all of the primary elements in a self-censorship for a failure which one himself cannot willingly accept as an element in his own life. The sternness with which Odysseus censures himself for his momentary weakness of consenting to so assertive an aspect of his nature is his remorse that he failed to respect his own more praiseworthy sensitivities.

As a spokesman for Homer's profound moral philosophizing, Odysseus points out to Eurycleia, his faithful nurse, that "men (fall) victims to . . . their own infamy". This explanation for what contributes to human misery is a thoroughgoing moral analysis. It accounts for human misery by a human deficiency to avert what brought about such suffering. In his moral philosophizing to his nurse, he declares that it is men's "own insensate wickedness" which brings "them to (the) awful end" from which they suffer.[127] The particular circumstance about which Odysseus speaks that provokes his moral philosophizing is of no philosophical significance. It does, of course, have literary or dramatic significance, since it is his reflecting on the tragic outcome of the princes of Argos for exploiting his possessions. The lack of all discipline which they might well have imposed upon themselves by virtue of their early training and their intelligence constitutes a "reckless" disregard for the rights of another. Lattimore's translation of this discourse of Odysseus points out how the tragic end of their lives is the penalty they have brought upon themselves: "By their own recklessness they have found a shameful death."[128]

Aeschylus continues the same type of reflecting on moral responsibility for the misfortunes from which men suffer that they might have avoided had they done differently. The spirit of Darius in *The Persians* reflects on the disaster of the Persians at Salamis which illustrates how "man hasteneth to his own undoing".[129]

Deianira, the wife of Heracles, in Sophocles' *Trachiniae*, is aware of a constant inclination to which a human being subjects himself to add to his difficulties by giving in to an impulse. Although there was dramatic reason for her to protest against the causes which brought about her sorrow, she, nevertheless, was keenly aware of how she herself could add to her own suffering. She declares: "Nor will I fondly aggravate my trouble by warring against Heaven."[130] Many people in Greek tragedies did just this, and in doing so, they augmented their plight by hurling their anger

61

against a possible source of help which, by their appropriate behavior, could have diminished their misery.

For dramatic reasons, Euripides has Hecuba declare that "there is not in the world a single man free; for he is either a slave to money or to fortune".[131] If this generalization were pressed for its implications, it would actually negate the possibility for the profoundest of dramatic tragedies. Tragedies of the greatest pathos derive from events which occur in the life of human beings that collide with a character that would have demonstrated merit had it not been for such events for which they themselves were not entirely responsible. Although ascertaining such responsibility is not one of the clear-cut features either of drama or philosophy, strength of character always is a praiseworthy aspect of a human being. If the expression of such character were totally negated by occurrences for which an individual was not himself responsible, there would be no tragic encounter of his character with events by the demonic vigor of which it was demolished. The generalization, therefore, which Euripides affirms would have to be qualified both for dramatic reasons and also for moral reasons. If it were the case that there were no human beings with capacities of character sufficient to prevent themselves from slipping into a bondage, then even the adverse impact of "fortune" upon human life would not constitute dramatic tragedy. If it were the case that everyone's effort to discipline himself by character were totally ineffective, all such effort would be morally futile. This would make every serious moral philosophy nothing more than wishful thinking. It would express only what might be thought, but which could not become actualized. It may well be that most human beings may be characterized by the generalization which Hecuba affirms. Yet, the very possibility for realistic moral philosophies, and for the most profoundly moving of dramatic tragedies, rests upon the fact that there are some human beings who do not come within the scope of this sweeping indictment of human weakness. The basis upon which reflecting comes to the realization of the pathos of human life is that there actually are great numbers of human beings handicapped by their own deficiency of character. But the redeeming encouragement with which reflecting on human history is brightened is what some human beings demonstrate about what can be done by human effort, notwithstanding every obstacle to its defeat. It is this "faithful remnant" of which the Bible speaks. It is this same segment of human history of which Emerson speaks when he declares that when he is discouraged by the "almshouse of the world", he turns to Plutarch's *Parallel Lives* for encouragement about what some human beings have done to demonstrate a wiser and a better way which others failed to achieve.

The same basic premise of a moral philosophy is affirmed in the Bible as it is affirmed in Greek literature, beginning with its mythology that circulated orally before being reduced to writing. One may assume that the same serious type of moral philosophizing took place among the earliest of the Israelites and circulated for their instruction centuries before it was formulated in religious literature. The earliest of the Israelites were aware of the tragic waste of human life in ceaseless warfare, and they were likewise aware of the tragic waste of human effort in building cities which were only to be destroyed by other human beings. It was this sobering reflecting which was carried on in the writings of Isaiah as he reflected on the destruction of Edom. He declares that "From generation to generation it shall lie waste, and no man shall pass through it ever again". (34:10) This commentary cannot even be thought about without sobering one by its pathos. The demolition of all that a people had worked for which gave them promise of their well-being is summed up by the Prophet when he declares that "nettles and briars shall cover its walled towns" which once were trusted for the defense they might offer to safeguard their homes. (vs. 12, 13)

Jeremiah thought of the history of his people and what it included that constitutes sheer tragedy, including the hatred and its expression in the warfare between the twelve tribes of one people. It was this history of which he speaks when he refers to "the evil which the house of Israel and the house of Judah have done".[132] The cause for their mutual suffering was their mutual failure to work for each others' welfare. Instead, the life and property of one part of this people were directed to the destruction of the life and property of another part. It is this type of internecine warfare which constitutes the aspect of human history for which Schopenhauer finds a parallel in the Australian bulldog ant which, when cut in half, engages in a struggle in which the tail stings the head and the mandibles of the head claw the tail until the creature is dead.[133]

One of the most sobering instances of reflecting on human history is expressed in the book of *Exodus* in which its historian takes account of the history of the Israelites in servitude to the Egyptians. He points out that "the more harshly they are treated, the more their numbers increased". (1:12) This fact is stern. Entirely apart from any specifically religious philosophy of history, in which the increase of their numbers was argued as making it possible for them to escape their servitude, and so again to "worship God" in their own synagogues, is the fact that parents could bring children into such misery. If there were no means what-soever by which the rate of birth might have been reduced for the sake of sparing children from going through the misery of their parents, then there would be no essential difference in determinants in the history of a people who "were fruitful and prolific" and in the animal kingdom in which, in spite of recurring starvation, whatever vitality remains in the crippled parent is expended in procreation. But if one reflects on the tragedy of suffering which is perpetuated by such procreation without limit, one despairs that even pity for children is not sufficient to make a differ-ence in what people do to mate under the pressure of instinct that totally paralyzes the human capacity to project its consequences beyond the moment in which reflecting is cancelled. Every other aspect of human life comes under reflective scrutiny and even censureship, but not the ele-mentary aspect of life in which life perpetuates its suffering by bringing other life into being. There are many sound recommendations retained in the biblical book of *Proverbs,* such as "Do not slave to get wealth; be a sensible man, and give up". (23:4) But there is not one proverb which considers the aspect of human life and its responsibility for perpetuating suffering such as is considered in *Exodus.*

What is morally sound in this quoted proverb is the awareness that a human being is confronted with alternatives in acting. He can devote his life to the extent of bondage in his pursuit of wealth. Or he can cultivate a moral freedom from such subordination to a goal which is as illusive as dipping the sea with the sieves of the cursed Danaïdes. Their curse, ac-cording to Greek mythology, was attempting to accomplish what *in principle* is incapable of being accomplished.

The tragedy of insatiable hungers is engaging in any behavior incapable of terminating a desire which presses for satisfaction. By their very nature of affirming demands which are without limit, they are *in principle* in-capable of being satisfied. It is this curse of the insatiable hungers of human life of which Isaiah speaks when he declares one may eat "his fill but yet is hungry" and "another devours but is not satisfied". (9:19, 20) The same sobering reflecting on the tragedy of spending a lifetime in pur-suit of ends incapable of satisfying the hungers which impel such efforts is also affirmed in the apocryphal writing of *Baruch,* whose author asks: "Where are those who have hoarded the silver and gold men trust in, never satisfied with their gains?" (3:17, 18) If an answer were given to this question, it would be that such human beings are everywhere. This fact is the basis for the reflecting upon the sense of futility with which so many are engulfed after devoting their lives to acquiring what leaves them

64

still unsatisfied. Their failure to be satisfied by what they do is in the very nature of the things for which they expend their efforts. Only an intrinsically good object of effort is capable of yielding a satisfaction which not only terminates an effort to acquire it, but what is far more significant, satisfies the individual himself, and not only one of his desires. It completes his nature by not continuing to refer beyond the fulfillment itself.

The tragedy of people devoting their lives in the pursuit of a type of good which is incapable of satisfying them, but only reinforcing the effort itself to continue to seek, is pointed out by Jeremiah: "They cannot retrace their steps." (9:5) What they have done determines what they become. And what they become, determines what they continue to do. This cycle does not stop of itself. It is the "Wheel of Ixion" in the mythology of the Greeks which expresses the sobering reflecting upon the tragic penalty of struggling for the satisfaction of insatiable wants. Such wants are reinforced by the energy with which their satisfaction is sought. Rather than diminishing their hungers, their hungers recur with the increased frequency that effort is directed to end them. This is the type of tragic life in which *Second Esdras* maintains that human beings "are entangled". The Prophet Ezra expresses his pity for them by declaring "Alas for those who are . . . overrun with their wicked deeds!" (16:77) Although his terminology introduces a consideration of men's relation to God to whom they have responsibilities which they do not respect, what is significant in this reflecting is the moral relation between what men do and what "entangles" them. It is this plight which confronts men so entrapped by their own failures that is the occasion for their turning beyond themselves to seek help from a reality transcendent of themselves. It is because the Prophet believes in the soundness of this type of release from the human plight of self-created misery that he declares: "Abandon your sins, and have done with your wicked deeds for ever! Then God will set you free from all distress." (vs. 67) The "distress" of which he speaks is created by human beings themselves. It is brought about by what he refers to as "sins" and "wicked deeds". Thus this type of analysis is in a terminology which is outside the scope of strict moral philosophy. It introduces a consideration which is not internal to a reflecting confined only to moral considerations. Reflecting limited to moral considerations alone would take account of what men themselves can do to liberate themselves from handicaps which they also have created, and so for which they are responsible. After creating handicaps for which they are responsible, they in turn would be considered as responsible for freeing themselves from such an impairment of their well-being. But when such an ability has itself

65

been lost by what a human being has done to limit his capacities to help himself, then a religious type of reflecting, such as is expressed by the Prophet, proposes a religious solution to the otherwise tragic plight of human life.

Such a religious proposal itself, however, raises problems in reflecting provided one continues to think about what is implied in affirming that a divine providence can do for human beings what they cannot do for themselves after destroying their own resources for helping themselves. This is the disturbing problem which Isaiah asks: "Why, Lord, dost thou let us wander from thy ways." (63:17) This question arises, of course, only for one who believes that there is a providence or a divine help available to do for men what they cannot do for themselves. But when this is believed, it is also a sobering aspect of reflecting that such a providence did not make itself available for men's help before they destroyed their well-being and before they impaired their capacities so completely that they could subsequently do too little to help themselves. Every sort of explanation can be given to resolve this problem of which reflecting becomes aware. A common type is offered by St. Augustine, who maintains that the more a human being destroys his own capacities to do what he ought to do, the more he demonstrates his final dependence upon God. If this type of explanation is proposed, it obviously goes entirely outside the scope of moral considerations. Even the tragic waste of life, which in a consistent moral reflecting would be looked upon as a moral tragedy, is not even regarded as tragic by such a religious explanation. The religious point of view is that no cost is too much if only it brings men to realize their final dependence upon God. Whereas this is cogent for one type of religious interpretation of human life, it is, nevertheless, entirely outside a reflecting on the moral tragedy of a human being who disregards what he might have done had he taken advantage of his own capacities to cultivate a character that would have oriented itself to a reality transcendent of human life, and would have done this before being so incapacitated by his own moral impotence that he was reduced to a moral helplessness of character.

One morally cogent type of reflecting which includes belief in the human being's relation to a divine reality, as the final source of trustworthy guidance in his life, is stated in the apocryphal writing of *Baruch*, which declares: "If you had walked in the way of God, you would have lived in peace for ever." (3:13) Even if one were to restrict his reflecting on human life within the scope of moral considerations alone, he could also agree with the profundity of this analysis. This type of religious analysis is not an abrogation of moral considerations, and so does not introduce

66

into a moral philosophy a consideration which is incompatible with it. It rather proposes a normative referent by which human life could bring about the cultivation of a character within whose nature is a stability made possible by its orientation to a type of guidance which is trustworthy.

Jeremiah offers this same type of sound religious thought to supplement whatever is consistent with a thoroughgoing moral philosophy when he declares: "Stop at the cross-roads; look for the ancient paths; ask, 'Where is the way that leads to what is good?' Then take that way, and you will find rest for yourselves." (6:16) This proposes what man himself should do. It directs him to orient himself to a dependable guidance. This, therefore, is not first acknowledging man's helplessness before he turns beyond himself. It proposes that if one were to begin his life looking for sound guidance, he would be spared a moral handicap to his own abilities by reaching out for every inducement which seems attractive because he had not already done his utmost to cultivate a capacity to reflect on what would be consistent with the cultivation of a character by means of which he would enjoy well-being for himself and for others influenced by his character.

II

Turning Beyond Human Resources

1. *Turning beyond human life for a help which is not believed to be available within human resources is a religious act*

An element within human life which accounts for its religious mode is a realization of its limited capacities to find within its own resources all that it requires for its well-being. A turning beyond human life, however, occurs only when a human being believes that there is a reality transcendent of human life which can fulfill its requirements as no human resource can do. This turning beyond human resources expresses a religious realization that there is a radical difference between two realities. Whereas human nature is regarded as deficient within its own capacities to fulfill its own requirements, religious faith affirms the belief that there is a reality transcendent of human life which is capable of completing human beings' otherwise incomplete lives.

Job states the nature of human life which accounts for its inability to provide for itself what it requires when he points out that men "dwell in houses whose walls are clay, whose foundations are dust, which can be crushed like a bird's nest or torn down between dawn and dark" (4:19, 20) If human beings did not require the security of a predictable source of good, their limited nature would not confront them with their own inadequacy. But the fact that human beings have a need for security which is not fulfilled within the transient order of their existing, they are confronted with a disparity between what they themselves can do and what they also cannot do.

Psalms continues the analysis of the nature of human beings which accounts for the disparity between their requirements and the resources within their own control for fulfilling such requirements. The Psalmist declares: "I look to my right hand, I find no friend by my side." Such unavailability of a trustworthy source for the fulfillment of a need expressive of human beings' social nature leaves them wanting. This persistent and irrepressible social need for a relation to another living being which supplements the loneliness of a life without companionship is described in the same psalm: "I cry to thee, O Lord, and say, 'Thou art my refuge; thou art all I have in the land of the living.'" (142:4, 5)

The pathos of this loneliness of a human being, needing a companionship which is not within his ability to control, is countered by the religious assurance that beyond human life is a help which can do for him in his need what no human being can equally fulfill. This reassurance thus diminishes the pathos and plight of a life which would otherwise hopelessly search for a good it requires and for which it hungers.

Thus the deficiency internal to the resources of human life is cancelled as a human being turns beyond human life with the trust that there is a reality other than human life which can help him as no aspect of human life or its resources can. The assurance that there is such a reality includes a consolation that it will "give heart to the orphan and widow" who are left without human help they require for their security. (146:9) This reality in which a religious trust is invested is believed to be capable of lifting the heavy load of discouragement of one who seeks within human sources but does not find what his nature requires. *Psalms* assure such troubled human beings that there is a Lord above who "straightens backs which are bent" by the burdens of sorrow undiminished by hope. (vs. 8)

This faith which orients a human being beyond human life liberates the discouraged from the oppressive load of their discouragement. The heavy weight of this oppressive burden is lightened for them by their assurance that "The Lord . . . set(s) the prisoner free" from his discouragement. (vs. 7)

The Prophet Isaiah reaffirms the same profound understanding as the Psalmist does of the plight of human beings who seek within human resources for a help they cannot find: "No help they find . . . only disappointment." (30:5) The recurring disappointments with which human beings are confronted understandably reaches a point beyond their endurance. And if it were not for a faith that there is a justification for them to turn beyond limited human resources, their life would be an unbroken despair. After becoming strengthened by their confidence that there is a trustworthy help available to them which human resources do not offer, they are freed from depending as they formerly had upon an unpredictable human help. Such human beings with the support of this trust ask themselves: "Why then fear man . . . man frail as grass?" (51:12) This complete reversal in their attitude accompanies the benefit they gained from the trust on which they reoriented themselves. The confidence with which a religious trust strengthens the former helplessness of a human being is affirmed by Isaiah in pointing out that even the mightiest of political powers are after all only men. Once cowed by the might of the Egyptians, a religious Israelite becomes confident that "The Egyptians are men, not God, their horses are flesh, not spirit". (31:3) This disparagement of the power of the Egyptians with which they exerted their oppressive cruelty in subjecting a people to servitude would not be forthcoming if such an Israelite were crushed by the fear of torture or death from such power.

But a reappraisal of what men can do accompanies their reorientations beyond human life to a reality upon which they trust as they trust no other reality. Trustworthiness is the esteemed property of a reality to which religious people turn for a help that reinforces their confidence that what human resources cannot give, such a reality can give. This reevaluation of all help internal to human life, however, could not come about apart from a metaphysic affirmed in religious trust. A religious trust is directed to what is believed to be a reality capable of justifying such trust. Confidence in its trustworthiness, therefore, accounts for turning from human life with an assurance that it can fulfill requirements which human resources can not fulfill. After this reappraisal of what human resources cannot do in contrast to a reality which is believed to be capable of doing, religious individuals ask themselves the question about the plight of others without such trust: "How can they raise themselves?" (*Is*, 2:9)

Greek tragedians of the fifth century B.C. were as clearly aware as were the Israelite authors of books in the Bible that there is a requirement within human nature which human resources are incapable of satisfying. This is pointed out many times in the various dramas of Euripides. In the despair from which Hecuba suffered the loss of everything in life which she once regarded as her possessions, she acknowledges: "There is something that doth seek, crying for God, when one of us hath woe."[1] In reflecting on the reverses of her life and the poverty of every available help to give her courage, she acknowledged that whereas "the cup of Death is empty," nevertheless, "Life hath always hope".[2] This is a mode within human experience that sustains the courage to seek beyond human life for a help which human resources cannot give. Another translation uses the expression "space for hope" to point out the basis internal to human life, which oppressed with despair, turns beyond itself and beyond human means of help.[3]

Iphigenia affirms the philosophy of Euripides about the unpredictability of human reverses and adversities when she declares "Who knows whom . . misfortunes may attend?" And she herself answers this question by declaring: "None can tell the ills to come."[4] The Chorus in *Iphigenia in Tauris* affirms: "Sweet is hope" when all of a human being's "pursuits are vain".[5] Hope itself is a saving factor internal to human life which is discouraged nearly to the extreme of total despair. But the basis for such hope is the trust that there is a reality other than everything which brings about such despair.

Hope is not generated by the mode of despair. It is generated rather by a belief that, apart from every cause for despair, there is a reality which offers a way to be freed from the circumstances which dominate life to the extent of such despair. The counsel which is affirmed by the Chorus in Euripides' *Ion* is "mid the greatest ills, never let mortal man abandon hope".[6]

Sound though this counsel is to propose such a way to be spared from a total despair, such counsel itself is impotent to bring about hope. The only factor which can support hope in occasions which would otherwise be unrelieved despondency is the belief or faith that beyond the occasions for such despair is another type of reality. It is this metaphysic or idea of a reality transcendent of the circumstances productive of despair which can alone support the initiative to be hopeful. Hope obviously is not brought about by the same evidence which negates hope. And the circumstances in which an individual reaches unrelieved despair is such a negation of the initiative to hope. Thus it is only as there is a hope which is not cancelled by despondency is it possible for a despairing person to be reoriented beyond the occasions for his despondency. Such a reorientation made possible by the emergence of a hope in what might come about to redeem the misery of despondency is an expression of a residue of courage which remains after reaching a point of near cancellation.

Whatever makes this possible is bewildering. Somehow the occasions internal to which despondency arises do not cancel the emergence of hope in a way that can cope with such despondency. It is, therefore, this triumph of hope over despair which demonstrates the capacities of character notwithstanding its confrontation with a test that often reaches a point of destroying it. Amphitryon in Euripides' *Heracles* affirms a sound moral philosophy when he declares "The bravest man is he who relieth ever on his hopes". Such ability to hope, notwithstanding despondency or despair,

71

is the redemptive factor internal to the resources of a human being's char acter which saves him from total despair which is said in this drama t be "the mark of a coward".[7]

Euripides' disparagement of an individual as a "coward" who canno maintain his hope notwithstanding the massive nature of discouragemen expresses a rationalistic moral philosophy which maintains that there ar no limits to which a character can be pressed that will bring about its tota destruction. This type of moral philosophy, therefore, is not capable o acknowledging the limits of human strength which so often are reached when the only redeeming source of help is a faith in a reality other tha one's character. Aeschylus and Sophocles are more capable than Euripide is of being sympathetic with the role of religious faith in occasions of defeat of the strength of character itself.

The apocryphal book, *Wisdom of Solomon,* acknowledges limits withi the resources of character such as a rationalistic philosophy does not. It author declares: "It was neither herb nor poultice that cured" a stricke people, but the "all-healing word" of the Lord. (16:12) The author of thi writing believes that there is a source of help transcendent of human lif which is "the guide of their uncharted journey". (18:3) The religiou faith with which this writer interprets the role of faith itself in human lif is affirmed in his declaration that "Let a man be ever so perfect in th eyes of his fellow-men, if the wisdom that comes from thee is wanting, h will be of no account". (9:6, 7) According to this religious faith, what i most worthy of being cherished about human resources is the faith itsel that can orient human life beyond itself.

2. Trusting a divine reality for its directing of one's life is also a moral act

It may be that the one-hundred-and-nineteenth Psalm is the profound est single interpretation in the Bible of the relationship between a religion and a morality. These two aspects of human life are expressed in the brief statement in this psalm: "How I long for thy precepts." (vs. 40) The Psalmist's awareness of his need for a trustworthy directive in his life is a manifestation of his serious moral reflecting. The confidence with which he believes that this need can be fulfilled by orienting his life beyond human directives to a divine reality is an expression of his religious faith.

The moral aspect of human life is doing all that an individual can do to acquire a trustworthy guidance for his life. This is achieved by those, such as the Psalmist, who have a religious faith that a trustworthy guidance can be introduced into life from a reality transcendent of human life. It is the moral effort itself to discover such a trustworthy authority for life which accounts for supplementing moral earnestness with religious dedication. This twofold aspect of a serious moral life which is also a devout religious life is expressed in the appeal of the Psalmist: "Teach me, O Lord, the way out in thy statutes." (vs. 33) The motive of the Psalmist for orienting himself to a reality he reveres as ultimate is that its authority in his life will not be superseded by another. As such, it will be a directive for his acting which is worthy of his unqualified trust. The motive for the religious act of orienting himself beyond the resources of his own life is acquiring a benefit in his life for which there is no other equivalent.

The constancy of well-being in human life is brought about by the constancy of its directive which is its moral authority. In seeking for a guidance in relation to a reality which is eternal, a religious individual thus is confident that he entrusts his life to an authority which is not capable of being superseded by another. His assurance in the trustworthiness of such guidance by which he seeks to order his life is a moral benefit that is derived from a religious act. This relation is pointed out by the Psalmist when he declares that "in keeping thy statutes, I shall find my reward". (vs. 33) According to this profound insight into the intrinsic worth of a trustworthy directive in life, the Psalmist does not seek a reward beyond life, such as a popular religious expectation of a paradise. His motive for orienting himself beyond his life for a directive of his life is for the enrichment of his life. The Psalmist's version of religion, therefore, is not a negation of life, but its affirmation. This type of religious dedication to a divine reality which is trusted for its guidance of one's life is supplementing all other moral resources for the achievement of its well-being.

The Psalmist's moral seriousness is affirmed in his search for "instruction" upon which he can depend. His religious faith fulfills this search by orienting him to a reality which is not subject to fluctuations in its dependability. Hence in his religious appeal, "Dispose my heart toward thy instruction," he acknowledges the inconstancy to which he is subjected by virtue of his own nature. (vs. 36) It is from such inconstancy of dedication to an authority for life that he desires to be free. But freedom from such inconstancy is only by means of being oriented to a reality whose worthiness to be trusted is its constancy. The constancy with which a religious human being directs his trust is, from his point of view, not entirely within his own control. It is the Psalmist's awareness of the limits

73

of his own integrity which is expressed in his appeal that his limited moral capacities may be strengthened by a wisdom granted him through turning to the reality he unqualifiedly trusts. Such awareness of his own limits is declared in the prayer: "Give me the insight to obey thy law and to keep it with all my heart." (vs. 34) If the Psalmist were confident in the constancy of his own commitment to what he respects as a trustworthy directive in his life he would not acknowledge his need for more dependable support than he finds within himself.

In this reflecting on what he most wants in life as the fulfillment of his utmost requirement, he is aware that this is a "law" or moral authority to which he can devotedly subordinate himself. Such an unbroken devotion to a single authority for life would, therefore, be a moral means to achieve a constancy in a pattern of living. But a reflective realization of the type of reality by means of which this requirement can be fulfilled includes an awareness that such a reality is other than oneself.

Believing there is such a reality which can fulfill one's most persistent need for trustworthy guidance is religious faith. Turning to it with a devoted willingness to acknowledge one's limited resources without it is a morally motivated act. It is relating oneself to a reality he trusts for enabling him to achieve the constancy in his life which he wants more than any other condition for his well-being.

The Psalmist declares his intention to devote himself to taking account of his dependence, and therefore he affirms the resolve: "I will meditate on thy precepts and keep thy paths ever before my eyes." (vs. 15) His pledge to do all that he himself can do to bring about the type of life that he wants more than any other good is not made to himself. It is not merely a resolution which he proposes among other suggestions of which he also should take account. It is rather a promise to the reality upon which he acknowledges his final dependence. Thus his moral resolve to "meditate on thy precepts" is an acknowledgement of his total dependence for a guidance which is other than his own meditating. If meditating were a clarifying of a pattern of acting, and therefore did not refer beyond the mental activity itself, there would be no such transcending of moral efforts by a religious act. There is, however, such transcending of an otherwise commendable moral resolve by acknowledging, as the Psalmist does, that the "precepts" are not products of his own meditating. They likewise are not his own insights into what he himself might do for his own benefit. The reality upon which he resolves to meditate is transcendent of himself, just as the "paths" are which he desires to "keep . . . ever before (his) eyes". (vs. 15)

In this particular resolve, however, to meditate, the Psalmist does not seek a help other than himself to enable him to be constant in his resolve. In this respect, he affirms a confidence in what he can do to carry out his resolve. But his resolve is not to propose ways by which he might live with a constant benefit of trustworthy authority. His resolve rather is to make himself obedient to an authority which confronts him with its ultimate nature. This, therefore, is a metaphysic which is basic to every genuine religious act of turning beyond human resources, because such orienting affirms a faith that there is a reality which can contribute to human life what human life cannot itself contribute.

The religious nature of the Psalmist's reflecting upon what he needs, which his resources cannot themselves fulfill, is expressed in his prayer: "Grant me the grace of living by thy law." (vs. 29) This prayer both acknowledges that there is a reality to which the Psalmist desires to orient himself, and it also acknowledges his dependence upon the grace of such a reality to enable him to live according to its authority. In appealing for such grace to supplement his own restricted capacities to remain loyal to the reality he trusts for doing for him what no other reality can do, he acknowledges a twofold dependence which is unqualifiedly religious. He is dependent both upon the directive of the divine "law" and also upon the divine grace to enable him to be spared from the mistake of turning to another source for guidance.

He is clearly aware that the moral benefit of a trustworthy authority to command his life is not contingent entirely upon his own resolve to be loyal to it. This is the same religious acknowledgement which St. Augustine affirmed. He prayed for God's grace to sustain his desire to be helped by God. In acknowledging that one himself is not even capable of sustaining an unbroken dedication to an authority for life which one trusts as supremely worthy of his dedication, one transcends a moral inventory of his own resources. He thereby passes from a confidence which he has in the adequacy of himself to an acknowledgment of his dependence upon a reality which he esteems for its worthiness to direct his life. This is a religious act. It is qualified by no confidence in what he himself is capable of doing for his own sustained orientation to a guidance which he trusts as supremely worthy for directing his life.

One request which the Psalmist makes of God which seems to abrogate his moral responsibility is his prayer: "Make me walk in the path of thy commandments." But this appeal is completed with his affirmation "for that is my desire". (vs. 35) The second part of this affirmation of a religious appeal is a declaration of a moral decision. He affirms that his acknowledgment of his dependence upon God is his own decision.

Thus what appears to be an expression of moral helplessness, actually is an affirmation of the moral wisdom of the Psalmist to acknowledge that his supreme desire is that he should be directed entirely by God's authority without any qualification that he himself might propose. His acknowledgment of his dependence upon God for becoming the sole authority by which he makes his decisions is itself a moral act. Such a moral act is acknowledging that there are no directives either of his or of other human beings which he trusts as he trusts the directives of God, referred to in the scriptures of his people as the "commandments" or the "laws" or the "will" of God.

The moral motivation in his religious acknowledgment of his dependence upon God's directives is unambiguously affirmed in his declaration "for through them thou has given me life". (vs. 93) In other words, the purpose for turning beyond human resources to a reality transcendent of such resources is that it is capable of doing in human life what human beings without such help are not capable of doing.

The constancy of principles which men themselves formulate as their rules for acting is no greater than is their competency to anticipate the change in their own requirements. Hence, insofar as a person regards the constancy of a directive for life to be the supreme good, he is confronted with the necessity to seek such a good from a source other than human life. This type of reflecting is basic to consistently devout religious people. It is also basic to the tradition of Platonic philosophy.

Plato esteemed the eternal nature of the ultimate Good as the one reality upon which human life might depend for its normative directing. Thus the metaphysic of Plato includes a philosophy of reality which in essential respects is basic to the Psalmist's religious life. But the Psalmist affirms a religious faith such as Plato does not insofar as the Psalmist acknowledges that the ultimate reality is mindful of his appeal to it to enter into his life. According to Plato's philosophy, the ultimate Good blesses life, but such a benefaction takes place as a result only of what a reasonable individual does in orienting himself to its nature. Its eternal nature, according to Plato, is inconsistent with its initiative toward the human being which directs himself toward it. Aristotle makes this relation of the human being to the ultimate reality thoroughly unequivocal when he compares the help made possible for human life in orienting itself to the Ultimate as the same type of help which a book can yield when an individual turns to it for its enlightening benefit. The attractiveness of a book for an ndividual who turns to it for whatever benefit he can receive from reading is his estimate of the book. The book provides a benefit in his life only pon the condition that it is sought. In other words, it does not seek an ndividual to take advantage of the benefit it can yield.

The religious trust which the Psalmist affirms in his relation to God is hat God will take the initiative to enter his life to give him strength to ustain his trust in God's help. This is a consistent religious faith. It is uch faith which accounts for a religious individual's orienting of his life o a divine reality. But the basis for such orienting beyond himself is his wareness of his own limited capacities to sustain any pattern of living vhich is consistently trustworthy. Thus turning beyond his own trust in vhat he himself can do for himself is the religious act which culminates , morally serious reflecting on relating oneself to a thoroughly dependable authority for life. If an individual were confident that he could formulate a directive that would not require reformulating, he would have no moral motivation to look beyond his own reflective abilities.

The Psalmist affirms a religious faith which is not qualified by an indication of his confidence in his own resourcefulness when he admits that "If thy law had not been by continual delight, I should have perished in all my troubles". (vs. 92) This admission by the Psalmist that he would have been unable to direct his own life without the guidance from a source beyond his own reflecting is itself a religious act. It acknowledges his helplessness apart from a source of help other than himself. Included in such a religious act is the affirmation of a metaphysic that there is a reality to which life can be oriented as an expression of moral wisdom.

Deciding to commit onself to what he acknowledges as the wisest way by which he can live is itself normative morality. The Psalmist exemplifies how such normative morality can pass into a religious act, and do so in a way which is the fulfilment of the moral quest itself for constancy in the directives by which he desires to live.

When the Psalmist declares that "It is by thy precepts that I find the right way", he affirms the moral purpose for his religious act of orienting himself to God for the constancy of God's directive in his life through the medium of God's commandments, as these are interpreted in the scriptures of the Psalmist's culture. (vs. 128) The explanation which the Psalmist gives for his religious act of trusting the commands or law of God is moral. By virtue of the Psalmist's attempt to have the benefit of "find-(ing) the right way", he orients himself to the only reality which he trusts for making such a discovery possible.

The Psalmist confirms the wisdom of his religious act of turning to the

77

eternal reality which he trusts as a directive for his life when he declares "I have found more joy along the path of thy instruction than in any kind of wealth". (vs. 14) The benefit from relating himself to a reality he reveres as trustworthy is the enhancement of the quality of his life. If the well-being or "joy" which he attributes to having discovered such an "instruction" is the highest possible good he can experience in his life then the consequence of his religious act is moral. This does not refer beyond his life. But it is achieved by what he does in turning beyond himself in order to find "instruction" by which to live for the purpose of achieving the completest degree of well-being of which he is capable.

The constancy of help which the Psalmist receives from what he reveres as the guidance of God's directives or "statutes" is acknowledged as his "continual delight". He declares: "In thy statutes I find continual delight." (vs. 16) Another expression of his gratitude for the "instruction" which he attributes to God's guidance in his life is his acknowledgment: "Thy instruction is my continual delight." He declares that he "turn(s) to it for counsel". (vs. 24)

The role of such trustworthy counsel in his life is the completion of his moral quest to find a guidance which is dependable. His confidence in its dependability is by virtue of the metaphysic with which he interprets such trustworthy "counsel" of God's "commandments". He declares: "I see that all things come to an end, but thy commandment has no end.' (vs. 96) The enduring character of an eternal directive for human life is the basis, therefore, for a religious faith that such a reality is the supreme good upon which a human being may depend, and depend for its role as "counsel" or "instruction" in his life.

There are also other references in *Psalms* which acknowledge an enrichment of human life by turning to a divine reality for its benefactions The thirty-fourth psalm declares: "Those who seek the Lord lack no good thing." (vs. 10) Such seeking is itself a moral benefit. It gives direction to a life that orients itself to a reality from which it seeks enlightenment. But the purpose for such seeking is not itself the benefit contributed by the seeking itself, although this does provide one type of direction to life. From the point of view of a religious individual, the purpose for so orienting himself is for achieving knowledge of such a reality. Thus there are two entirely different types of philosophies basic to an interpretation of the benefit of a religious act of seeking instruction from a divine reality. Philosophies of Existence maintain it is the seeking itself which is beneficial in directing a human life. Philosophies on the other hand, which do not hesitate to affirm a metaphysic of ultimate reality, are respectful of the metaphysic which is integral to the religious act of relating life to what is revered as a reality transcendent of human life.

Isaiah declares it is God who assures human beings that He instructs those who seek Him, and He does so for their benefit: "I teach you for your own advantage." (48:17) This interpretation of the justification for a religious act of orienting human life beyond iself is for the moral achievement of trustworthy guidance. Isaiah's interpretation of God's assurance to human beings includes a declaration of the necessity that human life should be so instructed; "I teach you . . . and lead you in the way you must go." At first glance this appears to be a type of coercion which negates the moral aspect of such instruction. It seems as if it denies a human being the option to decide whether to accept or to reject. Yet the necessity which is so affirmed is not a coercion of a human being to accept such instruction. It rather declares that if he seeks a guidance which will not be displaced by one that is more trustworthy, he has no alternative but to accept the guidance offered by God's instruction. This is made clear in declaring to human beings that if they had always oriented themselves to God's instruction through his commandments, they would not have engaged in activities which they subsequently regretted: "If only you had listened to my commands, your prosperity would have rolled on like a river in flood and your just success like the waves of the sea." (48:18) What would have thus accrued to men's activities would have been "just" in the sense that they would thereby have been spared a regret for their failure to take advantage of the wisdom available to them. Being so spared would have been the "just" consequence of their decision to live by a trustworthy counsel rather than pursuing the will-o-the-wisps of their own fancies.

Some religious persons are willing to give up life itself rather than be guilty of disloyalty to what they revere as the law of God. There is no more eloquent drama of such a trial of fidelity than is given in *Second Maccabees* which is an account of the torture of a mother and her seven sons for refusing to go counter to what they revered as the commandments given to them and their people by God. Each in turn declared: "We are ready to die rather than break the laws of our fathers" which they regarded as commandments given by God to their people. (7:2) In the face of torture, "the mother and her sons encouraged each other to die nobly". (vs. 5) The moral heroism with which this family confronted the decrees of an enemy ruler indicates the strength which some human beings have acquired through the fidelity with which they have persisted in

79

trusting the reality they revere as the ultimate authority for their life
This moving account includes the comment that after the death of the
first brother by torture, the second was offered the option to abrogate his
commitment of fidelity to the commandments he trusted as imposed by
God. Before "he in turn underwent the torture", "He replied in his native
language, 'Never!' " (vs. 8)

This account of what some human beings have been enabled to do by
virtue of disciplining themselves for heroic acting provides an encouraging
reassurance to others who have not trained themselves to be capable of
such acting. The mere willingness to respect such human beings as
demonstrating moral heroism is itself an expression of character. No one
could esteem this family of Israelites for their willingness to die by
torture unless he himself was capable of recognizing the praiseworthy
fidelity they exhibited in being faithful to what they honored as obligations they themselves had accepted. Their acceptance of such obligations
is an expression of their moral integrity. Their refusal to disrespect such
obligations because they regarded them as counsel and guidance offered
their forefathers by God is an expression of their religious dedication.

Such dedication, therefore, is a type of worship within the scope of
moral integrity. In other words, the cultivation of a character which is
capable of respecting an obligation notwithstanding every difficulty
entailed in doing so is a moral achievement which is the basis for the
type of religious fidelity exemplified by this family.

The relation between their religious acting and their moral preparation
for such acting is evident. Only as there is a cultivation of a character
capable of unflinching fidelity is there also a capacity to be unconditionally
faithful in fulfilling an obligation. A religious faith supports human acting
only to the extent that a human being has disciplined his capacities to
live by such faith. Religious faith as such does not cultivate character
although it encourages its cultivation and reinforces it. But the initiative
of a human being to discipline himself in forming his character is a
moral act distinguishable from religious faith.

The capacity of a human being to remain faithful to a commitment
which he regards as his religious obligation is cultivated by his own effort,
which includes his religious faith. His religious faith supports his effort
to cultivate a character-foundation for the fidelity with which he respects
his religious obligations. But the moral factor of character itself conditions
the degree to which a religious individual is prepared to affirm an unflinching fidelity to a commitment he makes to the reality he trusts as
having final sovereignty in his life. Such reverence for an ultimate sover-

eignty as the moral authority for human life is a religious act. The foundation for the constancy with which it is sustained in directing his life is the contribution of his character.

This relation between the moral cultivation of character and the fidelity with which a religious commitment is made is also pointed out in *Second Esdras*. This speaks of the Israelites "who have kept to the way laid down by the Most High", which they have done by virtue of a character achieved only by some of them. There is no book in the Bible which credits the entire Israelites as a people with such fidelity. On the contrary, the literature of this people is dominated with an awareness of their infidelity to what their prophets have affirmed as the commandments given to them by God.

It is the relatively few among them who therefore are spoken about when the Prophet Ezra declares, "During their stay on earth they served the Most High in spite of constant hardship and danger, and kept to the last letter of the law given them by the lawgiver". (7:90, 91) The interpretation of the source of this law to which the relatively few were loyal is religious. The condition which made the fidelity of this people capable of respecting their obligation to conform to the commandments is moral. It is the character they cultivated by their resolve to be faithful to their obligations. Their acknowledgment that such obligations had their source from God, whom they worshipped as ultimate sovereign of the world and of human life, did not as such account for their fidelity to fulfil such obligations.

If an Israelite's belief that the divine source of commandments imposing moral obligation were the determinant itself of his capacity to respect such obligations, the Israelite people would have had a very different history from the one which the Prophets record. The religious interpretation of such obligation was affirmed by the "faithful remnant" and by the many without a comparable constancy of dedication. Hence such a religious interpretation does not itself account for a constancy of dedication as was expressed by the relatively few. If a religious interpretation as such conditioned a fidelity which determined acting, there would have been an exemplary religious history among all of the Israelites. There is, however, no evidence for this in the biblical writing. On the contrary, it is the contrast between the faithful few and the faithless many which constitutes the spiritual cleavage among the Israelites as a people. Such cleavage is lamented in every book of the Old Testament prophets. What spared the few from living as did the many was a difference of characters which account for "their victory in the long fight against their inborn impulses to evil, which . . . failed to lead them astray." (vs. 93) There is no statement in moral philosophies which is less ambiguous than this It specifies a moral difference in the religious character of the Israelites Some were prepared to do what others were not prepared to do. The mora preparation therefore of some accounted for their sustained fidelity to respect the "law" they revered as coming to them from God: "Throughout their life they kept the law with which they were entrusted." (vs. 94)

Another apocryphal writing, *Wisdom of Solomon,* is equally clear in pointing out the moral act of those who resolved that they "will not sin" in the sense of doing what is inconsistent with the commandments they revered as given to them for their instruction by God. The religious motive for their moral resolve is made equally clear by the author of this writing: It is "because we know that we are accounted thine." (15:3) Thus the reciprocal relation between the moral conditioning of religious life and the religious conditioning of moral resolve is made clear by this writer In so doing, he reaffirms the same relation between two modes of life which were stressed throughout the writings of the early Israelites. Some of these have been included in the canon of the Old Testament. Others have not. But the profundity is the same with which both bodies of literature affirm the relation between the moral and the religious aspects of human life.

Aeschylus affirms as clear an understanding of the function of religious belief in human life as do the writers among the Israelites. The Danaides declare: "If the gods of Olympus hearken not unto us, we will perish."[8] The confidence in the moral rightness of whatever has its source in the ultimate determiner of men's life is likewise affirmed in this drama: "Zeus . . . by venerable enactment guideth destiny aright." The moral consequence for an entire people is likewise declared in this drama when the Chorus affirms: "Their State (will) be regulated well, if they hold in awe mighty Zeus."[9] This drama affirms a religious confidence in the inevitable well-being which follows men's fidelity to the requirements imposed upon them by Zeus. Danaüs in the drama declares: "If he but so vouchsafe, all will end well."[10] Although the terminology in the religious vocabulary of the Greeks differs from the terminology in the religious vocabulary of the Israelites, the meaning of terms for denoting the ultimate determiner of human well-being is basically the same.

Aeschylus' *Agamemnon* stresses moral conditions for human well-being without introducing a religious philosophy, although he does use a religious term when he declares that "to think no folly is Heaven's best gift".[11] This reference to "Heaven's best gift," however, is not serious

eligious philosophy. It merely declares that there is no greater good fortune for human beings under heaven than their freedom from folly. In
this reference, Aeschylus does not attribute to Heaven the means for
escaping such folly. "Heaven," as a reality transcendent of human life,
is not the agency which brings about the strength of character to avoid
folly. This is brought about by what men themselves do to introduce
intelligence into their lives as a means to save them from the mistakes of
the folly of their fancies.

Aeschylus likewise points out a correlation between the moral uprightness of a family-tradition and the moral blessings enjoyed by children in
the family. He declares: "When a house is righteous, the lot of its children is blessed alway."[12] Although he does not introduce a religious interpretation for the constancy of this correlation, he, nevertheless, believes
that there is a divine reality which is responsible for it. In other words,
there is a predictable relation between the moral worthiness of individuals
in a family and the moral well-being with which their influence continues
to determine the quality of life within the family. So stated, this is maintaining a correlation between moral goodness and moral well-being which
is the converse of the correlation affirmed in the early books of the Bible
that the "sins of the fathers" cripple the lives of their children and their
children's children. But basic to both of these ancient reflectings is the
same conviction that there is a moral determinant for human well-being.
And this determination is not confined to an individual's own life-span.
It is conditioned also by what others do which carries over into the conditioning of his life. One such conditioning contributes to the evils which
handicap an individual's life. Another such conditioning contributes to
the enrichment of an individual's well-being.

Aeschylus also takes account of the same correlation as does the Old
Testament between evil antecedents in an individual's family tradition
and in the evil from which the individual himself suffers. The Chorus in
Agamemnon declares: "It is the deed of iniquity that thereafter begetteth
more iniquity."[13]

In *Libation-Bearers*, Aeschylus devotes his reflecting to the moral relation between what an individual does that is morally censurable and the
penalty which he himself suffers from his misdeeds. The Chorus in this
play declares: "Calamity, racking his soul, distracts the guilty man so
that he is steeped in misery utter and complete."[14] The moral penalty for
an individual's wrongdoing is thus entailed in his own wrongdoing. In this
relation, Aeschylus does not consider the consequences of an individual's
wrongdoing upon others who suffer from it. In this respect, he therefore

maintains a moral philosophy which Ezekiel affirmed when he declare that the Israelites shall not again believe that the sins of fathers are inherited by their children. He declares: "The soul (itself) that sins sha die." (18:4)

Aeschylus accounts for the constancy between moral wrongdoing by a individual and the penalty for it from which he suffers in essentially th same way as the early writers in the Old Testament. Both the Greeks and the Israelites' interpretation of this correlation rests upon a meta physic that a reality transcendent of human life determines penalty fo wrongdoing and determines likewise the blessings accruing from huma effort to do what is morally worthy. The Chorus in *The Libation-Bearer* declares: "The balanced scale of Justice keepeth watch; swift it descendeth on some who still stand in the light; sometimes sorrows await them tha tarry in the twilight of life's close; and some are enshrouded by ineffectua night."[15] The same chorus affirms the inescapability of a penalty upo an individual who is faithless to another. For such infidelity, "there is n cure". The sternness of such moral guilt is stressed by Aeschylus whe he maintains that there is no way to cancel the fact of it from an indi vidual's life, "albeit all streams flow in one current to cleanse the bloo from a polluted hand, they speed their course to no avail".[16] This was als Lady Macbeth's discovery for her moral offense.

Euripides maintains the same inescapability of penalty for a mora wrongdoing. The Chorus in *Ion* declares: "The unholy wretch . . . neve can be happy."[17] Being denied happiness as the penalty for wrongdoing i moral judgment upon moral guilt. This correlation is one type of con stancy in human life which is affirmed in both Greek and Israelite reflect ing on the moral tragedy of human wrongdoing.

The same constancy of correlation between moral goodness and moral benefits is affirmed by Euripides in *Electra*. The closing statement of the play made by the Dioscuri is the assurance to men who endeavor to do what is morally worthy: "As we fly through heaven's expanse we help not the wicked; but whoso in his life loves piety and justice, all such we free from troublous toils and save."[18] This assurance affirms a version of salvation which is characteristic of religions. The salvation which is assured by the celestial agency in this drama is the moral benefit which occurs to acting justly and revering gods as they are entitled to be revered. Such "piety" by which human beings are assured salvation are their acts of reverence for the gods, since gods do not bestow benefits upon human beings irrespective of moral antecedents.

The constancy of a correlation between moral uprightness and moral blessings, however, is assured by the mediation of a reality other than human life. Thus the assurance that moral effort will be correlated with moral benefactions is based upon a metaphysic of a reality other than human life. Such a reality transcendent of human life is the basis on which such a correlation is assured between the character of human beings' conduct and the moral consequences of their acting.

Euripides affirms this type of religious interpretation of human life in *Rhesus* when Athena declares to Paris: "Go. And remember that thy fortunes still are watched by me, and they who do my will prosper in all their ways."[19] This assurance which is attributed to a goddess is essentially the same assurance which is affirmed repeatedly throughout the Bible. Both Greeks and Israelites who reflect seriously upon life, and in so doing take account of a determinant of human life by a reality transcendent of it, affirm the same type of reflecting. The religious literature of the Israelites might well be credited with the following assurance by the Chorus in Euripides' *Ion*:[20]

> "Though fortune's blackest storms
> Rage on his house, the man whose pious soul
> Reveres the gods, assumes a confidence,
> And justly; for the good at length obtain
> The meed of virtue."

3. *Orienting one's life to a reality which is trusted as an enduring good is a religious act which reinforces moral effort*

A verse in *Proverbs* declares: "The foundations of the righteous are eternal." (10:25) The metaphysic basic to this religious faith is also the basis for a moral assurance that an individual whose life is directed by a knowledge of an eternal reality will have a constancy in his own life. His pattern of living will be as constant as the reality is changeless after which he patterns his life. This way of interpreting the benefit of knowing a changeless directive is an expression both of moral wisdom and of religious faith. For a religious people, such as "the faithful remnant" of the Israelites, who were respectful of the requirements imposed upon them by their religious tradition, the combination of such moral wisdom and religious faith constitute both normative religion and also normative morality.

Isaiah stresses the same moral advantage of a stability of life made possible by its orientation to a directive which yields constancy of guidance. He declares: "My saving power shall never wane." (51:6) The

85

assurance itself that one is oriented to an authority for his life which will never disclose a deficiency is itself a moral blessing. It saves an individual from an apprehensiveness that he will be confronted with a regret for having trusted what subsequently discloses itself as untrustworthy.

The constancy of a direction of an individual's life is itself a moral stability. Such stability is made possible by a sustained confidence in the finality of a moral authority. Isaiah contrasts such stability and constancy of direction with the uncertainty and insecurity correlated with groping for a directive. He acknowledges the attractiveness and appeal of many transient goods which he characterizes as "flowering sprays, so lovely in their beauty". But he then points out the moral penalty for orienting life to such inducements. He declares: "Their bloom is gone while they lie in his hand." (28:3, 4)

There is no inconsistency in the Prophet's acknowledgment both of the attractiveness of many goods in life and also his acknowledgment that a penalty is entailed for pursuing them. Discontinuity in enjoyments of delights accruing from such attractions is regarded as a moral disadvantage by anyone who prefers an unbroken or uninterrupted quality of well-being. Such a benefit of equanimity would not, however, have a comparable appeal for one whose requirement for equanimity in his life remains undeveloped by virtue of never having been cultivated. This fact itself points out a problem which confronts a reflective person. It is the question of the worth of moral disciplining a character whose requirements in turn impose upon him a demand that is not equally experienced by others without such discipline. But after an individual has the quality of experience made possible by a stability of character cultivated through discipline, he also becomes morally incapable of regretting the character which imposes demands peculiar only to such character. For moral reasons, which are his own capacities for a quality of life made possible only by moral effort, he cannot seriously envy those whom Isaiah characterizes as trusting in "devious . . . practices" and then "resting on them for support". The Prophet interprets a penalty entailed in such a pattern of life by analogy to a structure whose weakness makes its duration impossible. He declares: "This iniquity will be like a crack running down a high wall, which . . . all in an instant, comes crashing down." Another analogy by which he stresses the unpredictability with which a future is faced by one without a trustworthy directive for his life is like "an earthen jar (which) is broken with a crash, . . . shattered, so that not a shard is found among the fragments". (30:14) This graphic description of the demolition of a reality which exemplifies a human life is the Prophet's way of emphasizing both the uncertainty with which one type of life faces its future and also the completeness with which its security can totally collapse.

Jeremiah affirms the same radical contrast between types of human life as Isaiah does. He declares that the individual is "strong" for whom "the Lord is on (his) side", whereas those without this support "stumble and fall". (20:11) The confidence with which he affirms this is reinforced by his assurance that a trustworthy directive for life yields a constancy of support which is a moral strength. Such moral strength, however, is not generated by the confidence itself. It comes about only as there is a confidence in the enduring nature of the reality from which one seeks the ordering of his life. This interpretation of such a reality is the metaphysical basis of a moral philosophy which correlates the quality of human life with the nature of a reality transcendent of it to which it is oriented for its directing.

First Maccabees reaffirms the same confidence which Jeremiah affirms in the moral effect upon human life of its orienting to a reality revered as eternal. The author of this writing declares: "No one who trusts in Heaven shall ever lack strength." (2:61) This type of religious faith in such a reality which supports morally devoted effort is not restricted to the Israelites and Greeks, whose literatures are being considered in this study. The very same religious assurance of moral benefit is affirmed by Confucius. In fact, this declaration from the author of *First Maccabees* could be inserted into the *Analects* and it would be consistent with affirmations of Confucius, such as "Only Heaven is great, and only Yao answers to its standard. . . . How sublime were his achievements! How brilliant his civilizing regulations!"[21] Another acknowledgment by Confucius of the supreme moral importance of an eternal reality that provides a directive for human life is: "Heaven begat the virtue that is in me."[22]

The apocryphal book *Judith* points out a graphic parallel of the inconstancy of a source of help to which many human beings orient themselves and the defenses constructed by the Medes which they presumed would yield the security they desired. (1:14-16) But just as such defenses collapsed under the pressure of an enemy, so the fabricated securities in which many human beings trust likewise collapse under the trial of adversities which demonstrate their inadequacy to justify the trust that people invest in them.

The author of *Second Esdras* affirms the same basic philosophy of history as well as a moral philosophy when he acknowledges that "Destruction will come upon us, the recipients of the law, and upon our hearts, the vessel that held the law". (9:36) But he then affirms a religious faith

87

which declares a metaphysic that there is a reality of a radically different nature which is not subject to the transient, such as the nature of everything which human beings either are or create: "The law itself is not destroyed, but survives in all its glory." (vs. 37) This assurance of religious faith is the consolation that although the destiny of dissolution is inevitable for everything other than the Eternal, a human being has the opportunity during the relatively brief span of life to relate himself to an eternal reality and thereby introduce into his life a knowledge of such an eternal reality. This religious faith, however, is not peculiar to this Israelite author. A religious faith of the same nature was affirmed by Confucius who declared: "He who heard the Truth in the morning might die content in the evening."[23] The Truth to which Confucius refers is not contingent upon any transient reality. It is eternal. The same confidence that during the relatively short length of a human life an individual can have knowledge of an eternal reality is affirmed in Hindu scriptures. The Vedas declare that whereas everything within the cosmos will be destroyed at the end of a Kalpa, or cosmic cycle, the Truth of the Vedas will not be destroyed. As eternal, it is not subject to transiency. Such confidence affirms a metaphysic of an eternal which contrasts with the nature of all that is not eternal. What is other than eternal comes to an end, which is the nature of human life and of everything that men create and to which they orient themselves.

By contrast to this mistaken trust, a religious faith testifies to the reality of an eternal reality. What makes this metaphysic specifically a religious faith is the relation of this eternal reality to transient human life. It is the source of an enduring directive for human life. And human beings who trust it for guidance acquire a stability or equanimity in their life which is supported by their confidence in the enduring character of the reality to which they relate themselves for its enlightenment of their life.

The Prophet Ezra sums up this foregoing analysis of a metaphysic basic to a religious faith which orients human life to an eternal reality with its benefaction of constancy when he declares: "My favour flows abundantly from springs that will never run dry." (2:32) Such faith itself is a benefaction in human life. But the human being who lives by this faith is convinced in the truth of his faith. He believes that his faith is justified because there is such a reality which he trusts.

The author of *Baruch*, writing in Babylon to a conquered people, sums up the foregoing philosophical analysis in his affirmation of religious conviction that there is an "everlasting God" who supports the human beings who prepare themselves to accept His guidance. On the basis of this religious interpretation of human life, he explains the tragedies of human beings as forgetting "the Everlasting God who nurtured" them. (4:8)

The great tragic dramas of Greece affirm a metaphysic such as is also affirmed throughout the religious writings of the early Israelites. This is the concept of an eternal reality transcendent of the order internal to which human beings struggle for a livelihood which confronts them with temptations to reach out for goods deceptive in the inducements they offer. The Chorus of Elders of Thebes in Sophocles' *Antigone* sums up much of this metaphysic basic to Greek tragedies in acknowledging a reality "untouched by Time".[24]

The utmost moral benefit of orienting human life to such a timeless reality is affirmed by Orestes in Euripides' drama when he declares: "God's help is enough of itself."[25] The sufficiency of a constant help in an otherwise inconstant context of human life is a religious faith affirmed in the serious reflecting of Greek dramatists about the tragic character of human life which is not effectively enlightened by a wisdom that otherwise might have oriented them to a trustworthy guidance in their search to find what alone is worth finding.

4. *Even a person devout in faith may at times question the warrant for his faith*

Character is not acquired without effort, and no single capacity of character is preserved without persistent effort. The same condition of diligence for attaining and preserving character is also a condition for the effective directing of human life by religious faith.

The struggle to preserve a faith even after it has been doubted is illustrated in the life of the Psalmist. Although the *Psalms* include examples of human life directed by religious faith, they also include expressions of a struggle against the inroads of a disbelief of the very assurance once affirmed in faith.

The seventy-seventh psalm is one of the eloquent expressions of this ambivalence in religious life between living by an unquestioned faith and subsequently being confronted with a doubting of its warrant. During one of the crises in his faith, the Psalmist remembered how remote such doubting once would have been for him. He mentions how his "thoughts went back to times long past" when his confidence in the providence of God seemed the most secure of all of his possessions. (vs. 5) Then in

contrast to the equanimity of this stage in his life, he became aware o:
the precarious character of his faith. He then points out the "deep distress"
he suffered while he reflected upon what had taken place in the weakening
of his faith that once seemed to him to be incapable of weakening. (vs. 6)
During the trial of his reflecting on what occurred in his life, he contrasted
his former confidence with the "despair" into which he admits his "spirit"
sank. This decrease in the vitality of a former faith by which he lived
with confidence and security was also a decrease in his confidence in hi
own capacity to have been worthy of such a former equanimity of life
The acuteness of his "despair" became the basis for his questioning i.
"the Lord will never again show favour". (vs. 7)

Such wavering of faith is an acute suffering for a person once so con
fident that there would never be such a questioning of his own integrity
to live by his faith. In addition to questioning his own deficiency for
being insufficiently critical of the faith he affirmed, he also indicts his
own infidelity to his former faith. His questioning of his faith, therefore
is an ambivalent doubting of the trustworthiness of the reality he formerly
trusted, and also a questioning of his own capacity to trust again as he
previously had trusted. The painful nature of the crisis both of his reli
gious faith and of his confidence in his own fidelity is expressed by his
question: "Has his unfailing love now failed us utterly?" (vs. 8) This de
clares his confrontation with the radical contrast between a former confi
dence and a subsequent distrust of the warrant for such confidence. In this
questioning, the Psalmist, therefore, both distrusts his own wisdom for
once believing without questioning its warrant, and also disbelieves in
the existence of a reality whose being he had never doubted.

In moving between distrust of himself and distrust of the divine provi
dence, he tends in this wavering to doubt the trustworthiness of the reality
upon which he had formerly depended with unwavering confidence. What
formerly would have distressed him as apostasy or infidelity to God is
later entertained as serious questioning: "Must his promise time and
again be unfulfilled?" In this mode of despondency, he disbelieves that
there ever was a warrant for his faith. This is thus a twofold doubting. It
is a disbelief in the worthiness of the reality to be trusted as he once had
trusted it for the constancy of its providence, and it is also a disbelief in
his own ability to be critical of the soundness of his own trusting.

Then as if he were reappraising the competency of his own questioning
which progressively became more and more an outright disbelieving, he
admits into his reflecting evidence for discrediting his own questioning
He declares: But then, O Lord, I call to mind thy deeds; I recall thy

wonderful acts in times gone by." (vs. 11) In permitting his own memory to enter into the defense as it were of his former faith, he takes account of evidence which, in his embittered questioning, he had for the time forgot. As he continues to recall the occurrences in his life on the basis of which he maintained his faith, he reappraises the warrant for such faith. And as he reflects upon the evidence in support of his former faith, in contrast to the evidence on the ground of which he had questioned it, he reevaluates both the warrant for his faith and also his own unworthiness to have slipped into such questioning with its intensified doubting and even its outright disbelieving. In moments in which he regains his equanimity after the crisis of troubled questioning, he again quietly reflects and confesses: "I meditate upon thy works and muse on all that thou hast done." (vs. 12) In regaining the balance within his own reflecting or meditating, he regained the confidence in his faith whose warrant he had permitted himself to question.

The sixtieth psalm is another expression of the struggle through which the Psalmist went in his attempt to preserve a faith which had once been his principal support for encouragement in his life that otherwise was not blessed with much encouragement. In this psalm, he contrasts the inadequacy of all other sources of help with the adequacy of the providence in which he had once been so confident of its unfailing help. He asks himself the disturbing question: "Who can guide me" as he had been guided before the crisis of disbelief had taken from him his trust in the guidance upon which he had depended with unquestioning confidence. (vs. 9) This troubled questioning of "who can guide" him arose only because he believed that there no longer was the providence of God upon which he had once trusted. He declares his total disbelief in God's providence when he addresses God: "Thou, O God, hast abandoned us." (vs. 10) The despair in this crisis of his faith is intensified by his disbelief that there is any other source of help to replace the one upon which he had so totally trusted. He declares: "Deliverance by man is a vain hope." (vs. 11) Thus his plight is his privation of a former help upon which he had been dependent, together with his clear awareness that there is no alternative of comparable dependability.

There would, therefore, have been no crisis of faith for the Psalmist had he believed there are various sources of help of equal worth. But his crisis was so intensely acute for the very reason that after being deprived of one source of help by his doubting, he had no other source of help to which to turn.

The eighty-ninth psalm is another expression of the Psalmist's ques-

91

tioning, doubting, and disbelieving. His questioning of the divine reality upon which he once had trusted is an affirmation of the loss of his faith, for he asks: "Where are those former acts of thy love, O Lord?" The temporal contrast between a past manifestation of providence and a later disbelief that it will continue is the Psalmist's reflecting upon what seems to him at the time to be a terminus of the warrant for orienting himself to the reality he once had trusted. In accusing God of perfidity when he asks, "Where are . . . those faithful promises?" he thereby takes no account of his own responsibility for the loss of his faith in the fidelity of a reality formerly trusted. (vs. 49)

Isaiah expresses the same type of wavering of faith in God as does the Psalmist when he declares: "Waiting for justice, and there is none!" (59:11) If Isaiah had qualified his complaint by specifying that there is no justice to be found among men, there would be nothing comparable in his complaint and in the despair expressed by the Psalmist. But included in the crisis through which Isaiah suffered is the admission that he once had believed that justice among men would be established by God. His confidence was that whereas there is no basis for expecting justice from a human source, there is a justification for depending upon it from a reality other than human life. Thus when his trust in the establishment of justice among men is doubted, it is disbelieving that there is an intervention of God in human life to establish justice, notwithstanding the human opposition to this.

The author of *Second Esdras* affirms another type of doubting which is not a weakening of his religious faith. Taking account of men's "ingratitude to the One who had put life within their reach", he censures human beings for the handicap they themselves impose upon the intervention of a divine reality to contribute a trustworthy direction which men themselves cannot provide. (8:60, 61) This expression of a troubled reflecting is not a result of questioning the soundness of religious belief in God's available authority for human life. It is rather a distraught questioning of how it is possible for human beings to bring "dishonour on their Creator" for living in a manner so unworthy of the nature with which the Creator has endowed them.

Although this questioning is not a disbelief in the trustworthiness of a divine source of direction for human life, it does, nevertheless, entail a religious doubting of God's creating a human being who is so capable of "ingratitude to the One who had put life within their reach".

A type of questioning of the warrant for a former religious faith is affirmed in the dramas of Euripides as it is also affirmed in the Bible.

Since earlier in his life, Euripides had been confident in the ultimate determining of human history by a divine reality, his progressively intensified doubting of the warrant for his faith became as painful for him as it was for the Psalmist. In his *Phoenissae*, Jocasta appeals to Zeus, "whose home is heaven's radiant vault", to "grant that (her) sons may be reconciled". And then simultaneously she doubts that her appeal will be granted because she doubts the wisdom of the deity in whom her trust would have warranted her appeal. She adds to her appeal the hypothetical of disbelief—"if thou art really wise". As if instructing the deity to whom she turns for the reconciliation of her sons, which she believes can be accomplished only by a help from a source other than human, she declares that if there really were a deity whose wisdom was equal to her trust, he would "not suffer the same poor mortal to be forever wretched", as she herself is, seeking such help, although also doubting her seeking can be justified.[26]

The same type of disbelief in the warrant for a religious trust in a divine source of help is also affirmed in Euripides' *Cyclops*. Odysseus addressed himself to Zeus, saying: "I am come to toils and depths of perils worse than all at Ilium." He then makes the appeal: "And thou, O Zeus . . . behold these things" which he himself regards as injustices and excesses in misfortune. Then he declares his doubt of the merits of his own appeal, saying: "For, if thou regard them not, in vain art thou esteemed the great god Zeus, though but a thing of naught."[27] His affirmation expresses an ambivalence internal to the act of orienting himself to a divine reality. His action includes opposite tendencies as radical as are affirmed in the intensest crises of doubting of which the Psalmist gives expression. Although Odysseus, in the extremities of his misfortunes, turns for help to the god upon whom the Greeks depended for his favorable providence, he also declares a disbelief in the soundness of the trust of the Greeks who built their temples to Zeus as an acknowledgment of their dependence upon him and their trust in his providence to contribute the help to them which they sought from him. Another translation of this part of the drama intensifies the contrast between the mode of Odysseus' turning for help to Zeus and his disparagement of the warrant for his trusting such a source of help when he declares: "If thou regard not, vainly we confess Thy godhead, Zeus, who are mere nothingness!"[28]

Euripides' increasing loss of confidence in the wisdom with which the government of Athens was conducted paralleled his increasing loss of trust in the soundness of his own religious faith that in spite of what men do to handicap the administration of justice, there is, nevertheless, a reality transcendent of human life which establishes a justice such as it is futile to expect of men. His drama, *The Trojan Women,* expresses his own discouragement and intensified disbelief in the justice of the Athenian government since it was at the time of this drama's production that Athens, without mercy and without scruples, destroyed the people of Melos because the Island's government did not want to be a party to the Athenian imperialism.

An Athenian government which had been admired for its rationality nevertheless became capable of unspeakable outrages such as massacring the adult male population of Melos and selling the women and children into slavery. The Athenian government had likewise demonstrated its low moral level in its outrages against other neighbors, such as its embargo upon Megara, and its tragically futile invasion of Syracuse. These repeated offences against the minimum morality of civilized life accounted for Euripides' despondency and for his despair that it was hopeless not only to expect justice in the acts of human government but also to expect it from any other reality.

The weakening of his religious faith after the total loss of his confidence in human sources for justice is expressed through the despondency of Hecuba who declares: "Ye Gods . . . Alas! Why call on things so weak for aid?" And yet, as has been pointed out in the foregoing, Euripides could not entirely accept the total negation of a possible divine help in the tragic plight of human life, confronted by the misery of struggling in a world devoid of justice. His ability, therefore, to accept this tragic conclusion both in a philosophy of human history and also in a religious life is affirmed in Hecuba's acknowledgment: "Yet there is something that doth seek, crying for God . . ."[29]

This confession indicates the struggle through which a religious faith sometimes goes to preserve the residue there may still be of a trust after the most demolishing disbelief, when such disbelief is supported by evidence so massive that a reflective individual cannot ignore it. The preservation of a religious faith entails a struggle when there is a challenge to its soundness. And as the evidence increases on the basis of which such faith is questioned, the struggle likewise increases for its life and death outcome. Yet the final submerging of faith by a massive evidence which constitutes a basis for its discrediting is, nevertheless, often coupled with the ambivalent longing to retain it. An individual who once has lived by a religious trust in the accessibility of a help which is not available within human resources cannot readily relinquish such faith, notwithstanding the most vehement of its challenges. And notwithstanding the most massive

94

cumulation of evidence to support the doubting of the warrant to believe what is contrary to such evidence, a pressure to abandon the hope which supports the faith constitutes the most painful struggle of which a human being is capable. When a defeat of faith comes about even against a weakened will to preserve it, a human being suffers the final tragedy of religious life.

III

Religious Faith Acknowledges a Final Dependence upon a Reality Other than the Physical World

1. *The basic metaphysic of religious faith is that there is a reality upon which human beings are finally dependent*

A metaphysic of an ultimate reality is implied in a question which Elihu asks in *The Book of Job*: "Who has prescribed His course for Him?" (36:23) This question implies that there is no reality more ultimate than what he reveres as God, who "towers in majesty above us". (vs. 22)

A metaphysic, however, which is basic to religious faith is not necessarily theistic, such as is the metaphysic affirmed by Elihu. Yet, the reality in which a religious life trusts for its dependability is ultimate in the sense that there is no reality prior to it upon which it depends. What makes this most general premise of a metaphysic the basic creed of religious faith is that the reality upon which human life depends in turn depends upon no other reality. Such an ultimate reality thereby completes the human quest.

A human being's awareness that he does not have within himself or within his resources the means sufficient to fulfill his own requirements is included in the religious act of turning to a reality revered as ultimate. Job asks: "How shall I find help within myself?" (6:12) This question

96

s subsequent to his analysis of his own resources when he declares: "The ower to aid myself is out of my reach." (vs. 13)

Turning beyond oneself for the fulfillment of a requirement which is ntegral to his nature expresses an acknowledgment that he does not have the capacities to fulfill some of his own insistent needs. It is this acknowledgment which is basic to the religious act of orienting oneself to a reality beyond oneself. But the confident justification for such a religious reference is that there is a reality which can fulfill this requirement. And, furthermore, it is believed to be capable of fulfilling such a requirement so that a human being will not be directed again to another reality to complete his quest.

Elihu declares the final dependence of every living thing upon God as the ultimate reality in whom he trusts. He maintains that if God were to "recall His life-giving spirit, all that lives would perish on the instant, and man would return again to dust." (34:14, 15) His religious faith thus is his acknowledgment that the reality which is essential for the maintenance of life is transcendent of life itself. As such, it is not contingent upon another living being. As the condition essential for every life, other than itself, it does not refer a living being beyond it. The religious quest, according to Elihu, terminates in the reality which is the condition for life. When Elihu declares, "All alike are God's creatures," he affirms a religious interpretation of life as contingent upon a source other than every other contingent life. (vs. 20) Job's friend, Eliphaz, affirms the dependence of every living thing upon God when he acknowledges that "God gives rain to the earth and sends water on the fields". (5:10) Thus whereas human beings depend upon the fertility of the fields for their life, the fertility of the fields depend upon the rain which is included in the Creator's scheme for the final dependence of every living thing upon Him.

But after Job acknowledges his dependence upon God to make life possible and to sustain it by all that is required by its created nature, he betrays a niggardliness of appreciation for life and its conditions which have been granted by God. With what seems on reflecting to be little less than blasphemy, he accuses God of punishing him "morning by morning" and testing his endurance "every hour of the day". (7:18) This change in Job's attitude thus expresses the very inconstancy of his nature which makes him realize how inadequate he himself is to live as he believes would be consistent with his dependence upon God for life and for the conditions which make life possible.

After his acknowledgment of his dependence upon God, he accuses God

of being antagonistic to human beings. He declares that God is as indi̇
ferent to their needs as is a "water (which) wears away stones, and
rain-storm (which) scours the soil from the land". He then declares th
by virtue of God's indifference to the plight of human beings, God actual
"wipe(s) out the hope of frail man", and dost overpower him final
(until) he is gone" and until "he is banished from thy sight". (14:19, 2(

It would tax the credulity of most people to believe that an individu
commonly regarded as an example of religious faith, such as Job, wou
be capable even in the hours of acutest despondency to rail against G(
as Job did. Yet when one is honest enough to acknowledge the nature (
"frail man", he understands how such inconstancy in the religious life (
Job is possible. The inconstancy in Job's acknowledgment of his gratitu(
to God for the conditions of life itself, notwithstanding the occurrence (
its misfortunes and its suffering, is consistent with a human capacity f(
infidelity. Human beings are capable of being faithless to each other, an
so it is consistent with their nature to be faithless to the very reality upo
which they also affirm their dependence and to whom they sporadicall
give their acknowledgment of gratitude.

The Book of Job fits into the scheme of a scripture which claims un
versality, because the conduct of Job, even in relating himself to God, .
consistent with a universal human nature. Something of the far fro
admirable nature of human beings is pointed out by one of the proverb
which forbids human beings to "encroach on the land of orphans"
(23:10) A type of life capable of dishonesty to the extent of exploitin
the helpless is capable of anything, including a faithlessness in ever
relation.

A realistic awareness of the nature often exhibited in human life spare
one from being surprised at Job's inconstancy even in relation to th
reality upon whom he is also capable of acknowledging his final depend
ence. The specific reason that the proverb referred to mentions the lo\
moral level of which human beings are capable is to remind them tha
the helpless orphans whom they would exploit "have a powerful guardia
who will take up their cause". (vs. 11) This account in *Proverbs* of wha
some human beings are capable of doing is a commentary upon the inade
quacy of human life to fulfill the human requirement to be related to
constant reality upon which it can justifiably depend.

Proverbs affirms one aspect of religious faith when it declares tha
whereas there is no ground for an assurance of justice within human lif(
there is a reality transcendent of human life by which justice is assured
The constancy with which God holds human beings accountable for thei

exploitation of other human beings is thus included in the religious faith affirmed by *Proverbs* that God "will requite every man for what he does". (24:12) Thus one aspect of God's sovereignty over human life is the justice with which God universally holds human beings accountable for their wrongdoing to others. This is a constancy in God's role within human life which is affirmed in the religious faith that turns beyond human life for what human life cannot provide. Human life cannot offer a ground to support its own moral requirement for an unfailing justice in judgment upon human wrongdoing. Hence when this moral requirement is an acute aspect of a human being who is also religious, a fulfillment of this requirement is sought transcendent of human life.

The Psalmist also affirms a religious faith of receiving "justice from God", but also upon the moral condition that he himself "has not set his mind on falsehood". He declares this moral responsibility for "the fortune of those who seek" God by acknowledging his own obligation to have "clean hands and a pure heart". (24:4-6) The Psalmist acknowledges his final dependence upon God for life itself when he appeals to God to "grant (him) life". (119:149) He acknowledges that everything which has made his well-being possible in the past has come from God, to whom he declares: "Thou, O Lord, hast been my help." (86:17) The trustworthiness of the ultimate source of life and its benefits is also confidently affirmed by the Psalmist for his future. He declares that "He shall receive a blessing from the Lord" when he becomes worthy of it. (24:5) Thus the Psalmist affirms an essential moral condition for receiving benefactions from God to whom he orients his life when he declares: "Thou art my hope, O Lord." (71:5) His hope that benefits will come from God when he turns to God with a trust in His constant readiness to give such help constitutes the essential condition for his religious orientation beyond himself. His trust in the constancy of God's response to the orienting of his life to God is affirmed in his faith that "none who seek refuge" in God are left wanting in time of their need. (34:22)

Yet after affirming his gratitude to God for having "set (him) free" from insecurities and uncertainties in life from which he would otherwise have suffered without the help he acknowledges from God, he, nevertheless, declares the unexpected qualification of his religious faith when he addresses God: "Give me proof of thy kindness." (86:17) Although this demand made by the Psalmist is for a particular manifestation of the intervention of God in the course of events in the precarious life of his people, nevertheless, it is a requirement which is hardly consistent with the affirmations of his faith that God is the constant source of help.

99

Isaiah, on the other hand, regards any qualified confidence in the wis dom and justice of God as a daring on man's part which makes man guilt of blasphemy. He confronts anyone who doubts the constancy of God providence with a question asked by God: "Would you dare question m concerning my children or instruct me in my handiwork?" This confronta tion of a human being's arrogance for doubting the wisdom and providenc of God is offensive for Isaiah who affirms the religious faith that it is Go who "made the earth and created man upon it". (45:12) Isaiah regard this religious faith which declares the earth as God's creating as incom patible with any disbelief in the wisdom with which God performs hi sovereignty over the earth. Isaiah declares his creed of faith in the wisdon and justice with which the earth is subordinate to the sovereignty of Go when he declares: "By righteousness the holy God shows himself holy." (5:16) On the basis of his faith in God's "righteousness", he condemn the presumption of human beings for discounting the sovereignty of Go as supreme. As the spokesman for God to the Israelites, he confronts hi people with the interrogation: "To whom then will you liken us, an whom set up as my equal?" (40:25)

Yet, after Isaiah repeatedly affirms his faith in the providence of Go as the source of blessings upon which human beings are dependent for every good in their life, he presses his religious metaphysic to an extrem which discredits his own faith in the unfailing providence of God for man kind when again, as spokesman for God, he declares to the Israelites: "I did indeed make you waste and desolate. I razed you to the ground." (49: 19) Attributing to God the "waste and desolation" from which a peopl suffer follows logically from the premise that God is the ultimate source of everything which occurs in human history. But the tragic consequence of pressing this premise of religious faith to the extent of attributing every occurrence as willed by God is a weakening of faith in the providence of God. Even though such penalty for human inconstancy in fidelity to God may seem to be just from the point of view of a prophet who is distressed by human infidelity, it nevertheless also functions as a reinforcement of a people's distrust that there is a providence which the Prophet also at- tributes to God.

If, as Isaiah maintains, God is the Creator, and therefore manifests his power and wisdom in his creation, it would also logically follow that such wisdom would include an understanding for the folly of which human beings are capable and for the inconstancy and infidelity they almost uni- versally express in their senseless patterns of life. A religious interpreta- tion, such as Isaiah's, which maintains that God is the trustworthy source

f help in every instance of men's supreme need, is not very convincingly
upported by his own interpretation that the same god is also the ultimate
ource of men's intensest suffering.

The same fundamental nature of religious faith is affirmed by Greeks as
t is affirmed by Israelites. As Scully points out, there is a "reverence for
hat which is outside the self" which is expressed in early Greek writings,
eginning with Homer and extending throughout subsequent reflecting on
he nature of human life in its total cosmic context.[1] So pervasive are the
eligious sensitivities of the early Greeks that there is hardly a feature of
he land itself on which they lived that they did not find a sign of some
livine reality. Scully refers to their "religious tradition in which the land
vas . . . a true force which physically embodied the powers that ruled the
vorld".[2] Their acute awareness of the final dependence of both human life
und the earth itself upon a sovereignty over life and the earth was ex-
oressed in the temples constructed in locations which the Greeks esteemed
is special opportunities for acknowledging their reverence for such sov-
reignty by powers other than the earth itself.

This religious acknowledgment of men's subordination to a reality
ranscendent of themselves and of the earth pervades the earliest of Greek
pics. Odysseus assures Eumaeus that "Zeus . . . never takes his eyes off
he world".[3] And Telemachus continued the religious tradition of his
father, Odysseus, when unaware of the identity of his father, he assured
aim that "the issue of all (that takes place) is on the knees of the gods".[4]

Homer's religious interpretation of human life in its relation to divinities
s expressed in the repeated instances in which gods or goddesses speak
directly to human beings, just as the religious faith of the Israelites
maintained that God spoke directly to his prophets. The goddess Athene
spoke as directly to Telemachus as the god of the Israelites spoke to his
prophets. She assured him that some of his understanding of events he
"will see in (his) own heart, and some the divinity will put in (his) mind".
Then the goddess declares Homer's own religious philosophy of human
life when she declares to Telemachos: "I do not think you could have been
born and reared without the god's will."[5]

Although Homer interprets human life as related to and dependent upon
the rule of gods over mankind and the earth, he gives no evidence in the
Odyssey that he regards such divine realities as any more predictable in
their relation to human beings than human beings are predictable in
their relation to the gods. Homer's gods are as ambivalent in their natures
as men are ambivalent in theirs. Thus there is no parallel in Homer for
the confidence of Israelite prophets in the constancy of their god. Although

the prophets among the Israelites are not always consistent in affirmi
their trust in God's constancy, they nevertheless do not attribute inco
stancy to their god as Homer attributes it to the Olympian powe
Odysseus, for instance, refers to Athene as "the giver of plunder", a
he attributes to her a caprice such as no Israelite prophet attributes
the god in whom he believes, notwithstanding the many times the proph
are bewildered by the absence of evidence of their god's providen
Odysseus maintains that Athene treats him as "she pleases".[6] Her trea
ment, according to his point of view, has no relation to what he hims
does. In this respect, therefore, there is a very great difference betwe
the religious interpretations affirmed in the Bible and those which Hom
affirms. Homer seems to find nothing incompatible about inconstancy a
caprice in the nature of a god or goddess. A reason for this is obvio
since his versions of the nature of such realities are projections of I
interpretations of the nature of human beings. Human beings are cap
cious in their acting, and so gods who are anthropomorphically interpre
by Homer are likewise capricious. The *Odyssey* affirms as a metaphy
about deities that "It is easy for the gods in heaven to make or mar
man's appearance".[7] The impairment of a human being is not necessar
affirmed as a punishment for his moral wrongdoing or for his infideli
to the gods. It may be merely an expression of the caprice with whi
gods treat men as if they were pawns in the game they often play wi
inhabitants of the earth. Another translation of Homer's metaphysic
"theology" is that "it is a light thing for the gods who hold wide heav
to glorify any mortal man, or else to degrade him".[8]

The Phaeacian princess, Nausicaa, explicitly declares this capricio
character of the acting of gods when she speaks to Odysseus and te
him that "Olympian Zeus . . . follows his own will in dispensing happine
to people whatever their merits".[9] This belief of Homer's, if it actual
does affirm his own metaphysic of the nature of divine realities, diffe
radically from the religious interpretations affirmed in the Bible. Su
interpretations of the nature of the god worshipped by the Israelit
acknowledge that a moral deficiency in human beings occasions ste
judgment upon them.

It, however, is difficult or even impossible to know just what Hom
believes about a god's relation to a human being insofar as there is
moral basis either for punishment for wrongdoing or for a reward f
moral uprightness. Homer affirms that there both is and also that the
is not a correlation between human merit and a god's acting in relati
to a human being. Since these position are contradictory, it is indefensib

o regard Homer as affirming a consistent interpretation about this aspect of a god's relation to human beings. After affirming that Zeus gives "to the good and the bad, just as he wishes," which thus expresses Homer's disbelief that there is any relation between men's moral merit and their treatment by a god, he also affirms an opposite view.[10] He declares that "Zeus . . . watches over suppliants that deserve respect".[18]

Homer expresses an unwavering confidence that men are not the final determiners of their own destiny. He believes that there are realities others than human beings which intervene in human behavior both beneficially and also maliciously. The latter notion is affirmed by Achilles in the *Iliad* when he declares: "Zeus makes havoc of the schemes of men."[12] A deity's intervention in human life is clearly affirmed in both the *Odyssey* and the *Iliad*, assuming that both of these express the beliefs of a single author. But there is no corresponding evidence in these writings attributed to Homer that there is a correlation between men's treatment by such divine beings and what men's conduct entitles them to receive. In this respect, there is a radical difference in the type of religious interpretation of an ultimate determiner of human destiny as this is affirmed in the Epics and as it is affirmed in the Bible.

Herodotus likewise interprets human history as influenced or conditioned by a reality other than human beings. As Godley points out, Herodotus believes there is a "divine ordering of human affairs".[13] But this point of view itself often seems to become a determinant of the historical account which Herodotus affirms. The tyranny of any bias or prejudice sooner or later manifests itself, and the religious point of view of Herodotus may be such a tyranny in his history. As Godley admits, "Herodotus may not be above the suspicion of twisting the record of events so as to inculcate a moral lesson" of the final dependency of human beings upon a divine intervention in their life.

Herodotus' interpretation of the story of the defeat of the Trojans is an example of his reflecting which is not consistent. He maintains that although the Trojans assured the Greeks that Helen was not within their walled city, the Greeks did not believe them, "though they (the Trojans) spoke the truth". Then after acknowledging that he himself believed the report of the Trojans to be true, he writes, "I am convinced and declare, the powers above ordained that the utter destruction of Troy should prove in the sight of all men that the gods do greatly punish great wrongdoing." He certifies that this is his religious interpretation by adding: "This is my own belief and thus I declare it."[14] Yet the merit for having such a religious belief and using it as the perspective with which

103

to interpret the destruction of Troy must certainly be questioned. In affirming his religious point of view of the justice for the destruction of Troy by the Greeks, he contradicts his own assertion that the Trojans had spoken the truth. In this particular instance either of history or of storytelling about Ilium and its destruction, Herodotus does not correlate wrongdoing with punishment by the gods, but he correlates the destruction of Troy with the refusal of the Greeks to believe the truth of the Trojans report.

An instance however of the consistency with which Herodotus proposes a religious interpretation is his account of the defeat of the Persians at Plataeae when they were "routed by the Lacedaemonians" and "fled in disorder to their own camp." He points out that in their flight "most of them fell near the temple in unconsecrated ground". He then offers his explanation for their defeat: "I judge—if it be not a sin to judge the ways of heaven—that the goddess herself denied them entry, for that they had burnt her temple, the shrine at Eleusis."[15]

Aeschylus continues the tradition of religious interpretation of human history. H. Weir Smyth maintains that "Homer, above all other of the older poets, set the mind of Aeschylus in motion".[16] He points out that it was the "legends of the national epic poet" which were "the means to body forth a world in which God directs the affairs of men". Aeschylus however, is a profounder interpreter of the religious significance of human history than is either Homer or Herodotus. He consistently affirms a metaphysic of a reality transcendent of human life which is the final determiner of human destiny. And he affirms this as a reflectively thought-out view of the nature of such a reality which is ultimate in relation to all that takes place in history. The Chorus in *Suppliant Maidens* declares of Zeus: "He doth not sit upon his throne by mandate of another and hold his dominion beneath a mightier. None there is who sitteth above him whose power he holdeth in awe." The second statement is a logically consistent restating of the meaning of the first statement. In other words, if the rule of Zeus is not "by mandate of another" and "his dominion" is not "beneath a mightier" than himself, then he is ultimate in relation to all others that might contend for sovereignty. The second statement is thus merely a reaffirming of the ultimate sovereignty of Zeus by the assertion that "none there is who sitteth above him whose power he holdeth in awe". An additional premise, as it were, in the theology affirmed by Aeschylus in this narration by the Chorus is that Zeus "speaketh and it is done". This again declares that the will of Zeus is not contingent upon any reality other than himself. The exercise of his sovereignty is unconditioned by any power, and therefore, he "execute(s) whatsoever his counselling mind conceiveth".[17]

H. Weir Smyth, the translator of this drama, points out a parallel between this theological affirmation in Aeschylus and a comparable affirmation in Isaiah. He declares: "The full force of this majestic and awe-inspiring passage, recall(s) the solemnity of Isaiah."[18]

Another parallel between the theology affirmed by Aeschylus and the prophets in the Old Testament is the interpretation of Zeus as "omnipotent upholder of the land!"[19] Prometheus himself acknowledges in *Prometheus Bound* that as supreme over other gods, Zeus holds "sovereign sway".[20]

Sophocles likewise continues in the Greek religious tradition of acknowledging that human beings are subordinate to a reality transcendent of themselves which is the final determiner of events in their history. Oedipus in *Oedipus the King* declares: "No living man can hope to force the gods to speak against their will."[21] So stated, this is the same theological premise of the supremacy of the gods over human history which was affirmed throughout the tradition of Greek religious reflecting beginning with the Epics. H. Weir Smyth points out that "Sophocles is more dependent . . . upon *Iliad* and *Odyssey*" than even Aeschylus.[22] Sophocles declares the same version of the gods of Olympus that Homer affirms. The aged servant, for instance, in *Electra* tells Clytemnestra: "When some angry godhead intervenes, the mightiest man is foiled."[23]

Frederick Grant points out that the "conception of power" of realities transcendent of human beings was affirmed "throughout the history of classical religion" and it was "revived . . . in the later Hellenistic age."[42] This comment on the history of religious reflecting in Greece takes account of the persistence of a philosophy of history among the Greeks for which there is a parallel in the religious reflecting of the Israelites.

Euripides also affirms the basic premise of a theology that a reality transcendent of human history is immanent in human history as a determining factor in what takes place in the life of human beings. He affirms this premise in *Iphigenia in Aulis*: "The will of the high gods(are) stronger than we."[25] Another such fundamental conviction which is basic to his religious philosophy of history is declared by Hecuba in *The Trojan Women*, notwithstanding the fact that this drama was written during the crisis of questioning his own religious faith that there is such a divine determining factor in human history. Yet the defeated Queen of Troy addresses herself to an ultimate reality when she declares: "Thou deep Base of the World, and thou high Throne above the world . . . Chain of Things that be."[26] But the trust which is affirmed in this drama is not

105

affirmed in *Orestes,* in which the Chorus declares a greatly qualified trust in the ultimate dispensation of justice among men who are under the final sovereignty of an order which is not respectful of their moral merits, and therefore does not assure a justice upon which they can justifiably depend. The Chorus affirms: "Great prosperity abideth not amongst mankind, but some power divine, shaking it to and fro like the sail of swift galley, plunges it deep in the waves of grievous affliction."[28]

What is questioned in this affirmation by the Chorus is not the reality of an ultimate determiner of what takes place in human life, but rather the respect of such a reality for the moral merits of human beings. As stated, there is no correlation between what men are morally entitled to receive by virtue of what they do and what takes place in their life which is an expression of "some power divine". It is this doubt of the justice with which human beings are treated by such powers that expresses the tragic impact of the history of Athens upon Euripides. It is thus an example of how the most clearly thought-out acknowledgment of men's dependence upon a reality transcendent of human beings can be subject to a weakening by adversities internal to which the strength of faith is threatened. It is as if it were impossible for a religious faith to endure a sustained evidence to the contrary of what it affirms under conditions which are more favorable for its flourishing.

2. *A reference to "Heaven" affirms the least specified metaphysics basic to a religious interpretation of human history*

Various terms are used in the vocabulary of the Greeks to refer to a reality they acknowledged as having a supreme importance in human life. One of these terms is "power". The meaning of this term, however, in Greek usage differs from its meaning in primitive cultures as a diffuse "dynamis" or dynamic in most physical realities to which people are related. One use of this term among early Greeks is for denoting "nether powers" which previously had been men of importance, such as kings, and who had become "deified spirits".[29] An acknowledgment that there is "some power" which conditions occurrences in human life which is less determinate than a god, is affirmed by Telemachus who believes that the return of his father after years of absence has been brought about by "some power . . . playing . . . a trick".[30]

The meanings of all terms are vague or ambiguous for acknowledging realities less determinate than a god who is denoted by a particular name. This is illustrated by translations which use the terms "divine" or "di

106

inity" rather than "power".[31] Herodotus, for example, uses a term translated as "divine" when he declares his belief that "there are many clear proofs of the divine ordering of things."[32]

In addition to these terms, whose connotations are less determinate than a named deity, is the term "heaven". When used to acknowledge a reality transcendent of physical realities, it does not mean the physical heavens. It is rather a reality such as is also denoted by "divine", "divinity", "power" which is other than physical. Aeschylus, for example, uses the term "Heaven" to take account of such a reality when he declares that " 'tis Heaven's gift for mortals to succeed".[33] It is with this same sense that he refers to "parents, reft of their children (who) in their old age bewail their heaven-sent woes."[34] In the same play, Atossa, the mother of Xerxes, speaks of "everything full of dread" which seems to her to be the visitation of Heaven".[35] The Chorus in *The Suppliant Maidens* maintains that "Heaven, if so it please, may still turn our utterances to sounds of more joyful tone".[35]

Sophocles likewise uses the term "heaven" to refer to a reality other than the physical heaven itself which in some way takes account of human beings and in some way makes a difference in their lives. He refers to the "omniscient eye of heaven".[36] And he also refers to "The hand of Heaven".[37]

The ambiguity of terms for denoting a reality which is not identified by a specific name accounts for the latitude with which the term "heaven" is used. In some cases, it is used interchangeably with "god", whereas in others it is not so used. It is not so used by Euripides in *Andromache* when Menelaus declares that "Helen's trouble was not of her own choosing, but sent by heaven".[38] It is used with the same non-interchangeable meaning in *Orestes,* when Orestes speaks of the "ill time" for him "to mention Heaven, when defending the cause of murder" for which he himself acknowledges responsibility.[39]

There are, however, other instances in which one translation uses the term "heaven" and another uses the term "god". In one translation, the Chorus addresses itself to Medea, acknowledging the "hopeless sea of misery heaven hath plunged thee!"[40] Another translation of the same passage uses the term "God" rather than the less determinate term "heaven": "God's hand on thine helm hath steered, O Medea, thy prow!"[41] The same latitude in translating occurs in *Heracles.* One translation refers to Heracles killing his children in a fit of madness as "heaven-sent woes".[42] Another translation refers to "the malice of Gods" for bringing about "these ills".[43] The same interchangeable terminology of "heaven" and "god" is used in translations of *Hippolytus*. In one translation, the Chorus refers to the source of "evil in the train by heaven sent".[44] Another interprets the same evil as sent by God: "God bringeth evil following hard on the track of evil!"[45] Still another translation indicates a source less specific than "God" by referring to "some god".[46]

The latitude of terminology for acknowledging an intervention in human life of some reality transcendent of human life is likewise indicated in *Andromache* in which the Chorus declares: " 'Tis Heaven's decree; God willed this heavy stroke."[47] Additional latitude is introduced in this same passage by another translation which attributes to the Chorus the declaration: " 'Tis God's doom", thus mixing the terminology of "fate" and "doom" with the theistic terminology "God".[48]

The only justification for pointing out the latitude in these translations is to support the point that their references to a reality transcendent of human life for accounting for occurrences in human life do not affirm a clear-cut or unambiguous metaphysic. The denotation, however, which the several terms do share in common is to a reality transcendent of both human life and the physical world.

The meaning with which the term "heaven" is used in any metaphysical reference to a reality transcendent of the physical world, therefore, is not to the physical heaven, to which Jeremiah refers when he speaks of "the heavens" as the source of "showers". (14:22) The sense, on the other hand, with which the author of *Second Maccabees* uses the term "heaven" parallels the sense with which this term is used in the Greek literature referred to in the foregoing. He declares: "For beyond doubt there is a divine power surrounding the temple. He whose habitation is in heaven watches over it himself and gives it his aid." (3:39) Both the terms "heaven" and "divine power" in this translation have connotations which are the same as these terms have in the Greek literature referred to above.

3. *An impersonal "Fate" or "Doom" or "Destiny" is a metaphysic commonly affirmed in Greek religious reflecting*

According to Homer, the one aspect of human life which no reflective person can ignore is the opposition which human beings encounter both by physical nature and also by a fate which works through nature, yet is other than it. The fact that it determines occurrences in the physical world is the metaphysical distinction between it and the world. According to Homer, the life of a human being is an encounter with such a reality referred to by interchangeable terms "Fate", "Destiny", "Doom".

108

The King of the Phaeacians gives Odysseus the stern counsel that "he must suffer whatever Destiny and the relentless Fates spun for him with the first thread of life" when he was born.[49] According to this counsel, fate determines a man's destiny from the moment he begins his life, and as Hector declares to Andromache, "No man yet has escaped it once it has taken its first form, neither brave man nor coward".[50] This is also the explanation Homer gives for the encounter of Tlepolemus, the son of Heracles, with "the godlike Sarpedon": He was "brought by the stern hand of Fate" into this conflict.[51] Another translation is that he "was driven by his strong destiny against the godlike Sarpedon."[25]

The ambiguous metaphysic with which Herodotus interprets history is likewise evident when he uses a battery of terms to refer to the determinant of history transcendent of the physical order itself in which men live and die. One term in his vocabulary for denoting such a reality is "Fate". He declares that "fate willed that Miltiades should be slain by Pisistratus' sons".[53] So stated, it would seem as if political events did not account for this death, although there is no incompatibility between the explanation Herodotus offers in terms of "fate" and an explanation in terms of political antecedents for this murder. Herodotus might actually mean that consequences which are entailed in a sequence of events are themselves invariant. And it is such invariance in a sequence of events which is the basic meaning of "Fate" as this term is used in early Greek discourse.

The inescapable character of Fate or Destiny or Doom is affirmed in Aeschylus' *Libation-Bearers* when Electra asks: "Is it not hopeless to wrestle against doom?"[54] If such "doom" is not objectified as an agency which is responsible for occurrences, it then may be regarded as the inevitability that consequences will follow antecedentes in the order of nature and also in the events of human life. Since there is no clarification of these terms in the writings of the dramatists, one must be satisfied with their nondeterminate characterization of such a reality. One meaning which is clear in their discourse is that there is a determination of events in the world and in human life which is other than both the world and human life. But further than this, they do not venture to reflect.

In the Chorus of Elders of Thebes, Sophocles acknowledges: "Strange are the ways of Fate. . . . Nor brass-prowed ships that breast the sea from Fate can flee."[55] Sophocles accounts for various events consistent with the premise that "Man is born to fate a prey". One of these was the death of Achilles "by the doom of Fate".[56] Another such event decreed or doomed by Fate was the fall of Troy in which the poisoned arrows of

Philoctetes played so definitive a part: "For when the fated hour h. come by them must Troy-town find its doom."[57]

The oppressive character of men's dread for the inescapable destiny doom which imposes the final limits upon life is expressed by Creon Antigone: "Whither to turn I know not; every way leads but astray and on my head I feel the heavy weight of crushing Fate."[58] The o pressive sense of an inescapable Fate with its pitiless doom is affirme by the Chorus of Elders in the same drama, and it counsels: "O pray no prayers are idle; from the doom of fate for mortals refuge is there none."

The latitude in translations of Euripides' *Heracles* makes it impossib to be confident of any care with which Euripides uses the term "fate The explanation which the Chorus offers for the madness during whic Heracles killed his children includes various terms which denote a reali transcendent of himself. One translation explains the "madness" as "hurle from heaven".[60] Another translation affirms a very different metaphys that the cause is "the malice of Gods". But the same translation al refers to "the fate with misery fraught".[61]

Euripides, however, was too critical in reflecting not to have been awai of the differences in the natures of realities denoted by these various term unless basic to the meaning of all of them is the inevitability of occu rences as consequences of their antecedents. If this is the basic meanir with which he denotes a reality transcendent of human beings that a counts for the inescapability of events in a causally related series, then tl particular term which is used to denote it is not metaphysically importan and may be a matter of poetry rather than of philosophy. But the phil sophical reflecting which is basic to Euripides' struggle to understand wh some events take place in human life includes the belief that there ai some sequences in series of events over which man has no control. Megar: the wife of Heracles, states such a philosophy of the inescapable charact in a sequence of events when she declares: "What must be, no one wi ever avail to alter."

The obvious reason that this explanation cannot be questioned is tha it is tautological. If it is the case that something "must be" then the ne cessity itself is merely reaffirmed by declaring that it cannot be altered. I Euripides were a physical scientist, he might affirm the same unalterabl sequence in series of occurrences. If he were a logician, he might affirm the same type of necessity in a logical sequence of inferences.

The same poverty of metaphysical analysis is affirmed in Megara assertion that "whoso struggles hard to escape destiny shows zeal n doubt, but 'tis with a taint of folly". This is not an explication of th

110

ature of necessity denoted by "destiny", but it is rather a condemnation
a human being for attempting to divert events in sequence, the nature
which is determined by antecedent factors. It would be the same sort
irrationality as affirming an illogical inference from a proposition the
eaning of which implies a very different inference.

Megara reaffirms this same censorship of human folly rather than com-
enting on the nature of a reality which accounts for the inevitability
a sequence of events. She admits that she regards "death" as "a dread-
l fate", and then reaffirms her point of view that "the man who wrestles
ith necessity (she) esteems a fool".[62] What is of metaphysical significance
this comment is not what she thinks about a human being who tries to
 what cannot be done, but rather the identification of "death" with
ate". The meaning of "fate", however, in this use may be nothing more
an the inevitability that any living being must eventually die. The term
ate" so used would also have no philosophical significance whatever to
note some causative determinant of events. Aristotle affirms the same
evitability of death of every living thing when he declares: "Whatever
ts must die." But Aristotle does not use the term "fate" or "destiny" as
these terms had explanatory significance.

Every philosophical Stoic would affirm the same point of view as con-
itutes the meaning of one translation of this same passage: "How base a
ing it is when a man will struggle with necessity."[63] So stated, this is a
oral philosophy, and not a metaphysic which proposes an explication of
the inevitability of certain sequences in human events.

Some of the terminology used in translating Euripides either expresses
poverty of philosophical understanding or it does not constitute very
pressive evidence for Euripides' philosophical intelligence. One transla-
on of Heracles' address to Theseus when he decided to endure the re-
rses of life after his madness is that "whoso schooleth not his frail
oral nature to bear fate's buffets as he ought, will never be able to
thstand even a man's weapon."[64] Another translation of the same pas-
ge uses the terminology of "misfortune's blows" rather than the termi-
logy of "fate's buffets".[65] The expression "misfortune's blows" ordinally
ggests "bad luck" or getting "the short end", but unless it is loaded
th a metaphysic referring to some factor other than a sequence of
ents causative of their invariance, it does not have a meaning such as
ate" ordinarily has.

Other references, however, to "fate" in the dramas of Euripides seem
 denote a "necessity" in the sense of a total absence of caprice in a
quence of occurrences, an initial factor of which determines the order

111

of subsequent events. It is used in this sense by the Chorus in *Hippolyt*
which declares "nor is there any escape from fate and necessity".[66] T
term "fate" and "necessity" are synonymous. Hence any explication
the meaning of "necessity" in such a vocabulary would also constitute
clarification of the meaning of the term "fate". The minimum of suc
meaning in a philosophy of reality is simply that there is an order in t
sequence of events which is not capricious, but it is a predictable orde
because the sequence is invariant. Another term for such an invaria
sequence is "lawful". It may, therefore, be the case that Euripides, as
rationalist, uses the terms "necessity", and "fate" as meaning lawful orde

The combination of terms such as "the doom of fate" may expre
merely an intensification of emphasis that a necessity of sequence initiat
by a causative factor is inescapable.[67] Any rationalistic philosophy wou
affirm this. And the same meaning would be affirmed in a science in whi
the terminology of "law" or "invariant" is used. If this is the meaning
"fate" as used by Euripides, then it would indeed be the case that as
purely impersonal order in events, it "knows not pity" and "will n
spare".[68] So likewise with this meaning, it would be understandable th
Electra should declare in *Orestes* that "fate runs counter to . . . hopes"
"short-lived men, full of tears and born of suffering".[69] When, for instanc
men are born in abject poverty, their hope for comforts and prosperit
are seldom more effective than are their prayers. Hope, in other words,
irrelevant to an invariant sequence, elements of which are determined b
antecedents, notwithstanding hope or prayer. The philosophical meaning
"fate" for Euripides would then be an order in occurrences which is dete
mined by the causal character of events themselves. That there is such
causally ordered sequence might, of course, be explained by taking accou
of a reality transcendent of the series of elements in such an order. If s
this would then be an unambiguous metaphysic of "necessity" or "fate

Some passages in the Old Testament affirm an inescapability in certa
sequences of events. But such inevitability in the sequence is not e
plained by a reality other than God. Job declares: "The days of (man'
life are determined." If this were separated from the following assertion
it would have a similarity to Greek thinking. But there is no such sim
larity as becomes clear in the following verse which is addressed to Go
"The number of his months are known to thee; thou hast laid down
limit, which he cannot pass." (14:4, 5)

The metaphysic so affirmed is a consistent theology. It maintains th
God has knowledge of human history, and nothing that occurs in suc
history is unknown to God. The reference in this acknowledgment to

limit" which is "laid down" by God may be construed to affirm that God's knowledge of history includes a foreknowledge of events in history. As such, it would then imply that God's knowledge of what will take place cannot be at variance with what takes place. His knowledge of future events would then be the determinant of such events. Or in other words, nothing would take place in a future which was not already anticipated by God. It is this type of explication of the meaning of "God's knowledge" of human history which supports the metaphysic of "predestination" or "foreordination". This, however, may well be reading into the faith of Job what is not included in his interpretation of the nature of God. His conviction, on the other hand, that God is the ultimate reality, and therefore nothing that occurs does so without relation to Him, would be a sufficient, even though not a detailed, explication of this passage. It would at least have the merit of religious faith, even if not of an expanded philosophical metaphysic.

A passage in *Jeremiah* is in a sense more bewildering than the passage from *The Book of Job*. Jeremiah declares that "These are the words of the Lord: 'Those who are for death shall go to their death, and those for the sword to the sword; those who are for famine to famine, and those for captivity to captivity.' " (15:2) This entire statement could be cited by anyone who thinks as Calvin does because there is an unequivocal affirmation that the length of life of a human being is not determined by aging, sickness, or accident. Rather, his death occurs in conformity to the limit imposed upon the duration of his life. It seems to affirm that if anyone were killed by a sword, there was no other way by which he could have died. In other words, the cause for the end of his life was determined at the beginning of his life. Although this may be argued on the basis of this passage, it would be pressing a meaning upon the passage that would not be warranted if one were to affirm a theology that whatever occurs in the history of human beings is not unknown to God. If the nature of such history is pressed for a philosophical explication, a corollary could be included either that God's knowledge of a future is itself a determinant of such a future, or nothing can take place in human history of which God is not eternally aware. If the meaning of this is not pressed into a philosophical analysis, it may be accepted as a religious assurance that human history is within the sovereignty of God. A weakening of such assurance then is not entailed in a more detailed philosophical explication of its possible meaning.

A comparable problem of meaning arises in a passage in Daniel which declares that for anyone who "utters monstrous blasphemies" against God,

113

"All will go well for him until the time of wrath ends, for what is determined must be done." (11:36, 37) Either this is ambiguous or it affirms that the final judgment upon what men do will be included in God's universal sovereignty. If the statement as such is pressed by an explication, the analysis could entail a surmise that there is a determination of events to which the sovereignty of God itself conforms. Or the analysis could maintain that since God is the ultimate reality, there is no determination of any event in history which is not within his sovereignty.

This same statement could support an analysis which argues on behalf of a meaning that parallels a Greek philosophy of "Destiny" or "Fate". And the same may be said of a statement in *Second Esdras* which declares: "For the Lord has weighed the world in a balance, he has measured and numbered the ages; he will move nothing, alter nothing until the appointed number is achieved." (4:36, 37) If this is regarded as ambiguous, it could yield one interpretation that God will conform to "the appointed number" which he himself does not determine. Or God determines "the appointed number", and therefore there is no reality other than God to which God's acting is subordinate.

The references above from the religious reflecting of the Israelites parallel the references from Greek literature which have been cited for a comparable ambiguity. None of the references themselves are expanded philosophies. And yet, it is only such philosophical explication which could provide an unambiguous analysis of realities denoted by the terms such as "Heaven", "Destiny", "Fate", either as ultimate realities or as included within the nature of a reality more ultimate than themselves.

4. *One metaphysic maintains that gods are subordinate to Fate*

The relation of Zeus to Fate is not clear in either the *Iliad* or the *Odyssey*. What, however, is perfectly clear in the Epics is that Zeus is sovereign over the other gods of Olympus. What is not clear, on the other hand, is whether Zeus is subordinate to Fate or whether his sovereignty has the inescapable character attributed to Fate. In Here's stern rebuke of Zeus who wishes to restore the life of Sarpedon, "a man who is mortal", she refers to his death as "doomed by his destiny".[70] A possible interpretation of this confrontation is that Zeus presumes to go counter to the "destiny" determined for Sarpedon, which is other than the wish of Zeus. According to this interpretation, Zeus would be subordinate to Fate. The same relationship of Zeus' subordination to Fate also seems to be indicated in the account of the death of Heracles, who was "dear to

Zeus". According to the account in the *Iliad*, "Even the mighty Heracles did not escape his doom, dear as he was to Zeus, the Royal Son of Cronos, but was laid low by Fate and Here's bitter enmity."[71] Although Here's part in his death is mentioned, her authority is subordinate to Zeus, who is sovereign over all other gods. The problem, however, is the role of Fate in relation to Zeus. If Heracles were "dear to Zeus" and yet "was laid low by Fate", it certainly seems as if Fate were more sovereign than Zeus.

A relation which may be less ambiguous is indicated in the *Odyssey* in a reference to "Zeus the Thunderer", "who knows so well what good and evil are allotted to each one of us on earth".[72] So stated, there is no explicit affirmation that the "good and evil" are "allotted" by a reality other than Zeus. They may well be his own decrees. This interpretation is supported by another translation that Zeus "well knows all things, the luck and the lucklessness of mortal people".[73]

Hesiod clearly affirms the ultimate sovereignty of Zeus without taking account of any other reality either equal in sovereignty or superior in sovereignty to him. He declares: "For those who practice violence and cruel deeds, far-seeing Zeus, the son of Cronos, ordains a punishment." Thus the decree of Zeus is the ultimate determinant of a penalty for human wrongdoing. The same ultimate role of Zeus is acknowledged in maintaining that "the son of Cronos either destroys their wide army, or their walls, or else makes an end of their ships on the sea". Rather than specifying Zeus as the ultimate reality of whom men should take account as imposing an inescapable punishment for their wrongdoing, Hesiod refers to "the deathless gods (who) are near among men and mark all those who oppress their fellows with crooked judgments." Hence when the "princes" are addressed and counseled to "mark well this punishment", they are warned to "reck not the anger of the gods".[74] In this entire analysis of human beings' subordinate relation to divine realities, Hesiod does not refer to an impersonal determinant of human history such as "fate" to which deities themselves are subordinate. Gods, and Zeus as their chief, are the only realities transcendent of the physical world and human beings to whom human beings themselves should take serious account as determining their destiny.

According to some Greek reflecting, even gods themselves are thought of as coming under the determination of a destiny over which they have no final control. This way of thinking is affirmed by "the priestess" to whom Herodotus refers in the first book of his *History*. He declares: "When the Lydians came, and spoke as they were charged, the priestess (it is said) thus replied: 'None may escape his destined lot, not even a god.'"

It is this same relationship which seems to be affirmed by Aeschylu in several references. In *Prometheus Bound,* the Chorus asks: "Who ther is the steersman of Necessity?" Prometheus answers: "The triform Fate. and mindful Furies". The Chorus then asks: "Can it be that Zeus hath lesser power than they?" And the unambiguous answer of Prometheus i: "Aye, in that at least he cannot escape what is foredoomed". But the answer of Prometheus does not seem to be the final thought of Aeschylu: since the Chorus asks the metaphysically significant question: "Why, wha' is foredoomed for Zeus save to hold eternal sway?"[75] According to thi: position, Zeus is not subordinate to a reality which restricts his sover eignty, such as would be the case if he were to rule within the limit: imposed upon him by another reality, whether denoted as "Fate" or "Destiny", or any other term indicating a reality other than Zeus' own sovereignty in determining events in the world and in human history.

In the same drama, however, the Chorus also refers to Fate as if it were the final determiner when it declares: "Alas, O Fate, O Fate, I shudder at beholding the plight that hath befallen Io."[76] Another transla tion is not a direct address to Fate but, nevertheless, acknowledges "fate' as a determiner of what will take place: "Alas, Alas, for your fate! I shudder when I look on Io's fortune.[77]

The relationship between Zeus and "whatsoe'er is fated" seems to be unambiguous as it is affirmed by the Chorus in *Suppliant Maidens.* The Chorus declares: "Whatsoe'er is fated, that will come to pass. The mighty, untrammelled will of Zeus cannot be transgressed."[78] But ac cording to this affirmation, Zeus is not subordinate to a fate more ultimate than his own "untrammelled will". Thus a fate which often is regarded by early Greeks as other than Zeus, is identified with the finality of the will of Zeus. It is this will that "cannot be transgressed".

This position of Aeschylus would not even be qualified by what the Chorus declares to Orestes in *Eumenides* after he murdered his mother: "Nay, be sure, not Apollo nor Athena's might can save thee from perish ing, spurned and neglected, knowing not where in thy soul is joy—a bloodless victim of the powers below."[79] It must be acknowledged in the first place that Apollo and Athena are subordinate in power or authority to the sovereign Zeus. And in the second place, "the powers below" are not the same as Fate. Hence the limited power of Apollo and Athena in relation to "the powers below" would indeed present a very different problem than the relation between Zeus and Fate.

116

The position of Euripides is anything but clear about the relationship between Fate and Zeus or the gods, since there is no single position affirmed in his dramas. In *Iphigenia in Tauris*, Athena declares: "The power of Fate o'er thee and o'er the gods prevails."[80] So stated, Fate is more ultimate than the gods. The same interpretation is affirmed in another translation of this declaration of the goddess: "For thee, for Gods, is Fate too strong."[81] This same relationship seems to be affirmed in *Hippolytus* when the Nurse maintains that it was "more than God, who hath ruined (Phaedra) and me, and all this house". The "something more than God" would then be Fate.

But a different relationship between Fate and other realities, whether interpreted as gods, God, or Heaven, is affirmed in the *Phoenissae* when Jocasta asks Polynices, "How was it thou didst go to Argos?" He answered: "I know not; the deity summoned me thither in accordance with my destiny."[82] According to this affirmation, it seems as if Euripides maintains that a god carries out the pattern of life which is destined for him by a reality other than the deity himself. Another translation affirms that it was "Heaven" which "summoned" him to his "fate".[83] According to this latter interpretation, it also seems as if his "fate" was prior to the act of Heaven in executing it.

The priority of Fate to the will of Zeus seems to be affirmed by Thetis, who addresses Peleus: "Fate's decree thou must fulfil; such is the pleasure of Zeus."[84] The same relation is affirmed in another translation: 'All the doom of fate must thou accomplish. Zeus' will is this."[85] In yet another drama, *Electra*, the point of view is also affirmed that "resistless doom" is brought about by fate. The Chorus asks the Dioscuri: "How was it that ye, gods too, did not ward the doom-goddesses from (Clytemnestra's) roof?" The Dioscuri answered: " 'Twas fate that brought resistless doom to her, and that thoughtless oracle that Phoebus gave."[86]

As if Euripides were not satisfied with this explanation proposed either in Greek mythology or in Greek popular religion, he has Electra press the Dioscuri for an explanation why the oracle of a god should decree that she should murder her own mother. She asked: "But why did the god, and wherefore did his oracles make me my mother's murderer?" The high probability is that the rationalistic Euripides was not satisfied with any of these explanations, and therefore for philosophical reasons, and not only for dramatic reasons, raises the questions about the conventional explanations most commonly proposed in the thinking of his contemporaries, who in turn reaffirmed the thought of an earlier tradition.

117

5. The basic premise of a theology is that a god is ultimate

A consistently thought-out philosophy about the nature of a god as the one ultimate reality is affirmed in the dramas of Aeschylus. Its basic premise is stated in *Prometheus Bound* when Oceanus declares to Prometheus that Zeus is established "on his throne omnipotent".[87]

Implied in such an "omnipotent" status in sovereignty over the world is that there is no reality to which Zeus is subordinate or upon whose power his own sovereignty is contingent. This ascription of omnipotence to Zeus is an unambiguous affirmation of the ultimate nature of Zeus in relation to every other reality, whether denoted by "Heaven", "Destiny" or "Fate". This unequivocal interpretation is also affirmed in *Suppliant Maidens* when the Chorus declares that "He doth not sit upon his throne by mandate of another and hold his dominion beneath a mightier". This affirmation of the ultimate nature of Zeus is expanded in a tautological character when the Chorus continues to declare that "None there is who sitteth above him whose power he holdeth in awe". Both of these declarations by the Chorus affirm the same proposition. It is that Zeus is the one ultimate reality.

The meaning of his ultimate nature is that all other realities are subordinate to him, and this implication is explicitly affirmed by the Chorus when it declares that "He speaketh and it is done—he hasteneth to execute whatsoever his counselling mind conceiveth".[88] So stated, Zeus both decrees what will take place and also executes his own decrees.

This theological discourse is an explication of the meaning implied in the term "omnipotent". If Zeus is all-powerful, he then likewise has a capacity to carry out his own decrees. His decrees are not duplications of a reality other than his own sovereignty, such as Fate, and he is not the agent for carrying out a destiny which is prior to his own decrees. The Chorus in the same drama maintains that by the "venerable enactment" of Zeus, "destiny" is guided "aright".[89] This does not affirm that Zeus decrees according to a destiny prior to his decree, but his decree or "enactment" is itself the factor that "guideth destiny aright".

The Chorus in *Agamemnon* declares an interpretation of Zeus as ultimate when it maintains that the "will of Zeus (is) author of all, worker of all". And then the Chorus affirms another tautological declaration, such as is common in the theological affirmations of Aeschylus, that nothing "is brought to pass for mortal men save by will of Zeus".[90] Both of these affirmations assert the same meaning. It is the theological premise that

us is the one ultimate reality whose sovereignty accounts for whatever
:urs in the world and in human history.

Since the theology affirmed by this Chorus is subsequent to the murder
Agamemnon by his own son, Aeschylus must have been troubled by
: implications of the premise that "What is brought to pass for mortal
n" is by the "will of Zeus". In the same drama, although in an earlier
:laration by the Chorus, it attributes to Zeus a guidance of human
ngs in "the way of understanding".[91] This qualification of the role of
us in human history would, therefore, constitute a very different
:ology, and so it was almost as if Aeschylus anticipated Plato's criticisms
the poets when he maintained that only good is decreed by God. Plato
uld, therefore, have specifically censured Aeschylus for maintaining
it everything which "is brought to pass for mortal men", including
: murder of a father by his son, is by the "will of Zeus". Aeschylus
nself, without the benefit of another's critique, was capable of thinking
arly enough to be aware of the indefensibility of attributing everything
ne by human beings to an ultimate reality, as if it were a sanction for
ls done by men.

Sophocles was as aware, as was Aeschylus, of the implications of the
nventional point of view which explained all occurrences in human
tory as interventions by some reality other than men themselves. What
ubled him by this conventional philosophy of history is that gods
uld thereby be regarded as responsible even for the death of heroes as
·y fight in battle, such as was affirmed by Tecmessa, the wife of Ajax,
o declares that "The gods were authors of his death".[92] And Neopto-
nus declares that his father Achilles was "Slain by no man but by a
1". He continues to describe to his friend Philoctetus how this came
out: "A shaft pierced him; by Phoebus (Apollo) sped".[93] Since Apollo
d other gods were subordinate to the sovereignty of Zeus, Sophocles
uld consistently reaffirm the traditional explanation that *gods* are
ponsible for whatever occurs in human life, and also affirm a theology
out Zeus as the ultimate god whose "will is ever best".

This particular thesis is affirmed by the Chorus of Mycenaean women
Electra, when it assures Electra that "Zeus still in heaven is king and
lers everything".[94] A bewildering problem, nevertheless, persists for
rely a logical reason. If Zeus "orders everything", even the acts of lesser
ds would come within the range of his final control. And then the asser-
n that "His will is ever best" would imply some sobering questions
out the moral justice of much which takes place in human history that
attributed to the "gods" in popular Greek reflecting.

119

It is, therefore, remarkable that Hesiod, centuries before Aeschylus a Sophocles, declared so clearly that omniscient Zeus "seeing all and und standing all . . . fails not to mark what sort of justice . . . the city kee within it", as if to acknowledge an ultimate criterion of justice by whi conventional versions of justice are appraised by Zeus.[95]

Sophocles, however, seems to struggle with a traditional Greek exp nation that whatever takes place of importance in human life, wheth favorable or not for human beings, is due to the intervention of goe Even the perverse Creon cites the gods as responsible for bringing abc what is favorable for human beings. He declares to the Elders of Thebe "The gods have righted once again our storm-tossed ship of state, ne safe in port."[96] This ascription to the "gods" would thus be consiste with the theological premise that the will of Zeus is "ever best", such the Chorus assured Electra.

Sophocles thus had to struggle in his reflecting with more than t relation between Zeus and Fate. He also had to struggle reflectively wi the relation of the "gods" to evil in human life. His problem was attemp ing to reconcile Zeus as both sovereign over gods and also as authorizi what is "ever best", although the gods under his jurisdiction were respo sible for what men regard as evil.

One resolution of this problem is proposed by analytical philosop which points out that some questions themselves create the probler which men subsequently struggle to resolve. Yet, if men affirm a theolog as Sophocles does, and also takes account of the fact of evil, they the are confronted with more than a problem which is generated by their ov questioning. The problem is encountered after a theology is affirme Hence the particular problem of evil would not arise in reflecting if different metaphysic were to be affirmed, or if no metaphysic, such as theology, were to be affirmed. But then a hesitancy to affirm a metaphysi such as a theology, would exclude one type of explanation for evil whie has persisted throughout the centuries.

Euripides wrestled with the problem which is entailed in both acknow edging that there are evils which blight human well-being, and also th; there are gods who are responsible for what takes place in the lives human beings. The Chorus in the *Suppliants* affirm that "the gods . . . ho. in their own hands each thing's allotted end".[97] This affirmation woul therefore, seem to attribute to the gods responsibility for what takes plae in human life which is both favorable and also unfavorable. Such an expl: nation thus dispenses with the traditional notion of an impersonal Fate ; the ultimate determiner of whatever takes place in human history, bot

120

eneficial and also detrimental to men's well-being. The closing affirma-
ions of several of Euripides' plays are essentially the same. *Andromache,*
he Bacchae, Helen, and, with a slight change, also the *Medea,* close with
he same pronouncement as does the Chorus in *Alcestis:* "O the works of
he Gods—in manifold forms they reveal them: Manifold things unhoped-
or, the Gods to accomplishment bring. And the things that we looked
or, the Gods deign not to fulfill them."[98] A less elliptical way of translat-
ng this passage is that "Many strange things are performed by the Gods.
The expected does not always happen, and God makes a way for the
unexpected."[99]

A philosophy of history is thus affirmed in these concluding declarations
of the several dramas, even if not a very explicit theology. What alone
seems to be explicit in several of Euripides' dramas is the elimination of
he traditional notion of Fate as the final determinant of events in human
history. The Chorus in *The Suppliants* refers to the gods, and asks: "For
who but they allot whate'er betides?"[100]

Euripides, however, also affirms the conventional explanation for what
akes place in human history as the intervention of gods. For example,
Orestes counsels his sister, Electra: "First recognize the gods as being the
authors of our fortune." But then he adds a significant interpretation of
himself in relation to the gods as their agency or as "their minister".
This introduces another point of view into Euripides' philosophy of
history. It is that men are not merely objects of the gods' activities, but
have a morally important role to be instruments of the gods. As their
ministers, men themselves thus make a difference in human history, and
they do so under the authority or the sovereignty of a reality transcendent
of themselves, which is not only "the gods", but also "fate".[101] Another
translation interprets the role of Orestes as a "minister of heaven and
fate".[102] What, therefore, is significant in the concept of men's relation
to a reality transcendent of them is that a human agency is also acknowledged in bringing about justice and so human "fortune".

Although the role of a god in human affairs is acknowledged, its exact
nature is not claimed as known. The Messenger in *Helen* admits "how . . .
inscrutable is the nature of God", since on the basis of the unpredictable
fortunes in human life, it is not possible to anticipate what a god's role
will be. Human fortunes are "now up, now down".[103] Rather than citing
this precarious feature of human life as evidence for a disbelief in a god's
sovereignty over human history, it is the basis upon which the inscruta-
bility of a god is argued. Another translation of the Messenger's comment

121

is that although "God's counsels are manifold", yet "His ways (are) pa: finding out".[104] The same point of view is affirmed in *The Trojan Wome* when Hecuba acknowledges the "Earth's Upbearer . . . whose throne : Earth", and then confesses her inability to understand such a deity role in human history. She declares: "Whoe'er thou be, O past ou finding out." Then she proposes some daring surmises about the natur of what "Zeus" may be. He may be "Nature's Law" or even the "Min of Man". But notwithstanding her awareness of how limited her know edge is of the nature of Zeus, she affirms her confidence that there is som factor in reality which establishes justice. This she proposes as the role c Zeus: "To justice' goal thou bring'st all mortal things."[105]

This is a religious assurance that justice is not merely conventional, a the later Cynics maintained, but is integral to the factors which hav sovereignty over human history. Even if the theology proposed in th various dramas of Euripides is not a thoroughly worked out metaphysic what is more important for a religious faith is the confidence that ther is a divine reality for whom justice is not indifferent, but for whom it establishment in human history is its essential role.

One aspect of human pathos is that no one "knows whom . . . misfor tunes may attend", and although "the god's will" works itself out i human history, yet "none can tell the ills to come". Men's "fortune" i unknown and unpredictable. Their "fortune from the sight obscures".[10] But bewildering as such limited knowledge of future occurrences in huma well-being may be, such uncertainty can be endured with the faith tha "to justice' goal thou bring'st all mortal things". This not only affirms : philosophical position which is later affirmed in Plato's philosophy, bu it also affirms a faith which is basic to the religious metaphysic of th Stoics.

Euripides also affirms a traditional view when it is said that "the god: have compassed (men) about with suffering" from which there is "n escape".[107] But what is especially significant in this religious belief, whicl is not traditional, is affirmed by Iolaus to the mother of Heracles: "Zeu: too, I feel sure, cares for thy suffering."[108] This assurance is an enrich ment of the content of traditional Greek religious faith. It is a trust tha: although men suffer, their suffering is not indifferent to God. Insofar as earlier reflecting upon human history maintained that Fate was the ultimate determinant of events in human life, there was no basis for a religious assurance that men did not suffer in an impersonal, indifferent world.

Another significant point which is also made in Euripides' reflecting
⟩on the pathos of human suffering in relation to a reality transcendent
 human life is affirmed by the mother of Heracles who declares: "Of
⟩us will I never speak ill, but himself doth know whether he is just to
⟩e."[109] Another translation stresses her doubt of the justice of her suffer-
g in stating her doubting as a question: "But is he just to me?" And
⟩en notwithstanding her perplexity or doubting, she affirms her trust in
⟩od's providence: "Himself knows!"[110]
 The reconciliation of human suffering with God's justice is also affirmed
⟩ Jocasta in *The Phoenician Maidens*. After acknowledging that "Some
⟩d with fell intent is plaguing the race of Oedipus", she admits she under-
ands how such misery began, and acknowledges that she "broke God's
w".[111] Even though there is a profound moral question about the basic
ɪfairness of the tragic consequences which accrued to what she did in
 ɪnorance of her son's identity, what is, nevertheless, significant in this
 ɾama is the correlation between human suffering and an infraction of a
 ɪvine law. In acknowledging "The God's will must we bear" for such an
 ɪfraction of His law, Jocasta affirms a profound moral understanding
 ɪat there is an invariant relation between human error or wrongdoing
 nd the suffering which it entails.[112] She also affirms a profound religious
 ɪith that even though the manifestations of God's justice in judgment
 ɾe beyond men's understanding, nevertheless, His justice is trustworthy.
 nd after the Chorus in *Hecuba* takes account of the "fearful curse"
 ⟩on the race of Priam, it acknowledges that " 'tis sent by God, and we
 ɪust bear it."[113] Although this may be construed as a Stoic's resolution
 ⟩ accept whatever takes place, it may also be looked upon as another
 cknowledgment of the immanence of God in human history, and so as
 ɪ expression of a religious attitude toward history notwithstanding its
 ɾagic character. The same religious philosophy of history is affirmed in
 'he Trojan Women by the Queen after the destruction of the kingdom
 ver which she and Priam ruled: "I have seen the open hand of God; and
 ɪ it nothing, nothing, save the rod of mine affliction."[114]
 If adversity in its acutest form constitutes a supreme test of religious
 ɑith that there is a divine reality working internal to human history,
 ɦen the declaration of the Queen indicates Euripides' profound under-
 ʈanding of the nature of religious faith.
 Writings among the ancient Israelites affirm the same supreme test of
 ⁀eligious faith in the justice of what takes place in human history. A
 ɾaditional example of suffering as a test of religious faith is, of course,
 ⟩ortrayed in *The Book of Job*. Basic to the religious life of Elihu, one of

Job's friends, is the primary premise of a theistic religion: "God is great« than man." (33:13) The same primary premise of religious faith of th monotheistic tradition of the Israelites is affirmed throughout *Psalm* One such affirmation of faith that the final determinant in human histor will be God's judgment and not men's is that "The Lord brings the pla» of nations to nothing". If the plans of men go counter to the intentio» of God for human history, then God "frustrates the counsel of the pe« ple". The intentions of God for human history are not only transcendei of such history, but they are eternal as human history is not. Th transcendence, the finality, the eternity of God's plans for human histor are concepts basic to the metaphysic of the religious faith of the earl Israelites. This entire metaphysic is condensed in the creed of the: religious faith: "The Lord's own plans shall stand for ever." (33:10, 11 This creed is subsequently reaffirmed in the following centuries in rel gions which appropriated the writings of the Israelites. Hence both th Christian religion and the religion based upon the *Koran* accept as th primary creed of faith the affirmation of belief as it is stated in this singl verse in *Psalms*. A corollary of this creed is that the eternal sovereignt of God transcendent of history is the basis for the final justice which wi be established in history. An instance of such faith is affirmed in *Proverbs* God "guards the course of justice." (2:8)

Faith in the finality of God's justice is affirmed throughout the tradi tion of the Prophets. Isaiah, for example, declares that there is only on final standard of justice by which men will be held accountable, and it i this alone which they "must fear". The reason for such "fear" is its final ity in the sense that no schemes or designs of men can alter the fina justice which is assured in human history. In relation to the finality o the justice assured by God's sovereignty over human history, men' schemes to the contrary are without enduring effect. Hence the Prophe declares: "Make your plans, but they will be foiled; propose what yo» please, but it shall not stand." (8:10) It is this same confidence in th« finality of God's sovereignty over history which is declared in *Lamenta tions* which asks: "Who can command . . . if the Lord has forbidde» it?" (3:37)

The contrast between the finality of God's justice and human plan. which are not respectful of it is affirmed in the *Wisdom of Solomon* whicl points out that the role of God in the world so surpasses the finality o men's decisions in history that they are like "a grain that just tips th« scale" or like "a drop of dew alighting on the ground at dawn". (11:22, 23

The Prophet Ezra in *Second Edras* maintains that "the strongest

se" for men's grief is their awareness of the contrast between their
worthy plans and the standard "of the Most High in his glory", in
trast to which "they break down in shame, waste away in remorse, and
ivel with fear remembering how they sinned against him in their life-
e". (7:87) Such self-accusation is the moral judgment which oppresses
man beings who recognize that their schemes for living go counter to
justice required of them by God.

The belief that human history is subordinate to the eternal sovereignty
God, whose requirements for men are the final norm of justice, is a
ral appraisal of history. It is also basic to a religious faith that, in
te of what seems evidence to negate a confidence in a final justice,
re, nevertheless, is an eternal basis for such justice which is transcendent
human history.

*A theology which maintains that God is the ultimate basis for justice
in human history is often inadequately expressed in anthropomorphic
imagery*

An anthropomorphic or mythological type of imagery is often used for
erpreting the means by which an eternal justice is established for
man history. Elihu, a friend of Job, employs such graphic or pictorial
guage when he declares: God's "eyes are on the ways of men and he
s every step they take; there is nowhere so dark, so deep in shadow,
t wrongdoers may hide from him." (34:21, 22) An imagery such as
s, however, is not essential to a religious confidence that there is a final
tice in human history. It is only a graphic way to state an account of a
ans by which justice in human history is established by a reality tran-
ndent of it. This graphic way is mythological in the sense that terms
ich are appropriate for speaking about temporal and spatial realities
used to interpret realities which are neither temporal nor spatial. An
rnal justice is not suitably interpreted by a graphic figure such as the
yes" of a god.

A nonmythological way of affirming a religious confidence in justice in
man history, for example, is affirmed by Isaiah, who declares for God:
ll is on record before me." (65:6) This is a nondescriptive metaphysical
ertion, free from anthropomorphic imagery, and yet it declares an as-
ance basic to the religious faith that transcendent of human history is
just appraisal of what has taken place for which human beings are
ponsible. When this religious assurance is pressed into the descriptive
agery of mythology, it loses its august character and, in turn, becomes

subject to a doubting and an eventual disbelief, because the inadequa‍
of such description negates the credibility of the spiritual profundity
the conviction itself.

A belief affirmed in early Greek literature is that there is a justi‍
which is not contingent upon human beings. Yet, this profound met‍
physical interpretation of history became impaired to the degree that t‍
anthropomorphic imagery of mythology was resorted to for its grap‍
character. Such an imagery occurs in the first book of the *Iliad* in whi‍
reference is made to the "all-seeing Zeus".[115] Hesiod likewise affirms ‍
metaphysic that justice in history is independent of a human agency wh‍
he declares that "with him who does wrong to a suppliant or a guest . .‍
truly Zeus himself is angry, and at the last lays on him a heavy requitt‍
for his evil doing".[116] The anthropopathic reference to the "anger"‍
Zeus actually detracts from the august affirmation that one who does su‍
injustice to others will suffer "a heavy requittal for his evil doing".

Hesiod also employs a nonanthropomorphic imagery to affirm his co‍
viction that there are spiritual means by which an ultimate accountii‍
is taken of human conduct when he declares that "upon the bounteo‍
earth, Zeus has thrice ten thousand spirits, watchers of mortal men, a‍
these keep watch on judgements and deeds of wrong as they roa‍
clothed in mist, all over the earth".[117]

On the other hand, an anthropomorphic imagery which is identical wi‍
the *Iliad's* is employed by Aeschylus in the opening chorus of *The Su‍
pliant Maidens* which refers to "the all-seeing Father".[118] Aeschylus us‍
still another anthropomorphic image in pointing out how Oceanus cou‍
seled Prometheus to be cautious of the way he protests against Zeu‍
since "Zeus may hear".[119]

Sophocles indicates how the jurisdiction of a god over human histor‍
can be acknowledged without also using mythological or anthropomorph‍
language. The Chorus in *Oedipus the King* declares:
"All wise are Zeus and Apollo, and nothing is hid from their ken; the‍
are gods."[120] Thus Sophocles points out that a religious conviction ‍
human history as under the sovereignty of an eternal reality need n‍
be expressed in a way which impairs its spiritual character by attemptin‍
to affirm a graphic description of how this is possible.

Euripides employs an anthropomorphic imagery in referring to a fin‍
accountability for wrongdoing when the father of Hippolytus reminds h‍
son of a "reckoning . . . of Zeus, whose aweful eye is over all".[121] Bu‍
unjustly accused by his father, Hippolytus appeals to the justice of Zeu‍

126

and does so also using anthropomorphic imagery when he asks: "Great Zeus, dost thou see this?"[122]

The rationalistic Euripides, however, indicates very clearly his disbelief in the adequacy of an anthropomorphic or mythological means for affirming a belief in a final justice when Amphitryon, the father of Heracles, addresses a skeptical questioning to Zeus: "O Zeus, dost thou behold these deeds?"[123] Talthybius, the herald of Agamemnon, likewise addresses himself to Zeus in what also indicates a skeptical disbelief that there is actually a god's sight which takes account of what occurs in history. He asks: "Great Zeus! what can I say? that thine eye is over man?" The skepticism about the soundness of this mythological version which is expressed by the Herald most likely is Euripides' own disbelief. The Herald asks if the belief that "thine eye is over man" is a "false opinion all to no purpose," such also as "thinking there is any race of gods, when it is chance that rules the mortal sphere?"[124]

Even though a reflective religious person were to believe that there is a final justice notwithstanding massive evidence to the contrary, his struggle to maintain his faith would be greatly handicapped by a mythological means commonly employed in affirming such a belief. The belief itself is maintained only with effort against the wavering of a faith that it is true. But the faith itself in a divine reality for establishing a final justice is done a great disservice by the mythological imagery of attributing to such a reality features which are incompatible with its nature. A spiritual faith can be maintained only by spiritual means, and such means include spiritual language. It is impaired by a language or an imagery which is incapable of conveying a spiritual meaning. This is merely affirming the incontrovertible principle of religious life which is affirmed in the Fourth Gospel: "They that worship god must worship him in spirit."

It may well be pointed out that the type of justice to which references have been made in the foregoing does not depend upon a "day of judgment" which the Prophet Ezra describes that "will be the end of the present world and the beginning of the eternal world to come". (7:113) The apocryphal writing of *Second Esdras* is historically important, however, for indicating the interpretation of the way that justice was believed to be established in religious reflecting of the centuries immediately before the Christian era and also during it. This included the imagery of a physical resurrection and the imagery of "the Most High (who) shall be seen on the judgment-seat". Such a resurrection is graphically described by the Prophet Ezra: "The earth shall give up those who sleep in it, and the dust those who rest there is silence; and the storehouses shall give back the souls entrusted to them." (7:31, 32) Although written before the Christian era, it anticipates a principal Christian notion of the conditions entailed in the establishment of justice at the end of human history. But such a notion of the method for establishing justice should not be read back into the earlier literature of either the Greeks or the Israelites.

IV

The Problem of Evil in a Religious Metaphysic

1. *Evil confronts a religious interpretation with its most bewildering problem*

The so-called "problem of evil" in a religious interpretation is not a single problem. It, therefore, is a misnomer to refer to it as such. Evil constitutes a battery of bewildering problems for a religious interpretation of human life in relation to a reality it trusts for establishing justice. Even the term "justice" so used includes more than one clearly defined requirement in a religious interpretation of a reality trusted for correlating moral merit with events in human history.

Isaiah was troubled by the indifference of human beings to the misfortunes of others; and this bewildering aspect of human life for him is entailed in his religious interpretation of the Creator. If he had not trusted such a creator which he believed would bring about what is fair or just in His creation, he would not have been disturbed by the fact that "The righteous perish, and no one takes it to heart; men of good faith are swept away, but no one cares."

It is not only the indifference of human beings to others' suffering which troubled Isaiah. He was also troubled by the nature of the reality internal to which human beings live which manifests the same indifference as human beings to the plight of those who suffer. Hence he complains, as it were, to the creator of such a reality: "The righteous are swept away before the onset of evil." (57:1)

129

Thus it is not only the occurrence of handicaps to human well-being which makes him question the affirmation that there is a providence in the world. It is the indifference both of human beings and reality itself to the suffering of people that constitutes a reason for his questioning a religious trust in the unfailing fairness or justice with which human history occurs in the wider context of a god's creation.

Jeremiah struggled with the same perplexity in attempting to reconcile his faith in God's goodness with the widespread occurrence of wrongdoing by people to handicap others when he believed that all men are under the sovereignty of God's justice. He actually indicts God for a defective creation in which people whom He created "are skilled in doing evil" to such an extent that they "know not how to do good". (4:22)

Jeremiah does not merely refer to a general evil or to evil in a sweeping generalization. He points rather to specific evils which constitute occasions for questioning a providence both in creation and also in guiding the created world. He points out that "Brother supplants brother and friend slanders friend". By mentioning relationships so close as members within a family and so intimate as friendships, he emphasizes the tragic nature of a creation in which infidelity comes about as if there were no limits to the extent of evil of which human beings are capable. An instance of this is that "They make game of their friends but never speak the truth". (9:4, 5) On the basis of such capacities of human beings to do what is morally offensive, the Prophet directs the question to God, whom he seems to hold accountable for such evil, since as the creator of men, He has created them with capacities for doing such evil. The Prophet's question is: "Why do the wicked prosper and traitors live at ease?" (12:1) The reason for his question is obvious. He believes they are not morally entitled to such prosperity and comfort in their lives, when others who are obedient to God's commandments, and are loyal to his expectations of them suffer every imaginable form of misery.

The unfairness of what takes place under such circumstances is the basis for the Prophet's complaint directed to God: "Thou plantest them, and they take root; they grow and bring forth fruit; thou art near in their mouth and far from their heart." (vs. 2)* In pointing out the hypocrisy of those who enjoy prosperity and apparent well-being, he expresses his doubt either that their hypocrisy is known by God or that if God is aware of it, he doubts if God treats it as a moral offense.

As Jeremiah takes account of the hypocrisy of people and of their indifference to the rights of others, he also takes account of their disrespect for the rights of God, such as the faithful respect and revere in their worship. He points out that "the sons of Judah have done evil in (God's) sight". "They have set their abominations in the house which is called by (God's) name, to defile it." (7:30)* And yet, their irreverence and outright blasphemy seem unrelated to a penalty which is just. In spite of whatever disapproval God may have for these offenses to Him, such people, nevertheless, seem to prosper as if their infidelity to God in no way makes a difference in their prospering, at least according to men's standards of prosperity. Hence the Prophet's question: "Why do the wicked prosper?"

The same type of questioning as occurs in the reflecting of the major prophets continues in a minor prophet such as Habakuk, whose writing in the Old Testament records a dialogue which he carried on with the god of the Israelites on the occasion of the oppression of the Israelites by the Chaldeans. The pointed question he directs to the god of the Israelites is "Why dost thou countenance the treachery of the wicked? Why keep silent when they devour men more righteous than they?" (1:13) What troubled him about such apparent indifference to the suffering of the Israelites is that the most faithful among them suffer no less than the least faithful. What greatly disturbed him, therefore, is the moral unfairness that there is no difference in suffering between those who are devoted to their god and those who are not. Even the "treachery of the wicked" is not correlated with a suffering that differs in any respect from the suffering of those who are faithful to their god.

A bewildered reflecting on the nature of evil in a world which religious faith interprets as under Providence continued throughout the centuries in Israelite literature. The second century B.C. *Second Esdras*, which is not in the Palestinian canon and so is not part of the Hebrew scriptures, continues the same questioning about the fact of evil as troubled the prophets whose writings are included in the Old Testament. The Greek speaking Jews in Egypt, therefore, are represented in the reflecting in this apocryphal book. The specific occasion for their questioning the justice of occurrences in human history is that the Israelites suffered from the cruelty of their enemies in total disregard of their trust in a providence working through their history. The specific question which the Prophet Ezra directs to the god of the Israelites is: "Why has Israel been made a byword among the Gentiles?" (4:23) The pointed question which expresses his sense of injustice in the history of the Israelites, presumably under the providence of a god in whom they trust, is: "Why then, Lord, have you put this one people at the mercy of so many?" (5:28) His question arising from his sense of injustice due to the evil from which

131

his people suffer is based upon his religious philosophy of history that the Israelites are entitled to be favored by a god in whose providence they trust. If it were not for this religious interpretation, the bewildering question would not have arisen. Ezra would instead have accepted the fact that the Israelites by virtue of their inferior military equipment and limited wealth were defeated by enemies numerically greater and possessing resources far in excess of those possessed by the Israelites. His perplexity as expressed in his question arose primarily from his belief that the Israelites are related to a particular god to whom other people are not also related. It is, therefore, this specific religious belief which accounts for his perplexity about an apparent indifference of a deity to the destruction of his nation by other nations. He declares: "I have travelled up and down among the nations, and have seen how they prosper, heedless though they are of your commandments." (3:33, 34) Thus it is the disproportion of prosperity enjoyed by other nations in contrast to the collective suffering of the Israelites which bewildered him.

He thus was not troubled about a general problem of the evil of suffering to which human beings are so universally subject. He was troubled rather about the suffering and misfortunes of his own people. It is specifically "the weariness of the race of Israel" which dominates his reflecting on evil. (5:35) The specific cause for his bewildering perplexity, which he characterizes as a "torture" from which he suffered "every hour as (he tried) to understand the ways of the Most High and to fathom some part of his judgements", is his assumption that he belongs to a people who have rights to the providence of their tutelary deity whom he believes should have a concern for them as he does not also have for other people.

The *First Book of Esdras* affirms a very different attitude toward the reverses suffered by the Israelites. This book does not question the justice of a divine judgment upon them. Its author, the Prophet Ezra, accepts as an unquestioned premise in his theology that the "Lord" transcendent of human history is just, and the reverses from which people suffer, such as the Israelites, do not impugn faith in His justice. The author of this book maintains that it is the unworthiness of a people which is the basis for their reverses and the ultimate cause for their suffering. In addressing himself to the divine reality upon whom he believes human history is finally dependent, he acknowledges, "O Lord . . . our sins tower above our heads . . . our offences have reached the sky, and today we are as deep in sin as ever. Because of our sins and the sins of our fathers, we and our brothers, our kings and our priests, were given over to the kings

132

of the earth to be killed, taken prisoner, plundered, and humiliated down to this very day." (8:75-78)

There, however, are radically different points of view expressed in *First Esdras* and in *Second Esdras*. *Second Esdras* questions the fairness or justice of the god whose providence is trusted. Its author declares: My heart sank, because I saw how you tolerate sinners and spare the godless; how you have destroyed your own people, but protected your enemies." (3:30, 31) *First Esdras,* on the other hand, acknowledges that the cause for the misery of the Israelites is their infidelity to their god. Whereas *Second Esdras* expresses the bewildering perplexity why such suffering should occur among the Israelites, *First Esdras* does not struggle with this particular problem. It acknowledges that the cause for the suffering of the Israelites is their own disloyalty to their god. Thus it is the failure of the people to relate themselves as they ought to the divine reality to whose providence they acknowledge themselves as subordinate. The problem, therefore, of evil is shifted from entailing a reality transcendent of human beings to human beings themselves; and in so doing, there is a human basis for coping with the evil of human suffering. The basis, in other words, is internal to human life. According to such an analysis, a religious faith is not confronted with a doubting of its validity, and the providence of a divine reality is not impugned by an evil the cause for which is acknowledged to be human.

First Esdras thus reaffirms a belief of long standing in the tradition of Hebrew prophecy, such as Isaiah's defense of the justice of God, and his accusation of the Israelites for their infidelity to Him which has brought about a divine alienation from them. He declares: "It is your iniquities that raise a barrier between you and your God, because of your sins he has hidden his face so that he does not hear you." (59:2)

Isaiah's analysis of the reverses suffered by the Israelites consists entirely of moral considerations. He maintains that the Israelites in relation to the god whom their forefathers worshipped "are a people without sense", and it is for this moral deficiency that "their maker will show no mercy". He affirms this moral analysis for the suffering of his people when he assures them that until they alter their ways of infidelity, "he who formed them will show them no favour". (27:11) Isaiah's theology thus is evident. There are moral conditions for a people's receiving the blessings of a divine providence. And unless such moral conditions are fulfilled, there is no justification for a people to complain about the injustice of such a providence. They themselves are responsible for handicaps to their well-being.

133

Isaiah's analysis of the tragic plight of his people affirms a position which is also stated in *Second Kings*. This explains the defeat of the Israelites by "Shalmaneser King of Assyria" as their infidelity to the god to whom they conventionally maintained allegiance, but did not do so as the utmost dedication in their lives: "All this happened to the Israelites because they had sinned against the Lord their God . . . and uttered blasphemies against the Lord their God." (17:7-9)

Thus one point of view about the cause for human suffering accounts for a problem of evil which bewilders those who reflect, such as is not brought about by another point of view. One interpretation of human suffering gives rise to an insoluble questioning, whereas another interpretation proposes a way by which such suffering can be diminished, if not eliminated. It can be coped with on the grounds of a moral analysis for human negligence in not doing what human beings ought to do. Such moral negligence may be regarded as a cause for human suffering even when a religious faith affirms the ultimate sovereignty of a divine reality over human history. According to such a religious interpretation, the wavering faith of human beings in a divine providence would itself not be subjected to doubt and disbelief if they themselves were to do all that they morally ought to do to prevent the occurrence of suffering in human life. Thus the general problem of evil as a philosophical topic changes to a very specific analysis of moral obligation. If human beings were to do what they might do to lessen the heavy load of misery from which so many suffer, religious faith itself would not be called into question for its soundness. In other words, such faith would not come within the scope of a doubting misdirected from a human cause to a cause transcendent of human life.

Thus reflecting would have one bewildering problem removed from its discouragement for its inability to find an answer to a question which ought not to have been asked in the first place. This way to be spared from asking questions which admit of no answer within the scope of the question itself is acknowledged also by the author of *Second Esdras*. He acknowledges that questioning a reality other than men themselves why men do as they do is directing a question to the inappropriate reality for an answer which cannot be given by it. He declares that an answer to such human questioning is as impossible as counting "those who are not yet born" or collecting "the scattered drops of rain", and making "the withered flowers bloom again." (5:36) He argues that if questions which come within the scope of reflecting on moral responsibility are asked within the scope of a theology, one can no more reasonably expect an

134

answer to them than if he were to ask that "the shape of a voice be made visible". Asking for this, he maintains, would be no less unreasonable than asking for answers to questions which by virtue of their very nature admit of no answer.

2. The "problem" of evil is partially clarified by removing it from a theological explanation

No one explanatory principle is adequate for analyzing any complex problem, and evil is one such problem. Some clarification of it, however, is possible by considering a cause for evil which is internal to nature itself rather than looking for such a cause transcendent of nature. This is the procedure which was introduced into Greek reflecting by the Milesian philosophers, such as when Thales sought for an explanation of natural phenomena internal to nature itself. He maintained that one element internal to the natural world could account for all aspects of the natural world. Thus his procedure of using one explanatory principle internal to the natural order itself to account for natural phenomena was a rejection of the mythological explanations which the Greeks for centuries had accepted.

Anaximenes of Miletus, also in the sixth century B.C., proposed a naturalistic rather than a mythological explanation. Instead, however, of the more determinate water, he proposed vapor or air as the basic explanation for all natural phenomena. His anti-mythological and anti-popular religious type of explanation for phenomena such as thunder, lightning, rain, and living beings themselves, was current among Greeks of the following century or more, as is indicated by Aristophanes' *Clouds*, in which the naturalistic explanations of Anaximenes were facetiously attributed to Socrates.

What is significant in the Milesian shift of explanation from mythological concepts of gods and goddesses of Olympus to natural realities, such as water and air, is the extension of this naturalistic point of view to explaining the nature of evil from which men suffer. This type of explanation, however, was already internal to mythological imagery, such as in the quarrel between two brothers, Danaüs and Aegyptus. The fifty daughters of Danaüs were demanded as brides by the fifty sons of Aegyptus, but their demands were refused, and Danaüs and his daughters fled to Argos for sanctuary with Pelasgus, the king. Since they were pursued and were unable to withstand such demands, Danaüs commanded his daughters to marry their cousins but to kill them during the first night of their marriage. The moral outrage of such murder committed by all the daughters, except one, was the basis for their punishment in the realm of Hades. According to this analysis, the tragic futility of the Danaides eternally lifting water in sieves is an instance of suffering accounted for by the human evil of murdering human beings. It is not accounted for by any act of a god. Thus mythology itself in the early centuries of Greece included an explanation for suffering which was brought about entirely by the wrongdoing of human beings. Notwithstanding the offense of the sons of Aegyptus for forcing a marriage upon unwilling cousins, the murder which the daughters of Danaüs committed constitutes an evil for which they and their father were alone responsible. No god or goddess prompted them to this moral offense from which the daughters eternally suffered.

The cruelty of human beings killing members of their own community or their own family by stoning is referred to in the *Iliad*. When Paris refused to fight a duel with Menelaus, his brother Hector accused the Trojans of being "too soft", since otherwise they "would have . . . stoned (him) to death".[1] Another moral outrage by human beings against other human beings is also referred to in the *Iliad* when Nestor, esteemed for his wisdom as a counselor, ordered the Argive soldiers: First "kill men. Afterwards, at your leisure, you can strip the corpses on the field."[2] This command was not given by a god, but rather by a king of Pylos. In this instance, therefore, the evils not only of killing in combat but also the brutality of stripping the dead are an expression of the meanness with which human beings contribute to the misery from which human beings suffer. Another example in the *Iliad* of human brutality accounting for human suffering is Agamemnon's declaring to his brother Menelaus that "we are not going to leave a single one of them alive, down to the babies in their mothers' wombs—not even they must live."[3] Another translation of this vindictive brutality of the Myceanaean ruler is "Let all of Ilion's people perish, utterly blotted out and unmourned for."[4] The same brutality with which Agamemnon treated the Trojans was directed against him by his wife, Clytemnestra, when he returned from Troy. She cut off his "hands and feet and suspend(ed) them to the armpits. This was done to prevent the victim from taking vengeance."[5] The evil of her cruelty thus was no more accounted for by an act of a god than the evil of Agamemnon himself in ordering the annihilation of a people who had no responsibility for an act for which only one of them was guilty.

The brutality of which Trojans and Greeks alike were capable as described by Homer differed in no respect from the brutality of which

136

thenians, centuries later, brought misery to others, whether to the people f Melos or Megara or even to citizens within the Athenian polis itself. Ierodotus gives such an account of cruelty of which the Athenians were apable even to their own fellow citizens. He says that "Lycidas, one of he councillors, gave it for his opinion that it seemed to him best to receive he offer brought to them by Murchides and lay it before the people". 'his proposal was sent by Mardonious through Murchides to the Athnians on the island of Salamis to which they had escaped when Mardonius returned to Athens to destroy it. Herodotus then continues: "But he Athenians in the council were very wroth; . . . and they made a ring ound Lycidas and stoned him to death." As if this moral outrage against ne of their own people was not evil enough, Herodotus narrates how the Athenian women learnt what was afoot, and . . . stoned to death his vife and his children".[6]

The evil of which human beings are capable is not confined to some nations or to some people. It is a universal blight upon human history. Iuman cruelty is an evil for which human beings are responsible, and he suffering and misery which accrue to their cruelty is from what they lo, and not from what some god prompts them to do.

Basic to Greek tragedies is the same type of human cruelty as is common in most ancient Greek mythology and in later dramas. In *Oedipus at Colonus*, Oedipus declares to Theseus, ruler of Athens, "dishonour flourishes, there is no constancy 'twixt friend and friend, or city and city".[7] The perversity of which a human being is capable is further indicated by Sophocles in *Philoctetes* when Neoptolemus betrays his promise to his 'riend, who already has suffered acutely from the heartlessness with which his comrades had treated him. Hence he turns upon his friend, declaring: 'Perdition on you all."[8] What is significant in some of his acutest suffering, in addition to his wound which didn't heal, is its cause in human faithlessness. So caused, the evil of this aspect of his suffering does not prompt reflecting to take account of a source for it from any reality other than human beings.

Euripides indicates something of the perversity of which human beings are capable when he points out what was entailed when, as a means to avenge Menelaus, Orestes spread rumors at Delphi that he was engaged in stealing gold from the "treasure-chamber" of Apollo. "The rumour . . . proved to have great weight", since the people "stabbed Achilles' unprotected son from behind" and "set to hurling stones . . . a storm of darts, arrows, and javelins, hurtling spits with double points, and butchers' knives . . . came flying at his feet". Euripides adds a sobering commentary on the depravity which prompted such brutality when he nar rates that "as he fell, there was not one that did not stab him, or cast a rock and batter his corpse. So his whole body, once so fair, was marred with savage wounds."[9] This incident of which the dramatist gives this sobering description is not merely a detail in a drama. It is a generaliza tion in a philosophy of human history. Included in such a philosophy therefore, is an explanation of the human responsibility for the massive evils from which human beings suffer.

The same philosophy of human history is affirmed by Aristophanes in *Lysistrata*, when Lysistrata addresses the Athenian with an accusation which is applicable to all of the Hellenes: "At Olympia, and Thermopylae, and Delphi, and a score of other places too numerous to mention, you celebrate before the same altars ceremonies common to all Hellenes; yet you go cutting each other's throats, and sacking Hellenic cities."[10] This philosophy of human history is well summed up in the generalization: "Man's inhumanity to man makes countless thousands mourn." It is this inhumanity which accounts for an evil whose curse cannot be attributed to any reality other than human cruelty.

Just as Greek poets, dramatists, and philosophers point out a human cause for evils from which human beings suffer, so likewise is there a long tradition in Israelite reflecting which points out the same human source for evil which oppresses human history.

The first book of the Old Testament records the beginning of the tragic nature of human history when one brother murdered the other. The narrative in *Genesis* is thus a graphic prediction of subsequent centuries of human life. "Cain said to his brother Abel, 'Let us go into the open country.' While they were there, Cain attacked his brother Abel and murdered him." (4:8, 9) The tragic character of this account is that the provocation for the murder of one brother by the other was sheer malice or unrelieved meanness. There is no mention of an impulsive element which brought about an accidental killing. It was deliberate. Thus the first account in the Bible of the evil of hate places the responsibility entirely upon a human being.

The second book in the Old Testament records the heartless uncharity of a father toward his own children: "When a man sells his daughter into slavery, she shall not go free as a male slave may." (21:7)

Numbers describes a type of hatred and cruelty of communities toward their leaders, such as the behavior of the Israelites toward Moses and Aaron: "Moses and Aaron flung themselves on the ground before the

138

ssembled community of the Israelites (which) . . . threatened to stone hem." (14:5, 10)

Just as communities are capable of destroying their leaders, so leaders r rulers of a people show the same indifference to the life and rights of he people. *First Kings* gives the graphic account of the relation of Rehoboam, son of Solomon, to the Israelites who had gone to Shechem 'to make him king". "The assembly of Israel came to Rehoboam and aid, 'Your father laid a cruel yoke upon us; but if you will now lighten he cruel slavery he imposed on us and the heavy yoke he laid on us, we vill serve you.' " (12:34) After this pledge by the people, he answered: 'My father laid a heavy yoke on you; I will make it heavier." (vs. 11) The tragic character of this confrontation of a ruler with a people il-ustrates the unrelenting evil of oppressive rule over others once it has ecome established. It illustrates likewise the unwillingness of some in ower over others to relinquish their oppressive leverage even when the ecurity of their own rule is not imperiled. It is done out of sheer cruelty, f which human history is an unbroken record.

The history of the Israelites in relation to the countries which overran heir territory is saturated with repetitions of cruelty by the powerful for he oppressed. *Second Kings* records the plight of the Israelites when the Assyrian Shalmaneser "captured Samaria and deported its people to As-yria". (17:6) Deportations with their suffering were repeated throughout he centuries. Such a history of suffering is recorded in *Second Maccabees*. The Egyptian king Antiochus "took Jerusalem by storm, and ordered his roops to cut down without mercy everyone they met and to slaughter hose who took refuge in the houses. Young and old were murdered, women and children massacred, girls and infants butchered. At the end f three days their losses had amounted to eighty thousand: forty thou-sand killed in action, and as many sold into slavery." (5:11-14) The same Antiochus "sent Apollonius . . . with an army of twenty-two thou-sand men, and ordered him to kill all the adult males and to sell the women and boys into slavery". (5:24) This, of course, is but a sample of history throughout whose centuries the cruelty of human beings for others have constituted evils more massive than any which mythologies or theologies have ever attributed to realities other than human.

Such cruelty of oppression was not only upon the Israelites by neigh-boring countries. It was also imposed upon Israelities by Israelites. Amos enumerates some of the wrongdoing by Israelites toward other Israelites when he refers to "crime after crime of Israel" such as "sell(ing) the innocent for silver and the destitute for a pair of shoes". Israelites themselves misused their advantage of power and wealth to bring suffering and misery to other Israelites: "They grind the heads of the poor into the earth and thrust the humble out of their way." (2:6, 7)

The Prophet Micah states this analysis with graphic vigor. He declares that among his own people, the Israelites, are those who "covet land and take it by force; if they want a house they seize it; they rob a man of his home and steal (his) . . . inheritance". (2:2) He directs the moral accusation against their willingness to commit every possible form of exploitation of others when he declares that people who "defile" themselves with wrongdoing toward others "would commit any mischief however cruel". (2:10) And then he specifies the cruelties of which such unscrupulous people are capable in bringing misery upon others: "You flay men alive and tear the very flesh from their bones; you . . . strip off their skin, splinter their bones; you shred them like flesh into a pot, like meat into a cauldron." (3:2, 3) He generalizes the extent of such evil, affirming it as a universal trait of a people: "All lie in wait to do murder, each man drives his own kinsman like a hunter into the net. They are bent eagerly on wrongdoing." (7:2, 3)

The author of *Ecclesiasticus* declares the same condemnation upon the unlimited capacity within human nature for imposing misery upon others. He maintains that if an individual without scruples and without charity for another were given "a chance . . . he will not stop at bloodshed." And what intensifies this human source of evil in human life is the duplicity and the hypocrisy of some who are so capable of cruelty: "He may have tears in his eyes" as if moved by pity, and yet, the realistic account by this author continues: "If disaster overtakes you, you will find him there ahead of you ready with a pretense of help, to pull your feet from under you." (12:16, 17)

A reason for listing this considerable number of biblical accusations against human beings for the evils for which they are responsible is pointing out that the Bible does not limit its analysis of the cause of evil to the mythological account given in *Genesis* of the subtle serpent and "the woman (who) said, 'The serpent beguiled me' ". (3:13) This myth, in spite of its naive charm, has no bearing whatsoever on the analysis of evil in human history. What does, however, have direct bearing on a critical analysis of evil in human history are accounts in the Bible of acts of human cruelty to human beings. Such acts of cruelty account for the most oppressive evil in human history.

What is significant in the accounts cited from the Bible is the realistic character of pin-pointing causes for human suffering and misery in the

140

acts of human beings. There is nothing mythological about this biblical analysis. It is a realistically informed inventory of human causes for evils from which human beings suffer. If such a human cause for human evils were removed from human history, the description of the Garden of Eden might well be a parallel of the religious vision of a Kingdom of God free from evils for which human beings themselves are responsible.

Isaiah speaks of the human responsibility for turning "light into darkness", and thereby destroying a way of life for human beings which is worthy of the plan of a god. (5:20) For such human responsibilities for the centuries of misery from which mankind has suffered, Jeremiah pronounces a moral judgment upon each individual guilty of doing this moral injustice to others: He "shall die for his own wrongdoing." (31:30) In cutting himself off from a history in which he might have devoted his life to human benefit, he condemns himself to a moral death. In his acting without justice and without charity, but only with cruelty and disregard for the rights of others, he condemns himself to a spiritual death. His insensitivity to human rights is the condemnation of "darkness" which he brings upon himself. This moral judgment is inescapable; and graphic means for stressing its inescapability are many. Among these are the graphic description of a final judgment when all mankind is brought to life again to have the record of their lives condemn them. What is spiritually profound in this graphic version is that each human being is judged by the record of his own life. As the author of *Second Esdras* declares: "All men will see everything that lies before them" which constitutes the record of their life. (7:42) The sternness of this moral judgment is the invariant relation between what an individual does and the record of his life in human history.

3. *There are fundamental differences in interpretations of the relation of human beings to a divine reality*

Hesiod cites effects brought about by Zeus upon human life which differ in their moral significance. If fame or its absence constitutes an influence in human life which is of moral importance in how it affects a human being's welfare, then Zeus, according to Hesiod, does have a morally significant role in human life. Hesiod declares: "Through him men are famed or unfamed, sung or unsung, as great Zeus wills."[11]

There is no question, on the other hand, about a preeminently moral role of Zeus in human life insofar as "true judgment . . . is of Zeus and is perfect".[12]

141

Zeus' role in human life, however, is not consistently of this moral benefit to human beings since he is capable of inconsistency in acting, such as human beings are, and therefore his relation to human beings is as unpredictable as is the relation of one human being to another. Hesiod declares that "the will of Zeus . . . is different at different times, and it is hard for mortal men to tell it".[13] Zeus often does not even relate himself to human beings according to a criterion of moral justice or fairness, since he is capable of punishing men for the acts of another god for which men obviously are not responsible. Hesiod points out that Zeus was angered when Prometheus "outwitted" him and stole fire for the benefit of human beings. Instead of punishing only Prometheus for "deceiving" him, he also punished human beings. Hesiod declares: "Because Prometheus, the crafty, deceived him . . . he planned sorrow and mischief against men."[14]

Hesiod does not portray Zeus as a moral ideal or criterion for human beings, but, on the contrary, he interprets him as capable of acting which would be censured as reprehensible by human beings. Prometheus warned his brother, Epimetheus, never to accept a gift from Zeus "for fear it might prove to be something harmful to men". But, as Hesiod points out, Epimetheus "took the gift, and afterwards, when the evil thing was already his, he understood".[15]

Zeus, according to Hesiod, is capable of being the ultimate source for every type of evil from which human beings suffer, such as "countless plagues". The Poet declares that "diseases come upon men continually by day and night, bringing mischief to mortals". The human plight, therefore, is men's relation to such a deity whose will is not only capricious, but also malicious: "There is no way to escape."[16]

Gods other than Zeus are likewise malevolent toward human beings as the Poet maintains when they "Keep hidden from men the means of life". If it were not for their ill-will toward human beings, men "could easily do work enough in a day to supply (themselves) for a full year without working".[17] Thus, according to this view, work is not a blessing, but a negation of well-being, such as it is also interpreted in *Genesis*: "With labour you shall win your food . . . all the days of your life." (3:17) "You shall gain your bread by the sweat of your brow." (vs. 19)

According to Homer, some effects of supranatural realities upon human beings are without moral significance. That is, they make no difference in an individual's character or in his well-being. He attributes the "comeliness and grace" of Odysseus to Athene who "made him taller and sturdier than ever". Although these effects of the goddess' acting upon Odysseus were advantageous in his relation to people, they were, accord-

142

ng to a common saying, "only skin deep". Although Athene "caused the bushy locks to hang from his head thick as the petals of the hyacinth in bloom", such "endowing his head and shoulders with an added beauty" did nothing to make a basic difference in his nature, such as would have changed his conduct in relation to other people.[18]

Homer mentions a number of times this nonmorally significant type of relation between Odysseus and Athene. One of these, however, suggests some moral benefit from the alteration of his appearance. A purpose for making him seem taller and broader" was that "he might inspire the whole Phaeacian people . . . with affection . . . and respect".[19] If, therefore, this change in their attitude toward him was brought about by his appearance, it might be argued that his appearance was of moral importance. But any further advantage, such as enabling him to "accomplish many trials of strength" by which the Phaeacians (Phaiakians) tested him is without any corresponding moral significance.[20]

The same type of change in a human being's strength brought about by a deity is attributed to Samson, the Israelite. But the significance of what Samson did with his strength made possible by a supranatural agency was very different. It was included in the plan of the god of the Israelites to punish the Philistines for their worship of Dagon. (*Judges* 6:23)

Athene likewise "endowed" Telemachus, the son of Odysseus, "with such grace that all eyes were turned on him in admiration".[21] A parallel account is given in the book of *Esther* in the Old Testament of a god endowing a human being with extraordinary beauty: "Esther found favor in the eyes of all who saw her." (2:15)* But the beauty with which she surpassed other women was significant in a plan by which the god of the Israelites would rescue his own people from the cruelty of Haman, an officer of King Ahasuerus. Thus Esther's beauty, which was given her by a god was intended as an indirect means for establishing justice.

Although Telemachus helped his father avenge the wrongs upon their property by the unscrupulous suitors of Penelope, his god-given appearance was not instrumental in ridding the palace of the suitors. If, on the other hand, Athene, had increased his strength to dispose of the suitors, as she had increased the strength of Odysseus for this purpose, her intervention would illustrate Homer's belief that supranatural agencies are instrumental in human history for establishing justice.

There likewise are differences in interpretations of the intervention of a supranatural reality guiding human beings. Odysseus acknowledged his debt to Athene for guiding him to the "rich land of the Phaeacians".[22]

And such guidance was included in her plan to return him safely to his home in order that he might bring about an end to the unjust exploitation of his property. But this type of guidance differs from the guidance of which Isaiah speaks when he maintains that God "will lead blind men on their way and guide them by paths they do not know". (42:16) This is for the enlightenment of their life by a wisdom which it would not be possible for them to acquire by their own unaided capacities. The moral benefit of such intervention in human life by the god of whom Isaiah speaks thus differs from the intervention of Athene in the lives of Odysseus and his son.

Isaiah's philosophy of history in relation to God is that God's guidance of human beings is for the enlightenment of human life. When so enlightened, men themselves are enabled to act justly. Their enlightened life is a difference in character brought about by God's acting upon them, both for their own benefit and also for the benefit of others made possible through their enhanced character-capacities for doing what is just.

Accepting divine guidance is a mark of religious fidelity to a deity. But such guidance can be rejected by men's decisions which express their own character. Hosea points out that "the more (God) called" his people, the Israelites, "the further they went" from Him in their determination to "sacrifice to the Baalim and to burn offerings before carved images" (11:2) As Hosea interprets the relation of the god of the Israelites to a faithless people, he points out how, by their own turning from their god to other gods, they rejected the superior guidance which they might otherwise have received.

Hosea thus interprets a guidance by a divine reality as compatible with moral responsibility. Human beings either could accept or they could reject such guidance. Such guidance, in other words, does not cancel their own initiative to accept a guidance available to them.

A very different interpretation, on the other hand, is placed upon the role of a supranatural being in human life when Athene declares to Odysseus that "it was I who made all the Phaeacians take to you so kindly".[23] This coercing them to be kind toward Odysseus is incompatible with the nature of moral goodwill. If the Phaeacians were to have been kind to Odysseus as an expression of their goodwill, their conduct would have been an expression of their character. But when their acting was determined for them by the intervention of the goddess, her intervention cancelled their capacity to act from a goodwill as a trait of character. When she declares "It was I who made you loved by all the Phaeacians", Homer removes all moral initiative from their acting.[24] So interpreted, their acting

144

is not "goodwill" as an expression of character. But it is favorable for Odysseus, and to this extent contributes to enabling him to return to his home to put an end to the injustices to his wife and to his property. This, therefore, would be a rather roundabout way to argue that Homer's interpretation of the agency of a god or goddess is for a moral benefit for those to whom such a divine reality is related.

An explicit negation of character by the intervention of a divine reality in human life is affirmed in the *Iliad*. Hector declares to Glaucus: "We are all puppets in the hands of . . . Zeus. In a moment, Zeus can make brave men run away and lose a battle; and the next day the same god will spur him on to fight."[25] In interpreting this role of a supranatural reality in human life, Homer negates the moral factor in human history. History becomes a puppet show of a god and is not determined by human decisions, either praiseworthy or censurable. This extreme version of a religious interpretation which negates all moral initiative as a determinant in human history is expressed in the translation that "always the mind of Zeus is a stronger thing than a man's mind".[26] Attributing to a god the final determination of what a human being does is incompatible with a philosophy of history which can even be regarded as "human" history. This total negation of the moral determinant in the behavior of human beings is expressed in Agamemnon's defense of himself for having taken what belonged to another. He argues: "I was not to blame. It was Zeus and Fate and the Fury who walks in the dark that blinded my judgment, that day at the meeting, when on my authority I confiscated Achilles' prize."[27] In attributing this act to the intervention of a god, Homer negates moral responsibility for an act which had vast consequences in subsequent events. In this sense, the subsequent history was an account of the consequences of a god's acting and not of a human being's decision. So interpreted, the following events in the Trojan War were not determined by human deficiency, failure, or evil. Pressing such a religious interpretation of supranatural agencies to an extent that they cancel human responsibility is morally offensive. This becomes evident in Agamemnon's admission of his total helplessness when he asks: "Yet what could I do? It is the god who accomplishes all things."[28] This, therefore, is pressing an interpretation in terms of a supranatural agency to such an extreme that it is not only morally offensive, it is also an offensive version of religious interpretation. This negation of the human aspect of so-called "human history" is made explicit in a translation of Agamemnon's declaration: "I am not responsible but Zeus is, and Destiny, and Erinys."[29]

Homer affirms the same total negation of human responsibility for behavior which has far-reaching consequences when he maintains that "Pallas Athene had destroyed (the Trojans') judgment", and it was because of her intervention that "the Trojans in their folly shouted approval" when Hector had "finished his speech".[30] Thus the Trojans' approbation for Hector's "counsel of evil" was not a "folly" for which they were responsible.[31] They merely did what puppets would be made to do when operated upon by an agent determining their activity.

The same negation of the human role in determining history is again affirmed in the *Iliad* when the supremacy of Zeus to human beings is so overstressed that human beings have no moral role in history. In declaring that "The thoughts of Zeus outstrip the thoughts of men", a supranatural agency determines history, and in so doing, negates human responsibility for human history.[32] This is also affirmed when Aias' "exhorting" of his men was prevented from having any effect because "Phoebus Apollo had filled (them) with supernatural fears."[33]

If these several interpretations of causes for occurrences were to be affirmed in a prologue to the *Iliad*, the epic character of the *Iliad* would be impaired, if not cancelled. It would tend to be looked upon as a determination of men's behavior by factors entirely outside of their control. As such, there would be no moral basis for heroism. And there likewise would be no moral basis for censuring men who do not do what would be worthy of a man with a character of a hero. Since this negation of moral responsibility occurs in various instances of utmost importance in the *Iliad*, its epic nature to this extent is subordinate to its over-stressed religious emphasis upon supranatural agencies as the final determinants of what men do. To the extent that men's moral responsibility is negated, their acting is not integral to a specifically "human" history.

This defect in the *Iliad* by virtue of its unrestricted ascription of influence to supranatural factors in human behavior is highlighted by the contrast of Aeschylus' way of interpreting the role of Zeus in human life. The Chorus in *Agamemnon* declares: "Zeus . . . leadeth mortals the way of understanding."[34] In this profounder version of the relation of human beings to realities transcendent of them, the moral stature of human beings is retained even when they are subordinate to the sovereignty of such a reality. And furthermore, in this relation as it is interpreted by Aeschylus, the sovereignty of a divine reality over human life is for the moral benefit of its enlightenment.

But Aeschylus also affirms an ambivalent relation of human beings to a supranatural reality when the Chorus in *The Persians* laments the massive losses of Persians "through disasters on the sea", and then also acknowledges that "we suffer in no doubtful wise this change of fortune

rom the hand of God".[35] After acknowledging that "The land bewaileth
her native youth, slaughtered for Xerxes, who hath gorged the realm of
Death with Persian slain", the other cause acknowledged in this ambivalent explanation is "powers divine have wrought . . . ruin".[36]

Euripides proposes the same type of ambivalent explanation for human
suffering when the Chorus in *The Children of Hercules* declares: "Without
the will of heaven none is blest, none curst."[37] The relation of human
beings to a divine reality, referred to in this instance as "Heaven", is
twofold or ambivalent. It is the relation in which both good and evil come
about for men, and the cause for neither is within the scope of moral
responsibility. The same type of explanation which absolves a human
being from responsibility for an act of evil is affirmed in *Hippolytus* when
Theseus falsely accuses his son, and then declares: "Heaven . . . perverted
my power to think."[38] In attributing to "the Gods" the cause for his "wit
to stumble", Theseus transfers all responsibility for such a moral offense
from himself to realities which, as transcendent of human life, cannot be
held morally accountable for offenses which, if caused by men, would be
moral outrages.[39]

This type of transferring responsibility to gods for acts that are morally
offensive in human life is also affirmed by the prophet Isaiah. After maintaining that "the chieftains of her clans have led Egypt astray", the
Prophet declares: "The Lord has infused into them a spirit that warps
their judgment; they make Egypt miss her way in all she does." (19:13,
14) According to this analysis, the plight of the Egyptians would be in-
correctly attributed to their "chieftains" since it was brought about by
"the Lord". Although the religious purpose is understandable which
motivates Isaiah to attribute to the god of the Israelites this reverse
from which the Egyptians suffered, it, nevertheless, introduces a grave
moral problem by absolving men for misdirecting a people. In attributing
to a god what the chieftains did, Isaiah qualifies the factor of moral responsibility in history, and thereby repeats the same questionable procedure which is exemplified in the literature of the Greeks to which
reference has been made.

The borderline between what is commendable in a religious interpretation and what is questionable, because impairing the moral significance of
such an interpretation, is affirmed for instance when Isaiah maintains that
"the Lord of Hosts", who is the tutelary deity of the Israelites, "has
planned for Egypt" what destroys the wisdom of the "wise men" who
counsel Pharaoh. (19:12) This borderline is precarious and is easily
crossed in a zeal to attribute credit to a divine agency for its role in
human life.

147

This is illustrated also in Euripides' *Hecuba*. Although Polymestor, the king of Thrace, was guilty of killing Hecuba's youngest son whom she had entrusted to him for his care, she, nevertheless, declares that "the gods confound our fortunes, tossing them to and fro, and introduce confusion." When she maintains that "the gods confound our fortunes . . . that our perplexity may make us worship them", Euripides construes such "confusion" in human experience as a cause which accounts for the origin of religion or for the worship of gods.[40] Although this is an attempt of Euripides to explain the genesis of religion, it, nevertheless, is a very questionable way of arguing in defense of religion. It actually impugns the integrity of gods in causing misfortunes among human beings so that human beings will believe in them and will turn to them. Included in such orienting of human life to gods, gods thereby use human beings for their own purposes. Such purposes are satisfied with the construction of temples and altars and the lavish and generous dedication of sacrifices to the gods. That the gods enjoy such sacrifices of food is affirmed time and time again in the literature of both Greeks and Israelites.

The ambivalent relation of gods to men is an impairment of a religious trust in the dependability of a divine source of unfailing good. Such ambivalence is affirmed, for instance, by Isaiah when he maintains that the god of the Israelites strikes men "down" in his "wrath" and subsequently shows them "pity and favor". (60:10) The *Iliad* likewise maintains that the cruelest occurrences in human life from which human beings suffer are witnessed by the gods without pity, such as sensitive human beings have for the suffering of others. Priam expresses his moral sensitivities in being unable to watch the duel in which his son fights "the formidable Menelaus". What oppresses him is that "Zeus and the other immortal gods" have less compassion for such human tragedy than he himself has as a human being. He attributes a knowledge to the gods of "which of the two (men) is going to his doom", as if the goods were totally indifferent to the waste of life of a highly intelligent and superior human being at the hands of another. The indifference of divine realities to human heroes is a type of religious interpretation which qualifies the epic character of heroes' superiority to other human beings, and thereby treats their heroic capabilities as essentially without moral significance.[41]

4. *The most profound of religious interpretations maintain the indispensability of a divine role in human life for moral reasons*

A religious interpretation of the relation of human life to a divine reality which is affirmed in the eighth chapter of *Psalms* might be credited to the most spiritually profound of Greeks writers, such as Aeschylus or Plato. The Psalmist addresses himself to God in acknowledging God's creating of the human being: "Thou hast made him little less than a god, crowning him with glory and honour." (vs. 5) The "glory and honour" attributed to the nature of a human being as created by God is his moral freedom, which is his ability to distinguish right from wrong and then to act according to his respect for what it is right for him to do. The Psalmist also affirms a morally profound interpretation of the "power" of God when he declares: "Great is his power to set men free." (130:7)

After acknowledging the moral capacities with which God created man, the Psalmist acknowledges man's dependence upon God for guidance. Acknowledging man's need for the continued providence of God to enlighten him is a religious interpretation which reinforces the moral nature of man as one worthy of a creation by God. This interpretation of the human being as morally responsible, and also as dependent upon God for enlightening him of a way to live which is worthy of a creation by God, is a high-minded moral philosophy which is compatible with an equally high-minded theology. It is an interpretation of man as worthy of an origin in relation to the ultimate reality, and it is also an interpretation of God as creating man with a requirement for the most spiritually august of essentials in his life, which is enlightenment. The Psalmist's reflecting both on the ultimate reality and on the supreme good of which man's nature is in need are united in this eloquent prayer: "Give me insight to understand thy instruction." (119:125) Another expression of the same spiritual orientation of the Psalmist to God for a moral reason is the petition: "Give me understanding of thy word." (vs. 169)

Jeremiah also interprets God as the Psalmist does. He gives credit to God for giving him the ability to know His nature. This implies that when such capacity is given its direction by God, there are no limits to the human capacity to know. The Prophet declares: "It was the Lord who showed me, and so I knew; he opened my eyes." (11:18) That the source of what is of supreme moral significance in human life should be contingent upon the human being's orientation to God is a normative theology which affirms that the supreme blessing which God can confer upon human life is an understanding of His nature. This religious interpretation credits human life both with a requirement to know this ultimate reality and also to be supported by it in attaining such knowledge.

This is a religious theory of knowledge. Rather than regarding a reality

other than human life as setting limits to human knowledge, this inter
pretation affirms that there is a reciprocity in man's knowing God. Ma▸
seeks such knowledge, and God directs his search. It is this mutuality
in the quest for knowledge which constitutes the highest version of a
religious interpretation of human life. It affirms that integral to man's
nature is a requirement which cannot be satisfied unless man's life is
directed toward the ultimate reality. It thus affirms a theological premise
that God's purpose in creating man is that man might live an enlightened
life, the norm of which enlightenment is the nature of the Creator himself

This interpretation of the purpose of human life to live for its enlightenment by a quest for a knowledge of the ultimate reality differs from the
equally religious, but morally very different, interpretation which Job
affirms of the relation of human life to its creator. In his despondency of
suffering, Job confronts God with the question: "What is man that thou
makest much of him and turnest thy thoughts towards him?" Although
the first part of his question would be compatible with the theology affirmed by the Psalmist, the second part differs radically from it. Job
declares that the purpose of God in creating man is "only to punish him
morning by morning". (7:17, 18) If it were not for the circumstance in
which Job affirmed this disparagement of the purpose of the creation of
man, one would understandably regard this as outright blasphemy. But
under the circumstances of his suffering, one is impelled to pity the
patriarch for having his faith in the providence of God subjected to a
testing which is almost beyond the reasonable range of human endurance.
It, nevertheless, is a tribute to Job's faith that he continued to acknowledge the sovereignty of God, notwithstanding his bewildered questioning
about the purpose of being created only to suffer.

The apocryphal book of *Ecclesiasticus* affirms as high-minded a religious
interpretation of human life in its relation to God as does the Psalmist. He
declares: "Praise the God of the universe . . . who from our birth ennobles
our life." (50:2) This is a declaration both about the nature of God as
creator, and also about the basic orientation of which man is capable from
his birth. This regards a capacity to be ennobled as a native endowment
of man. Such a capacity to use endowments for a continued ennoblement
of life, therefore, contrasts with the ascription of essential wickedness to
the human being which he himself cannot surmount. The nature which is
attributed to man by the author of *Ecclesiasticus*, therefore, differs radically from the doctrine of the essential wickedness and depravity of human
nature such as is affirmed in another apocryphal writing, *Second Esdras*,
which anticipates the Pauline doctrine, reaffirmed throughout the history

150

of the Christian Church, as it was influenced by St. Augustine and Luther.

The author of *Ecclesiasticus* interprets the human being's worship of God as "the outward expression of wisdom", and he interprets God as the basic inspiration for such worship. He declares: "The Lord himself inspires it." According to this interpretation, there is the same reciprocity of which the Psalmist speaks in the relation of the human being to his creator. Man's worship of God thus is not an escape from an enrichment of life, but is rather an orientation of life to a source which is capable of sustaining such enrichment as no other reality is capable of doing. Man is first enlightened by a wisdom achieved in his orientation to God, and then his wisdom in turn is manifested throughout his life as he continues in such worship. The mutuality so affirmed gives men credit for having a dignity which respects wisdom by using it to maintain a relation to the reality which is the condition itself for such wisdom.

The same mutuality of relation between God and man is also affirmed in this writing when its author declares: "The Lord gave me eloquence . . . and with it I will praise him." (51:22) In so orienting himself, a human being cultivates a capacity with which he began his life. So interpreted, he is not dependent upon God for reorienting him after a servitude to sin. The human being instead is credited with a wisdom sufficient to keep him from such servitude. In this interpretation of human nature, both a theology and an anthropology are affirmed which differ radically from later Christian doctrines about God and man.

The same high-minded version of human nature is also affirmed in another apocryphal book, *Second Maccabees*. The prayer of its author is that God may give human beings "a will to worship him, to fulfill his purposes eagerly with heart and soul". (1:3) This prayer, "May he give you a mind open to his law and precepts", thus also expresses an interpretation of human nature which differs radically from the version affirmed in *Second Esdras* and later in St. Paul's writings.

Another high-minded interpretation of human nature, which differs from the thought of St. Paul and subsequent teachings of the Church, is affirmed in the apocryphal book, *Wisdom of Solomon*. Referring to the wisdom of which human nature is capable, its author declares that "there was no way to gain possession of wisdom except by gift of God". This religious interpretation of human nature affirms that man's ability to gain wisdom is an endowment given to him by his creator. It also attributes to man's wisdom the "understanding to know from whom that gift must come". (8:21) This interpretation regards a religious orientation of human life beyond itself as an expression of an enlightenment achieved

151

in man's relation to the divine reality. Thus both the capacity to become enlightened and the content of such enlightened life are regarded as made possible in man's relation to God. A philosophy about human nature, and a theology about the ultimate source from which the supreme good or wisdom in human life is derived, are affirmed in the creed of faith of the author of this writing which is stated as a question: "Who ever learnt to know thy purposes, unless thou hadst given him wisdom and sent thy holy spirit down from heaven on high?" (9:18)

5. *A religious interpretation which explains everything as caused by a god weakens the moral significance of religious faith*

One type of religious interpretation maintains that whatever takes place in human life has a single divine cause, which is as capable of permitting misfortune among men as it is capable of blessing them. One religious explanation for such misfortune is that human beings bring a god's displeasure upon themselves by their infidelity to him. Such infidelity is expressed in as many ways as there are commandments formulated in religious interpretations about requirements imposed by a god. An infraction of a requirement imposed by a god is a sin, and according to one type of religious interpretation, such sin merits the handicaps which men suffer as a god's punishment for their failure to respect his requirements. Thus both the benefits which men enjoy as well as the misery they suffer are accounted for by this type of interpretation.

In a relation to a god in which men are obedient to his requirements, men have benefits which can also be taken from them when they impair such a relation by their infidelity. Such a religious interpretation of the twofold type of acting of which a god is capable in relation to human beings is affirmed throughout the Old Testament. It is also affirmed in the apocryphal book of *Second Maccabees* which gives an account of the alternating good and bad fortunes of the Israelites. When Antiochus defeated Jerusalem and took the wealth of its great temple, this historian maintains that it was "the sins of the people of Jerusalem (which) had angered the Lord for a short time, and that this was why he left the temple to its fate". (5:17, 18) "It was abandoned when the Lord Almighty was angry, but restored again in all it splendour when he became reconciled." (vs. 20) According to this type of interpretation, whatever takes place is either the approval or the disapproval of what men do in their relation to the commandments of statutes of a god.

This unrestricted character of a religious interpretation which attributes an ambivalence to the nature of a god confronts human beings with a type of uncertainty which is the very aspect of their life from which they seek to be freed by turning to a reality transcendent of the contingent order. An ambivalent nature, whether it is attributed to a god or whether it is the nature of most human beings, confronts human life with a degree of unpredictability which is one of the fundamental handicaps to its security.

Plato was aware of the hazard to man's faith which is entailed in a metaphysic that attributes an ambivalence to an ultimate reality. Hence he insisted that attributing both good and evil to the ultimate reality would be forbidden in the normative theology in the ideal state. The Manichaeans, with whose religious interpretations Augustine was favorably impressed for many years, were as clearly aware, as was Plato, of the handicap to an unwavering trust in the goodness of God if God is also regarded as the ultimate cause of evil. In their attempt, therefore, to avoid such a handicap to religious faith, they affirmed a metaphysical dualism, accounting for evil in the world from a source other than the god whose nature was incapable of a qualification of his total goodness.

A remarkable parallel of this type of dualism is also affirmed in Greek reflecting as early as Hesiod, who declares "there was not one kind of Strife alone, but all over the earth there are two . . . For one fosters evil war and battle, being cruel . . . But the other is the elder daughter of dark Night, and the son of Cronos who sits above and dwells in the aether . . . and she is far kinder to men."[42]

An explanation which is pressed beyond restricted limits, entails unfavorable implications. Pressing a religious interpretation to account for everything that occurs in human life as coming from a single source impairs the capacity of a human being to trust such a reality for its dependability. This impairment of religious faith, at least in theory, is explained away by maintaining that handicaps to human life come from a divine source only when human beings have not done what they ought to do in relation to it. But if the very reality to which they turn for help is as ambivalent as human beings themselves are, there is then no basis for their unqualified confidence that such a divine reality can help them as other realities cannot do. Any qualification in the dependability of the ultimate source of help for human life is a qualification also in a religious trust of such a reality. The struggle of Manichaeism throughout the early centuries of the Church was an attempt to prevent such an impairment of faith in the unfailing goodness of a god by maintaining that trust in him was justified by virtue of his unqualified goodness. Such goodness of God was thus regarded as the basis on which unconditioned trusting in his providence would save human beings from the very insecurity and uncertainty that constitutes some of the most disturbing of evils with which they are confronted in their lives.

Another theological basis for weakening a religious trust in the unqualified goodness of a god is the doctrine that there is a "rooted wickedness" in the human being whose creation is attributed to the Creator. The author of the apocryphal writing *Second Esdras* anticipates the Pauline doctrine of human depravity when he maintains that "the first man, Adam, was burdened with a wicked heart . . . and not only he but all his descendants. So the weakness became inveterate." (3:21, 22) This interpretation of a "rooted wickedness" in a creation attributed to the Creator entails a questioning of his unqualified goodness. Such questioning or disbelief is inevitable when both the creation of the human being, who is capable of evil, and also the goodness of the Creator are affirmed in one creed of faith. The interpretation that "every man alive is burdened and defiled with wickedness, a sinner through and through", attributes deficiency both to man and to his creator. Man's impaired capacity to cultivate character by his own discipline that would be a basis for predictable acts of goodness is, therefore, not man's deficiency. It is his creator's.

A religious interpretation which is motivated by a desire to give a god credit for everything that takes place is its own discrediting. It discredits the justice of a divine reality which imposes a handicap to a human being achieving goodness when he is limited by factors over which he himself has no control and so for which he is not responsible. It is a moral injustice to confront a human being with responsibility to prefer goodness to evil when his nature is incapable of preferring goodness. Yet this injustice is entailed in an interpretation of human nature in whose origin "A grain of the evil seed was sown . . . from the first". (4:30)

"This explanation may be cogent for the godlessness it has produced already", as the author of *Second Esdras* maintains, anticipating St. Paul. But such "godlessness" cannot also be attributed to the responsibility of human beings.

Although Jeremiah maintains that children shall not be accountable for evils for which their fathers are responsible, he strangely acknowledges that "man's ways are not of his own choosing; nor is it for a man to determine his course in life." (10:23) According to this emphasis upon the incapacity of a human being to choose his own conduct, and so "to determine his course in life" by his own decisions, a human being then is not morally responsible for what takes place in his life. A doctrine is not consistent which both discredits human competency to make intelligent decisions and then also expects men to have intelligence enough to orient themselves to a divine reality as an expression of their own wisdom.

Another type of religious interpretation maintains that some human beings are denied even an opportunity to live wisely enough to orient themselves to a divine help. Such an interpretation is affirmed in *Ecclesiasticus*: "In his great wisdom the Lord distinguished (men) and made them go various ways: some he blessed and lifted high, some he hallowed and brought near to himself, some he cursed and humbled." (33:11, 12) This is, therefore, a total negation of the justification for human beings to trust a god who has created some human beings incapable of receiving his blessings, and has created others who, notwithstanding their effort, receive benedictions from such a god. A religious interpretation of this sort affirms a theology which discredits the basis for a religious faith that when a human being prepares himself to receive a benefaction from a god, he can trust the god's dependability to bless him and thereby to confirm his trust. But a theological doctrine which maintains that a god decides who will not be capable of preparing himself even to be worthy of an enrichment of his life by such a god attributes to the god responsibility for the futility of moral effort itself to prepare himself to receive a god-given benefaction. This is pressing a theological doctrine in a way which discredits a religious faith in the unrestricted justice of a god. It attributes to a god the same sort of discrimination against which some people protest in the name of moral justice.

This recoil of theology comes about in part from the over-used analogy of a god to a potter who has final control over the clay with which he creates what he chooses, and does so without consulting the clay. Jeremiah presumes to speak for God when he declares "like the clay in the potter's hand, so are you in my hand". (18:6)* The author of *Ecclesiasticus* also uses this inappropriate analogy to compare men with "clay . . . in the potter's hands, to be moulded just as he chooses". The religious application of this analogy is that "men in the hands of their Maker (are) to be dealt with as he decides". (33:13) This analogy superficially seems to have some cogency for acknowledging the final dependence of human beings upon a god, but it actually negates their moral nature in maintaining that they themselves are not capable of choosing to trust the god as the most dependable source of help.

Another religious interpretation which attempts to attribute unrestricted providence to a god over human life also negates the moral capacity of the human being to prefer such a god's providence to any other type of direction in human life. Ezekiel affirms such an interpretation when, as a spokesman for God, he declares: "I will put my spirit into you and make you conform to my statutes, keep my laws and live by them." (36:27) Although this seems as if it were the god's desire to save men from the errors of which they are so capable, the god's activity upon men deprives them of their moral initiative to "conform" to his statutes. As stated, there is no option for human beings. They are incapable of doing other than they are made to do. Superficially this seems as if it were attributing to a god unconditioned providence in human life for human good. But in so doing, it negates men's responsibility for conforming to the "statutes" of a god.

Jeremiah affirms the same type of religious interpretation which negates a man's moral responsibility to orient himself to a god for a trustworthy direction of his life. Such wisdom in choosing to orient one's life to a god is denied to men by declaring: "I will give them one heart and one way of life so that they shall fear me at all times, for their own good and the good of their children after them." (32:39) On a first reading, this seems an ideal religious interpretation of the blessings which a god could bestow upon human life. But since it also maintains that it is a god's decision and not men's that he bless their life, it follows that this religious faith discounts the role of a human being to such an extent that he is not even given credit for a wisdom to prefer such a life oriented to a divine reality. Such a negation of moral capacities is also implied in Jeremiah's interpretation of a providence for men to "fill their hearts with fear of (god), and so they will not turn away from (him)". (vs. 40) This type of providence, eminently desirable though it may seem, yet entails a consequence in an interpretation of the human being which impugns the moral basis for preferring a religious life to any other type of life.

Although there is no comparable parallel in Greek reflecting for the type which is so extensive in the religious writings of the Israelites, there, nevertheless, are some expressions in Greek reflecting that men are born with a nature which prevents them from developing a character sufficient to prefer one way of life to another. Such an interpretation is affirmed by Hesiod when he maintains that "Zeus the Father made a third generation of mortal men, a brazen race, (which) . . . loved the lamentable works of Ares and deeds of violence . . . (who) were hard of heart like adamant".[43] A comparable view is affirmed in Aeschylus' *Agamemnon* when Clytemnestra declares: "It is born in men to trample the more upon the fallen."[44] And Iolaus in Euripides' *Heracleidae* declares: "I hold this true, and long

156

have held: Nature hath made one man upright for his neighbor's good, while another hath a disposition wholly given over to gain."[45] Although this is not a religious interpretation, it, nevertheless, affirms an interpretation of human beings which maintains that some are born with an incapacity to prefer a way of living which is wiser than another way of living. As such, they can hardly be thought of as moral beings who are capable of selecting between alternatives. Their entire life would have been determined by a nature with which they were born and over which they had no moral control. Euripides affirms this same determination of a human being's nature prior to any act for which he is morally responsible when, in *Electra*, Orestes maintains that "pity . . . is inborn in the wise".[46]

If Euripides were to maintain that by virtue of man's wisdom, he has the capacity to feel pity for others, he would thus affirm a very different philosophy about human morality. As stated by Orestes, however, the most praiseworthy expression of character, which is mercy or pity, is not a moral achievement, but is an endowment, just as is any nonmoral capacity of human nature. Euripides affirms the same point of view in *Orestes* when Menelaus maintains that some men "have a natural sense of pity".[47] This statement, of course, may be ambiguous since it may mean that the "sense of pity" is natural rather than effortful or deliberate for some people. If this is the meaning of "a natural sense of pity", then it may be regarded as a moral achievement that is cultivated by a character which progressively enriches a human being's sensitivities in all of the relations into which he enters. This interpretation then would be compatible with a moral philosophy which interprets a moral virtue, such as a capacity for pity, as an achievement of character. And character would in turn be regarded as an accomplishment which is possible within the range of human effort.

Just as one type of philosophy about human nature negates the moral capacities of a human being, so likewise does one type of religious interpretation. Hence both a nonreligious and a religious interpretation of human life are confronted with limits in affirming points of view about human nature which do not also negate what is essential to such nature, which is its capacity for making choices, and its ability to recognize the moral difference in alternatives.

This restriction should be respected as a general principle in affirming religious interpretations of human life, since a religious interpretation cannot both affirm that a religious faith is a tribute to human wisdom and also deny that there is a human ability to make such a choice.

V

The Problem of Moral Responsibility in Religious Life

1. *People who know what is right, nevertheless do wrong*

A problem which has continued throughout the centuries to trouble all who seriously reflect is that even when human beings understand what it is right to do, they nevertheless go counter to their understanding and do what is wrong. Hesiod points out that men may be cautioned against acting in a particular way, and yet ignore such counsel, and do so to their own harm. He illustrates this when Prometheus told his brother not to accept a gift from Zeus. "But he took the gift, and afterwards, when the evil thing was already his, he understood."[1] That is, he became aware of a mistake which he could have avoided by acting according to what he already knew before his mistaken acting. Taking account of such a common way that human beings bring handicaps to themselves, Hesiod declares that a man is "good who listens to a good adviser; but whoever neither thinks for himself nor keeps in mind what another tells him, he is an unprofitable man".[2] If this generalization were introduced into a reflecting on a human being's relation to a divine reality, it could be said he was equally unprofitable to such a reality.

Homer also was aware of this problem when he pointed out that Aegisthus deliberately "flouted Destiny" by his moral outrages "though he knew the ruin this would entail".[3] Knowing the consequences of one's acting, and yet ignoring one's own knowledge of them is the disturbing problem with which Greek reflecting was engaged as early as Homer and Hesiod. Centuries later, Aeschylus took account of the same disparity

158

tween a clear awareness of an act which is morally wrong and a deliberate ignoring of such an awareness. The Chorus in his *Agamemnon* points t that Agamemnon "hardened his heart to sacrifice his daughter that might prosper a war".[4] His act of "harden(ing) his heart" to the oral outrage he intended to do to his own child was his attempt to ignore the offense of which he was about to make himself guilty.

Sophocles makes the same deliberate immorality basic to his tragedy *hiloctetes*. When Neoptolemus was tempted to betray his friend, he knowledged the offense he was tempted to commit, and he censured mself for "knowing right" and yet being tempted to "do wrong". He dmitted to himself that "All is offensive when a man is false to his true lf and, knowing right, does wrong."[5]

Hebrew prophets were also troubled by this aspect of human life. Isaiah ntrasts opportunities men have to be enlightened with their refusal to enefit from such opportunities. He declares: "You have seen much but remembered little, your ears are wide open but nothing is heard." (42:20) here would be no moral basis for such censuring of men if they were not capable of learning. But when they have capacities to learn, and yet do othing to take advantage of them for influencing their acting, they are ensurable.

Isaiah, however, takes account of a very different basis for men's moral ailures when he refers to their "own deluded mind" which misleads them. e says that it is by virtue of their mental handicap that they "cannot collect" even so much of their behavior as to ask "Why" they continue to "feed on ashes" instead of more suitable sustenance. (44:20) If, therere, it were the case that men were unable to be critical of their own leas, which without their scrutiny become delusions, there would be a ery different moral problem. It would be the problem whether they ever ad capacities sufficient to be critical of ideas which subsequently were morally disadvantageous. If they once had such ability, and did less than ey could have done to take advantage of it, they then would be morally esponsible for the delusions by which they are subsequently "misled". f, on the other hand, their mental capacities were inadequate for them to be critical of their own ideas, they would not be responsible for the oral handicap of the delusions by which they were "misled".

Hosea declares a mere fact when he says that "A people without understanding comes to grief". (4:14) Taking account only of the relation between deficiency of intelligence and its handicap to well-being does not s such state a moral problem. A moral problem arises only in raising a uestion about the circumstances which enter into the poverty of their

159

understanding. If they either did nothing to impair their intelligence, or
there was nothing they could have done to prevent its impairment, the
then would not be morally censurable for the grief from which they suff
by virtue of their deficient intelligence.

When Jeremiah declares that a people is "corrupt to a man", he assum
they are morally responsible for their depravity. (6:28) If he did n
assume such responsibility, he would not even have used the term "co
rupt", whose connotation includes a moral basis. He supports his accus
tion with an analysis of a condition that leaves no doubt about the mor
responsibility for such a manner of living. He accuses his people of havir
cultivated one interest, and only one: "Each (is) intent on his own gai
wherever he can find it." Having "no thought for anything but gain
they become capable of "acts of tyranny" over helpless people. (22:17

Such a type of human evil could come about only on the condition tha
human beings have a capacity for wrongdoing which *Ecclesiasticus* refe
to as "propensity to evil". Yet, if there were no such capacity for evil,
choice for good would not even be morally praiseworthy. Kant points th
out when he explains that if there is only a "holy will" and no abilit
to do wrong, there is no temptation or inclination to go counter to wha
is right. Every act of such a "holy will" would be right, and so there wou
be no moral basis for praising it as worthy of approval, since there woul
be no inclination to do other than what is right.

The author of *Ecclesiasticus*, however, is distraught by the fact tha
there is such a "propensity to evil" in human beings. He, therefore, asks
"How did it creep in to cover the earth with treachery?" (37:3) Th
extent of such inclination to evil troubled the author of this writing be
cause he believed that the earth was created by a god whose intention fo
it differed so radically from what human history became. This type o
reflecting on the nature of human wrongdoing thus arises from contrastin
what one assumes human history might have been with its actual nature

It is this same type of contrast which underlies the lament of th
Chorus in Euripides' *Medea* which declares: "Gone is the grace that oath
once had." This notion of a better order than later came into being i
expressed in the generalization: "Through all the breadth of Hellas honou
is found no more."[6]

The same type of contrast is affirmed by Isaiah who points out tha
the inhabitants of Jerusalem deteriorated to a level which made them
morally no different from the people of Sodom, the proverbial city of
wickedness, He declares: "Like Sodom they proclaim their sins and do

t conceal them." (3:9) The moral tragedy of their level of life is that ey were not even troubled by their own wickedness.

It is this same contrast which Jeremiah points out between what rusalem once was and what it became when its citizens lived without a se of moral obligations. By virtue of their indifference to moral prin- les, the Prophet declares that "the city" deserved the name of "Licence" cause it tolerated an "oppression" which became "rampant in her". :6) This deterioration of the standards of life in a great city by the eer indifference of its people to right acting was the basis for the ophet's condemnation of them as "fools . . . one and all". (10:8)

But taking account of neglected moral obligations confronts reflecting th the disturbing problem of responsibility for such neglect. One cause r a moral deficiency of individuals is living in a community in which ere is a widespread disregard for moral principles. This type of context described by Isaiah in which "priest and prophet are addicted" to orally censurable behavior. They thus ignore obligations imposed upon em by the very nature of their ministry to people. If the leaders of a ople allow themselves to degenerate into a "drunken stupor" of which aiah speaks, the most impressionable of the young of the community n hardly be censured for doing what their priests and prophets do. This not excusing individuals who are capable of knowing the difference be- een the moral responsibilities of a genuine prophet and priest and the tual behavior of such unworthy human beings. But it is taking account a grave problem when individuals who ought to be examples in a com- unity are unworthy of being imitated, and yet are imitated.

If a community included individuals with capacities for moral standards gher than their assumed leaders, such individuals would be morally cen- arable for accepting such people as their standards. But the disturbing roblem is that many individuals know no standards other than the ones ey see manifested by people whom they are taught to respect as their amples. Under such social conditions, with leaders unworthy of instruct- g, it is unreasonable to expect that those who follow the blind should not so suffer the same disasters in life as the blind whom they follow. The eer moral tragedy of a community being subjected to leaders who are nworthy of their role is pointed out by Jeremiah when he declares that prophets prophesy lies and priests go hand in hand with them". The oral tragedy is that after they so influence a people, they cultivate in he people themselves a desire for a level of life which is the same as their aders'. It is this negation of the morality of a people by its morally nworthy leaders which the Prophet laments when he admits that "my

161

people love to have it so". (5:31) This collective moral handicap of people by virtue of the moral unworthiness of others who presume to b guides is one of the greatest of tragedies in human history.

It is tragic that individuals who, without the handicap of living und the influence of morally perverse leaders, might have cultivated a morall enlightened life. The moral poverty into which many slip by virtue accepting a leadership unworthy of being respected often occurs at an ag before individuals can even be held morally responsible for knowing bette The contrast of what they might have been under circumstances of different type of leadership with what they became is one of the hear breaking facts of history. When "prophets and priests are frauds", the do the disservice to a people such as Jeremiah describes when the "dress (a) people's wound but only skin-deep, with their saying 'A is well' ".

The contrast between what they affirm and what the facts actually ar is pointed out by the Prophet when he declares: "Nothing is well." (6:14 That is, "nothing is right" in a community in which its people are no challenged to be what they are capable of being. The leaders of such community destroy the very possibility within many of its members t surpass the low moral level of the community and its leaders. The problem then which confronts reflecting is who is basically responsible for th moral handicap which blights the life of impressionable individuals in suc a community when they themselves are not able to be critical of the im pressions by which their lives are conditioned and determined.

The moral tragedy in such circumstances is, as Jeremiah points out that "Lying, not truth, is master in the land". When this is the determin ing influence upon those who are not capable of being aware of such in fluence, it follows that such morally handicapped individuals "run from one sin to another". (9:3) The problem in reflecting on such circum stances is whether such handicapped individuals can reasonably be cen sured for their moral failure, since a failure is moral only when an in dividual could avoid it. But if the conditions internal to which ar individual lives are antagonistic even to the emergence in his life of moral sense of what is not right, such an individual cannot reasonably b censured for his wrongdoing.

Only an individual for whom the mores of a community are so distaste ful that he turns from them has the incipient leverage by which he ma transcend its mores and thereby become morally free from its handicap Only such an individual transcends the moral poverty of a context in which men "steal, murder, commit adultery, and perjury". (7:9) Jeremiah

162

numerates these patterns of life which are presented to impressionable individuals as standards to which they can conform. And in conforming to these, because incapable of subjecting them to moral scrutiny, they present reflecting with a grave problem. If it were the case, as Jeremiah declares, that "The shepherds of the people are mere brutes", it could not be expected that a people under such influence could differ very much from such influence. (10:21) If the so-called "shepherds of the people" destroy their own sensitivities to what is fair and just in their relation to the people who depend upon them for their influence, it can hardly be that people will manifest another type of living in relation to others of the same community. The prophet Habakkuk was aware of the consequences in the progressive destruction of moral bases for such a community when he pointed out that as "law grows effete", people's sense of "justice comes out perverted". (1:4) The prophet Joel was likewise clearly aware of the consequence of such disregard for the moral bases of corporate life when he appealed to his people to "Wake up" and to be aware of their "fate" entailed in such a negation of the elemental principles for corporate honesty and justice. (1:5)

But such appeal itself often seems futile when addressed to people who have committed themselves to a way of living without consideration for any moral responsibility to the community itself in which they live. Aeschylus refers to such apparent hopelessness of directing a moral injunction to people who have lost an awareness of moral obligation. Prometheus speaks of a people, before becoming enlightened by his help, as having no genuine human benefit from their capacities to see and to hear. He declares: "Though they had eyes to see, they saw to no avail; they had ears, but understood not." Such sensory capacities which might have moral benefit for the enrichment of life must be used with morally directed intelligence if there is to be such benefit. But as Prometheus points out, in everything they did "they wrought without judgment".[7]

The same uselessness of having capacities underexploited for moral benefit is pointed out by Jeremiah when he addresses himself to his people as "foolish and senseless . . . who have eyes and see nothing, ears and hear nothing". (5:21) The underexploitation of any capacity for moral benefit is a basis for accusing a people, as Isaiah does, of living "without sense". (27:11) And his analysis for this handicap to their well-being is due to the deficiency of intelligence they use in their acting. Failing to take account of consequences of their acting in terms of their own well-being is denying themselves the moral advantages otherwise possible in intelligently determined acting.

163

But when he maintains that "their minds (are) too narrow to discern" the consequences of their way of living, he takes account of a profoundly disturbing problem. If anyone's intelligence is too limited to make decisions which affect his life, then any censuring of his failure to "discern" what he ought to do would itself be unjust. Only when negligence in taking advantage of a native capacity is avoidable by effort, is such negligence a moral deficiency. If, therefore, anyone's capacity to benefit from the wisdom of another's counsel is impaired by an avoidable disregard for it, the consequences of such disregard are morally censurable.

Even the profoundest of wisdom can be rejected by a disregard which has never been checked by deliberate effort. Hence as Isaiah declares, for such human beings "prophetic vision" itself "has become . . . a sealed book". (29:11) Notwithstanding how great its benefit may be for the enlightenment of human life, such benefit depends both upon a willingness to learn and also upon an effort to cultivate an awareness of which counsel is genuine "prophetic vision" and which is fraudulent. Making such a distinction is itself a moral decision. Only as available counsel is evaluated for its moral worth is it a trustworthy source of guidance in an individual's life. An individual might be handicapped to the extent of "a curse", as Jeremiah maintains, if he were to trust counsel which was not worthy of being trusted, and if he were to "lean for support" on the counsel of others who are not capable of giving him the counsel he morally needs. (17:5)

2. *Human beings themselves set limits to what a god can do for them*

Jeremiah refers to his own people as "incurable in their waywardness". (8:5) This interpretation of human beings as incorrigible is one of the most disturbing concepts in religious literature. It raises bewildering problems not only about human beings but also about a divine reality whose potential benefit for human life is curtailed by human beings' own nature, or at least by their failure to do what they should do to benefit from such providence. This problem is gravely intensified when human nature is disparaged to such an extent that even its potentialities for goodness are denied. Yet, such capacities for goodness are denied by Isaiah when he declares that "there is not a sound spot" in the people to whom he directs his appeals for a change in their lives. (1:6)

A generalization of this sort confronts religious faith with a sobering question about the limits of a divine help for human beings. If human beings themselves can impose such limits upon a divine reality that it cannot even redeem them from their own evil or their wrongdoing, and so cannot reorient them to a sounder way of living, religious reflecting then wonders which reality is ultimate—the divine or the human. If human beings can handicap the extension of benefits to themselves from a divine source, reflecting cannot avoid entertaining the idea that men decide what a god can do rather than a god deciding what men can do.

This conditioning of a divine reality's potential benefit for human beings by what they themselves do argues in support of an interpretation of a god as finite rather than as unconditioned in capacities for benefitting human beings. It makes a reflective person doubt the soundness of a theology which affirms a so-called "omnipotence" of a god. Taking into account the limits which human beings are said by the Prophets to impose upon God, there seems no basis for attributing omnipotence to such a deity.

Such a theological doctrine, on the other hand, would be justified only if there were no realities external to a god which set restrictions upon the range of his capacities. But if men's "waywardness" can preclude the redemptive help which men might otherwise receive from a divine reality, then the sobering realization follows of having misdirected the tribute of "omnipotence" to such a reality.

A disparagement of human nature to an extent such as it is disparaged in the Bible raises disturbing questions not only about the potential goodness of human beings, but also about the restricted role of a god in enabling them to realize their potential goodness. Yet this troublesome question arises in reflecting on what is affirmed in the fifty-third Psalm which declares that men are "vile . . . depraved" and "not one does anything good . . . but all are unfaithful, all are rotten to the core". (vs. 1-3) This devastating denunciation of human beings is not only uncomplimentary to them, but what is far more disturbing is what it implied for a doctrine which attributes their creation to a god who is also affirmed in religious faith to be a providence immanent in human life and capable of directing it. But if the directing or the guidance from such a divine reality is thwarted by men themselves, its effectiveness in human life is contingent upon men's nature. It is contingent upon men's unwillingness to receive it. But such unwillingness on the part of human beings precludes the very type of help for human life which a religious faith affirms. Insofar as it affirms that the charity of a god is unrestricted, it is confronted with its own discrediting by the depreciation of human life as corrupt to its "core". Such a depreciation even for potential goodness is often looked upon, as it was by St. Augustine, as a backhanded way of acknowledging man's total dependence upon god. But if man's own nature can preclude the initiative of a god to change it and to make it want to receive his help, then the redemptive role of a god in human life is limited by man himself. Hence affirming such a depreciation of human nature entails the gravest of possible questions about a god's capacities in relation to human beings.

The intention of the Hebrew prophets was to threaten the Israelites with the terrifying danger of being alienated from the providence of their god. Thus the prophet Micah threatened them with the stern warning that "they will call to the Lord, and he will give them no answer". Micah assured them that there is no unlimited latitude permitted them in making their decision to alter their lives that they may be receptive of God's providence. He warned them that God "will hide His face from them", and the reason for such a threatened disregard of their belated appeal is that "their deeds are so wicked". (3:4)

There is no questioning that so stern a reprimand of human beings is morally justified in the light of human history, but what does constitute a basis for questioning is what this type of prophecy entails for a theology, or a doctrine about God. If a theology were not to include the assurance that God's grace is unrestricted and his providence is unconditioned, then it would not be contradicted by the type of prophecy which threatens human beings with a total denial of such providence. This does not raise the question of men's merit to be helped when they do not even want to be helped. But it does raise the gravest of questions about the theology affirmed in a religious interpretation of an unqualified availability of providence for men who need its redemptive help.

Human beings who are in need of a guidance which they do not have in their lives are the very ones who are blinded most completely by their own evil. But if it is maintained that evil in human life can reach a degree of such density that it can prevent the redemptive guidance of god, then the providence of such a god must be questioned.

The fact that there is such massive wrongdoing, evil, and unspeakable wickedness throughout history is a datum of which no one acquainted with history would question. But when a religious interpretation of human beings interprets their creation by a god, the wrongdoing of which they are capable then entails a disturbing question about the creator to whom credit is given for their origin and so for their nature. Such a religious interpretation is affirmed in *Second Esdras*: "Those he created have themselves brought dishonour on their Creator's name, and show ingratitude to the One who had put life within their reach." (8:60, 61)

If this interpretation were not pressed for its implications in a theology, t would be an exemplary affirmation of religious faith. But when the creation of human beings is attributed to a god whom such created beings ignore by withholding their gratitude and their reverence, it is their god-created nature which constitutes a basis for the most sobering of questions. Jeremiah asks the only appropriate question about this problem: "Who can fathom it?" The answer actually is that no one in reflecting can "fathom" the aspect of a theology that god creates what he himself subsequently cannot direct. According to this implied interpretation of the incorrigible character of a god's creation, the god himself made it so that it would be incapable of his own control. This implied interpretation of the restricted nature of a god's providence for his own creation would not perplex reflecting on religious faith if the faith itself did not affirm that human evil is beyond redemption by what god-created human beings can do.

The Neoplatonic tradition in Christian doctrine, therefore, does not maintain that any degree of evil is beyond redemption. According to its monistic metaphysic, no human being is cut off from its ultimate source. It is distinguished from it by its individuality, but it still retains its affinity with its source. It is never "cut off" to such an extent that it is separated from the source from which it has its derivation. On the other hand, a doctrine that a creator is totally other than his creation entails a difficulty for a reflective reconciliation of his unrestricted providence with limits set upon it by his own creation.

The restricted providence of a creator for his own creation is the most disturbing of theological problems for a religious faith which affirms trust in the unqualified goodness of a god. This problem, of course, does not arise in a religious interpretation of human life in relation to a god when his goodness is not affirmed as unqualified. If a deity is ambivalent so that his goodness is only one aspect of his nature, there is then no inconsistency in his indifference to the well-being of his creation. Such an interpretation is affirmed by the author of *Second Esdras*, attributed to the prophet Ezra. As a spokesman for the god of the Israelites, he maintains that their god declares: "I shall not grieve for the many who are lost; for they are no more than a vapour, they are like flame or smoke; they catch fire, blaze up, and then die out." (7:61) This ascription to a god of the irrelevance of a part of his creation is a profoundly troublesome point in scripture. Yet, it is not a farfetched inference on the grounds of much which has taken place in history when entire civilizations have been destroyed, and it certainly seems to be supported by historians' records of single battles in which hundreds of thousands are killed,

167

It is not only the prophetic tradition of the Israelites which consider this inference of the irrelevance of much human life to a god whom religious faith trusts for its providence. The Chorus in Euripides' *Troja Women* directs its questioning to "O Lord Zeus on high", and asks abou all who were killed in the years of the siege of Troy: "Were they all t thee as nothing, thou throned in the sky?" The destruction of a great cit and its people is as if they pass "in the wind and the flare".[8] The cor ditions attendant upon their cancellation from the earth, of which Eur pides speaks, parallel those to which the prophet Ezra refers. It is as the destruction of an entire people were of no more concern to a deit than the burning of wood is to the fire which consumes it. Yet, this ur limited annihilation of human beings is repeatedly affirmed in the Bibl such as when Zephaniah maintains that it is "the very word of the Lord I will . . . wipe out mankind from the earth." (1:3)

The tragic destiny in which so many human beings suffer is glossed ove or diminished by a derogatory interpretation of human life. After dis paraging its worth, it is assumed that the tragic aspect of its irrelevanc to its creator is reduced. Isaiah states such a depreciatory estimate of human being when he asks: "What is he worth?" And then the Prophe declares: "He is no more than the breath in his nostrils." (2:22) On th basis of this disparagement of the worth of a human being, the indiffer ence of a deity to him seems to be justified. But the theological problen reasserts itself that a creation which is without worth to its own creato impugns the deity more than it does the people internal to the creation

Isaiah multiplies the accusations against the human being, disparaging his cosmic worth on the grounds of his failure as a social being on th earth. He declares: "Man is of no account." And the reason for thi generalization, as if it includes the estimate from the perspective of deity, is that "Covenants are broken, treaties are flouted" into whicl human beings enter with other human beings. (33:8) But an accusatio of human beings' moral deficiency in relation to other human being hardly accounts for a judgment of their irrelevance to their creator, whose providence is affirmed in the religious faith of a people to which suck negligent human beings belong. Yet Isaiah's abusive disparagement o human "righteousness" as having the status of "a filthy rag" does no diminish the perplexity which considers a god's role in history. (64:6 If his creation is capable of no more than the Prophet gives it credit for it is indeed a pathetic miscarriage of creating. It would be impossible therefore, for a reflective person to reconcile such an inference about th incompetency of a creator with the religious faith of his unrestricted

ovidence for human beings. These interpretations are irreconcilable. If
ie is maintained, doubt cannot help being cast on the defensibility of
e other.

A most unconvincing argument is proposed by Isaiah when he first
ks: "Do you not know, have you not heard . . . that God sits enthroned
a the vaulted roof of earth?" And then he disparages the subjects over
hom such a cosmic sovereign rules when he declares that its "inhabitants
e like grasshoppers". (40:21, 22) Emphasizing the disparity between a
id and human beings as a means to stress the basis for their esteem of
• exalted a sovereign boomerangs as many doctrines do which are insuf-
ziently thought-out for their implied inferences. To the extent that the
gnity of human history is disparaged, to the same extent the sovereignty
: god is impugned. A ruler of inferior subjects has no august role in rela-
on to them; and the same parallel may be pointed out in the relation to
type of humanity of low level to a deity who has created it and then
iverns it.

The major prophets of the Israelites do not seem to tire of depreciating
uman beings as a means to emphasize their helplessness apart from a
od's providence. Yet, instead of persuading them by such an argument
iat they are worthy of orienting themselves to the noblest in reality, their
rguments would have the effect of persuading them to be content with a
vel of life commensurate with their own essential worthlessness. After
eclaring of a people that "What you conceive and bring to birth is chaff
id stubble", it is difficult to see how they could be persuaded to believe
iat a god's requirements of them imposed upon them the obligation to
irn to the god himself as the only reality capable of fulfilling their
iiritual requirements. If what men do expresses their requirements, and
'hat they do is of no greater worth than "chaff and stubble" and deserves
o more esteem from the perspective of a divine reality than "thorns cut
own and set on fire", it seems totally ineffective of a prophet to appeal
o them to orient themselves to a god as alone capable of doing for them
'hat realities of lesser merit cannot do. (33:11, 12)

The disparagement of human beings as one aspect of a prophetic
rgument for the urgency of human beings to orient themselves to a god
a a way which is worthy of them as their sovereign is not peculiar to
saiah. It is vigorously affirmed by Jeremiah, who also refers to his own
eople as "debased and worthless". (2:21) As a means to stress the
irgency of their need to change their way of living, and more worthily
.cknowledge their dependence upon their creator, he declares that their
leath will be of no loss to their god. This depreciation is stressed by

169

declaring that "The corpses of men shall . . . lie like dung in the fields . .
but no one shall gather them". (9:22) He repeats that after their deat
"there shall be no wailing for them and no burial; they shall be like dun
lying upon the ground". (16:4)

The purposes of this type of denunciation of human beings is obviou
from the point of view of a prophet, such as Isaiah or Jeremiah. It is t
stress the total helplessness of human beings apart from god's sovereignt
over their lives. But it is a very different thing to emphasize such help
lessness as men's worthlessness within themselves. It is, therefore, this wa
of stressing their need for god's sovereignty over their lives which has
very questionable effect. It disparages the worth of them to such a
extent that it could be understandably construed as denying they eve
have worth enough to be of concern to a god. Thus an argument intende
to persuade them to depend upon a god for a guidance worthy of them
rather than for depending upon ways of life unworthy of them, disparage
completely their merit even to presume to be regarded as worthy of
god's providence.

Jeremiah, however, does not confine his disaparagement of huma
beings to the Israelites. He generalizes such disparagement when h
declares people whom the Lord rejects from his favor "shall lie like dun
on the ground from one end of the earth to the other; no one shall wa
for them, they shall not be taken up and buried". (25:33) According t
this prediction, there would be a universal destiny for a vast part o
mankind which would be abhorrent for the Greek who regards neglect fo
burial of a corpse as the supreme offense against a natural obligatio
which any human being has for another.

Although there are various emphases in the prophetic tradition of th
Israelites which give rise to bewildering questioning, there is none mor
bewildering than the theological doctrine itself that "All nations dwindl
to nothing before" God. Isaiah affirms this disaparagement of humar
beings from the perspective of their creator when he declares that Goc
"reckons them mere nothing". He intensifies this disparagement by de
claring that God regards them as "less than nought" (40:17) This same
depreciatory estimate in the god's appraisal of his creation is maintained
by Obadiah in referring to "the house of Esau", that "they shall . . . be a
though they had never been". (1:16)

Zephaniah declares: "This is the very word of the Lord": "I will . . . .
wipe out mankind from the earth." (1:3) A disparagement of the worth
of human beings continues throughout the prophetic tradition, and is
affirmed in a late prophecy attributed to Ezra who refers to "the many

who were born in vain". He compares them to "one grape . . . out of a cluster, one tree out of a forest". (9:22) Although this is a sweeping disparagement of a vast part of creation attributed to God, it at least is not a universal disparagement. But it is a depreciation of the worth of the greater part of mankind, as if its creation was a mistake of the Creator. This vast part of mankind, in other words, sets such limits upon the Creator's satisfaction with his own creation that he could regard only a fraction of his creating as justifying his effort.

By virtue of what men do to negate the purpose for which they were given life by their creator, they defeat the purpose of a god in creating them. This theological doctrine that a creation defeats the intended purpose of a creator is also affirmed in early Greek reflecting. Hesiod describes the several attempts of a creator to create living beings. He disparagingly characterizes the "second order" as being unable to "keep from sinning and from wronging one another".[9] He then describes the plan of Zeus to create the present human race: "And again far-seeing Zeus made yet another generation, the fifth, of men who are upon the bounteous earth". This so-called "race of iron" consists of "men (who never rest from labour and sorrow by day, and from perishing by night". In expressing how unsuccessful even the fifth attempt of Zeus was to bring into being creatures with whose nature he was satisfied, Hesiod maintains that "the gods . . . lay sore trouble upon them".[10] This is another way of indicating the theological doctrine of a limited god in relation to a creation which is less than he intended it to be. It maintains in anthropomorphic terminology that what the god wanted to do was handicapped by his own creation, as if he were incapable of having created more successfully for his own approval.

Aechylus reaffirms this ancient notion recorded by Hesiod. In *Prometheus Bound*, Prometheus declares that "of wretched mortals Zeus took no need, but desired to bring the whole race to nothingness and to create another, a new one, in its stead". Prometheus maintains that "Against his purpose none dared make stand save I myself—I only had the courage".[11] Aeschylus thus affirms the same type of disparagement of human beings as the Israelite prophets do. The Chorus declares of Agamemnon: "He who aforetime was mighty, swelling with insolence for every fray, he shall not even be named as having ever been."[12]

The futility of the life of any human being implies a defeat in the purpose of a creator when a doctrine of such creation is maintained. The greater the number of human beings who go counter to such creating, the greater the disparity between what a creator had intended to ac-

171

complish and his actual accomplishment. The greater the obstacle which his own creation imposes upon his intention for it, the more limited his capacities necessarily are.

The prophet Ezra reaffirms the previous prophetic tradition's disparagement of a considerable part of mankind as coming far short of the Creator's plan. He contrasts the many who do not fulfill the Creator's expectation of them with the few who do, and then points out this contrast in the graphic figure of the abundance of "clay for making earthenware" with the scarcity of "very little gold-dust". Then he declares that "The same holds good for the present world: many have been created, but only a few will be saved." (II, 8:2, 3)

What is disturbing about this disparagement of so extensive a part of mankind as offering no justification for their creation is what it implies in a theology of a creator who is so limited in bringing into being the type of creation he himself intended. The reason conventionally given for defending a creator for dismissing the significance of so considerable a part of his own creation is the "countless offences" of human beings. But their "offences" express their nature as it was created, not by themselves, but by a deity. And it is this implication which is sobering for serious reflecting on religious interpretations affirmed in Scripture. Ezra declares that if the Creator were not to "blot out their countless offences" "of the entire human race only very few would be spared". (7:140)

The Prophet attributes this disparagement of the greater part of mankind to the judgment of "The Most High" who "made this world for many, but the next world for only a few". (8:1) What is sobering in this scripture is its parallel to a contemporary existentialist disaparagement of much, if not most, of mankind as "superfluous". Such disparagement of human history in a nonreligious philosophy, however, has a very different significance than it has in scripture. Scripture maintains that mankind was created by a god, and it is this theological doctrine which gives rise to the sobering awareness of a disparagement of mankind by its own creator.

This disturbing implication of a disparagement of mankind is certainly not lessened by a prophetic assurance that the Creator will "have joy in the few who are saved". This becomes merely another question about the Creator's capacity when the prophet Ezra, speaking for the Creator, declares: "It is they who have made my glory prevail." (II, 7:60) The disproportion between the few which justify a creation and the many who are rejects in it would raise questions even about the competency of a human craftsman. But the question is vastly more troublesome when this lisproportion in a creation is attributed to a deity whose so-called "om-nipotence" is a basic premise of prophetic religion.

The very confidence of a religious faith itself in the significance of human life is questioned by the position that a vast amount of mankind is beyond the scope of redemption by its own creator. Eliphaz raises this question in his conversation with Job. In the third cycle of their discourses, he asks: "Can man be any benefit to God? Can even a wise man benefit him? Is it an asset to the Almighty if you are righteous? Does he gain if your conduct is perfect?" (22:3) Such disturbing questioning arises in considering the god's disaparagement of so vast a part of mankind. If men are disparaged by a god for failing to conform to standards comprehensible to a human being's moral consciousness, then a question arises why another set of moral standards should constitute a basis for a deity's repudiation of human beings. The disturbing character of this question is not lessened by maintaining that the standards to which a god requires men to conform are the god's own standards, because their meaning for men as moral principles is within the scope of human mentality.

What troubles serious reflecting on a religious affirmation that only a fraction of mankind fulfills the expectations of a god is that such expectations are in terms of requirements which men themselves formulate as moral principles. It is, therefore, a legitimate question to ask why a moral difference in human beings should constitute a radical distinction in the worth of human beings from the perspective of a divine reality. Moral differences are significant in human appraisals of human beings, but why such criteria should also be the basis for a god's disparagement of the worth of human beings is a question which persists in reflecting on much of Scripture.

This problem, however, would not arise if a distinction between ways of living were only of significance for men's appraisals of human acting, and not also bases for a god's appraisal of success or unsuccess of his creating. If one way of living yields well-being to a degree that another way of living does not, it would have moral merit in terms of moral benefits. Then human beings who failed to have such benefits would differ from those who had them. But why those who were blessed with such benefits should also have favor from a god as others do not have is a question which is legitimately raised by Job's friend, and it persists in any serious reflecting on what Scripture attributes to a god as the basis for his disaparagement of human beings.

This disturbing question, however, does not arise in wisdom literature.

173

The author of *The Wisdom of Solomon* declares that he valued wisdom "above sceptre and throne, and reckoned riches as nothing beside her". (7:8, 9) Any person who also believes that the moral worth of wisdom in living surpasses every other good, could be grateful to a creator for such a moral possibility in human life. His gratitude for the opportunity which human life provides for such a moral benefit would then be the basis for his religious faith in the wisdom of a divine creating, and so a religious interpretation of human life would not be qualified by a disbelief in a creator's providence. Such a religious faith would regard the opportunity of human beings to achieve wisdom as the unquestioned evidence for the wisdom of a creation. On the basis of this religious interpretation, a divine role in creation would not be impugned by attributing to a creator moral requirements of men which are men's requirements of themselves. Hence the implied dilemma in a theology which regards these moral principles as god's criteria for appraising his own creation would thus be avoided.

If one were to follow the counsel of *Ecclesiasticus* to "seek wisdom's discipline while you are young", he would not have his faith impaired in the providence of god's wisdom. In enjoying the benefit of wisdom in one's life, one would be thankful that a creator had made wisdom one of the options of human choice. And this for him would be evidence of a divine providence. He would look upon the failure of others to take advantage of an enrichment of their life by such wisdom as their own punishment, and he would regard their own depriving of themselves of the benefit of this supreme good in life as their supreme loss.

An individual's gratitude to his creator for making it possible for the human being to live wisely would not disparage a god's creation even when vast numbers of people do not live wisely. Their rejection of their option to live wisely would be their own loss or their own condemnation. It would not be god's judgment as a condemnation of human beings after creating them. Having created them with a capacity to live wisely, their failure to do so would be their judgment, and such a judgment would take place internal to a human life for its own failure to take advantage of a capacity with which it was endowed.

The bitterness entailed in the prophetic disparagement of human beings would not have distorted a philosophy of human history if Scripture were to have affirmed this type of judgment rather than a mythologically interpreted judgment by a deity separated spatially from men as a transcendent judge.

Judgment is immanent in human history. Human beings judge themselves as deficient in wisdom when they do not live wisely. The possibility for living wisely is a good which can be chosen by men just as it can be rejected by them. In rejecting the option to live wisely, men condemn themselves to a tragic history. Such a tragic history is men's moral failure to take advantage of a creation in which they have an option to "seek wisdom's discipline". (6:18) Reflective and sensitive human beings may be saddened by the misfortune entailed in other's failure to live wisely, but their response to human failure would be radically different from the prophetic disparagement of a creation in which its divine creator is impugned.

Had this strand in the prophetic tradition of disparaging creation been replaced with the invitation proposed by the apocryphal writing of *Ecclesiasticus,* the history of the Church would have been very different. This invitation would have offered human beings an appeal that might have oriented them to good rather than to the wrongdoing which Scripture condemns. Stated as a simile, it is the invitation to "Come to her like a farmer ploughing and sowing; then wait for her plentiful harvest". (vs. 19) This is accompanied with the counsel: "If you cultivate her, you will labour for a little while, but soon you will be eating her crops." This counsel might be interpreted as compatible with a theology that affirms a universal providential goodness available to all who make themselves worthy to receive it. There then would be no universal disparagement of human history on the ground of the failure of human beings to benefit from the providence of their creator.

3. *Human beings determine a god's benefactions to them*

The Psalmist declares that men "broke faith with God", and it was by virtue of "their conduct" that they made themselves unworthy of God's continued guidance. (106:39) So stated, human beings take the initiative for being cut off from a divine blessing. Just as turning away from such providence is a human act, so likewise it is a human act to reorient oneself to such a divine reality and so prepare oneself to accept the providence which is available upon moral conditions. Zechariah maintains there are such conditions when he declares: "These are the words of the Lord . . . Come back to me, and I will come back to you." (1:3) What is of utmost importance in these emphases in the Bible is a confrontation of human beings with a responsibility for an initiative to make themselves capable of receiving divine help. Thus, this is an emphasis in Scripture which does not support the view that man is incapable of taking the initiative without first having received grace to want to reorient his life. It therefore, does not support the view of St. Paul, which St. Augustine reaffirmed, that apart from God's grace to enable men to turn to him, they would be denied his grace.

After the Church was influenced by St. Paul's emphasis upon the total inability of the human being to take the initiative to turn to God without first having been a recipient of his grace, it formulated a canon of scripture which was relatively consistent with the Pauline emphasis. Luther later pointed out that the *Book of James* should not have been included in the canon of Christian scripture because of its emphasis upon the moral obligation of the human being as essential to fulfilling a religious obligation to God. The inconsistency of both maintaining that the human being is helpless apart from God's grace and is also morally responsible to condition himself to receive such grace would not have occurred in Christian thought if the negation of man's moral ability had not first been so uncompromisingly maintained. If, in other words, the position which is affirmed in *Ecclesiasticus* had determined Christian thought, this inconsistency would not have occurred. The author of this apocryphal writing declares: "If you choose, you can keep the commandments; whether or not you keep faith is yours to decide. He has set before you fire and water; reach out and take which you choose; before man lie life and death, and whichever he prefers is his." (15:15-17) This emphasis became basic to the point of view of Pelagius in the early fifth century and was condemned by the Church as heretical. But it was heretical only because incompatible with the Pauline view which maintains that the human being is totally dependent upon God's initiative toward human life. The human being's dependence upon God is not denied by the view affirmed in *Ecclesiasticus* and reaffirmed in Pelagianism. What alone is rejected by both interpretations is the view that the human being is so incapable of himself to do any good act that he is not even capable of wanting to be benefitted by the divine reality.

The point of view affirmed in *Ecclesiasticus* is compatible with a religious faith that the human being is finally dependent upon a divine providence for the enrichment of human life. But it does not maintain that man is so alienated from it that he cannot even revere it as desirable enough to make the effort to prepare himself to receive it.

The mistake of the Church was to follow the extreme view of St. Paul about the total helplessness of the human being without the grant of God's grace. If it had reaffirmed the interpretations in the Old Testament and in Wisdom literature, it would have maintained the insistence of man's de-

176

pendence upon God without also maintaining that man was so devoid of moral capacity that he could not even prepare himself to accept God's providence without first receiving God's grace to enable him to do so.

This extreme version of the human being's dependence upon God has the merit of stressing the incompleteness of human life apart from a providence which can enrich it. But denying that the human being has even a capacity to take the initiative to turn to God without first being dependent upon him for such an initiative has no merit other than logical consistency with an initial theological premise that God is the only source capable of doing for man what man cannot do for himself. This theological doctrine as such is sound. But its soundness is negated by the inference which is drawn from it that, therefore, man is totally incapable of any praiseworthy act apart from God's initial grace. The inference of man's helplessness to such a degree that he is not even morally responsible impairs a religious relation of human life to God. The only relation consistent with this overemphasis is God's relation to men. But again, this relation of God to men would not exclude men's initiative to enter into such a relation if it were not negated by the premise which attributes to God an initiative that excludes the human initiative.

This negating of the human initiative, however, is not essential to a type of religious relation which is affirmed throughout scriptural writings. The Psalmist, for example, declares: "How great is thy goodness stored up for those who fear thee." This single affirmation includes an acknowledgment of the preeminent dependence of the human being upon the goodness available to human life only in its relation to God. But it also points out that taking advantage of this benefaction confronts the human being with a responsibility. It is acknowledging his dependence for this blessing. An awareness that the blessing made possible in this relation to God can also be lost by his own negligence is the meaning of "fearing" God.

The fear of God is an awesome awareness of how much is at stake in failing to do what one must do in order to prepare oneself to receive God's benefactions. The Psalmist points this out when he declares that the "goodness" of God is available "for all who turn to (Him) for shelter". (31:19) But the dependence for such a benefit is not contingent upon denying the human being's obligation to prepare himself to receive it. The Psalmist reaffirms the human being's obligation to relate himself to God's providence when he declares: "The Lord will hold back no good thing from those whose life is blameless." (84:11) And again he declares: "Unfailing love enfolds him who trusts in the Lord." (32:10) These af-

177

firmations assert a mutuality in a relationship to God which is denied by the position that men can do nothing of their own initiative to prepare themselves to receive God's blessings.

Isaiah affirms the responsibility of the human being in relation to God by maintaining that "Your own righteousness shall be your vanguard". Upon condition of doing one's part to prepare oneself to receive God's benefaction, the benefaction can be experienced as it cannot be apart from such preparation. Isaiah maintains this priority of the human being's responsibility when he declares: "If you call, the Lord will answer." (58:8, 9.) He stresses mutuality in the human being's relation to God by indicating what a human being can do to condition himself to understand the meaning of God's providence for him. This can be learned by being generous in goodwill to other human beings: "If you feed the hungry . . . and satisfy the needs of the wretched", then there will also be an understanding of the nature of God's greater providence. (vs. 10) Just as one must first learn to take one step before he can walk, so he must learn the meaning of charity to others before he is capable of understanding the far greater charity of a divine providence.

Jeremiah likewise points out the obligation of the human being when he declares: "If each of you will turn from his wicked ways and evil courses . . . then you shall for ever live on the soil which the Lord gave to you and to your forefathers." (25:5, 6) Although this counsel was addressed to the Israelites, it, nevertheless, constitutes a universally sound counsel of responsibility for the human being in his relation of dependence upon God's providence. The Prophet attributes to God a willingness to withhold an intended punishment for the Israelites' infidelity, but on the condition that they alter their conduct which alienated them from their god. As a spokesman for God, Jeremiah declares: "But if the nation which I have threatened turns back from its wicked ways, then I shall think better of the evil I had in mind to bring on it." (18:9) This statement confronts a human being with an obligation and also an opportunity. His obligation is to live as a morally responsible individual should live. His opportunity is to forestall a penalty for which he would otherwise be morally responsible. He can thus make a difference in a god's relation to him by altering his relation to the god. This type of acting is morally responsible conduct.

The same emphasis upon moral responsibility is affirmed in Jeremiah's *Lamentations*: "The Lord is good to those who look for him, to all who seek him." (3:25) This aspect of the mutual relation between the human being and the deity is man's responsibility to "look" to the deity for his providence and to "seek" such providence. It is upon this condition of man's initiative that the initiative of God to man is contingent. Malachi maintains the same mutuality when, as a spokesman for "the Lord", he declares: "If you will return to me, I will return to you." (3:7) The same moral responsibility in relation to God is affirmed in *Ecclesiasticus*: "The Lord keeps watch over those who love him." (34:16) As stated, the providence of God is thus contingent upon what human beings do in orienting themselves to God.

The only justification for citing these several passages from the Old Testament as well as from *Ecclesiasticus* is to point out the scriptural emphasis upon the human obligation in relation to God. This emphasis constitutes evidence for a more balanced interpretation of the nature of the human being's relation to God than is affirmed in the writings of St. Paul and reaffirmed by St. Augustine.

Taking account of these passages is also instructive to realize that there is a scriptural basis for the Pelagian emphasis upon human responsibility. This responsibility, therefore, is not limited to the Wisdom literature, such as the *Wisdom of Solomon*, which maintains that wisdom "enters into holy souls, and makes them God's friends and prophets, for nothing is acceptable to God but the man who makes his home with wisdom". (7:27, 28) This interpretation of the human being's preparation to become a prophet of God thus differs from the position which maintains that it is God who selects the prophet. This interpretation, by contrast, maintains that after a human being has prepared himself by cultivating wisdom, he makes himself a worthy medium for the prophecies of God: "He is found by those who trust him." (1:2)

A parallel of this emphasis upon the human being's responsibility in relation to a reality he worships is affirmed by Aeschylus who maintains that "with pure altars (men) . . . gain the grace of the gods."[13] The closing lines of the Chorus in Euripides' *Ion* are: "The man whose pious soul reveres the gods, assumes a confidence, and justly; for the good at length obtain the meed of virtue."[14]

A highly commendable balanced interpretation of men's relation to a god and a god's relation to them is affirmed by Hippolytus in Euripides' play: "Of Gods, of men, each maketh still his choice."[15] This same balanced version of the mutuality or reciprocity in relation between human beings and God is affirmed by the Psalmist: "The upright will worship in thy presence." (140:13) Isaiah declares the same mutuality: "The Lord is supreme . . . if you fill Zion with justice and with righteousness." (33:5) That is, under conditions for which human beings are responsible, they enable themselves to affirm a religious faith that "The Lord is supreme". And such certitude is reinforced by what men themselves do to cultivate a capacity to acknowledge themselves as dependent upon God for what He can do for them that they cannot do for themselves. But such a benefaction is contingent upon the human context to create "with justice and with righteousness".

Human beings impose handicaps upon themselves by what they do since what they do determines what they become. The Psalmist points out that the "crafty schemes" of "the wicked man" is "his own undoing". As he becomes "obsessed with his own desires" and disregards all other avenues into the abundance of life, he denies himself the goods he might otherwise enjoy. (10:23) Isaiah affirms this same type of moral conditioning of a human being's life by what he does. One has the character of a "scoundrel" when he "will speak like a scoundrel". His acting becomes his nature, and such a nature in turn conditions his acting. Encouraging "evil in his heart", he becomes "an imposter in all his actions". Such acting likewise conditions his relation beyond human beings. It determines what he is in relation also to "the Lord". As the Prophet points out, after creating himself "a liar" by his own dishonesty to others, he likewise becomes "a liar even to the Lord". (32:6)

Wisdom literature affirms this same type of moral conditioning of a human being's relation to God. *The Wisdom of Solomon* declares: "Dishonest thinking cuts men off from God." (1:3) After a human being has handicapped himself by his own dishonesty in all of his relations, his dishonesty determines the only possible relation he also has to a god. In the terminology of Wisdom literature, "This holy spirit . . . will have nothing to do with falsehood; she cannot stay in the presence of unreason". (vs. 5).

The traits of character which are esteemed as most praiseworthy in human life become the standards by which morally enlightened human beings think of their obligations to a god. And it is in terms of the same standards that they think of a god's expectations of them. Isaiah points out this relation between men's esteem for justice and their interpretation of God's requirement of justice when he declares that God "looked for justice and found it denied." (5:7) Jeremiah likewise points out that what is respected as the most worthy of men's relations to others becomes regarded as god's requirements of men. He refers to "deal(ing) fairly with one another"; not "oppress(ing) the orphan and the widow, shed(ding) no innocent blood" as God's expectations of men's fidelity to Him. (7:5, 6) These most esteemed principles of human acting in rela-

180

tion to other human beings are regarded as God's criteria for men's obligations to Him.

The relation between respect for justice to others and also to God is pointed out in *The Wisdom of Solomon* when its author combines the responsibilities to "love justice" and to "set your mind upon the Lord". He refers to these as "your duty". And in loving justice and "trust(ing) God", he assures human beings that God "is found". (1:2)

A parallel correlation of men's respect for justice and what it entails in their relation to the gods may be extracted from Greek sources by combining a statement from Hesiod with another from Aristophanes! Hesiod declares: "They who give straight judgments to strangers and to the men of the land, and go not aside from what is just, their city flourishes, and the people prosper in it."[16] And Aristophanes has Hermes censure the Greeks for their inclination to war rather than prefer the ways of peace, by declaring that "the gods . . . moved . . . at the furthest end of the dome of heaven" and did so "because of their wrath against the Greeks . . . they went as high up as ever they could, so as to see no more of your fights and to hear no more of your prayers."[17]

Both Greek and Israelite writers point out moral obstacles which men impose upon divine realities in relation to human beings. In other words, human beings handicap what divine realities can do for them. They create obstacles which deny themselves benefactions which might otherwise be forthcoming from divine sources. Aristophanes has Hermes declare that "Because (the gods) have afforded you an opportunity for peace more than once, but you have always preferred war," men have brought a curse upon themselves. This most tragic of curses is that they may never "see Peace again". [18] A parallel of this self-inflicted curse which human beings bring upon themselves is declared by Jeremiah in his condemnation of Judah for its wickedness. Speaking for God, he declares: "Offer up no prayer for this people; raise no cry or prayer on their behalf, for I will not listen when they call to me in the hour of disaster." (11:14) The Prophet thus interprets the disaster which fell upon the people of Judah as brought upon themselves by what they failed to do that they ought to have done. Their own failure imposed upon them a disaster from which their prayers could not free them. This is a type of self-imposed handicap to human life from which there is neither release by what men subsequently do to help themselves or by all they do in praying for a god's help. The finality of a self-imposed penalty for such an avoidable moral neglect is included in what the Greeks mean by "doom" and the Israelites mean by "perdition".

The converse of such self-imposed handicaps are moral benefits which accrue to what human beings themselves do and which therefore are not dependent upon factors over which they themselves do not have control. The Psalmist declares: "In thy commandments I find continuing delight." (119:47) This moral benefit to which he refers comes about within his life by virtue of his own decision to turn to such commandments for their instruction. Since such instruction is attributed to an eternal source, there is no temporal limit set upon their availability. In other words, whereas every temporal good is subject to the contingency of an order in which it is internal, the commandments of an eternal god are not so contingent. When the Psalmist declares "I put my trust in thy commandments", he orients himself to a source of help which will always be available to him in his need for dependable instruction. Making such a decision is bringing within his own control a good which he himself determines by what he himself does. Even the most elusive of human blessings is brought within the scope of a human being's own control by his own decision to relate himself to a reality which is trustworthy because it is not contingent upon any other reality. The Psalmist, referring to the commandments, whose source he attributes to God, declares: "Happy are they who obey his instruction." (119:2) Happiness, as the most elusive good in human life, is thus brought within an individual's own control. So analyzed, it is not dependent upon a relation to any transient reality, such as a human being.

In the Psalmist's orienting himself to a reality which is always available, he thus frees himself from trusting what is not totally trustworthy. He declares: "Thou has set me free." The freedom of which he speaks is a moral freedom from being driven in the pursuit of goods which reinforce desire without satisfying it. In maintaining that "The Lord . . . has granted all my desire", the Psalmist points out that by virtue of depending upon what he receives of God's providence, he frees himself from bondage to insatiable desires. (13:6) Thus by virtue of his own decision to look for no good other than the noncontingent providence of God, he brings within his own control the trustworthy reality of an eternal good. He does not liberate himself from the insatiable hungers which blight human beings, and deny them lasting satisfaction, but it is the reality to which he turns which accomplishes this in his life. He orients himself to such a reality, and thus by virtue of his acting, he determines what can be done in his life by such a reality transcendent of his life. When the Psalmist declares "I am satisfied as with a rich and sumptuous feast", he points out that the reality which satisfies him is not within his own nature, but it is a reality to which he orients himself. (63:5) The analogy, of course, is not entirely

182

atisfactory, since there is no enduring satisfaction from any "feast" no matter how "sumptuous" it may be. It would be more consistent, therefore, with what the Psalmist means if it were to be said that in relating himself to the trustworthy guidance of God's commandments, he has a quality of well-being whose freedom from insatiable hunger is a type of satisfaction which no "sumptuous feast" of perishable food could bring about.

The type of good of which the Psalmist speaks is intrinsic to what he himself does in relating himself to a reality which does not refer him beyond it. Thus he is spared from the sorrow of seeking without finding. He is freed from striving for goods which only elude his grasp. He declares: "Peace is the reward of those who love thy law." (119:165) In this affirmation, he makes the twofold condition for such a supreme benefit perfectly clear. The law which he loves is transcendent of himself, but his love for it is his own act. Loving the law of God is what he himself does, and in this act he receives the supreme moral good of "peace".

Such peace of which he speaks is freedom from seeking goods which do not satisfy, but which refer beyond themselves. And as this neverending series continues, an individual puts himself into the plight from which Ixion suffered. Just as such suffering was a possibility of which the Psalmist as a human being was capable, so likewise his freedom from it was also a possibility of which he not only was capable but of which he took moral advantage. The moral advantage was both by virtue of what he did, and also by virtue of the reality to which he related himself. Such benefaction in his life would not have been realized without both of these conditions.

Isaiah refers to the same type of moral benefit which is within a human being's control by what he does to orient himself to a reality other than himself which can yield him a blessing such as no other reality can. He declares: "Righteousness shall yield peace and its fruit be quietness and confidence forever." (32:17) The assurance that such a benefaction is not threatened with ending is by virtue of the nature of the reality to which he relates himself in cultivating righteousness of life. Such cultivating is a discipline within his control, but the quality of life which comes about as a result of such effort is not determined by his effort. His effort relates him to a reality which accomplishes this in his life by virtue of his relation to it. The twofold conditions for the "peace", "quietness", and "confidence" of which the Prophet speaks are basic to a religious relation to a reality which blesses him.

Although there is not the number of examples of such religious acts in

Greek literature as in the literature of the early Israelites, there neve. theless are some. Aeschylus, for example, takes account of the blessin which accrues to a moral act as its intrinsic nature when the Chorus i *Eumenides* declares: "From health of soul cometh happiness, dear unt all and oft besought in prayer."[19] In maintaining that happiness is a cor relation intrinsic to "health of soul", Aeschylus affirms a moral philosoph which Aristotle later expanded into his *Nicomachean Ethics*. Happines is the normative moral good according to both Aristotle and Aeschylu According to Aeschylus, it is "often besought in prayer", which Aristotl of course, does not consider as one of the means by which reasonabl human life can be achieved. The basic difference, therefore, is evident i the rationalistic moral philosophy of Aristotle and in the religious thinkin of which Aeschylus is so capable. But even as Aeschylus affirms the rela tion of "happiness" to "health of soul", he takes account of an intrinsi good which comes about in human life upon the condition of living in way of which the human being is capable and for which he is responsibl as the agent for bringing about "health of soul". The same intrinsic rela tion between what a human being does and what takes place in his life i pointed out in another translation: "The man who does right, free-willed without constraint, shall not lose happiness nor be wiped out with all hi generation."[20]

What occurs in the lives of human beings is correlated with what the do. What an individual therefore does which differs from what others d accounts for the difference in the qualities of their lives. This relation does not necessarily depend upon a religious interpretation. A religiou interpretation of the conditions for moral well-being specifically acknowl edges that there is a reality transcendent of the total context of the huma and the physical "worlds" to which a human being can beneficially relat himself which has properties such as human resources and the physica world do not have. And these properties are revered in a religious faitl as being eternal, such as no other reality is.

VI

Intrinsic Moral Judgment

1. *Human beings bring moral judgment upon themselves*

Human beings bring upon themselves the consequences of their own acting. The relation between what they do and what their acting entails in their own lives is a judgment upon the moral nature of their acting. This relation, therefore, does not include a reference beyond the human being himself. His acting and its effects upon the quality of his life are internal to himself. An individual may benefit himself by the moral soundness of his decisions, and he may likewise handicap himself by acting which is detrimental to his well-being.

Jeremiah takes account of this relation between what human beings do and what their acting brings about in their own natures when, speaking for "the Lord", he asks: "But is it I . . . whom they hurt?" And the answer which is given is "No; it is themselves, covering their own selves with shame." (7:19) So interpreted, what people do determines what either benefits them with well-being or denies them well-being. This same relation is affirmed by Hosea in reprimanding his people for their censurable ways of living: "You have ploughed wickedness into your soil, and the crop is mischief." (10:13) In other words, what they have done determines what they have a reasonable right to expect will be forthcoming from their acting.

The same type of relation between what human beings do and what is entailed for them by their acting is affirmed by Aeschylus when Hermes enjoins Prometheus: Do not "say that it was Zeus who cast you into suffering unforeseen. Not so, but blame yourselves. For well forewarned,

185

and not at unawares or secretly, shall ye be entangled in the inextricable net of calamity by reason of your folly."[1] Sophocles points out the same basic relation between acting wisely and enjoying the benefits of such acting when Philoctetes declares: "To those who fly from ill all winds are fair."[2]

The relation between what human beings do and what they thereby become is pointed out in *Second Kings*: "They followed worthless idols and became worthless themselves." (17:15) This interpretation of inevitable consequences entailed in ways of living is affirmed internal to human life itself: "Pursuing empty phantoms" a people "themselves become empty."

This stern interpretation of human life was current among Israelites and was preserved in their proverbs. One such proverb which takes account of the relation between what human beings do and what they themselves become by virtue of their acting cautions against answering "a stupid man in the language of his folly, or you will grow like him" (26:4) This relation was acknowledged through the entire tradition of the Prophets and was basic to the sobering reflecting in apocryphal writings. *Ecclesiasticus* declares: "Keep company with an arrogant man and you will grow like him." (13:1) When the author of *Ecclesiasticus* urged people to "Refuse ever to tell a lie" because "it is a habit from which no good comes", he was aware of the moral problem of cultivating habitual patterns of acting by the repetition of a type of acting until such habit in turn determines subsequent acting. Pointing out this relation is, therefore, merely reaffirming a moral principle stressed by Isaiah in maintaining that "the scoundrel will speak like a scoundrel", in the sense that a human being's nature is conditioned by what he himself does. (32:6) And what he continues to do becomes habit-formation which is his character.

The judgment of which the Psalmist speaks when he rebuked the Israelites for their practice of idolatry does not mention the displeasure of their god. It takes account rather of what the Israelites themselves become in the practice of such idolatry. He declared that "makers (of idols) grow like them, and so do all who trust in them". Just as idols worshipped by men have "eyes that cannot see", so men who worship them likewise lose the clarity of vision to be aware of their own folly. Hosea declared the same type of judgment upon Ephraim without also referring to the intervention of God when he maintained that "Ephraim became as loathsome as the thing he loved". (9:11)

The relation between what is done and what occurs to condition the

186

ature of a human being is basic to collective human life just as it is
asic to individual human life. Isaiah refers to "the proud garlands of the
runkards of Ephraim and the flowering sprays" with which they
ecorated themselves, "so lovely in their beauty on the heads of revellers
ripping with perfumes". (28:1) The moral penalty for what seems to
e such a delightful way to live is that they became revellers by virtue of
eir behavior. The aesthetic feature of their activities, referred to by the
rophet as "so lovely in their beauty", did not curtail the moral penalty
f losing what intelligence they might have had to direct themselves with
concern for a sounder basis for moral benefit than being "overcome
ith wine". When the author of *Ecclesiastes,* referred to as "the son of
)avid", maintains that "there is nothing good for a man to do here under
ae sun but to eat and drink and enjoy himself", he points out the moral
)nsequence of such a pattern of living when he says that "this is all that
ill remain with him to reward his toil throughout the span of life".
8:15) This is equivalent in moral significance to the repeated declara-
ons in Scripture that some ways of living constitute such a poverty of
fe that it is as if such life had never been. Such a way of living con-
ributes nothing significant to human history. As Hegel points out, periods
a which there is only a preoccupation with pleasures or happiness are
blank pages" in the history of spirit.[3]

A poverty of morally constructive conduct in a scheme of human life
; the negation of its moral worth. When actual wrongdoing by an in-
ividual is included in the pattern of his life, he handicaps the life of
very other human being affected by what he does. Isaiah points out that
rhen there is "no justice" which guides people, "all the paths they follow
re crooked". So stated, this is a judgment about the nature of an entire
fe conditioned by its acts of injustice. It becomes incapable of doing
ther than what it has become as a result of its own behavior. And the
dditional moral penalty of such injustice for which an individual is re-
ponsible is that he cannot "enjoy true peace" of mind. Isaiah declares:
No one who walks in (the steps of injustice) enjoys true peace." (59:8)
his is thus judgment upon an individual by what he himself does, and
he author of *The Wisdom of Solomon* points out the sternest penalty a
uman being can suffer when he maintains that "in our wickedness we
rittered our lives away". (5:14) The record of such a life is itself a
udgment that it would have made no difference in human history if it
ad never been.

Homer points out the same type of judgment upon human beings
rhich likewise does not entail the intervention of a reality external to

human beings themselves. After the return of Odysseus and his disposi‸ of the suitors of Penelope, she declared: "And now their iniquities ha▾ brought them to this pass."[4] Another translation affirms: "So they ha▾ suffered for their own recklessness."[5]

Entailed in every pattern of excess is the penalty that going beyor reasonable limit in any behavior motivated by desire is that the desi‸ itself is not satisfied in such excess. It is merely intensified. Such desir‸ entail their own penalty in becoming incapable of being satisfied. Isaia stresses this relation between excessive greediness and an insatiab‸ hunger for more when he maintains that the "greedy . . . can nev‸ have enough". (56:11) Hosea affirms the same type of moral judgme‸ upon desires incapable of being satisfied when he declares that his pe‸ ple "shall eat but never be satisfied". (4:10) Micah refers to such i‸ satiable hungers as "a signal punishment" inflicted upon men: It is th‸ they "shall eat but not be satisfied". (6:14)

The same moral penalty for doing what cannot accomplish what ‸ intended by such a type of acting is affirmed by Haggai when he a‸ dresses his people whom he characterizes as "clothed but never warm"‸ And to intensify the character of this sort of moral penalty, he refers t "the labourer (who) puts his wages into a purse with a hole in it". (1:7 This is the equivalent of many of the moral lessons in Greek mytholog‸ such as the ceaseless and futile dipping of water with a sieve or reachi‸ for water which recedes as one bends to drink it.

The sternest type of penalty for misdirecting one's life in a behavio‸ which consumes life without contributing to its enrichment is chara‸ terized in many ways in the *Book of Job* which considers the effect ‸ wrongdoing upon the moral light by which one might otherwise have live‸ Bildad the Shuhite, a friend of Job, maintains that "it is the wicke‸ whose light is extinguished, from whose fire no flame will rekindle'‸ (18:5) The pathos of this version of moral penalty is stressed by th‸ progressive decrease of an enlightenment in an individual's life until "hi lamp dies down and fails him". (18:6) A progressively decreasing mora sensitivity is the penalty entailed in moral wrongdoing. Such continue‸ behavior makes an individual incapable of being a critic of his ow‸ behavior. The opposite effect upon whatever moral light of conscienc‸ an individual may have is also pointed out when Job, in the secon‸ cycle of discussions with his friends, maintains that "in spite of all" th reverses and discouragements in one's life, "the righteous man maintain‸ his course, and he whose hands are clean grows strong again". (17:8, 9 In other words, even though one's life may be anything but an unbroke‸

equence of encouragements and achievements, still if he retains a capacity to pass judgment upon his own behavior, he retains his moral leverage over it. It is still within his final control notwithstanding the long struggle he may have had to preserve it. But when this last core of moral leverage internal to an individual's life becomes progressively reduced until it no longer functions, an individual is defeated beyond his own capacities to help himself.

The most graphic description of this progressive loss of moral leverage over one's own life is given by Isaiah when he declares that his people's 'wits are dulled, their ears are deafened and their eyes blinded, so that they cannot see with their eyes nor listen with their ears, nor understand with their wits, so that they may turn and be healed". (6:10) After an individual loses his capacities to censure a way of living into which he has slipped, he becomes helpless to free himself from such a cultivated handicap to his own well-being. The moral penalty entailed in this loss of leverage over one's life is that he cannot even "turn" from the bondage into which he has entered in order to be "healed" of the handicap to his well-being. A parallel of such a pathetic human being is suggested by Jeremiah who asks if it is reasonable to expect that "the Nubian change his skin, or the leopard its spots?" And then he makes the moral application of this parallel when he asks: "And you? Can you do good, you who are schooled in evil?" (13:23) This relation between what human beings do to destroy their own ability to liberate themselves from a bondage which they themselves create is not stated by the Prophet with reference to a judgment imposed upon human life from a source external to itself. In other words, it is not interpreted from a specifically religious perspective.

On the other hand, such a relation between what people do and the bondage into which they enter by their wrongdoing is interpreted by Amos from his religious perspective. He declares that "Men shall stagger from north to south, they shall range from east to west, seeking the word of the Lord, but they shall not find it". (8:12) Their handicap to such discovery is the way of living itself which they have practiced without taking into account the inevitable handicap that it precludes their reorienting themselves into a different way of life.

2. *Moral judgment may be independent of a divine reality*

When one of the friends of Job maintained that "the course of the wicked man" constitutes a "foundation flowing away like a river", he

did not take account of a reality transcendent of human life for establish‑
ing the relation between human conduct and the "foundation" or th‑
basis of human life. (22:16) The basis of human life is impaired o‑
destroyed by the wrongdoing itself of which human beings are capable
The same type of relation is maintained by Jeremiah when he declare‑
that "It is your own wickedness that will punish you". One type o‑
wrongdoing or wickedness which was especially grave from the Prophet'‑
religious perspective is the infidelity of the Israelites, and yet, he di‑
not even specify that this "wickedness" was penalized by the direct ac‑
of their god. He maintains rather that it is "your own apostasy tha‑
will condemn you". (2:19)

His omission of a reference to a divine judgment does not, of course
indicate that he did not believe there is such a source of punishment fo‑
the faithless. But what is significant in this particular condemnation o‑
apostasy is that its consequences would be evident in the impairment o‑
their own religious faith, and so it would deny them the benefits o‑
their own trust in divine providence. He affirms this type of penalty o‑
"punishment" when, in referring to their reverses and suffering as ‑
people, he maintains that "Your own ways, your own deeds have brough‑
all this upon you". And he tells them that "this is your punishment"‑
(4:18) What is included in the range of such "punishment" is not onl‑
their political and social reverses. It is also their "own ways" or thei‑
"own deeds" which constitute a punishment for those who are responsibl‑
for them. Becoming what they were as a people alienated from the god
whom their prophets trusted for providence, they incurred upon them‑
selves a handicap to their own blessedness.

Hosea pointed out to his people that the wrongdoing for which they
were responsible was their own "undoing". He declared: "Ephraim's
guilt is his undoing, and Judah no less is undone." (5:5) Thus condi‑
tions internal to their suffering were, according to the Prophet, directly
related to what they themselves had done to entail such a handicap to
their security and well-being. Although as a prophet Hosea believed that
his people are under their god's judgment for their wickedness, he did
not offer this religious explanation for their so-called "undoing". He
explained it entirely within the scope of their own responsibility for
bringing about the conditions from which they suffered.

Even the collective infidelity of the Israelites to their god is not in‑
terpreted by the prophet Ezra as a wickedness for which the only
penalty is a direct judgment by their god. Speaking for the god of his
people, he declared: "It is not I whom you have deserted, but yourselves,

says the Lord." (II, 1:27) Ezra thus explains that men, by their infidelity to their god, cut themselves off from the ultimate source of good. In other words, men's infidelity is their own penalty for their apostasy or their faithlessness to their god.

This profound understanding of the impairment of men's life by their own faithlessness to God is pointed out by the author of *The Wisdom of Solomon* who declares that "because they took no account of justice and rebelled against the Lord" they "shall meet with the punishment their evil thoughts deserve". (3:10) Their punishment is their turning from "the Lord", which punishment is invariant with ignoring their obligations to respect justice. Failing to respect justice as an ultimate moral obligation is itself a moral penalty they thereby "deserve". And disregarding their dependence upon God's providence is itself punishment for their infidelity. The moral penalty entailed in their infidelity to the ultimate source of wisdom is that in ignoring such wisdom, they lose "the power to recognize what is good". An additional moral penalty is that the record they "leave by their lives" is a "monument of folly". (10:9)

Living without wisdom is folly, and a religious interpretation of this moral penalty is that, living in folly, they cut themselves off from the providence of God which is a wisdom by which men may live enlightened lives. A life devoid of such providence, as the ultimate guide of human life, is without stability and security. It is as a tree which "For a time . . . may flourish, but as it has no sure footing . . . will be shaken by the wind, and by the violence of the winds uprooted". (4:4) The plight of a life without adequate foundation is its own instability.

Even when the relation between what men do and what may be interpreted as "penalty" for their wrongdoing is interpreted as an expression of divine judgment, men's own responsibility is always acknowledged. If it were not for this invariant relation between what men do and the consequences in their own lives, interpreted as judgment by a god, the god's judgment would be unrelated to men's moral desert.

This would be consistent only with the most primitive versions of religion, the principal ingredient of which is magic rather than moral sensitivity. *First Kings* affirms a religious interpretation of a human being related to a god whose judgment consists of "bringing his deeds upon his own head". (8:32) This religious interpretation affirms that a divine reality assures the invariance of relation between wrongdoing and impairment of human life by its wrongdoing.

The invariant relation as such between the type of acting for which human beings are responsible and its consequences in their lives is not established by God's judgment. Jeremiah affirms a religious interpretation of the role of God in human life when, as a spokesman for God, he declares to his people: "You provoked me to anger with the idols your hands had made and so brought harm upon yourselves." (25:7) Thus the Prophet does not maintain that God's judgment of men is creating the invariance between what men do and what is the consequence of their acting. Such invariance is intrinsic to human nature. It is the relation between what men do and what they become by virtue of their acting.

Ezekial affirms a religious interpretation of the relation between men's wrongdoing and the tragic consequences which accrue to it, such as when they "shed blood within" the city in which they wage war with other human beings. He declares: "These are the words of the Lord God: Alas for the city that sheds blood within her walls and brings her fate upon herself." The Prophet thus points out that war internal to a people entails the tragic fate or destiny of such a people. He declares: "The guilt is yours for the blood you have shed." (22:4) The religious character of this pronouncement is the Prophet's ascription of this judgment to God's decree. But the judgment of God does not establish the invariance between their acting and the fate it entails. God's judgment rather is expressed through such an invariant relation internal to human life.

Aeschylus illustrates this religious interpretation of an invariant moral relation between what men do and its conseqeunces in their lives when he refers in *The Persians* to the arrogance of Xerxes, "drawing on himself the punishment of Heaven by his vaunting rashness".[6]

3. *Intrinsic moral judgment is entailed in what human beings do*

Intrinsic moral judgments are consequences entailed in what human beings do. This moral invariance of the relation between antecedents which entail consequences is unlike the logical invariance which is entailed in consequents that are affirmed as implied in antecedents. Moral invariance is not a function of an assertion or a proposition. It is an aspect of human nature itself. The very condition for the moral seriousness of human acting is that acting itself entails consequences in human life which are invariantly related to such morally significant antecedents. This moral relation is affirmed in the fourth chapter of the first book in the Bible. This chapter in *Genesis* narrates the instruction given to Cain by his creator: "Then the Lord said to Cain . . . 'If you

192

do well, you hold your head up; if not, sin . . . crouch(es) at the door. It shall be eager for you, and you will be mastered by it' ". (vs. 6, 7) Thus a twofold relation is affirmed. One is between doing well, with the desirable moral consequences of such acting. Another is its moral opposite: it is being "mastered" or enslaved by a way of acting whose consequences are handicaps to well-being.

The *Book of Job* declares this moral relationship as a certitude: "This I know", Eliphaz, the friend of Job, declares, "that those who plough mischief and sow trouble reap as they have sown." (4:8) This moral relationship which is internal to human acting is so basic to the reflecting on human life in this book in the Bible that it is affirmed several times. In the second cycle of discourse between Eliphaz and Job, Eliphaz maintains that a human being's "iniquity dictates what (he) says and deceit is the language of (his) choice". (15:5) In other words, an individual becomes addicted to deception in what he speaks after he has disregarded a moral responsibility for integrity. Had an integrity of character been cultivated by persistent discipline, whatever he said would have been worthy of being trusted by another. But the very opposite occurs when an individual does not hold himself accountable to a moral principle of honesty in his relation to others.

Another friend of Job, Bildad the Shuhite, continues the discourse by enumerating various graphic figures to stress the impairment of human life which is entailed in acting that is censurable. He declares: "It is the wicked whose light is extinguished" in their own lives. (18:5) Thus a practice of wrongdoing progressively diminishes moral capacities for doing what brings about moral benefits. As "the light" of moral sensitivity or conscience "fades . . . and fails", an individual becomes progressively less capable of being able to direct his own acting by his own understanding of what it would be beneficial to do. Then the Shuhite ushers a considerable battery of descriptive figures to intensify his moral argument by pointing out that as an individual loses the capacity to judge his own behavior, his own inability "trips him up" and "he rushes headlong into a net" of handicaps to his own well-being. He becomes "caught in a snare", and in addition, a "noose", as it were, "grips him", and finally he becomes as incapable of moral freedom as one who is bound in "a trap". (18:5-10)

These graphic figures, however, are entirely inadequate in such a moral analysis since all of them are external to the individual himself. What on the other hand constitutes the nature of an intrinsic moral handicap is that it is entailed in acting itself. What acting itself brings about is

193

internal to an individual's life. What, on the other hand, is of hortatory value in the Shuhite's use of such graphic figures, is that an individual progressively loses his ability to select between moral options after he no longer sustains such an ability by persistent discipline.

The Psalmist continues the same sobering reflecting as occupied so considerable a part of the discourses between Job and his reflective friends. He reaffirms a relationship which had been pointed out in the discourses in *The Book of Job*, declaring that men are "destroyed by their own sinful words", and "what they have spoken entrap them". (59:11, 12) This is merely affirming a fact of which most people are aware as the penalty for declaring a falsehood. It is that one continues to support a falsehood with others, and the sequence is without end. It illustrates the ancient Greek principle that the unlimited is the nature of evil. As if the Psalmist were familiar with the conversations in *The Book of Job*, he uses another figure which had been used by Bildad the Shuhite: "The wicked fall into their own nets." (141:10) This is merely pointing out that there is no limit internal to what already is an unlimited. The nature of any evil is that there is no limit internal to it to restrict the indefinite extension of its moral handicap.

This itself is the moral penalty entailed in evil. Evil is a way of acting which does not include within itself a limit. The same moral penalty is entailed in types of acting which are censurable for corporate life, such as nations. The Psalmist declares: "The nations have plunged into a pit of their own making; their own feet are entangled in the net which they hid"—obviously for their enemies. (9:16) In other words, the very means by which one nation attempts to destroy another becomes the means by which it itself is destroyed. Jesus reaffirms this principle in declaring that "They who take the sword shall perish by the sword". A way of acting which is destructive of another's welfare entails the consequences of destroying one's own welfare.

Proverbs are highly condensed moral philosophies. One of these is that people "shall eat the fruits of their behavior". (1:31) This same principle which affirms an invariant relation between what is done by human beings and what later confronts them with their own handicaps is affirmed in the folk wisdom of every people whether primitive or civilized. It is one fact which people have learned, but learned too late to be a principle which enlightened their own acting. It is, however, a sound principle which they affirm in retrospect. It could, therefore, be of advantage to others provided others were to believe that they could benefit from the wisdom gained by others. But learning this much is itself a relatively rare occurrence in human history. Hence the cycle recurs of living without taking advantage of a wisdom which others acquired in the course of their living.

Proverbs preserves the same type of wisdom as was expressed in *The Book of Job* and *Psalms*. One such proverb declares that "The wicked man is trapped by his own falsehoods". (12:13) What is significant in taking account of this proverb is the soundness of a generalization that has been repeated throughout the centuries of reflecting on the nature of human life. *Proverbs* repeats the figure of being ensnared when it declares that "An evil man is ensnared by his sin". (29:6) One particular "sin" or wrongdoing in which a moral penalty is internal to acting itself is the case in which "rogues are trapped in their own greed". (11:6) A principle repeatedly affirmed in these ancient books of scripture is the same basic principle which the Greeks regarded as a metaphysical fact of reality that whatever is without a limit internal to its nature is an evil. Human greed is one such evil. It includes within its nature a momentum of moral handicap until an individual is penalized by a "surfeit" of his own acting.

The long tradition of the prophetic voice in the history of the Israelites repeats the same moral generalizations which had been formulated throughout the centuries in the reflecting of this people. Isaiah uses the figure of "weav(ing) cobwebs" to assure his people that "their webs . . . will never make cloth". (59:5, 6) This is reminding them that no foundation for life can be constructed out of materials which cannot carry a load intended for them. The weight of life's load of problems cannot be supported on the flimsy structure of fancies. Only sound moral principles can dependably carry the heavy burden of trustworthy direction for a human life confronted by the complexity of making difficult decisions. And the difficulty of making repeated decisions is diminished by the use of sound principles whose applications are inexhaustible, and therefore whose repeated applications confirm the wisdom of their continued use.

Jeremiah points out that a people who "have trained their tongues to lies" become incapable of honestly relating themselves to others. (9:5) The moral penalty for permitting oneself to slip into this pattern of dishonesty is that people "cannot retrace their steps". This is the sobering nature of ways of acting which disregard limit until they become incapable of being limited by an individual himself. The gravity of continuing a pattern of acting which progressively becomes incapable of being checked by an individual himself is a type of "iniquity" which Ezekiel declares "will be your downfall". (18:31) This penalty, in other

words, is the inability of an individual to alter what he himself has be
come in continuing a pattern of acting that increasingly makes him help
less to change it.

This same stern reflecting is formulated in many ways by the minor
prophets, such as Hosea, who declares that "Ephraim's guilt is his
undoing". (5:5) Obadiah addresses himself to his people, declaring:
"Your proud, insolent heart has led you astray." (1:3) And he assures
them that it will continue to be the case that "your deeds will recoil on
your own head". (vs. 15) Micah cautions his people against letting
themselves penalize themselves by their moral negligence of not being
critically aware of what is entailed for their own bondage by types of
insatiable desires: "You shall eat but not be satisfied." (6:13)

The philosophical prophet Ezra generalizes as a moral fact in human
history that a people "shall perish in their injustice". (I,4:38) And then
he interprets the wrongdoing of his people from his religious point of
view when he declares that "the wicked heart has grown up in us which
has estranged us from God's ways . . . and carried us far away from life."
(II,7:48) Thus the moral consequence of "the wicked heart", as the
Prophet points out, is twofold. It impairs man's relation to God by
"estrang(ing)" life from the ultimate source of its providential good, and
it thereby destroys the worth of life itself, "carry(ing) us far away from
life".

The Wisdom of Solomon includes a generalizing of moral principles,
such as "Evil . . . dims the radiance of good". (3:12) On the basis of
this moral wisdom, its author proposes the sobering moral warning: "Do
not draw disaster on yourself by your actions." (1:13) This warning is
on the basis of the moral principle of the invariance between what human
beings do and what they become as a consequence of their acting.

Homer defends the action of Odysseus in ridding his palace of the
unscrupulous suitors when he has "the aged lord Halitherses" address
the Ithacans, asking them for their "attention". Then he declares:
"Your own wickedness . . . is to blame for what has happened . . . your
sons . . . threw all restraint to the winds" in what they did to exploit the
undefended palace during the absence of its master.[7]

Hesiod likewise points out how blind human beings can be to a handicap entailed in their acting when they think only of an immediate
advantage of what they do. He takes account of the sobering fact that
men will eventually destroy themselves while they are preoccupied only
with what seems to be a present advantage. He has Zeus declare that
men will pay dearly for what they regard as the benefit they received

from Prometheus which went counter to the plan of Zeus: "I will give men as the price for fire an evil thing in which they may all be glad at heart while they embrace their own destruction."[8] Every detail of this declaration by Zeus might well be regarded as anticipating the eventual penalty the human race may pay for the specious advantages of nuclear energy. Hesiod likewise affirms another principle which is as applicable today as it was in the century in which he formulated it: "He does mischief to himself who does mischief to another, and evil planned harms the plotter most."[9] The validity of this principle is unrestricted in every application to human life, whether it be individual behavior or the collective decisions of a people in their corporate policies.

One of the most disturbing consequences of human wrongdoing is interpreted by Hesiod in a religious terminology when he predicts the tragic disasters among human beings which will accrue to the neglect of their obligations to the gods: "Reverence will cease to be." And when this becomes the spiritual blight of human life, "the wicked will hurt the worthy man, speaking false words against him".[10] The loss of reverence for an ultimate sovereignty over human life entails the dissolution of respect for moral obligations. Rather than respecting moral obligations, men ignore them, and in doing so, disregard considerations for the rights of others.

A stern moral penalty which, according to Hesiod, can blight human beings is destroying a feeling of reverence for a reality entitled to exert a restraint upon men from doing wrong. This trait of character is referred to in ancient Greek reflecting by the term *Aidos*. "Aidos" is the moral quality of an individual's attitude which acknowledges with reverence what he recognizes has a moral right to be revered. Another impairment of the moral capacities of which a human being is capable is his loss of indignation against a moral outrage. When an individual becomes indifferent to whatever takes place, so that evil acting no more raises a denunciation than good acting elicits approbation, an individual loses the moral trait of *Nemesis* in his life, which is a moral protest against a moral wrongdoing. Hesiod refers to both *Aidos* and *Nemesis* as having a precarious status in the moral fabric of the human being so that they are capable of being destroyed in human life with the resulting tragedy that a human being loses his moral nature. Hesiod declares: "Aidos and Nemesis . . . will go from the wide-pathed earth and forsake mankind to join the company of the deathless gods; and bitter sorrows will be left for mortal men, and there will be no help against evil."[11]

There could be no more eloquent expression in any philosophical literature of the moral tragedy of men themselves destroying their own moral sensitivities. This is intrinsic moral judgment. Men judge themselves as morally too helpless to preserve their own moral sensitivities as the essential conditions for saving themselves from the inroads of evil into their individual and collective lives. Since Hesiod interprets their moral penalty which men impose upon themselves in terms of a religious belief that Aidos and Nemesis are divine dispensations in human life, it is not indefensible to say that there is no affirmation in the Bible more eloquent than this reference to a divine judgment upon human life. Such divine judgment becomes an incapacity of human life itself to respect moral principles whose beneficial requirements of a human being are not conferred upon them by the human being. He is rather dependent upon them for his moral nature, and without them, his acting is without the benefit of moral enlightenment.

Hesiod interprets the sternest of moral judgment in a way which parallels the manner of the Prophets when he says that "Zeus will destroy this race of mortal men" just as he destroyed previous races which he had created. And Zeus will do so when the present race deteriorates to such an extent that a new born child will show the marks of ravage of old age. His expression for this sign of impending destruction of the human race is "when they come to have grey hair on the temples at their birth". The type of human behavior which will signal the end of the human race by virtue of its moral unworthiness to continue is that there will be discord in the most elemental of human relations such as between a father and his children: "The father will not agree with his children, nor the children with their father" and "brother will not be dear to brother". There will be a disregard of the basic obligations and right of hospitality: there will be discord between a "guest and his host". There will be a cancellation in human relations which constitute the essential condition for friendship: there will no longer be accord between "comrade and comrade".[12]

Aeschylus maintains that men will "be entangled in the inextricable net of calamity by reason of (their own) folly".[13] And he accounts for the genesis of such "folly" in living according to their own "delusions". The opening chorus in *The Suppliant Maidens* declares that "through delusions (men's) minds turned to folly", and such "delusion" internal to human life brings about human misfortunes and disasters.[14] The Chorus in *The Persians* describes the moral peril of delusion as "semblance of fair intent", and points out how this impairment of sound thinking "lureth man astray into her snares".[15] By virtue of the delusion of Xerxes,

198

hich was his belief that with his massive forces and equipment he could
:stroy the Greeks, he himself destroyed his vast armies which he had
:sembled for this military venture. In the same play, his mother
:knowledges that the arrogance of her son, which reinforced his delusion,
:ought "our whole host . . . to ruin".[16]

If an individual were to consider his own approval of his acting as its
nal moral justification, he would not be troubled about some additional
reward" or compensation. This attitude toward one's own conduct is
oncluded in a belief that conduct is self-justifying. That is, there is
o good in human life which supersedes the moral worth itself of acting
hich deserves to be approved by a morally honest person. Such an in-
ividual does not ask the naive, although commonly asked question,
hich Job directed to his friends: "Who will take account of my piety?"
.ware that after he is dead he cannot be conscious of his own acts of
everence for a divine reality, he points out to his friends: "I cannot
ake them down to Sheol with me, nor can they descend with me into
he earth." (17:16) This problem, however, would not have troubled
ob had he been aware that revering a divine reality is itself an act which
s merited by such a reality. Hence in giving reverence to a god, which
s the nature of piety, he would be doing what he himself acknowledged
.e ought to do insofar as he was aware of the merit of such a reality to
e revered. The same justification for morally worthy acting is internal
o all conduct. A person is loyal to another because he could not approve
of any other way of relating himself to the other. What another may do
n relation to him is not his moral responsibility. Another's disloyalty
nay obviously injure him, but it will not justify to himself his disloyalty
n return.

A friend of Job, Eliphaz the Temanite, has a far profounder understanding of the nature of the reason for conduct than Job has. Whereas
Job thinks of a compensation or justification for conduct as extrinsic to
such acting itself, Eliphaz regards conduct as its own justification. He
herefore asked Job: "Does your blameless life give you no hope?" (4:6)
Its basis for hope, according to Eliphaz, would be that it is itself a
ecurity upon which an individual can depend in his future. If such a way
of living were justified by something extrinsic to itself, there would be
no such security within a person's own control. One cannot control anything which is external to himself and so to his conduct. Hence if an
individual were to consider his conduct to be for some purpose or end
other than itself, he would thereby disparage it as subordinate to a good
more worthy than itself. When, therefore, a person is unwilling to qualify

his honesty or integrity, he is not primarily concerned with what other responses are. He is honest because it is the only way of acting that h can accept as his way of living. If comparable honesty were praised fc being a means to secure a position requiring integrity, honesty woul then be thought of as having instrumental worth for something beyon itself. That it has this entailed benefit does not by any means impair it moral worth. But it does not constitute the justification for a morall serious individual to discipline himself to honesty as a way of acting The same may be said of every other trait of character.

Proverbs selects the character-trait of kindness as a sufficient condi tion internal to life itself for entailing a blessing upon life. A proverl therefore, maintains that "The kindly man will be blessed for he share his food with the poor". (22:9) If such a way of relating himself t those who are in need of what he himself can give them were for som purpose other than for helping them to receive what they need, his actin would have significance other than his own approval of what he does If aware that there is a need, and he does what is within his abilities t respect his obligation to satisfy such a need, he acts for a moral purpose which is internal to the acting itself. Such an intrinsic justification doe not diminish the benefit of his acting to those whom he helps. But wha he does is the basis for his approval of himself for his acting. He doe what he believes will contribute to another's well-being. Acting as h does is the reason internal to his acting, although his acting as instru mental to bringing about some good for another refers beyond itself.

Isaiah's life was oriented beyond himself in doing what he regarded a his obligation to the god whom he revered. Nevertheless, he was aware o the moral merit of acting which is worthy of a person in relation to a reality he reveres. He therefore declares: "Your own righteousness shal be your vanguard." (58:8) Righteousness is a way of living which alone is appropriate for a human being who acknowledges his dependence upor a divine providence, and it is itself the only type of life that a religious individual could accept for himself in such a relation. Whatever blessing may come to him from the reality he trusts for its providence is the initia tive of that reality. What alone is his initiative is doing what he regards as worthy of himself in relation to such a reality. Acting in such a way is, therefore, the extent of his concern in determining what he himself does. What may eventuate in addition to his own acting is not within his con trol. His primary concern, therefore, is his worthiness in such a relation. His worthiness in such a relation is doing all that he regards as his obli gation to such a reality. And acting this way is the sole basis for his

cceptance of himself as worthy of doing what he regards as his obligation
to such a divine reality.

The nature of a reality to which one relates himself determines the
conditions which fulfill his obligation in relation to it. The nature of a
parent's child, for example, determines what the parent's obligations are
in relation to the child. The requirement imposed upon the parent is the
child's need of the parent, and doing all that a parent can to respect the
child's requirements in relation to him is the moral basis for a parent's
approval of what he does in relation to his child.

The relation of a parent to his child seems so elementary a type of
responsibility that a parent is disinclined to exalt such a relationship by a
terminology commonly used in religious or spiritual discourse. Yet, even
the most elementary relationships in human life can be lifted to a level
on which such discourse is entirely appropriate in commenting on their
moral significance. A parent who fulfills his parental responsibilities
"lives an upright life", to borrow the expression from Isaiah. (33:15)
All that the Prophet affirms of the integrity of such an "upright life" is
appropriately used in affirming a moral approbation for a person who
fulfills his responsibilities in such a relation. If one were to use the terminology of the Prophet, one might speak of such a parent as "stand(ing)
firm in his nobility". (32:8)

No serious person would question the soundness of the affirmation in
The Wisdom of Solomon that "Honest work bears glorious fruit". Yet,
if a person were to take account of his own motive for such "honest work",
he would maintain that it was his own honesty in his work which motivates him to act as he does. (3:15) The so-called "fruit" of his work as
other than his reason for acting as he does is an additional advantage
for having so acted. His desire to be honest in what he does is the basis
for his acceptance of himself as doing what an honest workman ought
to do.

The author of this writing indicates his clear understanding not only
of the intrinsic justification for an integrity of life whose work is honest,
but also whose relation to a reality he reveres has the spiritual merit of
"righteousness" or "holiness". He points out that "holiness of life (has)
its recompense" internal to itself. He thereby is free from a concern for
some justification beyond the quality of such a life itself. The author of
this writing therefore points out the mistaken notion which is widespread among those who entertain the "thought that innocence has no
reward". (2:23) It is this type of understanding of spiritual benefits
which are internal to a quality of life that is unimpaired by an accom-

modation to the standards of a so-called "world" which Jesus also ha
in mind when he said "for of such is the kingdom of heaven". (*Mat*
19:14)

If one were to select a reference from the Greek dramatists whi
illustrate an understanding of the intrinsic worth of a respect for i
tegrity in one's acting he might cite the splendid statement of Polynic
in Euripides' *The Phoenissae*: "The words of truth are simple, and ju
tice needs no subtle interpretations, for it hath a fitness in itself."[17] Th
single tribute to the moral role of truth and justice in human condu
sums up what has previously been said about the intrinsic moral wor
of conduct. A conduct which respects a moral obligation to speak trut
fully and to act justly has "a fitness in itself" which is its own justi
cation.

The same intrinsic "justification" or "reason" for religious living
internal to itself. The authors of wisdom literature show an understandir
for such a "defense" or "reason" for uprightness or righteousness. Th
author of *Ecclesiasticus* maintains that "Wisdom . . . cares for those wh
seek her", and "to love her is to love life" itself. "To rise early for he
sake is to be filled with joy." (4:11, 12) This way of dedicating onese
to the discipline of cultivating wisdom in one's living is not that one
life might be "filled with joy". This quality of life is the spiritual co
relative or accompaniment of living such a dedicated life. It is not a
end or objective for which one strives by means of his disciplined lif
The disciplining of life in gaining wisdom is the motive itself for such
way of living. Whatever additions there may be to such disciplining an
dedicating of life are spiritual gains, but such gains are not the objective
which sustain the disciplining of life. As Spinoza points out: "Blessednes
is not the reward of virtue, but is virtue itself; nor do we delight i
blessedness because we restrain our lusts, but, on the contrary, becaus
we delight in it, thereby are we able to restrain them."

Living a disciplined life, oriented to achieving as enlightened a life a
one can achieve, is the telos of such a life. It is the purpose itself imma
nent in such a life, benefits of which may well be more than the disci
plining or the enlightening. But such additional benefits are not the in
trinsic purpose for such a way of living. "Loving life itself" is what suc
a person does in the way he lives to enlighten his life. Such a "lovin
life itself" is the disciplining of its interests to respect Wisdom as
supreme good. And, as the author of *Ecclesiasticus* maintains, "To serv
her is to serve the Holy One". (vs. 14) Such a way of living is th
justification or the purpose for such living.

The prophet Ezra repeatedly manifests not only his philosophical bilities but also his spiritual nature in the writings attributed to him in *rst* and *Second Esdras*. He exhibits such understanding in characteriz-g the quality of living which is experienced by "those who have kept the way laid done by the Most High". (II, 7:88) "Their first joy is eir victory in the long fight against their inborn impulses to evil, which ave failed to lead them astray from life." (vs. 93) This has taken place ternal to the life of such a person by virtue of a discipline incompatible ith another type of living. In other words, he gave up one way of living order to cultivate another. And the quality of life he cultivated by his reference was itself the justification for the discipline required to achieve . The prophet Ezra characterizes "Their third joy" from a specifically ligious perspective. It "is the good report given them by their Maker, at throughout their life they kept the law with which they were en-usted". (vs. 94) But this interpretation points out that the response of their Maker" to them was in addition to the religious life itself which ey cultivated by conforming to "the law with which they were en-usted". Respecting the obligation with which "they were entrusted" was or them their religious way of living, and it was itself the "purpose" or he "reason" for what they did. They wanted to live by keeping "the law /ith which they were entrusted" because uppermost in their lives was ulfilling the obligation of revering "the law". They lived devoted to "the aw" because "they were entrusted" with its keeping.

. Human beings can help redeem the evil others do

Most human beings are capable of doing more for their own well-eing and for the well-being of others than they actually do. The fact of his disparity is basic to any serious reflecting about human life and its noral possibilities. Isaiah points out this difference between what people ould do that would enrich human life and what they actually do: "In tillness and in staying quiet . . . lies your strength. But you would have one of it." (30:15, 16)

More human beings are capable of doing good deeds than actually do hem. It is this confidence in the moral capacities of human beings which underlies the entire tradition of prophecy in the Old Testament. If the Prophets did not believe that human beings were capable of living more worthily than they most commonly do, they would not confront them with unfulfilled obligations. Jeremiah, for instance, commands his people to "Mend your ways and your doings, deal fairly with one another, do

not oppress the alien, the orphan, and the widow, shed no innoce
blood". (7:5, 6) If these several injunctions were to be respected in tl
daily practices of people, a new order of human life would come in
being to displace an order of cruelty, injustice, and disregard for tl
rights of the helpless and defenseless.

The basis for the Prophet's confidence that the people who "stea
murder, commit adultery and perjury" can do otherwise is that a totall
different pattern of living had been practiced in the history of the Israe
ites. (vs. 9) He therefore reminds them that they need only "think «
their fathers" who "dealt justly and fairly", who "dispensed justice t
the lowly and poor", to have evidence that the way of life he outlines ¿
their moral responsibilities had been practiced. It is not, therefore, a
unrealizable ideal.

The same contrast between what most people do and what some d
which differs in moral worthiness is pointed out by Euripides in Th
Phoenician Women when Menoeceus, the son of Creon, offered to ki
himself as a means to save the city of Thebes. His final address to th
citizens is that "If every man would take what good he can and give i
to his city's common good, cities would suffer less, be happy from nov
on".[18] This modest requirement of the citizens of a community woul
make so vast a difference in the quality of corporate well-being that
totally different type of community would come into being than the on
in which people live. It would indeed be what Isaiah envisioned for hi
people, "a new earth". (65:17)

The basis on which this hope rests for an improvement in the genera
level of corporate life is more than mere hope. It is an evidence interna
to the nature of human beings themselves that many, and likely most
are capable of praiseworthy acting which they however do not make th
effort to bring about. Crises in community life demonstrate what huma
beings are capable of doing which is so far in excess of what they ordi
narily do that it would seem as if for the time they had become a dif
ferent people in their willingness and zeal to sacrifice to help those i
need. It is on the basis of such actual demonstrations of what people ar
capable of doing for the enrichment of human life that it is an empiri
cally sound generalization to maintain that the good of which people ar
capable outweighs the evil of which they are also capable. Euripides ha:
Theseus, King of Athens, affirm in The Suppliants: "I believe the goo
outweighs the bad in human life." And the argument by which he sup
ports his belief is simply stated: "If it did not, the light would not be
ours."[19] But the fact is "the light (is) ours"; only it is not a determinan

actual practice as often as it could be, and surely as often as it morally ought to be.

Most people are morally capable of recognizing ways of acting which are right rather than wrong, and they are also capable of determining their own acting by the clarity of their awareness of what is right for them to do. Because the prophet Hosea believed that his people were capable of doing more worthily than they actually did, he addressed them with the injunction: "Sow for yourselves righteousness and justice." And he assured them that they would then "reap the fruit" of such a way of living. (10:12)

As Hosea confronted his people with the radical contrast between what they do and what they ought to do, because they have the moral capacity so to act, so the Laws addressed themselves to Socrates who was confronted with the appeal by his friend Crito to break the laws of Athens in order to save himself from the death-penalty. Socrates reflected upon the disproportion between the worth of extending his life and what he would have to do in going counter to the laws of the state. The Laws appealed to him: "Ah, Socrates, be guided by us who tended your infancy. Care neither for your children nor for life nor for anything else more than for the right." The decision which Socrates made pointed out to others what could be done by a human being who conforms to a way of acting which he himself respects as worthy of his approval.

It is not only a rare person, such as Socrates, who deliberately gave his life for the collective good. Herodotus, for instance, states the substance of a conversation between Demaratus, formerly King of Sparta, and Xerxes, ruler of Persia, who underestimated the capacity of the Greeks to sacrifice their lives in defense of their political freedom. "O King", said Demaratus, "in Hellas poverty is ever native to the soil, but courage comes of their own seeking, the fruit of wisdom and strong law; by use of courage Hellas defends herself from poverty and tyranny . . . the Lacedaemonians . . . will never accept conditions from you that import the enslaving of Hellas . . . they will meet you in battle, yes, even though all the rest of the Greeks be on your side."[20]

Thus Demaratus points out the impressive aspect of human history that there are some human beings who will do what they regard as worthy of themselves even though it entails the loss of their life. As he says, the Lacedaemonians would decide what they themselves would do in the life and death struggle against the Persians, and they would not have to wait to find out what other people of Hellas would first decide to do. The final authority for them was what they themselves regarded

as their obligation to their own heritage and to all who would li
after them. An entire political philosophy thus was basic to the mo
authority by which they lived and by which they sacrificed their liv
in defense of the principles of such a political philosophy.

Proverbs affirms a parallel of a moral authority for individual a
collective acting which is based upon a political philosophy. It declar
that if a people were to "rid the king's presence of wicked men . . .
throne would rest firmly on righteousness". (25:5) The alternative
an existing corrupt rule which is pointed out by this incisive reco
mendation is what a people themselves could do to establish justice
their nation. If they were to have the moral courage to oppose t
wrongdoing practiced by those in the service of the king, they wou
eliminate the injustices from their country which are the consequenc
of the "wicked men" in "the king's presence". *Proverbs* also affirms
profound political philosophy when it declares that "Where there is
vision or no one in authority the people run without restraint". B
there is an alternative to this self-destructive scheme of corporate li
and this is proposed in the same proverb. If there were "a guardian
the law", he would keep the people "on the straight path". (29:18) H
own uprightness as a ruler would have this effect upon the people.

In maintaining this relation between the integrity of a ruler an
the people over whom he exercises sovereignty, *Proverbs* affirms the san
faith which is basic to the political philosophy affirmed by Plato in t
Republic and by Confucius in the *Analects*. "The Master said: 'H
who governs by his moral excellence may be compared to the pole-sta
which abides in its place, while all the stars bow towards it.' "[21] Th
political philosophy is based upon the confidence that, when a peop
recognize the absolute integrity of a ruler, they respect his right to
their sovereign. Such a normative ruler is characterized by Confucius
having "religious attention to business and good faith, economy in e
penditure and love of his people".[22] In other words, these are the co
ditions upon which a wisely ruled state comes into being. The uprigh
character of a ruler sets a standard for the people whom he rules. In s
doing, he fulfills his responsibility to them, irrespective of what they i
turn do to benefit from his rule.

Plato also believed that it is the obligation of the ruler of a people t
do all that he himself can do to make himself worthy of their respec
And the procedure for this achievement consists of a discipline for be
coming a dialectician or ideal philosopher. As a "lover of wisdom", hi
life will be an "associating with the divine order", and in so doing, h

will himself become orderly".[23] The faith which Plato had in what people can do, and so what they could be, is expressed in his confidence that it is impossible "not to imitate the things to which anyone attaches himself with admiration".[24] In other words, the sole possibility for bringing an order of intelligence into being as the pattern of a community or state is that there is an example of unprightness and justice which the people can see. And then out of respect for such a way of living, that way of life would come into being. If it does not come into being, notwithstanding the normative character of a ruler, it is not a moral failure of a ruler. In being worthy of the respect of his people for his uprightness, he fulfills his responsibility as a ruler in relation to them.

Plato was realistic enough not to assume that when there are models of life worthy of respect there will also be people who will respect such a way of life to the extent of conforming to its conditions. But he was convinced that if an ordered state were to come into being, it would be in conditions such as he outlined, which include the worthiness of a human being to be the ruler of a people.

The author of *Ecclesiasticus* points out the correlation of the moral qualifications of a prophet with the trustworthiness of his predictions. He declares that "Because of his fidelity, he proved to be an accurate prophet". The same correlation, of course, holds for any individual of authority in a country. The competency of his plans for its future rests upon his anticipations of what such a future will be, and the adequacy of what he prescribes for such a future will be determined by his own capacity to make true judgments. The author of this writing affirms another profound principle when he declares that "the truth of his vision" is "shown by his utterances". (46:15) In other words, the competency with which he is able to anticipate developments in a future is manifested in the truth-character of what he affirms about a future. That is, what he is enlightened enough to anticipate in his predictions will be substantiated by what takes place in a future about which he makes such predictions. The condition for such verification of his predictions is moral: it is his integrity to interpret a present state of affairs in light of what can be learned of comparable conditions in a past. And on the basis of such knowledge, judgments about a future can be affirmed. Such verifiable judgments, however, would not be possible if an individual were biased by his desires, his prejudices, and his antipathies. Only as he can understand what has taken place which parallels what takes place at a present time is he capable of making sound predictions about the high likelihood of what occurrences will develop in the future.

207

Herodotus contrasts the characters of three famous rulers as their characters were correlated with the nature of their rule. "The Persians called Darius the huckster, Cambyses the master, and Cyrus the father." The moral nature of their rules was in turn conditioned by their own morality. Herodotus points out that "Darius made petty profit out of everything, Cambyses was harsh and arrogant, Cyrus was merciful and ever wrought for their well-being".[25] Thus the people of empires were affected by the character of their ruler. Blighted under the rule of Darius and Cambyses, as interpreted by Herodotus, they were blessed with benefits correlated with the merciful character of Cyrus.

Human beings can be merciful to others even though such manifestation of mercy is not as frequent in human life as it could be and should be. *Leviticus,* which is a record of the laws of the ancient Israelites, includes an injunction of a moral obligation, conforming to which would bring into existence an entire community blessed with merciful acting.

"When you reap the harvest of your land, you shall not reap right into the edges of your field; neither shall you glean the loose ears of your crop; you shall not completely strip your vineyard nor glean the fallen grapes. You shall leave them for the poor and the alien." (19:9,10) These conditions for acting which are stated as obligations of a people to others in their community would be sufficient to fulfill some of the elementary needs of "the poor and alien". If charity of this type were to become the practice in a country, it would itself determine the relation of concern of those who have for those who do not have, and it would constitute a basis for bringing about a moral response of gratitude rather than a tragic attitude of ill-will, resentment, and embitterment against property itself and against those who own it.

Human beings likewise are capable of forgiving others, and their ability to do so unfortunately is not always exploited by what they do. But having such a capacity constitutes the basis for a hope in a future in which men with moral capacities will use them to their utmost effort. The Old Testament book of *Second Samuel* includes an eloquent record of what the high level of character of a single man accomplished. It is the record of King David, against whose rule some of his subjects rebelled. One of the tribe of Benjamin who had rebelled, repented and "fell down before the king and said to him, 'I beg your majesty not to remember how disgracefully your servant behaved when your majesty left Jerusalem.'" Another subject of the king, however, insisted that the repentant man "be put to death". "David answered: . . . 'Why should any man be put to death this day in Israel?'" "Then the king said: 'You shall not die', and confirmed it with an oath." (19:19-23) King David thus demonstrated to his people the highminded nature of forgiving one and thereby relieving him of the oppressive weight of remembering his guilt.

An equally eloquent account of the charity of forgiveness is the act of Hippolytus toward his father as this is narrated in Euripides' play. Theseus had unjustly accused his son, and to punish him, had appealed to Poseidon to send a sea monster which frightened the horses driven in a chariot-race by his son. Hippolytus was fatally injured, and the final conversation he had with his father indicated his admirable character. He forgave his father both for the false accusation and also for the fatal injury. Theseus lamented: "And so you leave me, my hands stained with murder." Whereupon Hippolytus answered: "No, for I free you from all guilt in this." This act of forgiving his father demonstrated to his father the noble nature of his son, whereupon Theseus declared: "Dear son, how noble you have proved to me!"[26]

What is important in this single relation between these two men is the possibility of a human being to forgive so vast an injury as a false accusation and, in addition, to forgive another for his responsibility for one's own death.

Although it is not a common trait of human acting, nevertheless, it is possible for human beings to be thankful for another's good fortune and do so without envying them. Aeschylus affirms his faith in this human capacity when Agamemnon declares: "For few there be among men in whom it is inborn to admire without envy a friend's good fortune. For the venom of malevolence settles upon the heart and doubles the burden of him afflicted of that plague: he is himself weighed down by his own calamity, and repines at sight of another's prosperity."[27] A sad commentary on the nature of human life is that there are few who have this capacity of character to rejoice in another's good fortune without a malice of wishing it were they instead of another who had the good fortune. But being aware that there are some who have this trait of character is a basis for esteeming the possibilities of human beings. The reason that there are relatively few who can be aware of others' good fortune without being embittered that one himself does not have it is that such a capacity is cultivated only by moral discipline. It is an achievement of character. Spinoza closes his *Ethics* with the comment that "It must indeed be difficult since it is so seldom discovered". And then he points out that if being free from such an impairment of character, which is "salvation", "lay ready to hand and could be discovered without great labor, how could it be possible that it should be neglected almost b everybody?" And the assurance with which Spinoza ends this great wor is that "All things excellent are as difficult as they are rare".[28]

Greeks affirmed their moral faith in what human beings can do no only in their literature but also in other expressions of their art. Th subjects of sculptured metopes of their temples are as eloquent as ar their dramas of the faith in what human beings can do to impose thei enlightened will upon the otherwise unenlightened drives of their nature Vincent Scully points out this medium of sculpture for affirming thi moral faith when he says that the "sculptured groups" of the metope usually represent "the triumph of human will, assisted by the Olympia gods, over the beast power of nature".[29]

The art which affirmed this faith thus is a tribute to the character o human beings notwithstanding all they did which could not be approved They, nevertheless, had a vision of what might be, and had a confidenc in the capacities of the human mind to direct the massive inclination of human nature to act in ways which go counter to reasonable under standing.

This ambivalent nature of the human being accounts for the difficult with which human life is confronted in bringing the unordered and un directed aspects of native endowments within an order proposed for ther by a reasonable intelligence. The difficulty of this constitutes the natur of the praiseworthy human accomplishment of imposing an order of in telligence upon a considerable aspect of human nature which of itsel does not include this ordering factor. But what is a basis for encourage ment is that in spite of the difficulty, it is achievable. A comment witl which Spinoza ends the discourse of his *Ethics* is that "If they . . . seen very difficult, it can nevertheless be found".[30]

Basic to his *Ethics* is thus the same confidence in the moral capacitie of the human being which is affirmed in the sculpture of the Greek tem ples and in the plays of the Greek dramatists. The same confidenc obviously is basic to the moral philosophies of Greece, which are amon; the notable achievements of the human mind. Even the briefest commen upon them would itself require a separate study.

A confidence which underlies the extensive body of Greek mora philosophies is that the imposing of order upon an otherwise unordered material is an achievement which constitutes a satisfaction for whicl there is no equivalent among other forms of human victory. The victory of a reasoned plan over a massive vitality without such direction is tribute to what the human being can do in directing himself in ways tha e can accept or can approve. Such acceptance of oneself is the moral triumph of which Socrates speaks which is made possible by the reasonable procedure of knowing oneself. In taking such an inventory of one's own nature, one is enabled to understand the problem which he himself encounters in proposing for himself a way of living which he regards as worthy of his approval. Even occasional accomplishments in directing one's inclinations by a pattern which is not native to their nature is one of the encouragements of which a morally earnest person is capable. The author of *Second Esdras* refers to such an achievement as a "joy" which morally sincere individuals experience in their "victory in the long fight against their inborn impulses to evil, which have failed to lead them astray from life". (7:92)

Directing native vitalities into some sort of ordered scheme which is productive of well-being is an enrichment of life. Some of a human being's resource are thereby given a direction by intelligence which they otherwise would not have had without the advantage made possible by an individual's own understanding of their potential uses for consistent moral benefit. Insofar as an individual can bring the diverse components of his own nature into an ordered pattern of living, he is also capable of benefitting others with whom he is related as he could not do without his moral discipline of himself. Such an individual is referred to by the author of this writing as "one man here, one there" who can do for others what they themselves without such help could not do. (3:36) He is one who helps to lessen the handicaps from which others themselves would suffer who do not have the benefit of comparable intelligence in directing their own willing or desiring. In the language of the Old Testament, those who can help others by virtue of what they have done to order themselves are a "faithful remnant". And the moral importance in human history of what the relatively few can do for enlightening the life of others is expressed by Isaiah who declares if there had not been such a body of devoted persons among his people "we should soon have been like Sodom", a city which had floundered from one excess into another until it had destroyed its own justification for existing. This is the moral tragedy narrated in the Old Testament which occurred because the redemptive help offered by the faithful patriarch Lot was inadequate to redeem the folly of the many of that great city.

This is one of the many crises of moral faith recorded in the Old Testament. The story of Noah is another such account which expresses how, in periods of supreme moral crisis, a few human beings alone would be capable of helping the many. But the refusal of the many to accept the available guidance of an enlightened few is a recurring tragedy i human history. The prophet Ezra refers to this tragic contrast betwee those who are capable of redeeming and the many who deny themselve such benefit: "The lost outnumber the saved as a wave exceeds a dro of water." (II, 9;16) This writing thus anticipates the same soberin philosophy of history which is affirmed in the New Testament account c the teaching of Jesus: "Wide is the gate, and broad is the way, tha leadeth to destruction, and many there be which go in thereat." Th contrast, on the other hand, to this sobering comment on human histor is the encouragement affirmed in the moral faith that there is "a narrov gate and a hard road that leads to life". (*Matt.* 7:13, 14) The fact tha "a few find it" is the basis for supporting the moral faith in what can be

Faith in what can be is the element in history which is the basis fo its human character. Plato declares that this redemptive element is "; very small remnant." And in maintaining this sobering view of history he affirms a view which parallels the philosophy of history as it i; repeatedly formulated in the Old Testament.[31] But the numerical dispro portion between those who witness to what life could be and those whe do not offer evidence to support such moral faith is not what is mos' significant. What is of utmost moral and so historical importance is th redemptive role of the relatively few. This is the faith which Isaiah affirmed in declaring that "Justice shall redeem Zion and righteousnes; her repentant people." (1:27)

VII

Divine Sanction of Moral Obligations

1. *An ultimate reality is attentive to human history*

The first book in the Bible affirms the redemptive role of human goodness. It narrates a conversation between the patriarch Abraham and the deity of his people about the threatened destruction of Sodom for its excessive follies. Abraham spoke on behalf of the City for the sake of its faithful few. At first he considered fifty, but aware of the unlikelihood that there was even this number in the entire city for the sake of whom it might be spared, he progressively reduced the number which might be sufficient to redeem the many others until it was reduced to ten. The significance of the redemptive role of the faithful few is then eloquently declared when Abraham was assured: "For the sake of the ten I will not destroy it." (18:32, 33)

This remarkable narrative in *Genesis* affirms not only the redemptive role of human goodness, but also the respect which a reality transcendent of human history has for human goodness and its role for redeeming an evil for which others are responsible. It begins with the question that the Patriarch asks of "the Lord": "Wilt thou really sweep away good and bad together?" (vs. 23) And he affirms his trust in the respect which the Lord has for even this limited manifestation of human goodness when he declares: "Far be it from thee to do this—to kill good and bad together; for then the good would suffer with the bad." This faith of Abraham is thus a basic premise of a theology: "Shall not the judge of all the earth do what is just?" (vs. 26)

With this faith, a human being is reconciled to much that occurs in human life which is otherwise bewildering and totally beyond his understanding. This faith itself redeems a human being from discouragement as he tries to understand what otherwise bewilders him.

Another significant feature of this affirmation of Abraham's faith is the metaphysical premise that a reality transcendent of human life is a basis for the validity of moral principles which are universally effective for establishing justice among human beings. The faith that "the judge of all the earth" establishes the moral criterion of justice reassures a human being that whatever he himself does to bring about justice is significant not only in a limited social context, but also in the total scope of human history. He likewise aligns himself with a reality transcendent of human history, and in so doing, his final approval is not by human beings, but by a sanction which is beyond them.

The religious faith affirmed in *First Kings* also constitutes a theological premise that what takes place in human history is known to a reality transcendent of it. This faith maintains that this reality "knows a man's heart" and is aware of "his deeds". And the essential nature of this faith is that there is no reality in human history itself with such knowledge. What makes this theological premise also morally significant is that "Thou alone knowest the hearts of all men". (8:39)

Psalms likewise affirms the religious faith that there is a divine knowledge of all that enters into human history. This faith is that "the Lord's . . . eye is upon mankind, he takes their measure at a glance". (11:4) The special consolation which this faith contributes to the moral struggle of human beings who try to do what they regard as right is that the Lord "is turned towards the upright man". (vs. 7) The assurance that the struggle in which they are engaged is known to "the Lord" is thus the final religious justification of a sustained moral discipline of human life.

The religious faith affirmed throughout the book of *Psalms* is that the decrees of God are "straight and true" and therefore have no similarity to the capricious judgments most often made by human beings. (119:137) This faith that "thy law is truth" declares a metaphysical premise about the validity of moral principles which are effective for directing human beings into well-being. (vs. 142) Thus according to this faith, the preferences of human beings on behalf of ways of living are not the final criterion for their trustworthiness. There is rather a criterion of truth beyond what human beings believe is true. When their beliefs are enlightened of this truth, they then have a nature which is not determined alone by what men think, but rather is informed of a reality whose nature is not contingent upon the thinking of human beings. This metaphysic affirmed as religious faith is that the "commandments" of God are "justice itself". (vs. 172)

This religious faith is not merely a philosophically significant point of view, but it is a moral basis for living itself. It is the assurance that "the instruction" which is given to men by the god in whom the psalmist trusts is "just". (vs. 138) He declares: "Thy justice is an everlasting justice." (vs. 142) This faith thus reinforces an often faltering belief of human beings and renews their confidence that their struggle to do what they esteem as right is not misspent effort. Its sanction is not merely what others think, but is from a reality beyond human estimates which too often are biased by ignorance and its follies.

The eleventh psalm adds another note to reinforce an encouragement affirmed in a religious faith. It is that "the Lord" not only is just, but also "loves just dealing". (vs. 7) Thus notwithstanding what occurs to otherwise discourage one who tries to do what is fair, he has a profounder encouragement than can ever be forthcoming from what other human beings think of his efforts. A basis for encouragement to sustain devoted effort to do what one himself can approve is the assurance affirmed in the psalm that "The Lord weighs just and unjust". Whatever one himself may do to reduce the tendency to hate and violence in human relations is reinforced by his faith that "The Lord . . . hates with all his soul the lover of violence". (11:5) Hence the conciliatory efforts of some human beings to lessen the destructive weight of so much that many others do are supported by their faith; and so their efforts come under a judgment which is other than human judgment. This is declared in the thirty-fourth psalm: "The Lord sets his face against evildoers to blot out their memory from the earth." (vs. 16)

This stern judgment is itself intrinsic to their own way of living: what they do is not included in the constructive aspect of human history. By virtue of their opposition to efforts for establishing goodwill and justice, they are excluded from this moral tradition, which is the nature of whatever is essentially "human" in history. In other words, they themselves "blot out their memory" from the spiritual tradition of the earth which includes all that every human being does to bring about an enduring good to enhance the lives of others.

All that men do which is directed to an enrichment of human well-being may be encouraged by the assurance affirmed by Isaiah that "the Lord God . . . will use justice as a plumb-line and righteousness as a plummet" in determining the merit of human beings to be included in the history of the moral struggle to redeem the evil brought about by others. (28:17)

The early poets of Greece, Homer and Hesiod, are approximately of the same historical period as the Israelites whose thoughts have been recorded in the earliest writings in the Old Testament. And there is a remarkable parallelism of thought in the writings of both of these ancient people. The Epics attributed to Homer affirm a religious faith that there is a divine approval of morally praiseworthy human conduct. An instance of establishing justice in a human context is construed by Homer as evidence that there is an undergirding for such justice by a divine reality. Laertes, the father of Odysseus, declares this belief when he affirmed: "By Father Zeus, . . . you gods are still in your heaven, if those Suitors have really paid the price for their iniquitous presumption."[1] The indignation of the elder Laertes against the moral outrage of the princes for disrespecting the rights of hospitality in his son's home is, according to his point of view, justified by what he regarded the just treatment which they received. In other words, his faith that there is a divine sanction for the efforts of human beings to establish justice was supported by what took place through the acting of Odysseus to penalize those who violated the sacred principles of hospitality.

Another expression of Homer's religious interpretation of human acting in terms of its accountability to a god's standard of what is right for men to do is affirmed by Penelope, the wife of Odysseus. She addressed Antinous, a friend of the family, with the stern censuring for his faithlessness in plotting against the life of her son, saying: "How dare you plot against Telemachus' life and dishonour the obligations that a past act of mercy imposes—bonds that are ratified by Zeus himself?" The moral outrage of such faithlessness of a human being toward another who trusts him as a friend is referred to as "a sacrilege".[2] Thus what takes place between one human being and another has a significance which is beyond a human relation. Instead, it comes under a scrutiny of a final criterion of what is right. In her condemnation of Antinous for his disregard of the rights of hospitality and of friendship, she accuses him of still another moral outrage which is his disregarding of the right of suppliants for mercy. And she reminds him that this long established obligation which morally sensitive Greeks respect as sacred is sanctioned by a god. She confronts him with the question if he is not aware that in ignoring the "heed of suppliants" he is defying the sovereignty of a god over human history.[3]

Even if it were the case that the *Iliad* is not by the same poet as the

216

Odyssey, it nevertheless affirms the same interpretation of the gravity of human behavior in relation to a divine reality which constitutes a judgment upon what men do. The reason for proposing that men "find out . . . why Phoebus Apollo is so angry" with them is the suspicion that "He may be offended at some broken vow".[4] This proposed analysis acknowledges the accountability of men to a reality which is other than themselves. Thus a broken vow entails an offense which is not limited merely to a human estimate. It is judged by a god. This type of religious faith is a confidence that "Perjurers will get no help from Father Zeus". It is thus a confidence that "men who go back on their word and break a truce" will be accountable to more than men.[5]

The sternness with which a divine judgment is passed upon the wrongdoing of men is as vigorously affirmed by the poet of the *Iliad* as it is affirmed by the author of *Psalms*. He declares that Zeus' "anger is roused because . . . (men) have misused their powers, delivered crooked judgments in a public session and driven justice out".[6] His poetry likewise includes a premise of a political philosophy that a ruler who exhibits principles sanctioned by Zeus is entitled to a respect which exceeds that to which other human beings are entitled. If a king, for instance, should rule "through the authority he derives from Zeus", he "has more than ordinary claims on our respect".[7] The ground for a subject's respect of such a king is not his personality or his access to power to enforce his decrees. It is rather his reverence for the sovereignty of a god to whom he acknowledges his final obligation.

Hesiod considers a type of questioning of the justification for one's effort to do what is right which parallels the type of questioning that troubled Job. Hesiod declares a resolve that neither he nor his son "be righteous among men" if it were the case that "it is a bad thing to be righteous—if indeed the unrighteous shall have the greater right". But then he is far too sensible a person and too religiously oriented to believe that this notion is entitled to serious consideration for he adds: "But I think that all-wise Zeus will not yet bring that to pass."[8] Then after overcoming the momentary questioning of the worth of righteousness, notwithstanding so much evidence to support such questioning, he affirms his recovered faith: "For whoever knows the right and is ready to speak it, far-seeing Zeus gives him prosperity."[9]

What is morally significant in the recovery of his confidence in the final merit of an acting which endeavors to do what is right is not the prospect of its entailed "prosperity". What rather is far more significant is the sanction by a god for what a man tries to do that is right when

217

there are countless inducements to do otherwise. Although the struggle to do what is right is difficult when there are inducements to the contrary, still the reason for disregarding these inducements is also pressing. There is the reminder which one cannot ignore that "bitter sorrows will be left for mortal men" if they do not restrain themselves from wrongdoing and permit themselves finally to become indifferent to it. In other words Hesiod had the moral confidence supported by a religious faith that when human beings lose a sense of moral shame (*Aidos*) which restrains them from doing wrong, and lose the feeling of righteous indignation at the sight of wickedness in human behavior (*Nemesis*), "there will be no help against evil".[10] By their own moral apathy they will have lost the capacities disapproving of wrong which might have saved them from "bitter sorrows" had they made the effort to retain these moral sensitivities.

A religious faith in the final justification for moral earnestness to do what men can do that is fair and just, which is affirmed in the Epics and in *Works and Days*, is reaffirmed in all that Socrates maintained about the divine sanction of human righteousness and justice. His religious faith that there is a divine sanction for what is worthy of approval in human life is summed up in his appeal to the Judges who decided whether he was to live or die: "But you also, judges, . . . must bear in mind this one truth, that no evil can come to a man either in life or after death and God does not neglect him."[11]

2. *A standard of moral right is transcendent of human beings*

The *Iliad* declares that "However bold a man may be, he cannot run counter to the will of Zeus, who is far more powerful than we are".[12] This acknowledgment of the limits with which human beings are confronted in what they may presume to do is basic to the thought which is affirmed throughout centuries of Greek reflecting. It is affirmed as premises in their metaphysics, and it is maintained as a fact which is repeatedly exemplified in the great tragedies of the dramatists. Diomedes, therefore, declares a wisdom characteristic of the reflective Greek: "I am not the man to fight against the gods of heaven."[13]

Works and Days declares that justice as a moral demand upon human beings cannot be brushed off as if it were no more than a convention having its origin in a social context. This notion of its nature, which was affirmed centuries later by the Cynics of Athens, would have distressed the morally serious Hesiod who maintains that if men ignore their obligations to do justly in relation to others, they will be pursued by

218

ustice. In other words, justice is not contingent upon what men think about what is permissible for them to do, but is a demand which the nature of human life itself imposes upon men in the social contexts in which they live. And when they disregard this minimum condition for human dignity in corporate life, they are penalized by their own acting. Hesiod maintains that "Justice", although fragile in the sense that it can be destroyed as a basic order in human relations, nevertheless, persists in its inflexible demands upon those who presume to be exempt from its jurisdiction. He declares that it "follows to the city and haunts of the people, weeping" when rejected by men. But its sorrow for its rejection is not its final form of making itself evident in human life. It "brings mischief to men, even to such as have driven her forth in that they did not deal straightly with her".[14] In interpreting in this graphic way the relation of justice to human beings, Hesiod affirms the same basic belief as Homer does that "However bold a man may be, he cannot run counter" to a requirement of human life which is other than such life itself, but is a limit within which human life alone can achieve well-being.

This stern metaphysic which maintains that there is a condition for well-being which is not of men's own choosing is basic to the dramatists who reaffirm the moral philosophy of Homer and Hesiod. The Chorus in Aeschylus' *Libation-Bearers* declares that "the balanced scale of Justice keepeth watch: swift it descendeth on some who still stand in the light; sometimes sorrows await them that tarry in the twilight of life's close; and some are enshrouded by ineffectual night".[15] The accountability of human beings to this requirement imposed upon them continues throughout the span of life. In other words, there is no time in a human being's life when he is exempt from obligations imposed upon him. The latitude of his choice includes either accepting such obligations or rejecting them. But the consequences of either act are not within the scope of his choice. These are entailed in what he does. And such entailment is inescapable. It is this sobering awareness of the human being's confrontation with obligations other than his own choosing that conditions the serious reflecting in a long tradition of Greek literature.

Aeschylus reaffirms this finality of a moral judgment upon human life which is not within human control, but is entailed in the nature of the ultimate reality itself. The Chorus in *Suppliant Maidens* declares of Zeus that "He speaketh and it is done—he hasteneth to execute whatsoever his counselling mind conceiveth".[16] The contingent nature of human life is thus affirmed in this metaphysic of a reality to which human beings are subordinate. In their relation to this reality, they are not in final control of what takes place in their life when they ignore the limits imposed upon them by this reality. The Chorus affirms this warning: "Verily the wrath of Zeus, the suppliant's god, awaiteth such as will not be softened by a sufferer's plaints."[17] It repeats this warning of what will be entailed for those who disregard such rights of suppliants: "Look unto him that looketh down from on high, unto him, the guardian of mortals sore-distressed, who appeal unto their neighbours, yet obtain not the justice that is their due right."[18]

The relation of the human being to an order transcendent of human life thus confronts the human being with obligations which are not his choice. They rather set limits within which his choice is either an expression of his wisdom or his folly. Any act which goes counter to such obligations with which he is confronted is a judgment upon his folly. Respecting such obligations, on the other hand, is an expression of his wisdom, and is itself the condition for his wisdom.

The wisdom affirmed by the Chorus that "gods of our race . . . regard with favour the cause of righteousness"[19] is respected by Danaus in instructing his daughters to "be minded not to neglect the gods" under any circumstances, even those in which they are most distraught.[20] The crises in life which confused the clarity of an individual's thinking should, in other words, never be permitted to be the final determinant of what he does. If he were to be respectful of the limits compatible with his obligations to "the gods, the peril of crisis would be controlled."[20] It would be controlled by his own wisdom to take account of the priority of such obligation to any disorder in his distraught life.

Basic to Sophocles' *Antigone* is the metaphysic that "the eternal laws of Heaven" set the limits within which a human being either acts with wisdom or in folly. It is this ultimate reality of which Antigone reminds her sister that it is her liberty to "Scorn, if thou wilt, the eternal laws of Heaven", although in so doing she will impose upon herself the peril of her folly.[21] Antigone herself is not deflected from respecting the priority of the "eternal laws" to the laws of Creon, the king. And yet, the folly of her sister, Ismene, is the impiety with which she thinks only of the fact that Creon "rules". Antigone, on the other hand, is convinced that the scope of his rule is subordinate to another rule. Hence the arguments of the two sisters express two totally different philosophies of life because each bases her philosophy upon a different metaphysic. This contrast of metaphysics is pointed out by Antigone in her confrontation with Creon. She points out to him that the laws which decree his authority over his subjects are subordinate to laws which are not contingent upon a human ruler whose laws are as transient as he is. The Chorus in Aeschylus' *The Seven Against Thebes* declared this fact: "What a state approves as just changes with changing times."[22]

Antigone believes that only "The immutable unwritten laws of Heaven" are entitled to respect, and this belief expresses her metaphysic that the "laws of Heaven" "were not born to-day nor yesterday".[23] They are independent of time, and their transcendence of a temporal order is the priority of their right to be respected. This metaphysic defines for Antigone the decision to defy the rule of the King.

Antigone's father, in spite of his tragic life, is convinced of the soundness of the same metaphysic which she herself affirms. He declares: "The eye of Heaven beholds the just of men, and the unjust."[24] Thus both Antigone and Oedipus represent a type of religious faith which acknowledges a human being's subordination to an order transcendent of human life and having a priority to human respect such as human conventions, including human laws, do not have.

The entire set of beliefs affirmed in the dramas of both Aeschylus and Sophocles are reaffirmed in the dramas of Euripides, although this constitutes only one of his points of view about religious beliefs and the warrant for religious faith. Hecuba acknowledges the radical contrast between her weakness as a human being, subject to the injustices of those who are stronger than she is, and the superior sovereignty of the gods. She affirms her faith that "the gods are strong" and "set up bounds of right and wrong for our lives".[25] This faith provides her a courage and a strength with which to accept the reverses in her life which are transient in contrast to the "law of Heaven" by which the evil will be judged that brought them about. The Chorus reaffirms her faith that "the rights of justice and the law of heaven are one".[26]

A comparable reassurance is affirmed by Theseus in *The Suppliants*: "One thing alone I need, the favour of all gods that reverence right, for the presence of these things insured victory" and insures the final establishment of justice. Such establishment may be deferred or delayed by what men do to impede justice in human relations, but the faith he affirms is that notwithstanding whatever men do to deflect a final justice, it will be established. The time within which it operates is not always the time with which men reckon what is right and fair. And the same disparity of what men regard as right, in contrast to what is right, is also affirmed in the faith of Theseus when he declares that men's "valour availeth men naught, unless they have the god's goodwill".[27]

The Chorus in *The Heracleidae* affirm the same religious faith, based

221

upon a metaphysic that there is an ultimate justice which is other than what men regard as justice :"The majesty of Justice shall not suffer" when men do what goes counter to what is decreed as right in Heaven's laws.[28] One such principle of just acting is the right of suppliants at altars, whose rights are established by the gods to whom the altars are dedicated. Hence " 'tis but right we should reverence the gods' suppliants, suffering none with violent hand to make them leave the altars, for that will dread Justice ne'er permit".[29]

The metaphysic or theology affirmed by Hesiod that a man "cannot run counter to the will of Zeus" is also affirmed in *The Book of Job*: "Wisdom and might are his . . . If he pulls down, there is no rebuilding; if he imprisons, there is no release." (12:13, 14) These two cultures thus acknowledge that man is subordinate to a reality whose sovereignty cannot be challenged without disaster to human presumption.

Psalms disparages the folly of boasting of self-sufficiency with its vaunted independence of such an ultimate reality. And for such vanity of wickedness, its author maintains there is inevitable regret in what takes place in those who so boast. "To the boastful", he warns, "Boast no more", and to the wicked, "Do not toss your proud horns: toss not your horns against high heaven nor speak arrogantly against your Creator." (75:4, 5) Included in human wisdom, according to the Psalmist, is a clear understanding of the limits with which a human being is confronted in his relation to "high heaven". Such a relation is the same ultimate fact to which Sophocles refers as "the immutable unwritten laws of Heaven" or "the eye of Heaven (which) beholds the just and the unjust". The wisdom expressed in this psalm of acknowledging the limits with which one is confronted in his relation to such an ultimate reality is the wisdom also affirmed by Diomedes in the *Iliad*: "I am not the man to fight against the gods of Heaven."[30]

This religious acknowledgment of the human being's subordination to a reality transcendent of every other reality is affirmed by Isaiah when he maintains that "the Lord" declares: "What I do, none can undo." (43:13) Speaking for "the Holy One" in whose service Isaiah regarded his mission to his people, he affirms: "I the Lord speak what is right, declare what is just." (45:19) The validity of the injunction which he addresses to his people is, therefore, independent of his pronouncements. His pronouncements rather are true by virtue of affirming the god's requirements for men.

Zechariah regarded his role as a prophet in the same way as Isaiah regarded his role. He maintains that "The word of the Lord came" to him, and "These are the words of the Lord: 'Administer true justice, show loyalty and compassion to one another, do not oppress the orphan and the widow, the alien and the poor, do not contribute any evil one against another.' " (7:9-11)

Even if one were not to believe that there is such a direct revelation of the so-called "word of God" to a prophet, one, nevertheless, would almost be coerced by the soundness of such stated moral obligations to admit that if they were not so formulated by a god, their moral validity would entitle them to such an interpretation of origin. Even if one were not to have the religious faith of Zechariah that he is in direct relation with a god who speaks through him, yet, one would be pressed to find any aspect of his pronouncement on behalf of God unworthy of an ultimate standard of moral obligations. The Prophet declares: "These are the words of the Lord . . . 'This is what you shall do: speak the truth to each other, administer true and sound justice in the city gate. Do not contribute any evil one against another, and do not love perjury, for all this I hate.' " (8:16, 17)

In spite of the anthropomorphic aspect of this statement of prophecy, the soundness of the pattern of acting it affirms as obligatory for human beings has a universal cogency irrespective of differences in cultures. It is this cogency of its universality as a way of living which constitutes its worthiness to be attributed to an ultimate wisdom or deity transcendent of the limited wisdom of human beings.

3. Human beings cannot change divine demands upon them

A dominant emphasis in the writings of Isaiah acknowledges an irrevocable relation between human beings and the god on behalf of whom he speaks. He confronts his people with the question: "Who shall frustrate" a plan which "the Lord . . . has prepared?" (14:27) Another expression of the irrevocable character of this relationship is "the Lord . . . in his wisdom . . . does not take back his words". (31:2)

Although the imagery with which this unalterable relationship is affirmed is anthropomorphic, it nevertheless is a vehicle for affirming the Prophet's metaphysic that there is a reality transcendent of human beings which is not within the scope of their options. He points out the moral significance of this stern fact in his assertion that "thou has hidden thy face from us and abandoned us to our iniquities". (64:7) The moral basis for this response attributed by the Prophet to God becomes evident if the order in this assertion is converted. Human beings would be

223

"abandoned" to their own "iniquities" if God should turn from them. When this stern judgment occurs upon them, they are cut off from an enlightening by a reality of a totally different nature from theirs. Human beings who are inclined so readily to do wrong would thereby be denied the guidance of a reality external to their own initiative to do wrong. In the anthropomorphic imagery used by the Prophet, the "face" of God is "hidden" from men who destroy their own capacities to be respectful of a divine reality which imposes requirements upon them which they refuse to regard. And the detriment to themselves which their own refusal entails is that they destroy within themselves their capacity to orient themselves beyond their own evil. Such moral judgment upon themselves is inescapable.

Jeremiah's ministry to the Israelites continued the same stern condemnation upon the wrongdoing of his people. He warned them that "The Lord's anger is not to be turned aside, until he has . . . fulfilled his deep designs". (23:20) This warning confronts them with the stern reminder that their liberty to do evil terminates their own initiative to do good. After they destroy their own initiative to do good, they themselves cannot restore it. Such limits upon what they can do to redeem an evil for which they took the initiative confronts them with the gravity of a judgment before which they have no option. The Prophet addresses the people of Judah with this sobering reminder of the relation between what men do and what they thereby become when he declares: "The sin of Judah is recorded with an iron tool, engraved on the tablet of their heart with a point of adamant and carved on the horns of their altars to bear witness against them." (17:1) This is one of the many condemnations in Old Testament prophecy of the ineffectiveness of human evil to be camouflaged by rituals and sacrifices. Even such "altars bear witness against" a people who presume that something external to them can cancel an evil they have brought about internal to their own nature. The vigor of the image with which the Prophet indicts the superficial morality and hypocrisy in the religion of his contemporaries stresses the futility of their efforts to gloss over the gravity of what they themselves became by what they continued to do. Continuing in their hypocrisy under the gloss of religion created them into the pattern of their own dishonesty, which is an inescapable moral judgment.

An emphasis upon the irrevocable character of human acting by virtue of the consequences it entails underlies the tradition of the Prophets. Ezekiel confronts his people with this tragic aspect of their lives by warning them of their accountability for their acting. Speaking for the god of his people, he declares: "I will call you to account for your doings." (7:8) In this religious interpretation of their relation to a judgment upon themselves, the Prophet stresses the irrevocable character of the impairment of their lives by their own evil acting. Basic to the entire prophetic tradition is this sobering awareness of the tragic consequences entailed for human life by men's own acting.

Each prophet affirms a version of judgment which is characterized by his personality. It is this feature of prophecy to which John Locke refers when he points out that "God does not unmake the man when he makes the prophet". The violence, for instance, with which Ezekiel hurls his condemnations against the Israelites is radically contrasted to the more gentle way that Hosea reminds his contemporaries of their accountability to God for what they do which entails an impairment of God's creation. Rather than attempting to frighten his auditors with the violence of a threat about impending punishment, he invites them to be reasonable in taking advantage of the opportunity they have to relate themselves to their god as they ought to do. He proposes: "Let us humble ourselves, let us strive to know the Lord." And then he assures them of the unfailing certainty upon which they can depend for the benefactions of God's justice, "whose justice dawns like morning light, and its dawning is as sure as the sunrise". (6:3)

Before the tradition of the Prophets had begun in the history of the Israelites, the priests who wrote the book of *Deuteronomy* affirmed a theological belief which is comparable to an aspect of the Greek notion of the inescapability of Fate. It declares: "There is no rescue from my grasp." (32:39)

The *Iliad* affirms a parallel both to the theological concept affirmed in *Deuteronomy* and to the prophetic tradition's acknowledgment of the confrontation of the human being with an ultimate reality in relation to which he becomes aware, often too late, of his limited nature. Diomedes acknowledges that "not even the powerful Lycurgus . . . survived his quarrel with the gods of Heaven for very long".[31] This reference in the *Iliad* takes account of the disparity between the range of activities which is within men's control and the far greater scope of their consequences which are not within their control. This sobering metaphysic persists throughout the following centuries in Greek reflecting and in Greek religion. It thus has a continuity which is comparable to the continuity of the same type of metaphysic in the history of the Israelites.

Theseus in Euripides' *Madness of Heracles* declares a sobering reminder which reaffirms the stern acknowledgment made by Diomedes in the *Iliad*.

225

Theseus declares to Heracles: "Thou, a man, canst not pollute what is of God."[32] In the violence of his madness in which he killed his own children, he committed an outrage which desecrated the most elemental basis of human nature and thereby alienated him from the tolerance of "the heavens".[33] The heavens are the embodiment in Greek reflecting of the limits within which men alone can live well. Going counter to these limits sanctioned by the divine nature brings about men's own destruction.

Euripides does not question the validity of the traditional Greek belief that there are limits within whose strictures men can live wisely and in defiance of which they destroy themselves. But he became increasingly critical of the mythological vehicle with which this belief was expressed. He questioned the warrant for a religious version of the moral strictures which are not of men's choosing, but rather are limits within which they may chose to live well by living wisely. He thus acknowledges that there is a final factor with which human wisdom must reckon in deciding what is admissible for them to do without destroying their well-being. But he questions, if not outrightly rejects, the theology which maintains that "the bounds for right and wrong for our lives" are imposed upon men by gods. In his *Hecuba*, he ventures the explanation that it is "by custom . . . we believe" in the gods and by custom likewise we believe that they "set up bounds of right and wrong for our lives".[34] His shift from a traditional religious explanation to a sociological explanation does not, however, lessen his characteristic Greek acknowledgment of the limits which are imposed upon men that are not their option. Their option is only what they do in relation to such limits which confront them either in their deciding to live wisely and so well, or ignorantly and so cursed with the consequences of their own folly.

Euripides thus introduces a type of "demythologizing" in his reflecting on versions of popular Greek religion. He thereby distinguishes the spiritual or moral soundness of a belief from the pictorial or mythological imagery with which it is affirmed. The Chorus in *Electra* expresses his own view about some of the spectacular accounts of which Greek fancy was capable, just as the fancy of the Israelites likewise was capable. The story in *Joshua* of the sun standing still and the moon halting "until a nation had taken vengeance on its enemies" (10:13) may have some parallelism to the mythology which the Chorus disparages when it declares "'Tis said, though I can scarce believe it, the sun turned round his glowing throne of gold, to vex the sons of men by this change because of the quarrel amongst them". What Euripides did not question was the fact of a disparity between men's acting which is worthy of respect, and so of a reverence for its sanction by gods, and the moral outrages of hate in warfare of which the Greeks were as capable as were the Israelites.

The Chorus affirms another point of view of the dramatist when he acknowledges that "tales of horror have their use in making men regard the gods".[35] Euripides thereby introduces into a more conservative tradition of Greek religious interpretations of men's relations to gods a less religious type of explanation which takes account of principles of psychology or sociology. In so doing, one can respect the preeminent need internal to Greek mythology and mythological versions of religion for a criticism such as the major Hebrew prophets introduced into the priestly tradition of the Israelites.

Aeschylus points out an aspect of Zeus which could not help being morally abhorrent to reflective Greeks when the Chorus in *Prometheus Bound* refers to the "direful sway by self-appointed laws" which characterize his reign.[36] The notion of "self-appointed laws" was repellent to the reflecting of serious Greek intelligence. Their critique of this notion was one manifestation of the secularizing of Greek religion, and with this secularizing there was a progressive decrease of reverence for gods as the ultimate moral standard.

Plato's stern criticism of the tales about gods in the Epics and in the writings of Hesiod formulated this critical attitude into a philosophical criticism of religion which was inevitable for anyone capable of distinguishing amusing fantasy from sober reflecting on principles whose soundness is beyond questioning. The concept of Athena Poliuchos, for instance, as the incarnation of law and so of civic virtue, contrasted in serious Greek reflecting with the follies and caprice which fanciful mythology attributed to some of the lawless and irrational activities of the gods.

The Athenians, according to Herodotus, commissioned Solon to codify a system of laws for them. And by virtue of his understanding of the inclination of many people for lawless behavior, he formulated laws with the provision that "the Athenians themselves could not repeal them . . . for ten years". Understanding the nature of men as well as understanding the type of laws beneficial for them, he left Athens for the ten years "lest he should be compelled to repeal any of the laws he had made since the Athenians themselves could not repeal them, for they were bound by solemn oaths to abide for ten years by such laws as Solon should make".[37] An ambivalence is thus expressed in people's disinclination to subordinate themselves to laws which admit of no latitude in their options and, on the other hand, in their respect for their own honor to

conform to their oath as a binding obligation. Thus the moral respect c
the Greek for his oath, notwithstanding his impulsive opposition to th
constraint of laws imposed upon him, indicates the survival of a mora
restraint in Greek corporate life even after the weakening of a religiou
reverence for a divine sovereignty, whether personalized as a god o
revered as the Heavens. Reflective Greeks, such as Euripides, distin
guished between laws which merit being attributed to a divine source fo
their validity and the type of arbitrary laws imposed by Zeus upon othe
equally capricious gods of Olympus. A mythology of the caprice of suc
gods is the final dissolution of the high-minded character of a Gree
religion which was expressed in its noble temples. A Greek tragedy, whic
is also a universal tragedy, is that the nobility of temple architectur
outlived the piety which was expressed in the building of such temples.

4. A penalty for human beings is entailed in transgressing sanctions o a divine reality

Hesiod defends the basic appropriateness of human beings to rever
the gods. He declares that "it is right for men . . . wherever they dwell
to "serve the immortals" and to "sacrifice on the holy altars of th
blessed ones". Acknowledging that this reverence is a reasonable obliga
tion of human beings makes it credible that they should be held ac
countable for their negligence or unwillingness to respect such piety a
one of their moral responsibilities. He, therefore, regards it as one aspec
of intelligence to understand the basis for the penalty men suffer whe
there is an initiative of such a reality to "put them away because they
would not give honour to the blessed gods".[38] Hence he gives a religiou
counsel for moral reasons when he says "as far as you are able, sacrifice
to the deathless gods purely and cleanly . . . both when you go to bed an
when the holy light has come back, that they may be gracious to you
in heart and spirit".[39]

This counsel of what human beings should do in relation to the gods
expresses a piety which was an established or respected way of living o
long standing. This is illustrated by a pre-Dorian religious festival o
Hyacinthus celebrated by the Lacedaemonians, which according to Her
odotus, expresses that "their chiefest care was to give the god his due".[40]

Homer likewise maintains that piety includes human "decency and
moderation", since these are ways of living which the gods "respect ir
men".[41] And when men do their part to conform to such expectations of
them, they bring about an enrichment of their own well-being. He main-

228

ins that "The blessed gods . . . reward justice and what men do that is
wful".[42] According to this interpretation of human beings' relation to
ivine realities, the lawful or ordered aspect of human life conforms to
divine criterion of what is most worthy for human beings. In other
ords, it is an ultimate criterion of what constitutes right acting, the
rmal pattern of which is acting within limits. This ancient version of a
rmal criterion for right acting in relation to the gods is reaffirmed by
ristotle as a basic moral criterion. In his *Ethics,* however, he does not
tain the religious sanction for such a criterion. He maintains that acting
cording to a mean is a scheme which human reason itself recognizes as
referable to acting without a restraint of limit. What is significant,
erefore, in this celebrated Athenian moral philosophy of the fourth
entury is a primary moral criterion which for centuries was respected as
religious obligation as well as moral imperative.

The combination of both of these considerations is expressed in the
unsel given by Odysseus: "Never disregard the laws of god." If the
oral imperative were extracted from the religious obligation so stated,
would be the principle of lawful acting as the nature of conduct. The
orrelate of such lawful acting is well-being, as Odysseus points out when
e formulates a universal moral imperative as "a lesson to every man
ever to disregard the laws of god but quietly to enjoy whatever blessings
rovidence may afford".[43] This counsel was not pulled out of thin air,
nd it was not a principle of practice at which he arrived merely from his
eflecting, abstracted from the ordeal of his many years of wandering.
lthough "anxious . . . to get home," he was detained, and he acknowl-
dged that the reason for this was not his own decision. It was rather
he decision of the gods to detain him because he "had omitted to make
hem the correct offerings". Then he formulated the basis for piety as
bligatory: "They never allow one to forget their rules."[44]

The religious emphasis in the dramas of Aeschylus thus had a back-
round of centuries in the *Epics* and writings of Hesiod. The Chorus in
rometheus Bound reaffirms the essential meaning of the counsel of
dysseus when it declares: "Never shall the counsels of mortal men
ansgress the ordering of Zeus."[45] The Chorus in *Suppliant Maidens*
lso declares: The "will of Zeus cannot be transgressed."[46] Aeschylus
tates the same reason for making piety basic to human life that Homer
nd Hesiod stated: "For the appraiser of our work is severe."[47]

Piety, as reverence for the gods and their requirements of human
eings, cannot be physically coerced upon men, since it is a moral act,
nd therefore expresses men's decision. It is what they choose to do

229

rather than the alternative of disregarding the rights of gods to their reverence. But entailed in men's unwillingness to revere the gods is a consequence in human life which is not a matter of men's option. This occurs without their consent, and occurs even though it destroys their well-being. But it is a consequence which is entailed in their decision not to respect obligations to the gods because they seem tangential to men's primary concerns. The Chorus in *The Suppliant Maidens* urges human beings to "Consider the righteous ordinances of God". And it does not make this appeal as if it were a matter of indifference, the alternative to which is without paramount importance for human beings. It, therefore, declares the warning: "Beware the wrath of Heaven."[48] And it characterizes the inescapable judgment upon men's irreverence for a god's rights to men's respect by declaring "heavy in truth is the wrath of Zeus" for an infringement upon basic moral obligations, such as honoring the rights of suppliants.[49]

In this expression both of his religious and his moral sensitivities, Aeschylus does not dissociate them as if they are separable or independent of each other. According to him, in keeping with the long tradition in which he is included, primary moral obligations, such as those to a guest or to a suppliant at an altar, are also basic religious obligations. Their obligatory character is derived both from a human being's relation to others and also from his relation to a divine reality transcendent of human life. As a morally serious religious person, Aeschylus regarded the sternest of judgments upon men's immorality as reasonably entailed in the nature of justice as a property of a divine reality. He recognized even in the popular mythology of folk wisdom an understanding of principles compatible with the moral and religious sensitivities of erudite literature. One of these beliefs, "so men tell", is that among the dead another Zeus holds "a last judgment upon misdeeds". Thus "not even in the realm of Hades, after death, shall (a human being) escape arraignment for outrage" committed against the basic moral principles of ordered human life.[50]

Although Euripides questioned the defensibility of many religious beliefs which had been affirmed in the previous centuries of his country, there were some whose soundness he did not doubt. At least one of these is the inescapable penalty for a moral outrage of murdering a defenseless child. When Menelaus threatened to kill Andromache's child, she asked him: "Thinkest thou God's hand is shortened, and that thou wilt not be punished?"[51] A moral offense of this nature is so abhorrent even to the most undeveloped conscience, that entirely apart from any embellishment of a basic religious acknowledgment of a divine order, it can readily be believed that there will be a "reckoning-day" for such offense.[52] Another offense which went counter even to the most elementary conscience of a Greek about what is right was the burial of soldiers from Argos; and the Argive women appealed to Theseus, ruler of Athens, to negotiate with the Theban authorities on their behalf. The aged mother of Theseus in turn appealed to him, saying: "My son, I exhort thee give good heed to heaven's will, lest from slighting it thou suffer shipwreck."[53]

Another moral offense which even the most skeptical about religion could believe would meet with an inescapable penalty was Pelop's murder of Myrtilus in revengue for a grudge he held against him. Electra recalls this of "hurling the corpse of murdered Myrtilus into the heaving deep" as the basis for a curse upon "the race of Pelop's sons" which expressed "the wrath of God . . . on them".[54]

"Heaven's light" is the least specified designation for a reality transcendent of human history which Euripides employs to acknowledge the accountability of human beings for a grave moral offense such as the infidelity of Phaedra to Theseus. The Chorus in *Hippolytus* addresses her with the sobering accusation that "Thou hast disclosed thy sin to heaven's light".[55] Thus in spite of any disbelief Euripides had about the intervention of a divine agency to establish justice among men with an unerring accuracy, for which such a reality was often credited, he nevertheless continued to regard some moral offenses as meriting, and also receiving, an inescapable penalty commensurate with their evil.

The entire tradition of the centuries-long culture of the Israelites, as it is recorded in the Old Testament, is keenly aware of an inescapable judgment upon human evil. In this respect, the moral conscience of the Israelites parallels the moral sensitivities of the Greeks, as this is expressed in their early literature. But other than this parallel, there is a vast difference in the vehemence with which the threat of divine judgment upon human wickedness is expressed in the two literatures. There is no parallel in Greek writings for this aspect of divine judgment. But with this exception, there is a comparable acknowledgment of a final inescapability of penalty for moral offenses. Both Israelites and Greeks acknowledge the inevitability of moral penalty for evils which men deliberately commit when they have an alternative way of acting. By virtue of selecting one alternative rather than another, when both are open possibilities for them, their acting comes within the scope of moral accountability. And by virtue of the religious metaphysic of the Israelites,

231

such accountability is interpreted as coming within the province of a divine sovereignty over human history.

The fourth book of the Old Testament affirms a spiritual version of divine judgment which is without the bombast characteristic of much of the Bible's later version of judgment. It maintains that a penalty for infidelity to God is his abandonment of his people: "You will not have the Lord with you . . . because you have ceased to follow the Lord, and he will no longer be with you". (14:42, 43) This spiritual insight into the type of penalty which is entailed by a people's infidelity is internal to the faithless life itself. The severity of this version of spiritual loss by making oneself incapable of a spiritual benefit could not be made more convincing even by the most violent of imagery, such as occurs in some of the biblical accounts of judgment, which often become as revolting as the offenses which are being credited with warranting divine judgment.

First Kings stresses the inability of human beings to forestall a penalty entailed in their moral offenses, and characterizes their ineffectiveness in resisting it to "a reed" which "trembles . . . in the water". In contrast to the characteristic vehemence of the Israelite version of judgment, this book affirms a profoundly spiritual interpretation of it when it declares that "The Lord . . . will abandon Israel for the sins that Jeroboam (the wicked ruler) has committed and has led Israel to commit". (14:15, 16) Being abandoned by a reality which is worthy to be revered is itself the sternest of possible penalties.

Second Kings continues an account of the tragedy entailed in the history of the Israelites by virtue of their infidelity to their god which was entailed in their persisting "in all the sins that Jeroboam had committed". They "did not give them up, until finally the Lord banished the Israelites from his presence". (17:22, 23) This is another spiritual version of judgment free from the mythological embellishment of terrifying imagery. No punishment of human wrongdoing could supersede in severity the penalty pointed out in this reference in which "the Lord banished" a people "from his presence". Cutting them off from the ultimate source of well-being is the supreme version of penalty that could be correlated with human offenses against what it is right for men to do. This same profound version of divine judgment is again affirmed in this same book when it points out that the "tribe of Judah . . . followed the practices adopted by Israel; so the Lord rejected the whole race of Israel . . . and . . . flung them out of his sight". (vs. 20, 21) Denying a people their relation to the ultimate source of trustworthy good is the supreme form of penalty entailed in the deliberate type of evils of which human beings are capable. They cut themselves off from the source from which they can be liberated from their practices of evil. There therefore could be no punishment more severe entailed in infidelity than alienating themselves from the benefactions which religious faith acknowledges as having a providential origin.

Isaiah maintains that human beings are "destroyed" who "do not regard the majesty of the Lord" and who "never learn justice". Their incapacity to be faithful is the offense of their impiety. Their failure or refusal to learn "justice" is the moral offense which denies them the quality of human life made possible only on moral conditions. Thus intensifying the imagery with which judgment is described does not add to the soundness of a spiritual version of it. His declaration carries its own credentials: "The wicked are destroyed, they have never learned justice; . . . they do not regard the majesty of the Lord." (26:10)

Hosea likewise interprets the human failure to respect justice as entailing an "unalterable" penalty. In accusing "Ephraim (as) an oppressor trampling on justice", he declares that disregard for justice is itself the destruction of a people: "Ephraim shall be laid waste." (5:11) Such destruction need not be envisioned as external to the disorder and eventual disintegration of a society itself which is entailed in its own injustices. Insofar as justice in human relations is the minimum condition for social stability, and so for well-being in a social context, a people destroy themselves by their own injustices.

Jeremiah maintains that deceit is a moral offense of which human beings are capable in their relations to others who trust them, and for such offense, they are accountable. He declares: "One speaks amicably to another, while inwardly he plans a trap for him." And the Prophet's comment on this offense is attributed to the Lord: "Shall I not punish them for this?" (9:8, 9) The theological premise on the basis of which he makes this prediction with a prophet's characteristic confidence is that the Lord is mindful of men's way and therefore "their wrongdoing is not concealed". (16:17, 18)

Ezekiel reaffirms the prophetic rubric which is basic to the tradition of the prophets in the Bible. He declares a warning which he attributes to the god of Israel: "I will call you to account for your doings." (7:8) He declares that it is the "Lord God" who decrees that "As I live. I will reign over you with a strong hand, with arm outstretched and wrath outpoured". (20:33)

Habakkuk specifies a type of moral offense for which men will be unfailingly penalized by the consequences of their own offenses when he

233

declares: "Woe betide you who have built a town with bloodshed and founded a city on fraud." (2:12) The morally insubstantial structure of any social organization internal to which are bloodshed and fraud is incapable by its own nature to yield well-being to its citizens. It is incapable of an endurance such as would be assured a society whose fabric is free from such offenses against human rights.

5. *Religious faith in the justice of divine judgments*

Whereas Job questions the justice of his suffering which he attributes to the indifference of a divine reality, his friend, Eliphaz the Temanite, affirms an unwavering religious faith that whatever is sanctioned by such a reality is just. Furthermore, be believes that even adversities in human life are indirect manifestations of a providence which works for men's benefit. He declares this unqualified religious faith when he says : "Happy the man whom God rebukes! . . . For, though he wounds, he will bind up; the hands that smite will heal." (5:17, 18)

The Psalmist also affirms an unquestioned trust in the justice of God's judgment, declaring: "He it is who will judge the world with justice and try the cause of the peoples fairly." (9:8) His confidence in the justice of God's judgments is as unqualified as is his faith in the worthiness of God to be trusted. He declares: "Thy unfailing love, O Lord, reaches to heaven, thy faithfulness to the skies." (36:5) Included, therefore, in this dependability of God is the dependability of whatever expresses God's providence, such as his guidance or his instruction of those who trust his providence. The Psalmist maintains that "The Lord's instruction never fails", and "The Law of the Lord is perfect". Its perfection "revives the soul" of the human being who turns to it. (19:7)

These affirmations of faith in the trustworthiness of God's providence constitute what may be regarded as a norm for religious life. But, as all norms, it contrasts with the nature of actual human life. And this normative nature of religious faith, as it is affirmed in *Psalms*, is also contrasted with a questioning of its defensibility. The Psalmist honestly admits he was in "deep distress" and his "spirit was sunk in despair". (77:6) In this ordeal of distress and despair, he asked himself: "Will the Lord reject us for evermore and never again show favour? Has his unfailing love now failed us utterly. . . . Has God forgotten to be gracious." (vs. 7-9) This questioning of the truth of affirmations of God's unfailing dependability is a qualification of the type of normative faith which the Psalmist himself affirms. In this respect, his religious faith has an ambivalence which is all too human.

After questioning the justification for confidence in the dependability of God's providence, his attitude changes, and instead of being preoccupied with his distress and his despair, he recalls the blessings for which he had previously been thankful. His entire point of view changes, and he addresses himself to the god whom he both alternately trusts and distrusts, saying: "But then, O Lord, I call to mind thy deeds; I recall thy wonderful acts in times gone by. I meditate upon thy works and muse on all that thou hast done." (vs. 11, 12) Thus internal to his own ambivalent way of interpreting his relation to God is a corrective for his own disbelieving. His disbelieving, in other words, is only one aspect of his experience. If it were the entire nature of his attitude, he would not have had the redeeming help within himself to overcome such an unqualified disbelieving.

It, therefore, is instructive to take account of the contrast between the normative type of religious faith of which the Psalmist was capable and the tentative suspension of such faith. In points out an unstable character of faith even in individuals who at times have an unwavering faith in the availability of a providential help to diminish what otherwise would be an ordeal of unending distress and despair. The instruction in other words which one can gain from the *Psalms* is thus twofold. It is both an ideal of religious faith, and it is also an actual case study of a human being subject to discouragement, distress, and despair. And during such occurrences in his life, he questions or disbelieves what he sincerely believed during other conditions within his complex life, which may be characterized as ambivalent because capable of experiences which are essentially different orientations of life itself. One orientation is a trust in a reality external to oneself, and another orientation is its opposite: It is a distrust. One attitude is unquestioning faith, and another attitude is disbelieving the justification for having such an attitude.

Isaiah affirms a version of religious faith which, although normative, nevertheless, differs from the norm affirmed by the Psalmist. Isaiah's orientation to a future which he believes will include the providence of God in an unqualified manner contrasts with his view of the time in which he lived. Looking to a future, he declared: "On that day the plant that the Lord has grown shall become glorious in its beauty." (4:2) This is the type of religious faith characteristic of all apocalyptical versions of human history. These versions include a radical contrast between what is possible when there is an unrestricted manifestation of God's providence, and what constitutes the nature of human life denied such po: sibility by its own unworthiness to receive it.

Both Jeremiah and Ezekiel affirm a confidence that whatever the pa: ticular responses of God may be to human life, they will be just. Suc justice is determined by what men themselves deserve, and in this sens the judgment is determined by what men do, although the initiative f imposing such judgment is not within men's control. Jeremiah declar that God "will pour down upon men the evil they deserve" by virtue their wrongdoing. (14:16) Ezekial declares the same confidence tha "the punishment men had deserved" is the treatment they received b God's initiative. (22:31) Basic to the prophet Ezekiel's religious fait is an unwavering confidence in the justice of God's judgment upon me irrespective of the severity of penalty which such justice may entail. H declares: "The Lord . . . will bring you to justice." (11:9)

The apocryphal writing of *The Wisdom of Solomon* expresses one the profoundest versions of a religious faith in the justice of God withou resorting to the violence of threats so characteristic of canonical propheti writings. The author of this writing interprets "the dreams that to mented" human beings "before they died" as having a providential fun tion of disclosing to them a judgment upon their lives. Such dream made it clear to them "why they suffered", and the justice of God i providing such dreams for human beings is "that they should not di ignorant of the reason why they suffered". (18:19)

This most subtle version of the justice of God is also a spirituall sensitive way of interpreting the justice of God's providence in the cor relation of "tormenting" dreams with the wrongdoing in human lif that occasions them. By taking account of one's dreams, one thus ha an inventory of his own acting which he refuses to acknowledge durin his waking consciousness, but which asserts itself in his dreams. Th correlation, therefore, between the tormenting character of a dream an the wrongdoing which is the occasion out of which it arises is a versio of justice that occurs in human life without men's consent and agains their own wishes. It comes about because it is a just judgment upon wha they themselves do.

The author of this apocryphal writing stresses the justice expresse in the spiritual poverty of human life that comes about when men d not take notice of the manifestation of the Creator in a world whos divine creating should be so evident. He points out the moral respon sibility for a poverty of religious interpretation by reminding huma beings that, although they have "enough understanding to speculate abou

236

ve universe", they do not use the same capacities to revere the Creator
of the universe. For their insensitivities to the divine origin of the universe, they are, therefore, responsible. Hence "they do not deserve to be
excused" for the spiritual poverty which blights their life because of
their own moral failure to cultivate a richer spiritual life. (13:8, 9) Men
pass judgment upon themselves as "fools" who "live in ignorance of
God, who from the good things before their eyes could not learn to know
him who really is, and therefore fail to recognize the artificer though
they observed his works!" (vs. 1-3)

This writer affirms his own religious faith that "it was by the prime
author of all beauty that they were created", and he therefore believes
that other men also "should have learned from these how much more
powerful is he who made them". He infers men's moral responsibility for
their religious insensitivities to the origin of the world from the so-called
"cosmological" argument for the existence of God. This argument, as he
affirms it, is that "the greatness and beauty of created things give us a
corresponding idea fo their Creator". (vs. 5) But since men are responsible for interpreting the world as created by God, they are likewise
responsible for the impoverishment of their life by failing to make this
belief central to their life. The spiritual poverty of their lives is thus a
judgment upon themselves for their failure to give God the reverence to
which, as the Creator, he is due.

A parallel ambivalence is expressed in Greek reflecting upon what takes
place in human life that is religiously interpreted as an expression of its
relation to a divine reality. In addressing himself to Pallas Athene, Odysseus declares: "I could fight against three hundred with you beside me,
sovereign goddess, and with your whole-hearted help to count on."[56] A
comparable type of religious trust in a divine help is also affirmed by his
son, Telemachus, who assures his nurse that there is no reason to have
fears about his father's return since "There's a god's hand in this".[57]

Homer's religious interpretation of the relation of human beings to a
divine reality which expresses itself in their life is also expressed in the
assurance that Athene gave to Telemachus: "Where your native wit fails,
heaven will inspire you."[58] Another translation of Athene's relation to
him is the comment: "Some of (your wit) you yourself will see in your
own heart, and some the divinity will put in your mind. I do not think
you could have been born and reared without the god's will."[59]

Homer expresses his religious way of interpreting what is extraordinary
in human life as a manifestation of divine favour to human beings. He
characterizes Amphiaraus as "a man whom Zeus and Apollo loved and

237

blessed with every mark of their favour".[60] Such favor, however, was not continuous or unbroken, since in spite of both gods' generous attitude toward him in giving him capacities for leadership and "every favour", "he never came to the doorsill of old age, but perished in Thebes, because his wife had been bribed with presents".[61] Thus Homer points out how limited divine agencies are in bestowing benefactions when human beings impair what gods are capable of doing. This is another acknowledgment characteristic of both Greek and Israelite reflecting that human beings themselves set limits to what a divine reality could otherwise do for them.

The *Iliad* offers an instance of a religious interpretation of a human capacity to be strengthened by a divine favor upon the condition of permitting such a favor to benefit one's life. Bellerophon "succeeded in killing" the Chimaera because he "let himself be guided by the gods".[62]

Aeschylus in *The Suppliant Maidens* expresses a religious interpretation which is essentially as unquestioned as is affirmed in the *Epics*. The king of Argos is uncertain about what to do to give sanctuary to the Danaides when the Chorus affirms the religious faith that "Both sides alike in this dispute doth Zeus . . . survey with balance poised impartially, apportioning, as is due, unto the wicked, their wrongdoing and to the godly their works of righteousness".[63]

The impartiality of a judgment for which Zeus is trusted is thus an acknowledgment of his justice. The counsel which the Chorus proposes to Pelasgus, the king, is "Look upon him that looketh down from on high, unto him, the guardian of mortals sore-distressed, who appeal unto their neighbours, yet obtain not the justice that is their due right".[64] This counsel thus affirms a contrast between what a divine reality can be trusted to do that human beings cannot equally be trusted to do. Such a contrast is in one form or another basic to a religious faith in a reality transcendent of human life which is more worthy of trust than human beings are. An entire metaphysic basic to religious faith is, therefore, affirmed by the Chorus: "Without Thee what is there that cometh to its accomplishment for mortal man?"[65] This may be regarded as an irreducible core of religious faith. It is an unembellished or unexpanded creed of religious trust in a reality transcendent of human life which is worthy of the trust directed to it by human beings. Directing such trust is the nature of religious life.

What is essentially religious in such a human life is its freedom from questioning or disbelieving, which is characteristic of the ambivalent human life in which religious faith is one element, but its dominance in

238

life is qualified by a questioning of its own warrant. The drama of Sophocles' *Oedipus Colonus* affirms an ambivalence of believing that what takes place in human life is fair or just, and also of disbelieving this. Oedipus contrasts his confidence in Zeus and Apollo with his distrust for the justice of Creon. He asks: "Are not my teachers surer guides than thine?"[66] But the Chorus affirms a very different attitude. It expresses a disbelief that there is justice in what has taken place in the life of Oedipus and asks: "Who of all our townsmen gazed not on his fame with envious eyes?" Such freedom from pride should have merited only the approbation of gods, and yet, in spite of his virtues, he suffered in "a sea of troubles sunk and overwhelmed".[67]

The same type of ambivalence is expressed in *Philoctetes*. Philoctetes affirms an unqualified faith that "the gods are just".[68] He therefore regards his appeal to heaven to be justified: "God in heaven requite in kind the wrongs that they have done to me."[69] But he affirms a very different attitude when he declares: "For pirates no wind's adverse."[70] This is a disbelief that there is any correlation between moral merit and what is favorable in human life. He thus affirms a philosophy which maintains that the reality in relation to which human beings live is indifferent to any standard of right rather than wrong. Hence if he were to have interpreted reality as under a sovereignty which establishes a final justice in what takes place in the world, he would not have affirmed this disbelief.

The Chorus of sailors of Neoptolemus' crew, thinking of the crippled and helpless Philoctetes, acknowledges "how piteous thy lot, luckless man, by man forgot". And on the basis of this obvious instance of injustice entailed in his suffering from the unscrupulous treatment he received from men, affirmed: "O the crooked ways of heaven." The Chorus' denunciation of heaven is provoked by the sailors' sense of the injustice of "Lots so changeful, so uneven" which are "given" to "hapless men"[71]

This acknowledgment of the "uneven" lots given to men, in which men suffer adversities intensified by human cruelties, cannot be regarded as having been incorporated into the drama merely for dramatic reasons. It rather expresses the dramatist's own attitude toward the type of religious belief often affirmed about a justice in human life that can unfailingly be depended upon because sanctioned by a divine reality.

Each reader of the drama will, of course, decide whether the extended denunciation of the injustice of Heaven affirmed by Philoctetes is Sophocles' own questioning of the justification for religious faith in an ultimate justice or whether it is introduced into the drama purely for dramatic

239

reasons. So much, however, occurs in human life which is described by Philoctetes that it would be understandable to assume that the reflective Sophocles affirms his own point of view when Philoctetes declares: "evil never dies,

> Fostered too well by gods who take delight,
> Methinks, to turn back from the gates of hell
> All irredeemable rascality,
> But speed the righteous on their downward way.
> What should I deem of this, how justify
> The ways of Heaven, finding Heaven unjust?"[72]

The Trachiniae by Sophocles also indicates an ambivalence of attitudes in which there is a vacillating between believing and disbelieving. After Heracles has become a "piteous spectacle" from being nearly burned to ashes, he addresses himself to Zeus:

> "O altar on Cenaean height,
> How ill dost thou requite
> My sacrifice and offerings!
> O Zeus, thy worship ruin brings.
> Accursed headland, would that ne'er
> My eyes had seen thine altar-stair!
> So had I 'scaped this frenzied rage
> No incantation can assuage."

After this declaration of his regret that he had ever worshipped Zeus—as if apart from such worship he might have been spared his plight—he then acknowledges that "no art a remedy could teach, save Zeus alone".[73]

Whereas Heracles may be regarded as vacillating in disbelieving and in believing, or in denouncing the injustice of Zeus and yet admitting that Zeus alone can offer a help which no other source can offer, there is no comparable ambivalence in the response of Hyllus, his son, to his father's tragic plight. He declares an unconditional disparagement of any religious faith which affirms a confidence in the justice of the gods:

> "We are blameless, but confess
> That the gods are pitiless.
> Children they beget, and claim
> Worship in a father's name,
> Yet with apathetic eye
> Look upon such agony."[74]

The Chorus in Euripides' *Medea* assures the distraught Medea that Zeus will judge" the infidelity of Jason.[75] Therefore "It is Zeus that shall right thee".[76] Medea herself trusts the justice of Zeus in her appeal: Forget him not who is cause of this."[77]

The closing chorus, however, affirms a more qualified confidence that the gods respond to appeal according to men's belief of what it is just and right for the gods to do. While not indicating a disbelief in the justice or fairness of the judgments of gods, it affirms a caution that a human being should not presume that his own version of what is right or just is also the version of it which is maintained by the gods—if there actually are such gods whose versions of right or justice supersede the soundness of human judgments of what is right or just. At the end of the play, the Chorus counsels: "The things that we looked for, the Gods deign not to fulfil".[78] The same conclusion is affirmed in other plays by Euripides, such as *Helen, The Bacchae,* and *Andromache.*

Since this type of conclusion is ambiguous, it is impossible to infer from it any estimate about the dramatist's own attitude toward the warrant for a religious trust that there is a more dependable dispensing of justice than any of which men are capable. The very ambiguity of the conclusions of these several plays most likely indicates Euripides' own questioning of the defensibility of traditional beliefs about the role of any reality transcendent of human life which enters into human life to establish a justice that men themselves do not establish.

In Euripides' *The Madness of Hercules* there is no such ambiguity of the dramatist's point of view about the defensibility of popular trust in the justice of gods. Amphitryon appeals to Zeus to spare the lives of Hercules' children, but when there is no evidence of the god's intervention in the tragic madness of their father, Amphitryon resigns himself to the futility of his petition. He declares: "Yet often hast thou been prayed; in vain I toil."[79]

After the fit of madness in which he killed his children and their mother, Hercules himself vents his bitterness against heaven for its remorseless indifference to the plight of his innocent children and to the evil of a madness which made him unaware of what he was doing. He declares: "For me God cares not, nor care I for God!"[80]

That his madness was attributed to the goddess Hera implies a disbelief that there is any respect by a god or goddess for rationality as the supreme good in human life. Iris cynically declares that "'Twas not to practice self-control that the wife of Zeus sent "madness into the mind of Hercules.[81] This is a negation of the popular religious belief that there is

241

a respect on Olympus for what is most noble in human life, which is man's self-control by means of his reasonable intelligence. This is, therefore, a disparagement of a traditional religion as it became corrupted in the myth-making fancies of popular mentality uncontrolled by any genuine piety for a divine reality worthy of respect and reverence.

The Chorus most likely affirms Euripides' own critique of popular religious beliefs of the nature of gods which are not within the scope of the most enlightened of human beings' moral standards. The Chorus declares: "Had the gods shown discernment and wisdom", as they should have done, there would have been a very different manifestation of their role in human life. It complains that there is no evidence among human beings that there is "a visible mark of worth" by which it is "possible to distinguish the good and the bad". The fact that there is no such obvious distinction between good and evil men is the basis for the Chorus' inferring that "the gods have set no certain boundary 'twixt good and bad" in what human beings do.[82] Thus men who will to do good are at the mercy of those without such will and for whom there are no scruples which limit what they do. The moral outrage, therefore, of this nature of human beings in relation to each other is that the good suffer for the unrestrained evil of those who live without respect for what is right and just.

Euripides' critique of the low moral level to which popular religion degenerates in its mythological versions reaffirms another tradition of long standing among reflective Greeks. This is the conviction that there is an essential reasonableness of the universe. This is taken for granted in all of Greek philosophies other than its cynicisms and skepticisms. It is also basic to its most influential moral philosophies of Stoicism and Epicureanism, before the high-minded teachings of Epicurus became as corrupted in popular interpretations as sober traditional religion became corrupted in popular mythology.

Homer and Hesiod reaffirm an early Greek tradition of reflecting which maintains that there is a lawful order in the world, objectified as a reality distinguishable from the vast number of ordered phenomena. Such a factor other than ordered phenomena themselves was identified as *themis*. And in the mythological embellishment of this deified factor manifested in the lawful order of the physical world, Themis was identified as a wife of Zeus and mother of Prometheus. And the fantasy continued without limits of reason, as is the characteristic nature of fantasy.

Apart from the pictorial mythology, which corrupted the profound Greek insight into an explanation for the lawful character of phenomena was a reflective inclusion of moral order in an explanation for all order. This more sober metaphysic of the orderliness of nature extended also to human society and then to individual morality. When so extended, it became identified with the *Horae*, anthropomorphically interpreted goddesses of the seasons as instances of ordered nature.

When Apollo was interpreted by people who were capable of reasonable restraint in their reflecting and in their conduct, he was identified with traits that high-minded Greek reflecting could respect and honor. But when he was interpreted by Greeks without either the intellectual or the moral qualification adequate for conceiving of any reality as upright, his figure became encumbered with the same type of projected irrationality as did Zeus and the other gods. The same tendencies which characterize human life also characterize human beings' versions of divine realities. And the upshot of their interpretations is that gods are reduced to their own level, which is characteristically impoverished of respect for order and so for justice.

Notwithstanding the widespread extent of popular corrupting of religion, as every other aspect of human life, there always remains the "faithful few" whose reflecting is conditioned by their own uprightness. Such human beings are impressed with the preeminent desirability of rational order in human relations, and such a rational order includes a proportionate relation between moral merit and the moral quality of human life. The formal basis for this relation is *dike,* or what is right and just. When this formal basis is reified, or thought of as a reality other than every particular relation itself exhibiting the nature of justice, it becomes thought of as a divine being, Dike.

Reflective Greeks, such as Aeschylus, dissociate the notion of justice from its mythological versions and even from its reification as a deity and regard it as a reality unembellished with the clutter of pictorial imagery. Aeschylus speaks of it in this way when the Chorus in *The Suppliant Maidens* declares that "Justice protects her champions".[83] This high-minded moral faith is independent of the imagery of popular religion or popular mythology. It has a metaphysical status such as Plato later attributed to all normative archetypes, one of which is Justice.

Reflective Greeks thought of Law as the universal condition for all lawful relations, including the essential nature of laws of an ordered society. Herodotus narrates the conversation of Demaratus with the Persian Xerxes in which Demaratus praises the Lacedaemonians for being "as brave as any man living" and acknowledges that "together they are the best warriors on earth". Then he points out to the Persian, who was incapable of understanding what he said, that "Free they are, yet not wholly free for law is their master, whom they fear much more than your men fear you . . . what the law bids them, that they do".[84] This analysis by Demaratus, himself formerly king of Sparta, affirms a moral and political philosophy which had persisted for centuries among the reflective Greeks. This long tradition in Greece was formulated by Plato into his normative moral and political philosophy in the *Republic,* and became basic to Aristotle's *Politics* as well as to his *Nicomachaean Ethics.*

The mother of Theseus, king of Athens, in Euripides' play *The Suppliants,* affirms the nonmythological and nonreligious tradition of the reflective Greeks when she declares: "This it is that holds men's states together—strict observance of the laws."[85]

A strictly moral way of supporting character which sustains a human being throughout his adversities is affirmed by the Chorus of Myceanaen women in Sophocles' *Electra.* The counsel it offers to distraught Electra is an expression of a moral wisdom which Stoicism maintained is the final source of trustworthy dependability in human life: "Abate excess of hate, for time can heal, a gentle god and mild."[86] This counsel might well be regarded as Sophocles' moral philosophy which points out to human beings a source of help internal to their own resources. This counsel, however, is not incompatible with a morally enlightened religious interpretation of the validity of such counsel. But it is incompatible with the mythological imagery characteristic of popular religious belief which are accommodations to the moral level of many human beings.

VIII

Limits to What Men May Do

1. *A limit is set by a divine reality beyond which men may not go*

A prohibition against trespassing upon an area made sacred by the presence a divine reality is affirmed in *Exodus*, which includes a narrative of the descent of the Lord "upon Mount Sinai in the sight of all the people". The area thus made holy was thereby also made tabu to people, whereupon the demand was made that they "must put barriers round the mountain and say, 'Take care not to go up the mountain or even touch the edge of it' ". The penalty entailed in defying the prohibition was death: "Any man who touchs the mountain must be put to death." (19:12)

The *Book of Job* includes an account of Job's confrontation with his creator in which he is reminded of the principle upon which the world itself was created: "Bounds were established" to which every part of the creation must conform. The Creator instructed each part of his creation with the inflexible law: "Thus far . . . and no farther." (38:11) Human beings included within the creation were likewise confronted with limits within which they may live and beyond which they may not go without a penalty entailed in their defiance of their Creator's decree. The range of permissible acting for human beings, therefore, is not determined by their choice, but by the ultimate reality to which they are subordinate. This is acknowledged by Job as an expression of his religious awareness of his subordinate status: "Thou has laid down a limit, which (man) cannot pass." (14:5)

Job's philosophy of life within his more comprehensive metaphysic of

245

an ultimate reality to which human life is subordinate is basic to the reflecting of the ancient Israelites. It is likewise paralleled in ancient Greek reflecting. As Frederick Grant points out, the "Delphic maxim, 'Know thyself,' . . . meant simply, 'Acknowledge that you are a mortal, and do not overstep the limits of your lowly estate.' "[1]

A dialogue between Athena and Diomede in Euripides' *Rhesus* is very much a parallel of the dialogue between the Creator and Job. Diomede, for the moment, forgot his subordinate status and presumed to tell the goddess what he was going to do. Whereupon she reminded him that there is a sovereignty more ultimate than his will: "No! beyond the ordained . . . thou canst not go."[2] In other words, what he was inclined to do was confronted by a reality which he dared not ignore. Such confrontation was a warning for a sensible Greek as well as for a sensible Hebrew.

Every aspect of human life can approach a limit, and such limit is an occasion for a sobering warning not to go beyond what is permissible for human beings. Even the happiness of human beings is confronted with a reflective awareness that as it approaches more than most human beings enjoy, it also runs the risk of being curtailed for the same basic reason that exceeding limits is not permitted to human beings. Homer's *Odyssey* includes a narrative of Odysseus' return to his home after nineteen years for a reunion with Penelope, whereupon she acknowledged that the long denial of their happiness together was "due to the gods, who couldn't bear to see us share the joys of youth and reach the threshold of old age together".[3] Although such happiness seems a good to which human beings are entitled, a more than common span of such good fortune runs counter to the basic principle that there are limits for everything. This principle is so basic to the reflecting of the ancient Greek that there is no exception to its application. It, therefore, is manifested in setting limits even to the supreme good of happiness between human beings who are loyal to each other, and therefore who respect one of the fundamental moral obligations.

Herodotus narrates a conversation between Croesus, king of Lydia, and Solon, in which the King was anxious to learn from Solon what he regards as the most important of principles basic to living well. Solon replied that one truth of which he is certain is "Heaven" is "jealous" of men and troubles them upon every occasion that men forget the limits within which they otherwise might live well.[4]

Solon inferred this moral principle from observed occurrences in nature. In this respect, his reflecting is as empirically based as is the reflecting

246

of the Milesian naturalistic philosophers who were his contemporaries. He points out: "It is ever on the tallest buildings and trees that lightning strikes." And then he affirmed the metaphysical generalization that "It is heaven's way to bring low all things of surpassing bigness". Since his metaphysic is also one of his religious beliefs, he points out that "the god smites with his thunderbolt creatures of greatness more than common", and a reason which he offers for this occurrence is that "the god" does not permit men "to display their pride".

The universality of this principle which is implied in his religious metaphysic also applies to men's military ambitions: "Thus a numerous host is destroyed by one that is lesser, the god of his jealousy sending panic, fear of thunderbolt among them, whereby they do unworthily perish; for the god suffers pride" in no human being.[5] This generalization was thus applicable to the defeat of Xerxes by the armies of Greece, notwithstanding his massive superiority of men and military equipment.

The thought which is expressed in the third chapter of *Genesis* parallels the thought of the reflective Greeks that there are limits with which human beings are confronted that they may not defy. And when such penalty is interpreted within a religious orientation, it is regarded as punishment imposed by a divine reality. In this chapter in *Genesis,* the deity protests that "Man has become like one of us, knowing good and evil". And then he asks: "What if he now reaches out his hand and takes the fruit from the tree of life also, eats it and lives for ever?" Aware that the prerogative of endless life would trespass upon the nature of the creator himself, he decided that the human being had gone as far in his daring as he could be permitted to go, and "So the Lord God drove him out of the garden of Eden". (3:22-24)

2. *Men may not trespass upon sacred precincts*

The precinct of a temple is sacred to a god who inhabits the temple. This precinct or *temenos,* therefore, is a limit which a human being may not disregard. And when he does, either with or without intending to do so, he is subject to a punishment imposed by the god. A temple which is dedicated by men to a god becomes the sacred dwelling place of the god. Its sacredness, therefore, is a property of such a building created by men which no other structure has that men themselves build. After its dedication to a god, it passes beyond the jurisdiction of men and comes under the sovereignty of a god. The religious acknowledgment of men's subordination to a divine reality upon whom they are finally dependent makes

247

it possible for them to accept this transition of jurisdiction from themselves to a god by virtue of dedicating the temple to its god.

People were not permitted to enter the innermost sanctuary in the ancient temples. This was a shrine in which oracles of the god were disclosed to men, but only through the media selected by the god who deemed them worthy of this mission. The term for such a sacred area of the temple is derived from the Greek "adytos", which means "not to be entered". Hence the *adyton* is a part of the temple which is closed to all but to those who were permitted by the god to enter. Frederick Scully thus points out the ambivalence in the nature of the temple from the point of view of the religious Greek. It "both invites and sets a limit". It is "approachable and inviolate".[6]

Although it was built by human beings, their religious orientation to the gods enabled them to be thankful that they had among themselves the presence of a god who would honor the temple with his presence. This transition from what men themselves build to what later imposed inviolable limits upon them was certainly not regarded by them as a process of objectifying their reverence upon the object of the temple. This may be an explanation which is cogent to one who is external to the religious attitude toward a temple revered for the presence of a deity. But such an explanation is not included within the set of beliefs with which a religious person esteems a temple and its precinct as sacred. Their sacredness for him is a property entirely separable from any aspect of human life. In other words, it is not a property conferred upon the temple and its precincts by men's reverence. It is rather by virtue of the god's presence. The god confers the sacredness. Not men. Hence the god sets the limits to what men may do in relation to it after they have had the honor to build it for the presence of the god.

The door of the cella of a temple was closed to the very people who previously had been its workmen, bringing the temple into existence. Thus it appears as a paradox to all who are not internal to such a religion, that a temple, its cella, and its adyton, which men have created, should constitute limits beyond which they themselves were not permitted to go. But the reverence of a religious person is the religious interpretation itself of the rights of a divine to a human being's dutiful subordination. And it is within the conditioning by such an attitude of reverence that the interpretation becomes cogent to a religious person.

One for whom this religious orientation is not his way of thinking and of living is likewise incapable of understanding as cogent the awesome significance of opening the sacred doors of the cella on holy days in which nen have the honor to give special reverence to the deity. Other than being granted this honor on these extraordinary days, the religious individual is aware of the right of the god to be set entirely apart from human beings.

From the point of view of a Greek religious orientation, gods have sovereignty over the earth as they also have over human life. Hence, it is understandable to such an orientation that there are places on the earth which are suitable for temples such as other places are not. A site thus determines the location of a temple rather than human beings' decision. Even its accessibility to human beings on the special days of religious festivals is not a primary consideration in locating it. What alone is considered in the site of a temple is its suitability to the nature of the deity whose presence will be honored by the temple.

Herodotus understood the religious attitude of the Greeks who dedicated temples to gods. He, therefore, respected the heroism of the Greeks for resisting the invasion of both Darius and Xerxes, because he was aware there was a religious reason for their heroism. It was to defend the temples. Temples had a property for the religious Greek which was more than architectural beauty. Their destruction would entail the dislocation of the presence of the god in relation to whom the religious Greek acknowledged his final dependence for his well-being. Herodotus, therefore, records the Persians' invasion as something more than a military undertaking. He regards it as basically a sacrilegous offense to the gods worshipped by the Greeks that the Persians destroyed all that came within the path of their campaigns, "setting fire to towns and temples".[7] Their plundering and destruction of the temple of Apollo, which was "a place of divination", was especially disturbing to Herodotus.[8] He was confident that the Persians were punished both for this sacrilege and also by the goddess Athene Pronea when they came near her temple for "they were smitten by thunderbolts from heaven, and two peaks broke off from Parnassus and came rushing among them with a mighty noise and overwhelmed many of them".[9] Even the Persians were aware that they had trespassed upon the precincts of a goddess who would not tolerate their impiety, since as Herodotus points out, they fled. And "the Delphians, perceiving that they fled, descended upon them and slew a great number".[10] The defeat of the Persians was thus regarded by Herodotus as their punishment for their sacrilege of entering into the sacred area of Delphi.

Herodotus narrates events, presumably historical, from his religious perspective, such as when he refers to the Scythians pillaging the temple on Cythera. He maintains that they "who pillaged the temple, and all their descendants after them, were afflicted by the goddess" with a permanent disability.[11]

Aeschylus repeatedly expresses in his dramas a religious interpretation such as Herodotus affirms in what he regarded as "history". As if Herodotus were commenting on the invasion by the Persians, Aeschylus thinks of the spirit of Darius returning to pass judgment upon the folly of Xerxes for invading Hellas and destroying its temples, the punishment for which was that his armies were destroyed by the gods, and he himself was brought to total ruin. "For, on reaching the land of Hellas, restrained by no religious awe, they ravaged the images of the gods and gave their temples to the flames. Altars have been destroyed, statues of the gods have been overthrown and their bases in utter ruin and confusion. Wherefore having evil wrought, evil they suffer in no less measure."[12]

Clytemnestra declares in Aeschylus' *Agamemnon* that if soldiers "keep them clear of guilt towards the gods of the town—those of the conquered land—and towards their shrines, the captors shall not be made captives in their turn". The gods, in other words, will defend men who respect temples of the gods. But the provision to such a protection by the gods is that the army which plunders a conquered city may not by "mad impulse . . . overmastered by greed, ravish what they should not".[13] The Chorus in this drama affirms that "It hath been said . . . the gods deign not to be mindful of mortal who trample underfoot the grace of inviolable sanctities".[14] The Chorus again affirms a religious interpretation which is cogent to Aeschylus when it declares that "riches are no bulwark to the man who in wantonness hath spurned from his sight the mighty altar of Righteousness".[15] The opening Chorus of *The Suppliants* declares: "Stronger than a castle is an altar—'tis a shield invulnerable."[16] And the King of Argos maintained that he "beheld yon company of assembled gods marking their assent beneath the shade of fresh—plucked boughs" which had been placed by the suppliants upon the altar as tokens of their appeal for divine mercy.[18]

In Aeschylus' *The Seven Against Thebes*, Eteocles affirms his religious respect for the role of the gods in the welfare of his people, and enjoins them "to succour the city and the altars of your country's gods that their worship may never be blotted out".[19]

In Sophocles' *Philoctetes*, the apparition of Heracles to Philoctetes urges him before going to Troy to revere their gods even though the Trojans are his enemy. Reverence even for the gods of one's foes thus supersedes every other nonreligious consideration: "Only take heed, in laying waste the land to reverence its gods; all else by Zeus . . . is less regarded."[20] The severity of a penalty for ignoring the respect due to whatever is sacred is stressed by Neoptolemus when he points out to his friend Philoctetes that the wound he suffers which does not heal is "heaven-sent". It is his punishment for profaning a shrine: "For this sin wast thou stricken."[21]

3. Men are held accountable for infidelity

There was no more demanding obligation among either the early Israelites or the early Greeks than respecting an oath, whether it was between one individual and another or between a person and his god. The absolutely binding character of a vow which a human being makes with a god is illustrated in *The Book of Judges* that records the "vow to the Lord" made by Jephthah who was "judge over Israel for six years". (12:7) He promised that he would sacrifice the first creature that comes out of his house to meet him when he returned, and the first to meet him was his only child. Because his vow was unconditionally binding, "he fulfilled the vow he had made". Out of respect for his fidelity to the sacredness of his vow, his daughter consented to die. To commemorate her willingness to die rather than to have her father break his vow, "It became a tradition that the daughters of Israel" should honor Jephthah and his daughter "four days in every year". (11:40)

The gravity of obligation which a person's promise imposes upon him is indicated in Ezekiel's declaration that anyone who has "violated a covenant and made light of a solemn oath" will be held accountable by "the Lord God". (16:59)

The Chorus in Euripides' Medea refers to Themis as the goddess who is "witness of oaths" to whom Medea appealed for the "grievous wrongs" she suffered from the infidelity of Jason.[22]

The obligation of a host to his guest is one expression of a promise or vow, and therefore it has the same unconditional character of obligation as the oath by which one declares he will respect his word. The individual who offers hospitality to a guest thus likewise commits himself to the obligation of fidelity for the security and safety of his guest. The Chorus in Aeschylus' *The Suppliant Maidens* expresses the confidence that a state will "be regulated well, if (its citizens) hold in awe mighty Zeus, and, most of all, Zeus the warden of guest-right."[23] The Chorus also warns the King of Argos of the penalty imposed upon anyone who does less than he can to offer sanctuary to those in need of refuge from an

251

oppressor: "Heavy in truth is the wrath of Zeus, god of the suppliant."[24] And the Chorus repeats: "Verily the wrath of Zeus, the suppliant's god, awaiteth such as will not be softened by a sufferer's plaints."[25]

Aeschylus regards the offense of Paris against Menelaus as twofold. He not only took the wife of Menelaus, but he also disregarded his moral obligations to Menelaus for the hospitality he was offered. This moral offense is pointed out in *Agamemnon*: "Paris . . . came to the house of the sons of Atreus and did dishonour to his host's hospitable board." The Chorus declares the gravity of this offense for a human being as a sacrilegious act against Zeus, "the guardian of the rights of hospitality": "To his prayers all gods are deaf." The penalty for one violating his sacred obligation as a guest is that he "who is conversant with such deeds, him (the gods) destroy in his unrighteousness".[26]

Euripides stresses the rights of guests and the obligations of one who offers them hospitality, which is the same basic relation that binds Zeus to suppliants at his altars. Demophon, king of Athens, points out the peril to anyone who dares "spurn the guests" of Zeus at his altars,[27] maintaining that "A temple of the gods is an asylum open to the world".[28]

By virtue of the divine character of its sanctuary to those who seek its protection, anyone who disregards the sacred sanction opens himself to an inescapable punishment by the deity. Hecuba appeals to Agamemnon to revenge Polymestor, king of Thrace, for killing her youngest son, Polydorus, whom she had entrusted to him for safety during the siege of Troy, characterizing the King as "this most godless host . . . fearless alike of gods in heaven or hell".[29] The Chorus declares to the King: "A fearful penalty for thy foul deed hath the deity imposed, who'er he is whose hand is heavy upon thee."[30]

4. *Arrogance or pride is a disregard for moral restraint*

A disregard for limit is offensive to human beings who are injured by others who trespass upon their rights. It is also offensive to divine realities in relation to whom human beings are subordinate. And insofar as human beings deny their subordinate position to such realities, they subject themselves to the penalty entailed in disregarding any limit.

Ignoring a limit is the essential nature of moral evil. It likewise is the essential nature of impiety. Men who presume they are not subordinate to a divine reality therefore bring upon themselves a handicap to their well-being, such as moral evils entail. Disregard for moral restraint is an expression of ignorance in those who do not have intelligence sufficient to

252

order their behavior. But disregard for moral restraint by those who have mental capacities which would be sufficient to order their life, and so to enable them to live well, is a very different type of offense. It is an arrogant disregard for limit as the principle of moral order. Such insolence or arrogance to presume that one is exempt from strictures to which other realities are subject is *hybris* or *hubris*.

As is the case in Greek popular mythology, every moral principle is objectified, and so Hybris becomes anthropomorphically interpreted as the mother of Pan. But such a mythological version does not occur in the serious moral reflecting of the Greeks. Hybris as a moral disregard for reasonable limit in acting is, for example, acknowledged by Homer as a basis for the disastrous outcome for the princes of Argos who exploited Odysseus' property during his long absence. Commenting upon what took place to destroy them, Penelope says: "It must be one of the immortal gods that has killed the young lords, provoked, no doubt, by their galling insolence."[31] In everything they collectively did, they exhibited their arrogance in disregarding the rights of the absent Odysseus, of his son, and of his wife. On the basis alone of the Greek conviction that hybris entails penalty, the support given to Odysseus by Athene fit into the ancient Greek framework both of religious and of moral reflecting. It was for reasons, therefore, other than merely a literary resolving of a problem in the Epic that the princes were destroyed. According to the ancient Greek way of thinking, their destruction was entailed in their own hybris or disregard for every restraint of reasonable behavior.

Lattimore's translation points out this moral entailment in their acting: "They suffered for their own recklessness." According to this interpretation, the assistance by the goddess in reinforcing the strength of Odysseus has both religious as well as moral significance. Homer's belief expresses his religious point of view that human hybris is offensive to gods because it manifests a disregard for the limits within which human beings must respect their subordination to the gods. And it is morally significant for refusing to restrict oneself within limits in any activity. Such refusal is moral evil, which entails its own handicap to well-being.

A principal theme in the *Iliad* is resolving the offense of Achilles' unlimited pride, and therefore his pride without restraint constituted a problem with which Homer struggled through several books in the *Iliad*. Its offensive character finally is resolved by his relenting, which was a morally motivated decision brought about by his reflective awareness that he was thereby destroying himself. It was likewise a religious act, since

253

giving up his offensive pride was a condition for acknowledging his subordination to the gods.

Homer affirms a theological premise in declaring that "When a man decides, without the goodwill of the gods, to fight another who enjoys their favour, he has disaster coming to him".[32] But a profounder moral insight than the belief that some human beings are favored by divine realities more than others is the acknowledgment that all human beings are confronted with limits beyond which they cannot go without an impairment of their well-being. This is a principle basic to the metaphysics of the Greeks. It therefore is logically included in their moral philosophies.

An exception to such entailed handicap for pride seems to be affirmed in Odysseus' comment that although "Kings . . . have their pride", they, nevertheless, are not subject to the same handicap as other men are. The reason for their exemption however is pointed out by Odysseus: "Kings are divine . . . upheld and favoured as they are by . . . Zeus."[33] By virtue, therefore, of having a pride within the limits acceptable to the god, such pride is not subject to a divine curtailment, as is every other instance of pride that goes beyond limits of restraint, and consequently is offensive to a divine reality to which a human being is accountable.

Herodotus interprets history from a religious orientation, just as Homer interprets human life. He maintains that it was the arrogant pride of Xerxes which made it impossible for him to listen to any proposals that did not conform to his own plans. He points out that Xeres refused to be restrained by a "great portent" which appeared at the Hellespont, "though it was easy of interpretation", nevertheless, "Xerxes took no account" of it. "The meaning of it was" that "Xerxes was to march his army to Hellas with great pomp and pride, but to come back to the same place fleeing for his life."[34] Knowing what took place in the several major encounters in which the massive Persian forces were progressively destroyed, Herodotus believed that such a portent had a source other than human fabrication. He believed it was a disclosure from a source transcendent of human beings and was given to them for their instruction. But when their pride refused to take account of such a divinely sent warning, it was the preface to their fall.

The arrogance of Xerxes prevented him not only from taking account of a divinely sent portent, but also of the advice of men older and more informed than he was. His uncle Artabazus, referred to by Herodotus as Artabanus, was well informed of military procedures, and warned him not to fight at Plataea, "But Xerxes answered in wrath, 'Artabanus, you are my father's brother; that shall save you from receiving the fit reward of foolish words. Yet for your craven lack of spirit I lay upon you this disgrace, that you shall not go with me and my army against Hellas, but abide here with the women; and I myself will accomplish all that I have said, with no help from you."[35] As events turned out, Xerxes learned of his folly to have ignored the wise counsel of a general who knew much more than he did, but of whose intelligence his pride prevented him from benefitting.

Herodotus points out another instance of how the pride of Xerxes entailed his final defeat. Artemisia of Halicarnassus, respected for her extraordinary military ability, counselled "Mardonius . . . against a sea-fight" at Salamis, but the hybris of Xerxes again prevented him from taking such counsel. He explained the defeat of his naval forces "off Euboea" as a result "of his absence", and so he "purposed to watch the battle himself" at Salamis.[36] But as he soon found out, his presence made no difference in the disastrous defeat of his naval forces in the encounter against which Artemisia had cautioned. Herodotus thus cites Xerxes' refusals to respect the portent and to listen to the counsels of his uncle and the queen of Halicarnassus as factors contributing to his defeat. Thus his own hybris was the basis for his folly of ignoring counsels whose wisdom far exceeded his own. In other words, his armies were destroyed by his unrestrained arrogance, which was the moral handicap to his ability to seek counsel and to respect it when it was more informed than any judgment of which he himself was capable. His arrogance was his unwillingness to learn from others who were more enlightened than he himself could be by virtue of the handicap of his own pride. His pride in what he himself knew made it impossible for him to believe that he was capable of being surpassed either by divinely sent portents or by others who had previously demonstrated their superior abilities.

Aeschylus interprets the defeat of Xerxes from the same basic religious philosophy of history which was maintained both by Homer and Herodotus. This philosophy of history is based upon the conviction that human beings can live well only when they respect limits. But when they defy such limits, they go counter to more than moral convention. They go counter also to the divine reality to which they are subordinate. Hence any refusal on the part of a human being to acknowledge himself as mortal, and therefore as confronted with finitude, entails a handicap to well-being such as is inevitable for every transgression of limits. In Aeschylus' drama *The Persians*, the spirit of Darius returns to Atossa, the mother of Xerxes, after the destruction of the Persians both at Salamis and in Macedonia. The Spirit declares: "Mortal though he was he thought in his folly that he would gain the mastery over all the gods, aye even over Poseidon."[37]

His offense against Poseidon began at the Hellespont, when not achieving what he wanted, he ordered the sea to be flogged. The Chorus acknowledges that it was not only Poseidon who was incensed by the hybris of Xerxes, but it was also Zeus. It declares: "O sovereign Zeus . . . thou hast destroyed the armament of the high-vaunting and multitudinous Persians."[38] Implied in this twofold reference is that notwithstanding the vast numbers of the Persians, they were defeated by virtue of the hybris of their ruler. The "high-vaunting" attitude was penalized by "Zeus . . . chastiser of overweening pride" who "corrects with heavy hand".[39] Such penalty is regarded by Aeschylus as entailed in the arrogance itself of Xerxes, "drawing on himself the punishment of Heaven by his vaunting rashness".[40] And such punishment was not entailed only for him who returned to his palace "in tattered robes and attended by a scanty retinue". It was also for his empire: "The land bewaileth her native youth, slaughtered for Xerxes, who hath gorged the realm of death with Persians slain."

Aeschylus affirms a religious philosophy of history when the Chorus declares: "Alas, alas, ye powers divine, ye have wrought us ruin."[41] The human cause for such ruin, assured by a divine order as entailed in the moral offense of hybris, is explained by Aeschylus in the chorus in *Agamemnon*: "Ruin is the penalty for reckless crime when men breathe a spirit of pride above just measure."[42] The Chorus affirms the same relation that Herodotus affirmed between excess and the peril it entails: "Glory in excess is fraught with peril; 'tis the lofty peak that is smitten by heaven's thunderbolt."[43]

The reflective Greek was constantly aware of a peril entailed in any manifestation of a pride that trespassed beyond the limits permissible for men. When Agamemnon, for example, returned to his palace after ten years of absence, he was welcomed with an extravagance made possible only by his wealth. Precious tapestries covered the walk on which he entered his palace. But when he noticed them, he expressed his displeasure for fear that such manifestations of pride in using wealth to honor a man rather a god would entail stern disapproval by the gods. He therefore warned: "Draw not down envy upon my path by strewing it with tapestries. 'Tis the gods we must honour thus; but for a mortal to tread upon broidered fineries is, to my judgment, not without ground for dread."[44]

The offensive character of arrogance in any of its many manifestations was likewise feared by Eteocles, prince of Thebes, in *Seven Against Thebes*. He refers to "Onca Pallas, whose abode is high" as "loathing the arrogance of man".[45]

The Messenger in Sophocles' *Ajax* quotes the prediction made by the prophet Calchas that "O'erweening mortals waxing fat with pride fall in their folly, smitten by the gods with dire disaster". The reason for such "disaster" is that human beings disregard the limits to which their nature entitles them, and in so doing, trespass upon the rights of gods. Ajax ignored this barrier between what men may do and what they may not do. He "exalt(ed) himself in thoughts too high for man". He thus began early in his life, as did Xerxes, to disregard the wisdom of those older than himself and enlightened by years of experience which therefore eclipsed his intelligence. "In folly (he) spurned his father's monishments", which were that he "Seek victory . . . but seek it ever with the help of heaven". Yet, this is what he in his arrogance refused to do, regarding himself the subordinate neither of men nor gods. "In his wilful arrogance", he replied: "Father, with gods to aid, a man of naught might well prevail, but I without their help." "Such was his haughty boast", and it was these "vaunting words" which "drew on him the dire wrath of the goddess— pride too high for mortal man".[46] The sad lament of his wife Tecmessa acknowledged the vast disparity between which his pride for a short time had elevated his boastful life and the inevitable penalty entailed in his own ill- founded boasting: "Ah me! How high thou stood'st my Ajax, and how low thou liest here!"—forbidden even burial, which was the minimum version of Greek respect for the dead.[47]

Menelaus, who forbad his burial, ordered that "He shall be cast forth on the yellow sands to feed the carrion birds that haunt the beach".[48] And he defended his decree by declaring, "The State where arrogance hath licence and self-will, though for awhile she run before the gale, will in the end make shipwreck and be sunk". Then he gave the counsel which reaffirms the wisdom repeatedly declared by the reflective Greeks: "Let us not fondly dream that we can act at will to please ourselves" such as "this man lorded it in insolence".[49] After Athena had punished Ajax with madness, she affirmed the principle by which a human being not only might avoid disapproval by the gods but could actually enjoy their gift of well-being: "A day can prostrate and a day upraise all that is mortal; but the gods approve sobriety and forwardness abhor."[50]

Lichas, the herald of Heracles, declares in Sophocles' *Trachiniae* that "gods no more than men can suffer insolence".[51] In affirming this, he points out that the arrogance of overestimating oneself is an offense not only in relation to the gods but also in relation to other human beings whose intelligence enables them to have an enlightened awareness of their own nature. Human beings, in other words, who apply the Delphic maxim, "Know thyself", are offended at the insolence which betrays the ignorance of vanity and conceit which are without limits. Without limits, they are a moral evil to a man who is thereby cut off from approval by his fellows. The social consequences of the offense of "braggarts of outrageous tongue" is "their towns enslaved", because misguided by ignorance presumed in folly to be intelligence.[52] Misinformation provides a foundation which is secure neither for individual human beings nor for them in their corporate life.

In addition to the tragic consequences in relation to other human beings of an individual's overrated poverty of intelligence is the tragic impairment of his life in relation to a reality transcendent of human beings: "Swelling words of high-flow might mightily the gods do smite." The closing lines of the chorus in this same drama, *Antigone,* are: "Of happiness the chiefest part is a wise heart: and to defraud the gods in aught with peril's fraught . . . Chastisement for errors past, wisdom brings to age at last."[53]

The extant dramas of Euripides repeat the same judgment of the centuries of Greek reflecting that arrogance or insolence which is the excess of unjustifiable pride entails an impairment of well-being. Such impairment is brought about not only in human beings' relation to realities transcendent of human life, but also in the relation of human beings to other human beings. An elderly friend of Hercules, seeing the plight of the cursed man, declared: "Zeus chastiseth overweening arrogance."[54] And the chorus in the same drama of the *Children of Hercules* declares: "For the god proclaims it clearly, by cutting short the bad man's pride in every case."[55]

Euripides offers an explanation for the emergence in human life of the offense which alienates a human being both from gods and from other men when he maintains that "Success makes them forget how to bear their fortune".[56] The particular event which was the occasion for this generalization was the Thebans' victory over the Argive forces which made them insensitive to the rights of the dead soldiers for burial. Hence this is the event to which the Chorus refers when it declares: "How insolent the villains are, when Fortune is kind to them, just as if it would be well with them for ever."[57]

A reason that an arrogance which disrespects the rights of others also entails its own penalty in relation to others is its shortsightedness. The

258

ignorance upon which it is based includes a failure to understand the brevity with which any excess of good fortune is confronted. If an individual were intelligent enough, or sobered sufficiently by a wisdom gained in living, he would know that there is no indefinite extension either in the physical world or in the good fortune which sometimes comes to human beings. Basic to this understanding both of the precarious nature of good fortune, and also the impossibility of its indefinite extension in time, is the Greek metaphysic that the world is finite, and as such, there are no durations or extensions without definition or limits.

When it was reported that Capaneus, even before beginning his attack on Thebes, was making plans for what he would do after defeating it, Antigone appealed to the deified Nemesis "to silence such presumptuous boasting".[58] His arrogance was repugnant to Antigone who had been so severely disciplined by life's stern lessons. Hence she appealed to the goddess to intervene to bring an end to his offensive arrogance. The same repellent nature of offensive boasting is disparaged by Theseus, king of Athens, in *The Suppliants,* who declares: "Our presumption seeks to lord it over heaven, and in the pride of our hearts we think we are wiser than the gods."

An undisciplined life tolerates an uncontrolled pride as one manifesation of its low level of morality. When, on the other hand, good fortune occurs in the life of an individual with character, matured by discipline, and so having the benefit of wisdom, there is an appreciation for such good fortune. Theseus points this out when he asks: "Are we not then too proud, when heaven hath made such preparation for our life, not to be content therewith?"[59] He thus affirms a moral philosophy which is akin to Stoicism. And this Stoical aspect of his reflecting was based upon his piety.

Just as Capaneus offended Antigone for his presumption that he could make plans for a future, as if he himself were the sole determinant of it, so Hector was offended by the boasting of Rhesus, king of Thrace, who claimed that when he attacks Troy, he would do in one day more than the total forces of the Greeks accomplished in years of besieging Troy. Instead of appealing to a goddess for rescue from such boasting, as Antigone did, Hector offered Rhesus the sound moral counsel: "Lose not thy path watching a distant view."[60]

Euripides was aware of the arrogance to which boasting might go under the gloss of piety. The self-righteous Hippolytus conferred upon himself a superiority to the morality of all others so that he presumed he was entitled to relate himself to the goddess Artemis on a level to which only

259

another deity was entitled. But in his hybris of distorted religious attitude, he regarded himself as an equal of Artemis, and thereupon addressed her with an irreverence of familiarity: "Accept, I pray, dear mistress, mine this chaplet from my holy hand to crown locks of gold; for I, and none other of mortals, have this high guerdon, to be with thee, with thee converse."⁶¹ A commentary hardly needs to point out that there is more than one way to express a lack of reverence for a divine reality. An outright disavowal of one's obligation to such a reality is even less offensive than an arrogance which presumes that the universal disparity between a human order and a divine order is transcended only in one's own exceptional case. The counsel affirmed by the chorus in *The Heracleidae* might well have been included in the *Hippolytus* as sound instruction for the arrogant youth who mistook his pride for piety: "This must no man wrest from thee, thy reverence for the gods."⁶²

The Israelites' belief that there are limits beyond which human beings in their arrogance of pride cannot go is affirmed throughout their entire early literature. It is expressed in the first book of the Bible and is expressed in nearly every book thereafter, finding expression even in the late historical writing of the *First* and *Second Maccabees*.

Genesis includes the naive but nevertheless impressive religious explanation for the vast variety of languages which are spoken. The story begins with the announcement that "Once upon a time the world spoke a single language", but human beings became overconfident in their abilities and planned to construct a tower "with its top in the heavens". This expression of their presumption, however, came to a halt when "the Lord came down to see the tower which mortal men had built", and he expressed his displeasure for their excessive confidence in what they could do without consent or approval by their creator. He thereupon "confused their speech" so that they could not converse with each other and had to give up their ambitious project.

The second book in the Bible stresses the annoyance of the deity for his people, the Israelites, because they did too little to acknowledge their total dependence upon him for his tutelary role in their corporate life. He declared to them that he had permitted them to continue to live "only to show" them his "power and to spread (his) fame throughout the land", and so beyond the limited area which they occupied. (9:16) The tribal character of "the Lord the God of the Hebrews" is thus evident in *Exodus* in a way that is paralleled in the Greek chauvinistic idea about their tutelary deities. Such tutelary deities are gods of one particular people. Yet, as the reality to whom the Israelites are subordinate and upon whom they are dependent, their deity, according to the reference in *Exodus* is primarily concerned to impress his people with their dependent status. His concern, therefore, is less to impress the Israelites with their status as mortals than it is to impress them with his superiority to other tribal or local gods. This becomes evident in the translation in the *Jerusalem Bible* in which the Israelites are told by their god that he "shall win glory" for himself by defeating the Egyptians, whereby they "will learn that I am Yahweh". (14:4) The more explicit expression of this deity's annoyance with the pride of his people is affirmed in *Leviticus* in which priestly book he threatens to "break" their "proud strength" for not doing enough to acknowledge their final dependence upon his protective providence. Their penalty will be that they "shall wear out (their) strength in vain; (their) land shall not yield its produce any longer nor the trees their fruit". (26:19, 20) The jurisdiction over the fertility of the earth which the Greeks attributed to one of its many deities, such as Demeter, was thus credited to the one and only tutelary deity of the Israelites.

The *Book of Job* affirms a more spiritual religious orientation which is comparable to the profoundest of such orientations in the literature of the Greek dramatists. It thus is very different from the priestly writings of the first books in the Old Testament. In the first cycle of speeches, between Job and his friends, Eliphaz the Temanite addresses himself to Job, telling him of "an apparition" which appeared before him, and in "a low voice" asked him, "Can mortal man be more righteous than God, or the creature purer than his Maker?" (4:17) This interrogation thus stresses the subordinate status of the human being, without also emphasizing as the priestly writings do, the pride of the tutelary deity rather than the pride of human beings.

Eliphaz stresses the helpless nature of human beings without the providence of their god. He declares that apart from his providence they "dwell in houses whose walls are clay, whose foundations are dust, which can be crushed like a bird's nest or torn down between dawn and dark". (vs. 19. 20) In acknowledging the helplessness of the human being apart from the charity of God, the friend of Job affirms a religious interpretation of total dependence upon God for whatever is trustworthy in fulfilling his need for security. Elihu, the second friend of Job, likewise stresses the subordinate status of human beings in relation to God, and therefore is clearly aware of the offense of human arrogance to presume to be self-sufficient or independent of God's providence. He assures Job that "God . . . repudiates the high and mighty". (36:5) And he offers evidence

261

to support this assurance by citing how "kings on their thrones . . . grow arrogant" after they have "sovereign power", but then soon lose their power. Rather than continuing to exert their power, they are "loaded with fetters (and) held fast in captives' chains". As Elihu points out, God "denounces their conduct to them, showing how insolent . . . was their offence". (vs. 8, 9) He explains that the offense for which they were punished was the arrogance of their pride: "Proud men rage against (God) and do not cry to him for help." (36:13) In other words, their pride prevents them from acknowledging their need for the reality upon whom they are finally dependent, which is the ultimate source of benefactions, and it shares this providential nature with no other reality. Hence the folly of human beings who presume that there are other sources of well-being. One of the benefactions a human being could receive from such a reality, if he were to accept its help, is that it would "turn him from his reckless conduct" by checking the unjustified presumption of his self-sufficiency, which is an offense of "the pride of mortal man". (33:17)

The Psalmist explains that the arrogance of a human being is an offense against God because it "leaves no place for God in all his schemes" (10:4) In other words, "he scorns the Lord" as the final source of trustworthy good, presuming that he can live without acknowledging his dependence upon such providence. The Psalmist's religious orientation is the acknowledgment of his total dependence upon God's charity toward human life. Hence he declares: "There is no place for arrogance before thee." (5:5) He acknowledges that it is right that the "Lord give man no chance to boast his strength" and to "let the nations know that they are but men". (9:19, 20) He thus disparages the folly of all who are "full of bluster" about their self-sufficiency, and in their sacrilegous lives parade their "boasting and swaggering". (94:4) He therefore believes it is right that they should be called to account for their arrogance in disclaiming their dependence upon any reality other than themselves. And he addresses himself to the ultimate reality whom he reveres as "judge of the earth": "Punish the arrogant as they deserve." (vs. 2)

Such presumption on his part for telling "the Lord" what should be done, however, exemplifies the same arrogance which he himself condemns in others for their failure to acknowledge their subordinate status in relation to "the Lord". Regarded as literature, such inconsistency would indeed be an instance of irony, expressing arrogance in his condemnation of it. But notwithstanding such irony, the Psalmist is consistent in affirming a religious faith that the divine reality "high as he is, cares for the lowly, and from afar . . . humbles the proud". (138:6) He affirms like-

262

vise the Greek confidence in the inescapability of retribution for hybris: 'The Lord . . . pays the arrogant in full." (31:23)

Proverbs records centuries of reflecting. Much of the reflecting it preserves is universal in its wisdom. Thus when it declares that "Pride comes before disaster, and arrogance before a fall", it condenses the wisdom affirmed throughout centuries of reflecting. (16:18) It regards pride as entailing its own penalty, and in this respect it likewise reaffirms the basic Greek conviction of the inevitability of retribution. In declaring that "Pride will bring a man low", it maintains that such a corrective is entailed internal to human life itself even without the functioning of any reality transcendent of it. (29:23) But the religious orientation of the Psalmist maintains that the inescapability of relation between human pride and its penalty within human life is assured by the role in human life of a reality transcendent of it. This religious belief is expressed in the proverb: "Proud men, one and all, are abominable to the Lord" and "will not escape punishment". (16:5)

The very nature of religious faith itself accounts for the belief that there is a stern correlation with pride and its offensive arrogance. It is offensive because it disparages the religious humility itself expressed in the acknowledgment of man's dependence upon a divine reality for every trustworthy good.

Since pride is an expression of an individual's presumption that he is not dependent upon a source of help external to his own capacities or his own resources, it is understandable that *Proverbs* should regard "a proud heart" and the "haughty looks" which are expressed by one having such pride as "sins (which) mark a wicked man". (21:4) His wickedness is an appraisal of his nature from the point of view of a religious perspective that human beings are not independent of a source of help beyond their own.

The aspect of human beings which exercises Isaiah's indignation is their arrogance which disregards their status as subordinate to a reality transcendent of themselves. Their refusal to acknowledge their subordinate status is stressed by the Prophet's repeated use of similes. Human beings who regard themselves as self-sufficient, and therefore as independent of a reality transcendent of themselves, are like clay in relation to a potter. If the clay were to affirm an arrogance comparable to the arrogance which the proud affirm in relation to their creator, it would declare of the potter: "He did not make me." And if the created pot were to have an arrogance comparable to boastful men, it would turn upon the potter with the insolent comment: "He has no skill." (29:16) If "the axe" were to "set itself up against the hewer, or the saw claim mastery over the sawyer" it would indicate the extent of the presumption affirmed by men who in their pride refuse to acknowledge their creature-status in relation to their creator. They would be like "a stick" if it were "to brandish him who wields it, or a staff of wood to wield one who is not wood". (10:15) On the basis of these repeated similes of realities without life or selfhood in relation to a human artificer, Isaiah affirms a theological interpretation of creation and human history which is the basis for his prophecies that "the Lord . . . has a day of doom waiting for all that is proud and lofty, for all that is high and lifted up". (2:12) The rubric of such predicted judgment upon the arrogance of human beings is that their "pride shall be brought low, and the loftiness of man shall be humbled". Then Isaiah declares what he regards as the only just outcome of such judgment upon human beings: "The Lord alone will be exalted on that day." (vs. 17) This is another way Isaiah maintains that the arrogance of the human being is a trait of life over which he does not have final approval. As the Prophet declares, it will be "due punishment upon the wicked" in which "the pride of the haughty" will be checked and "the arrogance of ruthless men" will be brought low. (13:11)

Isaiah cites history to support his religious interpretations of history itself, and in this use of occurrences in history he may be compared with Herodotus who does likewise. He cites reverses encountered by the Assyrian king which he interprets as punishment for his arrogance and vainglory, because the King had said: "By my own might I have acted and in my own wisdom I have laid my schemes." (10:13) The offensive character of such conceit was regarded by Isaiah as justifying the resentment which "the Lord" manifested in his judgment upon the King.

Isaiah cites another occurrence in history to support his prediction of inescapable penalty for the arrogance with which human beings affirm their pride in their own overestimated resources. He declares: "We have heard tell of Moab's pride, how great it is, we have heard of his pride, his overweening pride." (16:6) And after stressing by such repetition the arrogance of Moab, he predicts the inevitable judgment upon such arrogance: "The glory of Moab shall become contemptible for all his vast numbers; a handful shall be left and those of no account." (vs. 13, 14)

This prediction affirms a Greek maxim that the high shall be brought low. Thus if there is one premise basic to the philosophies of history both of the ancient Greeks and Israelites, it is the inescapable penalty which is entailed in an arrogance which refuses to acknowledge the contingent nature of human life, dependent upon a reality other than its own capacities.

Isaiah, who depends so heavily upon the use of simile to stress the application of a principle, declares that "Moab shall be trampled under (the Lord's) feet as straw is trampled into a midden." "Moab shall spread out his hands as a swimmer spreads his hands to swim, but he shall sink his pride with every stroke of his hands." (25:10, 11)

These various ways of stressing the futility of human pride to fabricate a fiction of its self-sufficiency is reinforced by a reference to the futility of what are too frequently regarded "impregnable" walls of defense upon which people trust for security, until the walls themselves are destroyed, demonstrating thereby the folly of peoples' mistaken presumptions that they can work out their own security. Isaiah reminds the Moabites and all who think as they do in their mistaken notion of themselves that "The Lord has thrown down the high defences of your walls, has levelled them to the earth, and brought them down to the dust". (vs. 12)

Isaiah affirms his faith in the justice of a divine judgment upon human life as one aspect of human history when he maintains that the penalty is the same for all "people without sense" enough to acknowledge their subordinate status. For such human beings who do not recognize that they do not have the final judgment upon what they are and what they do, the Prophet declares: "Their maker will show them no mercy, he who formed them will show them no favour." (27:11)

Jeremiah repeats Isaiah's comments about "Moab's pride", and he affirms his agreement that "proud indeed he is, proud, presumptuous, overbearing, insolent". When the comment attributed to "the Lord" is added to Jeremiah's own appraisal of the offensive traits of Moab, the entire vocabulary of terms is exhausted for denoting this boastful attitude. "I know his arrogance, says the Lord! his boasting is false, false are his deeds." (48:29, 30) It is the falsity of exaggerated notions which is morally offensive about the trait of pride.

If, however, there were a correlation between the nature of whatever is a basis for pride and the pride itself as its accurate appraisal, pride would not be morally offensive. It would, on the other hand, be meritorious for anyone to be competent enough to understand the worth of whatever he values. But the disproportionate appraisal expressed in pride or boasting is morally reprehensible because it desregards the actual nature of whatever is so overestimated for its worth or its merit to be esteemed. It is this disparity between the nature of whatever is appraised and the disproportionate estimate of its worthiness to be so praised which constitutes a principle that is universally applicable in human life. Jeremiah points out the scope of application of this principle when he maintains that "These are the words of the Lord: Let not the wise man boast of his wisdom nor the valiant of his valour; let not the rich man boast of his riches." (9:23)

Each of the goods to which reference is made is worthy of high regard when properly appraised, since there is no greater good for yielding well-being than wisdom. But overestimating the wisdom which an individual may have is offensive because it is presuming credit for having what one does not actually have. If one were as wise as proverbial Solomon or Solon, and were not to overestimate the extent of his wisdom, he would be entitled to be regarded as the most envied of mankind. But when wisdom is less than it might be, it is indefensible to appraise it as all that could be.

Since wisdom has a fecundity of increasing its own fund by reflecting upon itself, there is no upper limit to what reflecting on wisdom itself might yield for the enlightenment of a human being. But overestimating the wisdom which one already has achieved through his reflecting is not only depreciating the justification for further reflecting, it is doing the already achieved wisdom the dishonor to be given credit which it does not deserve.

Ezekiel follows the precedent of Isaiah in citing familiar examples from the history of surrounding nations to illustrate the principle that their arrogance based upon their wealth and power was the antecedent of their destruction. The Prophet maintains that "the Lord" delivered to him the judgment against the "prince of Tyre" in whose arrogance he claimed: "I am a god; I sit throned like a god on the high seas!" (28:1-3) The basis for his boasting was that Tyre had "vast resources and (its) imports . . . enriched the kings of the earth". (vs. 33) As its "commerce grew so great, lawlessness filled" the heart of its prince and he "went wrong". (vs. 16)

The actual wealth and power of Tyre, therefore, were the basis for the boasting of its people that it was one of the wealthiest and most beautiful cities of the earth. But the offense of Tyre was not its real wealth or its real power. It was the overestimate of its wealth and power that was the ground upon which its prince presumed he was a god and sat "throned like a god on the high seas". The commerce of Tyre made it wealthy, and its great wealth made possible its great beauty. But the tragedy was that its "beauty made (it) arrogant" and its ruler "misused (his) wisdom to increase" the power about which he boasted. (vs. 17)

266

Notwithstanding his wisdom and his power, he was not a god. It was, therefore, his overestimate both of what he was and of what he had accomplished in his rule which were offensive to an impartial judgment upon his claims. Hence the Prophet maintains that "the words of the Lord God" declared the judgment that "Because you try to think the thoughts of a god . . . your fine wisdom" will lie "in the dust" together with "your pride". (vs. 6, 7)

The sequel to the power and fame of Tyre was, as Ezekiel points out, a "dirge: Who was like Tyre . . . with your vast resources and your imports you enriched the kings of the earth. Now you are broken by the sea in deep water . . . the merchants jeer in derision at you; you have come to a fearful end and shall end and shall be no more for ever." (37:32-36) If the great city of Tyre had been a great person, its history, as the life of a person, would have been a subject for Greece's great dramatists, because it was a tragedy. It rose to power, but misused its power. The wisdom of its prince was misused for boasting rather than for the spiritual enlightening of his people. Thus the span of its history is the scope of a tragedy. This history and its tragic character are summed up by Ezekiel: "You have heaped up riches, and with your riches your arrogance has grown." (28:5)

The great city of Sodom "grew haughty" in misusing its wealth and luxury to deepen its perversity. Ezekiel points out that it became "abominable" in the sight of God, and he "made away with them". (16:51) The same judgment was decreed against the great city of Jerusalem: "You will be disgraced for all you have done." (vs. 55) The same stern judgment upon misused wealth and power was directed against Egypt. "Her boasted might" was disproportionate to the power it was presumed to have. And the penalty for the disproportion between a vaunted boasting and a reality about which there is such arrogant appraisal is the falsity which brings about its own discrediting. The penalty entailed in such falsity of estimate of its real nature is that it is "brought low". (30:6)

Boasting is fraudulent because it claims that something is more than what it actually is, and the fraudulent character of such exaggerated estimate is its irrelevance for actual practice. If there were no real world to constitute a criterion for the truth or falsity of judgments about it, a tissue of false judgments could constitute a world of fantasy. But such a world of fantasy collides with a world of reality. It is the disproportion between reality and a fantasy about it which discredits the fantasy and destroys the well-being of those who make a futile attempt to live according to such fantasy. Ezekiel points out that "Pharaoh king of Egypt" lived and ruled in the world of fantasy rather than in the sterner world of reality. His fantasy was that there was no sovereignty even of heaven which was the equal of his authority. But he was brought to account by "the Lord God" for his fantasy and the arrogance it supported, and was accused by his Judge for having claimed "My Nile is my own; it was I who made it". (29:3) Instead of admiration for his power, even without its boastful exaggeration, the estimate of him credited by the Prophet to "the Lord God" was "You great monster". Since his boasting was monstrous, the estimate of "the Lord God" is true, and its truth is its justice.

The prophet Daniel wrote the history of Chaldaea from a religious perspective, as Herodotus wrote the history of Persia in its relation to Greece. Daniel, however, wrote such history as only a great dramatist could, and therefore his account of the history of Nebuchadnezzar and his son Belshazzar reads with the appeal of Aeschylus' *Agamemnon*. Daniel narrates how Nebuchadnezzar, the king, "was walking on the roof of the royal palace of Babylon, and exclaimed, 'Is not this Babylon the great which I have built as a royal residence by my own mighty power and for the honour of my majesty?' " The Prophet points out that "The words were still on his lips, when a voice came down from heaven: 'To you, king Nebuchadnezzar, the word is spoken: the kingdom has passed from you. You are banished from the society of men and you shall live with the wild beasts; you shall feed on grass like oxen.' "

The reason for this severe judgment upon the king was the offense of his arrogant boasting of all that he had done without the support of another whom he should have acknowledged as mightier than himself. He was told that "seven times will pass over you until you have learnt that the Most High is sovereign over the kingdom of men". (4:30-33) This was to remind the boastful king that in spite of his belief that he was sovereign, there nevertheless was another to whom he was in turn subordinate. The lesson he was late in learning is that no matter how exalted men may regard another for his status in life by virtue of his wealth, wisdom, and power, there is a judgment upon him by a reality other than the myopic view of human beings. The reason that the mighty king was "deposed from his royal throne and his glory was taken from him" was that "he became haughty . . . and presumptuous". (5:20) Instead of using his power and his wealth for the benefit of his kingdom, he presumed it had only one purpose and that was "for the honour of (his own) majesty". (4:30)

The arrogance of Nebuchadnezzar can hardly be understood apart from what is affirmed in the book of *Judith* which characterizes the insolence of Holophernes, his commander-in-chief. Holophernes destroyed "sanctuaries and cut down sacred groves . . . so that Nebuchadnezzar alone should be worshipped by every nation and invoked as a god by men of every tribe and tongue". (3:8) The irreligious Holophernes expressed the arrogant impiety of his king when he asked the insolent question: "What god is there but Nebuchadnezzar? . . . lord of the whole earth." (6:2-4)

Daniel continues the history of Chaldaea as if it were a drama destined to a tragic ending. After Nebuchadnezzar "was banished from the society of men", he was succeeded by "his son, Belshazzar". (5:22) Like his father, he "did not humble (his) heart, although (he) knew all this". The Prophet therefore declared the stern accusation against him: "You have set your self up against the Lord of heaven . . . and you have not given glory to God." (vs. 23) This accusation by the Prophet against the offense of impiety due to arrogance was confirmed by the writing on the wall of the palace during a lavish banquet "for a thousand of his nobles", for which he sacrilegously used "the vessels of gold and silver from the sanctuary of the house of God at Jerusalem". (vs. 3) Daniel interpreted the writing which was that "God has numbered the days of your kingdom and brought it to an end; you have been weighed in the balance and found wanting". (vs. 26, 27)

The prophet Zephaniah reminded the people of Judah what had been the stern penalty for the great Assyrian city of Nineveh which also had once "exulted in fancied security, saying to herself, 'I am, and I alone.'" (2:15) The contrast of what it once was for which it had prided itself and what it became as "a waste, a haunt for wild beasts", was a reminder to his people of a penalty they too should anticipate for duplicating the same folly of arrogance for which Nineveh was destroyed. On the basis of what had taken place in Nineveh, he affirmed a prophecy of what would take place among the people of Judah. Referring to Jerusalem, the capital of their kingdom, he predicted what would be the judgment of their god against them: "I will rid you of your proud and arrogant citizens, and never again shall you flaunt your pride on my holy hill." (3:11)

In referring to what had taken place in Nineveh as the basis for what would recur in other cities of wealth and luxury, Zephaniah exemplifies the principle of Hebrew prophecy, which is also the principle of all empirically based predictions. Taking account of what has occurred under a set of circumstances, such as is subsequently repeated, becomes the factual basis on which a prediction may be made about what will likely again take place. Such prediction, when it is ordinarily affirmed, is qualified with an assessment of some degree of probability. But no comparable qualification was appended to a prophecy affirmed by the Hebrew prophets. Their predictions rested not only upon comparable circumstances, but upon a philosophy of history. The basic premise of this is that there is an inevitable judgment upon the impiety of human beings which expresses itself in their arrogance that they are subordinate to no reality. They flaunted their self-sufficiency as evidence that they would be exempt from humbling themselves in an act of piety by which they should acknowledge their subordinate status. The penalty for such arrogance was repeated in the history of so many cities of wealth and luxury such as Babylon, Sodom, Tyre of Phoenicia, that the similarity therefore between the excesses of Jerusalem of Judah and Nineveh of Assyria was the ground on which Zephaniah predicted a parallel judgment, which as a prophet, he interpreted as divine judgment.

Thus as Jonah was sent to warn Nineveh against the penalty impending for its pride, so Zephaniah regarded himself as sent by the god of his people to warn them of what they should guard against, and do so by replacing their pride with piety, and their sense of self-sufficiency with gratitude for their god's providence. Zephaniah, therefore, declared a warning to the arrogant people of Jerusalem, such as Jonah declared to the arrogant of Nineveh.

The prophet Obadiah warned the Edomites of the inevitable penalty entailed in their "proud, insolent heart" which "led (them) astray" from revering the god upon whose providence they ought to have acknowledged themselves as dependent. (1:3) Such piety ought to have continued in their conduct, since as descendants of the patriarch Isaac, their tradition traced to Abraham, the model of submission to the will of a god, and so the example of what a people ought to be.

The offensive character of the impiety of the Edomites is indicated in the Prophet's reminding them of what they say to themselves: "Who can bring (us) to the ground?" His reply to such arrogance, which negates every trait of piety, is that "Though you soar as high as a vulture and your nest is set among the stars", the "word of the Lord" declares: "I will bring you down." (vs. 4)

The pride affirmed by a people who had the benefit of a tradition that included the faithful patriarchs was offensive to every religiously oriented Israelite. The *Wisdom of Solomon* thus affirms a rubric which is basic to the entire tradition of Hebrew prophecy: "Judgment falls relentlessly upon those in high place." It is the penalty for the excess of pride in their vaunted self-sufficiency. Hence the philosophy of history affirmed in this wisdom-literature is basic to the tradition of Hebrew prohecy: "The powerful will be called powerfully to account for he who is all men's master . . . is not overawed by greatness."

The theological premise basic to the philosophy of history is that "It is the powerful for whom (God) reserves the sternest" rebuke. (6:6-8) Such rebuke is an inevitable check entailed in the excess of their power which is basic to their pride. The excess of pride thus is confronted with the inescapable limit that expresses the principle declared in Job: "Thus far and no farther." (38:11)

Basic to the philosophy of history which underlies the tradition of Hebrew prophecy is the principle of the pendulum, the arc of whose movement is established by its own nature. The nature of a human being establishes the limit within which its vaunted arrogance entails its own penalty. This entailment occurs with a predictability which is interpreted by the Prophets as evidence that human beings can live well only by acknowledging the framework within which they live. No human being therefore can presume to trespass beyond the limits of his own nature without destroying himself and thereby demonstrating that the final judgment upon his folly is entailed within his own folly. Such moral judgment interpreted from a prophet's religious orientation is entailed in the nature with which men are created, not by themselves, but by their Creator. The author of *Ecclesiasticus* declares: "Pride was not the Creator's design for man." (10:18)

2. An ordered life saves human beings from handicaps entailed in excesses

Proverbs is a moral manual or an enchiridion, such as Epictetus' and St. Augustine's. It consists of digests of good sense which are helpful suggestions in giving guidance to those who are willing to listen to such wisdom. As is common in such digests of wisdom acquired through centuries of human experience, there are similarities in the proverbs of the Israelites and the Greeks. One proverb affirms the prosaic but sensible counsel that "If you find honey, eat only what you need, too much of it will make you sick". (25:16) The principle it illustrates is basic to Aristotle's *Ethics* which expands the applications of this principle of moderation into a systematic moral philosophy.

The sound moral insight affirmed in *Psalms* that anyone who "scoffs at all restraint" brings about "his own undoing" applies to every excess which disregards limits. In failing to impose limits upon every aspect of one's life, one subjects himself to the peril of insatiable desire. When desires are no longer capable of conforming to limits, they likewise become incapable of being satisfied. The more that is done to satisfy their insistent demands, the more the demands themselves become reinforced until they are no longer within the limits of an individual's own control. One slips into such bondage by a failure to take account of the nature itself of desire. And when there are many diverse desires, each pressing for its satisfaction, an individual comes under a tyranny of demands which no longer is within his control.

Aeschylus affirms a religious interpretation of the moral benefit of a reasonable supervision of multiple desires which enter into a human being's nature. He declares: "To moderation in every form God giveth the victory."[63]

Sophocles, on the other hand, affirms a nonreligious metaphysical version of the Greek moral principle of moderation when he declares: "All that exceeds the mean by Fate is punished, Love or Hate."[64] So analyzed this is not a religious interpretation, such as is affirmed by Aeschylus. It maintains rather that a handicap to human life is entailed in either loving or hating without reasonable restraint.

The nurse attending Medea in Euripides' drama maintains: "Sweeter name than The Mean shall ye say not, and to taste it is sweetness untold."[65] In maintaining this, Euripides affirms a strictly moral principle without the religious explanation offered by Aeschylus or the metaphysical explanation given by Sophocles. In other words, it is simply a fact of human life that there is no sounder condition for well-being than moderation. In maintaining this as a moral principle which is effective in human life by virtue of human nature itself, Euripides anticipates the treatment which Aristotle gave to the "Mean".

The effectiveness of living within the strictures of limits demonstrates the soundness of the principle of the mean as moral counsel. Its effectiveness can thus be regarded as its own credentials. Insofar as this attitude is taken toward this principle, one does not believe that its validity or workability is assured by taking account of any reality other than human behavior itself. It is such an attitude which accounts for Aristotle's humanistic or naturalistic moral philosophy. And it is this same attitude which is affirmed in Euripides' *Medea*.

The stress in moral philosophies upon the desirability of moderation in human wants rests upon a clear understanding of human nature. It such moderation were a feature native to human inclinations, there would be no such emphasis in moral philosophies. But the fact that there is such an emphasis indicates the acknowledgment of the ease within human nature to disregard moderation. The seventy-eighth psalm gives an account of a time when the Israelites were confronted by a shortage of food. And the religious orientation of the Psalmist explained the occurrence of great numbers of birds in their camp as an expression of their god's providence. He points out that "the people ate and were well filled". Whereas one might reasonably have expected that they would have been grateful for their rescue from near-starvation, they instead were still dissatisfied. The Psalmist points out that "they did not abandon their complaints, even while the food was in their mouths". Their incapacity to be satisfied even after receiving what they had wanted is an instance of the insatiability of human wants. Unless a want is disciplined to terminate its demands upon an individual, the individual's selfhood becomes, as Spinoza points out, an appendage of his own wants. He becomes driven by them into a type of dissatisfied life for which there is no remedy other than his own self-imposed discipline.

Proverbs expresses as clear an understanding as does the Psalmist of the tendency internal to undisciplined human inclination to remain unsatisfied even after they receive what they demand. Receiving what is demanded only terminates a momentary requirement. It does not eliminate the recurrence of an insistence intensified by previous satisfactions. The wisdom of *Proverbs* acknowledges that the severest curse of which human beings are capable is "Abaddon", which in Hebrew means bottomless or without limit. Hence Abaddon is identified with Sheol. A proverb, therefore, declares that "Sheol and Abaddon are insatiable". And it points out the moral meaning of this identification of Sheol with the curse itself of insatiability by declaring that "a man's eyes too are never satisfied". (27:20)

The same comment is affirmed in *Ecclesiasticus* upon the nature of the human curse of having wants which are incapable of being satisfied by conforming to the demands of the wants themselves. It declares: "A covetous man's eye is not satisfied with his share." The moral penalty for subordinating the well-being of a total self to one demand in its complex nature is that such "greediness" of demand "shrivels the soul". (14:9)

Greek reflecting as early as the *Iliad,* and most likely much earlier before it was reduced to literary form, was aware that "People tire of everything". This sound insight into the difficulty of the human being to be satisfied without a special effort of moral discipline is pointed out by

273

Menelaus who says: "People tire of everything, even of sleep and love, sweet music and the perfect dance."[66]

A capacity to be satisfied is cultivated by a deliberate moral discipline. Such discipline is taking account of the tendency itself to be unsatisfied irrespective of the amount of what is made available to meet the demands of a want. When this tendency itself is recognized, an individual knows enough of himself to be aware of the folly of supposing that by yielding to the demands of an inclination he will be freed from its goading pressure. Liberation from an insistent want is not native to such a want after it has usurped its rights and has subordinated other requirements in an individual's life to its sole insistence.

Herodotus understood the nature of people whose follies constitute a major part of human history. He narrates the conversation of Artabanus with his nephew, pointing out to him that "when two opinions were laid before the Persians, the one tending to the increase of pride, and the other to its abatement", the Persian Xerxes "preferred that one which was most fraught with danger to himself and the Persians". And then Artabanus exhibits his profound understanding when he declares that in making such a choice, Xerxes showed "how evil a thing it is to teach the heart continual desire of more than it has".[67]

The "evil" to which Artabanus refers is the insatiability of desires when not brought within the range of a reflective awareness of what they entail in terms of moral handicaps. Such a reflective awarenes is a condition for imposing upon them reasonable limits. Herodotus was aware that the evil of an insatiable aspect of a human being can blight the life of anyone irrespective of his accomplishments and his possessions. He narrates the plight of Themistocles, the distinguished general in the Peloponnesian war, whom "all Hellas glorified (as) the wisest man by far of the Greeks". Yet, notwithstanding the type of wisdom for which he was credited, he ruined his life by virtue of not having sufficient moral wisdom to live free from the tyranny of insatiable greed. He misused the naval forces of Athens to pressure the islands to give him vast sums, threatening them that "if they would not give what he asked he would bring the Greek armada upon them and beseige and take their islands".[68]

The penalty for his illegal acts dominated by his insatiable greed was intrinsic to his vice. He made himself unworthy of the Athenians' esteem and trust. He exemplified the type of a greed-driven human being of whom Chremylus in Aristophanes' *Plutus* speaks: "If a man has thirteen talents, he has all the greater ardour to possess sixteen; if that wish is achieved, he will want forty."[69] The sound insight expressed in this play indicates that even the borderline between comedy and tragedy in literature is often as ambiguous as is the borderline between a blessing and a curse in human life.

The discourse of Helen with Aphrodite in Euripides' *Helen* includes her questioning of the goddess: "Why art thou so insatiate in mischief, employing every art of love, of fraud, and guileful schemes?" But without waiting for an answer, she declares that included in the ambivalent character of love which Aphrodite inspires in human beings is also life's greatest blessing, provided that love is within reasonable limits. Hence she addresses herself to Aphrodite: "Wert thou but moderate, only that! —in all else thou art by nature, man's most welcome deity."[70]

In so contrasting the blessings which may be entailed in a reasonable type of human love with its "spells that bring bloodshed on families", Euripides points out the vast disparity within a single human capacity between a supreme good and a tragic curse. The difference between these two potentialities immanent within a single human capacity is pointed out by Aristotle who argues that good and evil of any aspect of human life are in relation to their uses. A so-called "goodness" entailed in one use is a function of its reasonable character. The so-called "evil" entailed in its contrasted use is an expression of the poverty of its reasonable nature. The degree to which reflective intelligence is expressed in ordering and directing aspects of human nature, which of themselves are without order, constitutes the factor that determines their moral goodness. The absence of such ordering constitutes their evil nature, which is their impairment of well-being.

The same borderline between the ambivalence of a blessing and a curse is pointed out by Euripides' Andromache, who declares: "A curse is youth to mortals, when with youth a man hath not implanted righteousness."[71] The difference, therefore, between the delight in living and the sorrow which so often impairs such delight is the balance or the order whose role in directing vitality is imposed upon it. If only it were intrinsic to vitality itself, human life would universally be without tragedy! But the fact that the dynamic itself of vitality is devoid of order accounts for regrets that provide so much material for life's heartaches and tragedies.

IX

Retribution as a Philosophy of History

1. *The idea of retribution is based upon a metaphysic*

One feature of the world which Greek reflecting regards as essential to its nature is its ordered character. Even the emphasis of Heraclitus upon change as an essential nature of the world is compatible with his point of view of the lawful feature of such change. In reflecting upon the ordered character of occurrences, such as the cycle of day and night and the cycle of the seasons, he distinguished their individual ordered character from a property of order. Their individual order, in other words, is an exemplification of order as a universal property.

The two are distinguishable in reflecting, but not in the nature of the world itself. In distinguishing the ordered feature of each natural event from the universal ordering in which each event is included, Heraclitus understandably selected the terms "Mind" and "Wisdom" to refer to such universal ordering. Universal ordering has a feature which is the property of reasoning or rationally ordered reflecting. Such reflecting is connected in a way that one distinguishable element in it is related to another. Heraclitus describes this relationship internal to every ordered sequence or event as "consistent with itself". Its various component elements are distinguishable or separable in reflecting, but they are not separate from each other. Each "flows", as it were, into the other. Each element can be "divided" from another, but such an operation is a feature of thinking, just as an arithmetical division is an operation upon a unit. A unit's own essential nature as an entity is not fragmented or fractured by such reflecting.

Every reality distingushable from other realities, such as a "bow" which is distinguishable from a "lyre", nevertheless, has properties in common. Each coheres as an entity which is "a harmony of tensions".[1] The internal tension which is its coherence as an entity is thus ordered. Every entity making up the totality of the world shares in common both the properties of a "tension" and also a "harmony". These are not radically separated from each other, such as are basic properties in a dualistic metaphysic. According to the metaphysic of Heraclitus, there is one reality. But when it is reflected upon, reflecting becomes aware of more than one of its features.

Reflecting itself is ordered, and therefore is an instance of the same ordering character which is universal. If the universal order of the world were designated by the term "Logos", then human reflecting would exemplify the Logos as does every other ordered entity internal to the world. The ordered world is not ordered by a reality separated from it, as if having a status prior to or independent of the totality itself of the ordered world.

The concept of Logos is basically the concept of Law. Heraclitus declares: "All things take place in accordance with this Law."[2] Law, as a universal property of lawfully ordered occurrences, is distinguishable in reflecting from such ordered occurrences, but it has no existence apart from them or prior to them. The lawfully ordered world is a totality, including the philosopher's wisdom, whose ordered thinking is essentially the same as the so-called "wisdom" or "logos" of the world. Heraclitus declares: "Wisdom is a single thing. It is to understand the mind by which all things are steered through all things."[3]

Heraclitus' metaphysic is a version of the Greek idea of Limit as a condition for the existing of a reality. A reality is internally coherent in the sense that it is an entity whose identity is its own nature. The sun is one such entity. But "the sun will not transgress his measure" or limit which constitutes its identity as distinguishable from other heavenly bodies.

After formulating a metaphysic of the lawful character of the totality of the world or Nature, Heraclitus condescends, as it were, to use mythological imagery to convey his otherwise "dark" or profound philosophy. Since his statement that "The sun will not transgress his measure" is perfectly comprehensible, he would not have needed, therefore, to add the mythological reference that "if he does, the Erinnyes, the supporters of justice, will find him out".[4]

If this mythological notion were pressed, it would actually be inconsistent with his metaphysic. But if the reference merely means that the property which mythology attributes to the spirits that bring retribution to those who violate natural laws is the same property internal to the nature of the sun itself, then the sun would not violate its own lawful nature. The same type of pictorial imagery is used by Heraclitus when he refers to the regularity or ordered sequence with which every dawn of a day is followed by an evening of the same day. He says: "The boundary between dawn and evening is the Bear." That is, the rotation of the constellation is a measure of the duration of a day. The notion that there is such a limit which exemplifies the universal Law or Logos of the lawfully ordered world is thus given a graphic vehicle in the figure of the constellation "Bear". Then Heraclitus adds still another graphic figure to this highly condensed metaphysical statement when he says "and over against the Bear is the confine of bright Zeus".[5] But this is another concession in the metaphysician's vocabulary, and he admits his hesitancy to introduce the mythological notion of Zeus into his otherwise abstract philosophy: "The one thing which alone is wise is willing and unwilling to be called by the name of Zeus."[6]

This admission, therefore, should be reconstructed to clarify his meaning that he is not willing to identify the universal Logos with a particular deity which popular mythology locates on spatial Olympus. Yet, in order to express his position about the sovereignty of Law, he mentions the mythological term "Zeus", since the nature of Zeus as sovereign over gods made him ultimate as other gods are not.

The Logos likewise is ultimate in the sense that there is no reality which has created the lawful character of the world. The lawful world is itself the ultimate reality. Heraclitus specifically affirms this nonmythological or noncosmogonic concept when he declares: "This world . . . neither any god nor any man shaped it, but it ever was and is and shall be."[7] In maintaining this position, he thus anticipates the metaphysic of Aristotle.

Another affirmation of its noncreated nature is that it is eternal: "This Law holds forever."[8] Heraclitus is aware that if any reality has an endurance "forever" or without time limit, it likewise could not have had a beginning. It always was; and this type of analysis is affirmed by the Eleatic Parmenides. Both Heraclitus and Parmenides formulated metaphysics which differ in every respect from popular mythology and popular versions of religion. Heraclitus uses the term "God", which is borrowed from popular religion, but his use of this term is devoid of theistic meaning. He declares: "God is day, he is night; winter, and summer."[9] If

he meaning of this assertion were to be affirmed in Aristotelian terminol-
gy, it would become the declaration that "What is, is". Day, night,
inter, and summer are what they are. Each is a lawful ingredient in a
lawful world. Such a lawful world is the ultimate reality, and as ultimate,
has the character with which popular religions interpreted God. The
rst fragment which introduces the sayings of Heraclitus thus sums up
is entire metaphysic: "All things are one."

Apart from the world which includes day, night, winter, and summer,
here are no gods or goddesses which have sovereignty over each of these.
Heraclitus thus did what Thales already had done in Milesian philosophy.
He took the jurisdictions attributed to each of the many deities on
Olympus and identified them with natural realities themselves. Thus
rather than a god controlling the sun, the lawful nature of the sun itself
controls the sun. Rather than a goddess determining the movements of
the moon, the limit internal to its own nature determines its eternal
identity.

As is common in philosophies, one premise may create problems insoluble within the scope of another premise. Such certainly is the case
hen Heraclitus tries to incorporate the long established Greek notion of
retribution into his own philosophy of identity which maintains that "All
things are one", and therefore, there is no radical difference between
good and evil, right and wrong, just and unjust. He declares this philosophy of identity when he says: "All things are fair and good and right
• God; but men think of some as wrong and others as right."[10] He thus
contrasts the human point of view about reality with reality itself, identifying reality itself with "god". According to this terminology, "god" is
synonymous with "ultimate reality". His metaphysics of an ultimate iden-
ty of whatever human beings regard as distinguishable is affirmed in
his premise that "Reality is One". This type of monistic metaphysic
•gically implies there is no essential difference between realities which
human beings regard as basically different. Metaphysical dualisms or
luralisms, on the other hand, maintain that there are essential differences
• some realities. The concept of retribution is based upon such a
dualistic or pluralistic metaphysic which maintains there are essential
differences between some realities, such as right and wrong, good and evil,
just and unjust.

Denying the identity of goodness as exclusive of evil and right as exclusive of wrong, denies also the very notion of retribution. Heraclitus'
emphasis upon Identity as the basic principle of metaphysics, however,
implies that "good and evil are the same".[11] Yet, the basic principle of

279

retribution maintains they are radically different and therefore enta
radically different moral judgments upon them.

Thus whereas one aspect of his philosophy is compatible with his i
sistence that "good and evil are the same", another aspect, which is b
moral philosophy, and so his conviction of the validity of the notion
retribution, is not compatible with this insistence that "good and evil a
the same". Basic to the Greek notion of retribution is the belief that goc
and evil are different, and Heraclitus also believes this when he declar
that "Surely justice will overtake the fabricators of lies and false wi
nesses".[12] Justice and wrongdoing are exclusive of each other. The
therefore, do not share the same imperceptible difference as does "Tl
way up and the way down (which) are one and the same".[13]

Both Homer and Hesiod affirm the Greek conviction that there a
essential differences in the properties of human conduct which are referre
to as "good" and "evil", "right" and "wrong". But Heraclitus, as Pla
later, was impatient with the ancient Poets. He declares that "Home
deserves to be thrown out of the lists and whipped".[14] He also depreciat
the critical intelligence of Hesiod by declaring he "did not know day an
night!" Whereas he treated them as different parts of a day, Heraclitu
in stressing his own metaphysic of identity, maintained: "They are one
Thus he depreciated the estimate of people who believed that Hesic
"knew a great many things", and therefore deserved to be respected
"the teacher of many"[15]

Classical Greek philosophies reaffirm many ideas which are basic
earlier popular mythologies. Mythologies and philosophies differ less i
their ideas than they do in the ways their ideas are expressed. Mythologi
are pictorial. Philosophies are nonpictorial. An idea, for example, of tl
lawful and harmonious character of physical phenomena is personifie
as Themis, an earth-goddess. The term itself for this goddess mea
"that which is laid down or established", and it is this meaning which
basic to the metaphysical philosophy of Heraclitus, of the Pythagorean
and later of Plato.

Popular mythology attributes this metaphysical property to an anthr
pomorphically interpreted goddess, who is represented as a wife of Ze
and mother of Prometheus. But this embellishment in a pictorial versic
completely conceals the basic philosophical meaning of the term wi
which the goddess is denoted. Yet, such meaning is affirmed in the ter
itself by which the goddess is identified, since the meaning of the lawf
character of events includes the idea of limit, which in turn impli
boundaries beyond which no reality may go.

An inescapable penalty is entailed for going beyond limits, and its inescapability is the meaning of "doom" or "fate". Such fate is a fact according to Greek mythology and to all sober Greek reflecting which is expressed in its Epics and later in its tragic dramas.

This particular aspect of the inescapability of penalty for going beyond limit became personified in the goddess Nemesis, and, when not so personified, it was regarded as a power of Zeus. So interpreted, it is on the borderline between pictorial mythology and a more abstract philosophy.

Nemesis and Themis share a common property of representing the lawful character of an ordered world. The nature of such order is limit, and the thesis that limit is essential to the nature of the ordered world became the basic premise of Pythagorean philosophy, and in turn the basic premise of Platonic metaphysics. In popular mythology, Nemesis was identified with a power transcendent of individual human beings which imposed limits upon the aspects of their life which were most often subject to excess. One of these is pride, and so Nemesis was thought of in popular Greek reflecting as a law, which set limits to human pride. As a power capable of restraining human beings, it was also thought of as a power capable of penalizing them for disregarding its sovereignty. Thus Nemesis became feared as a factor with which lust for power was inescapably punished. Such lust for power and its inevitable penalty became the bases for the great Greek dramas oriented around the ancient myths associated with the rulers of Mycenae. The murders of Agamemnon and Clytemnestra thus are included in this tradition of final accountability for lust for power, which as lust, defies all restraint of moral limits.

When these myths became basic to later dramas, their moral significance was stressed. As such, the storytelling role of myth was enriched by the reflective profoundity of which the dramatists equalled the ablest of Greek philosophers. In the vehicle of drama, the Greeks thus saw portrayed the inevitable working of Nemesis. The aspect of inevitability of penalty entailed in violating limits had, however, already been personified in popular mythology as Adrastia, a goddess of inevitable fate, who thus embodies the sober awareness of the reflective Greek that disregarding limits which are established by a reality other than human beings also entails an accountability to such a reality. The chorus in Euripides' *Rhesus* introduces this goddess whose ambivalent nature includes both imposing penalty entailed in exceeding limits and also guarding human beings from going beyond such limits. She is appealed to by the plea: "Now Adrasteia be near and guard our lips from sin, lest the end be hard."[16]

281

Such ambivalence is a characteristic trait of deities in ancient civilizations. The god of the Israelites, for example, both creates and destroys, both protects and punishes. The goddesses of love in ancient Mesopotamian civilizations were also goddesses of war and so of cruelty.

Human cruelty, like human arrogance, is capable of being expressed without limits, and such unlimited cruelty is brought to account in an inevitable retribution. Odysseus assures Eumaeus that a "special office" of Zeus "is to call cruelty to account".[17] His nature as "Protector of Strangers" is "outraged at evil dealings" which violate the rights of guests and disregard the obligations of a host.[18]

The *Iliad* likewise takes account of the fact that there is divine judgment upon human behavior which either insolently or ignorantly disregards the limits set for men by virtue of their own nature. Such nature is not of their own making, and therefore they likewise do not define for themselves the limits beyond which they cannot go without penalty. Their nature, as the nature of every reality, exists by virtue of an order or limit. Its individuality is its limit, and, when such order is disrespected in acts of folly, the folly itself entails its own accounting. When such accounting, however, is objectified or personified, it is thought of as judgment by a god. Dione, to whom the *Iliad* refers as a "gracious goddess", the mother of Aphrodite, declares that the hero "Diomedes is a fool" because "he does not know how short life is for the man who fights against immortals".[19]

Chryses, priest of Apollo in the *Iliad*, appeals to the god to "let the Danaans pay . . . for my tears", which were brought about when Agamemnon refused to return his daughter, whom he held as a captive.[20] The *Iliad* then takes account of the retributive justice assured by Phoebus Apollo who "heard his prayer".

Hesiod acknowledged the retributive entailment for men who acquire wealth by dishonest means. He declares: "If he steal it through his tongue, as often happens when gain deceives men's sense and dishonour tramples down honour, the gods soon blot him out and make that man's house low, and wealth attends him only for a little time."[21]

Without referring to any deity in popular mythology, Aeschylus points out that men cannot escape a penalty for achieving what they regard as "success" when it disrespects limits that should be acknowledged as a condition for every human good. When men regard their success as "God and more than God", they will be confronted by the fact that "the balanced scale of Justice keepeth watch".[22]

Thus without referring to a personificaiton of justice as a deity, Aeshylus reaffirms the conviction affirmed in traditional popular mythology that men are not ultimate. They are subordinate to an inevitable accounting for their wrongdoing, the essential nature of which is excess. A justice ther than conventional justice operates internal to human life to bring hose guilty of injustice to account, and such accounting is according to he ancient belief that the "mills of the gods grind slowly, but sure".

The Theban seer Teiresias in Sophocles' *Antigone* confronted Creon vith the stern reminder that he will be held accountable for his arrogance y "the avenging spirits of Heaven and Hell who dog the steps of sin".[23] And the chorus of Elders of Thebes likewise reminds Creon that the Vengeance of the gods is swift to overtake the impenitent".[24]

The throne of Thebes was usurped by Creon who was killed by Lycus, vho then usurped the throne. It was again usurped by Heracles after killing Lycus. This sequence of outrage against lawful succession to a hrone is the basis for the confrontation of Heracles by the chorus in Euripides' *Heracles,* reminding him that although "Evil has changed ides", "Justice and heavenly retribution" still have final sovereignty ver human life and hold such evil accountable: "He who was erst a mighty king is now turning his life backward into the road of Hades."[25] The Chorus repeats the stern judgment with which it had warned Heracles vhen it declares: "Swiftly hath fortune o'erthrown him who sat on high."[26]

Thus, notwithstanding all the feats of strength and skill which Heracles aad exhibited in achieving the tasks imposed by Eurytheus, and after reeing the throne of Thebes from its most recent usurper, he himself uffered the "vengeance" of Zeus, "exacting a full penalty".[27]

The Chorus in Euripides' *Hecuba,* predicting what will take place with Polymester, King of Thrace, for his moral outrage of violating the obligations of a guardian to his ward, declares: "For where the rights of justice and the law of heaven are one, there is ruin fraught with death and doom."[28]

Second Samuel in the Old Testament includes a story which in every detail might have become the basis for a drama by Aeschylus or Sophocles. It affirms that "No one in all Israel was so greatly admired for his beauty as Absalom; he was without flaw from the crown of his head to the sole of his foot." (14:25) Yet, this very endowment was the basis for an arrogance which expressed itself not only in rebellion against his father, King David, but also in moral excesses until his death. His death itself was an instance of what a Greek would have regarded as retribution, since one aspect of his "beauty" was his extraordinary hair. And it was this which caught in the branch of a tree by which he hung until he was killed by soldiers of the King's army, who "took Absalom's body and flung it into a great pit in the forest". (18:17) This was the end of one "without flaw from the crown of his head to the sole of his foot"!

This story illustrates every principle basic to the Greek concept of retribution. His beauty could have been stressed by the Greeks as the envy of the gods for having more than a human being is entitled to have. It could have been regarded as the "height" from which the arrogant fall. But in addition to retribution entailed in the excess of his beauty, was retribution also for his infidelity to his father, the King.

Elihu in the *Book of Job* affirms a metaphysic which in every respect could have been affirmed by Homer and Aeschylus. He declares that there is a god who is aware of all that men do: "His eyes are on the ways of men, and he sees every step they take; there is nowhere so dark, so deep in shadow, that wrongdoers may hide from him." (34:21, 22) What he says about this soverignty of a deity over human life might well have been regarded by a Greek as retribution for arrogance and for insolence entailed in flouting one's superiority to others: "He . . . breaks the powerful and sets up others in their place." (vs. 24)

Eliphaz the Temanite, in the first cycle of speeches with Job, declares a theological premise which is repeatedly affirmed throughout the tragic dramas of the Greeks when he maintains that a god "frustrates the plots of the crafty, and they win no success, he traps the cunning in their craftiness, and the schemers' plans are thrown into confusion. In the daylight they run into darkness, and grope at midday as though it were night." (5:12-14)

When Job resumed the discourse with his friends, he also declared a version of retribution which might have been repeated many times in the reflecting of the Greeks, whether by Homer, Herodotus, or the dramatists. He maintained: "This is the lot prescribed by God for the wicked, and the ruthless man's reward." "He may have many sons, but they will fall by the sword, and his offspring will . . . be brought to the grave." (27:13-15) This might have been affirmed by a chorus either about Pelops or about Laius. The tragedies based upon the retribution entailed in the moral outrage of Pelops include those oriented around his son Atreus, the father of Menelaus and Agamemnon. If one were to consider the tragedies alone of the children of Agamemnon, he would see that a considerable part of the corpus of extant Greek dramas exemplifies the metaphysic affirmed by Job. And then if one were to take account of the tragedies based upon Oedipus, the son of Laius, he would see that these two traditions, which exemplify retribution, constitute the chief subject matter for the greatest number of the known dramas.

Psalms affirms a principle which likewise could be considered as basic
Greek reflecting on retribution when it declares that men "shall founder
1 the rock of justice". (141:6) This retributive principle is likewise
firmed in *Proverbs*. This fact itself is significant because it is a record
centuries of reflecting among Israelites. The counsel affirmed in one
the proverbs is "Never rob helpless man because he is helpless, nor
l-treat a poor wretch in court; for the Lord will take up their cause and
b him who robs them of their livelihood." (22:23) Greek reflecting
ould have summed up in the same way the retributive justice for such
enalty inflicted by a god upon a human being for his evil acting: He
ould have received the same treatment he gave others. So interpreted,
ere is no subjective element of bias or prejudice in the retributive judg-
ent imposed by an ultimate sovereignty over human life. It is deter-
ined by the acts themselves of which human beings are guilty. Thus
ccording to this metaphysic, basic to the Israelite and Greek concept of
tribution, there is no latitude of error in penalty. Penalty for evil is
etermined by the evil itself.

Jeremiah affirms a metaphysic in terms of a god, which therefore may
e regarded as a theology that is identical with the metaphysic affirmed
1 the long Greek tradition beginning with Homer. The Prophet declares
1at "the Lord, a God of retribution, will repay in full". (51:56) So in-
erpreted, there likewise is no latitude for the penalty for an injustice,
ince the penalty entailed in wrongdoing is correlated to the specific in-
tance of such evil. As a spokesman for the god of the Israelites, Jeremiah
eclares: "I will make her princes and her wise men drunk, her viceroys
nd governors and warriors, and they shall sink into unending sleep, never
o wake." (vs. 57) The finality of such judgment is thus affirmed, as well
s the total disregard for the relative status which men may enjoy for a
ime in relation to others, who for a brief time regard them as superior.
uperior though they may be in relation to other human beings, such
tatus does not intimidate an ultimate justice. The justice of judgment
pon arrogance of power is not respectful of a threat by its insolence. Its
nsolence intimidates men, but not retributive justice.

The history of the Israelites which is recorded in *Second Maccabees*
ncludes an account of Nicanor, the commander of the Syrian army who
ad been appointed by Demetrius I as governor of Judea. The ruler whom
Nicanor represented owed the Romans two thousand talents, which he
lanned to repay "by the sale of the Jews he would take prisoner; and
e at once made an offer of Jewish slaves to the coastal towns, undertak-

285

ing to deliver them at the price of ninety to the talent." The author of this account then makes a comment which might have been made by Herodotus had he been the historian of this segment of history: "But he did not expect the vengeance of the Almighty which was soon to be at his heels." (8:10, 11)

This historian records another incident which also might have been commented on in the same way by Herodotus. He narrates how Antiochus Epiphanes was hurrying on his way to Jerusalem to destroy the Jews, but "After he had given orders to speed up the journey, it happened that he fell out of his chariot as it hurtled along, and so violent was his fall that every joint in his body was dislocated." (9:7, 8) The comment which is made about this accident affirms a conviction about retribution which would have been affirmed by Herodotus as well as by the dramatists: "He, who in his pretension to be more than man had just been thinking that he could command the waves of the sea and weigh high mountains on the scales, was brought to the ground and had to be carried in a litter thus making God's power manifest to all." An eloquent comment, in every respect a parallel of a comparable Greek comment, is that "only a short time before (he) had seemed to touch the stars in the sky". (vs. 10)

2. *Retribution when interpreted within a religious orientation is regarded as a divine judgment*

Although there are obvious parallels in the version of retribution as interpreted by the early Israelites and the ancient Greeks, there is at least one fundamental difference. Retribution is regarded by the Israelites in their religious interpretations as coming to human life from a source external to the natural world. The world itself from their religious orientation is created by a god who is other than the world, and in this respect is transcendent of it. The general meaning of "transcendent" is "other than", and in this most general sense, one reality is transcendent of another insofar as each is an entity or an individual. Thus this most general sense of "transcendence" does not connote an exclusion of two realities from each other. The creator of the world, for instance, is other than the world he creates, in the sense of prior to it and independent of it, but not excluded from it in the sense of being cut off from it. Yet, according to Israelite theology, the Creator in no way shares a nature in common with any of his creation. In this sense, therefore, God is "wholly other" or completely separable from the world of which he is the creator.

There is no parallel of this version of transcendence in Greek metaphysics. The only comparable parallel is in the pictorial cosmogonies in which the world is referred to as made by an artificer who is other than the world he creates. Even Homer affirms a nonmythological metaphysics when he regards divine reality as the natural course of the world. Yet, as distinguishable from phenomena in the world over which men have control, it is transcendent of such a world. But its transcendence is merely its distinguishable nature, and is not its separation from the world in the sense of being independent of it. Any individual in the *Epics* who refers to a god thinks of such a divine reality as other than human beings and transcendent of them in the same sense as the Israelites think of the Creator as other than his creation. But the Homeric gods are not creators of the world. They are in the world, and so not cut off from it as "wholly other", to use an expression common in the discourse of Rudolf Otto's *The Idea of the Holy*. Amphinomos in the *Odyssey* acknowledges that the gods are other than human beings when he declares to the princes of Argos that before they do any violence to Telemachos, they "should first have to ask the gods for their counsel".[29] When Odysseus "looked down" from a balcony on the assembled princes and accused them of moral outrages within his home, he maintained that they had "no more fear of the gods in heaven than of the human vengeance that might come".[30]

Thus Homer distinguishes two types of penalty from which a human being may suffer. One is "human vengeance". The other is "of the gods". Both are transcendent of the wrongdoer in the sense that they are other than him. Whereas one is effected by human effort, the other is brought about by powers or agencies that are divine.

The *Iliad* likewise acknowledges that the gods are of an order entirely apart from human beings. Although their location on Olympus is purely mythological in its pictorial character, their final sovereignty over human life is anything but mythological. Zeus "sends down the most violent waters in deep rage against mortals" which expresses his indignation against them for their immoralities. "Mortals . . . stir him to anger because in . . . assembly they pass decrees that are crooked, and drive righteousness from among them and care nothing for what the gods think."[31] This manner of the gods' punishment for men's wrongdoing is pictorial and so mythological. But the effect upon human society by the unjust decrees which assemblies pass is not pictorial. Its profound meaning is spiritual. Such wrongdoing destroys social life itself. This is moral judgment, and such judgment is intrinsic to the wrongdoing itself.

In addition to the category of moral offenses for which there is retribution, interpreted as divine judgment upon human beings, there is also a specifically religious category of offenses for which there likewise is retributive penalty. This is human failure to do less than ought to be done to acknowledge men's reverence and respect for the gods upon whom they are finally dependent. When Aeneas in the *Iliad* saw "what havoc Diomedes was making of the Trojan lines", he hurried to Pandarus, urging him to "put up a prayer to Zeus" to interfere. But he first gave the word of caution to be sure that Diomedes himself is not "one of the immortals, annoyed with us for some shortcoming in our rites". "Shortcoming in rites" is an offense of impiety, and impiety is a deficiency of the human being in not relating himself to the gods as it is right that he should do.

Aeneas acknowledges that "Perhaps we are being punished by an angry god". The displeasure of a god for men's negligence in performing appropriate rites entails retribution in which men suffer the consequences for such disrespect. And the penalty they suffer is correlated with the gravity of their offense against a deity. Stern as retributive penalty is for moral offenses against other human beings, it differs from the severity of penalty for an infraction of piety. Gods are of a higher order than men, and therefore offenses against them are more grave than offenses against human beings.

The last words of the heroic Hector reminds Achilles of the retribution he will suffer if he does not do what is morally right for one human being to do to another, even though an enemy. The final obligation of such a human being to his heroic enemy is to provide for his burial. Hector specifically wanted to be returned to his parents after his death, and he addressed himself to Achilles: "Pause before you act, in case the angry gods remember how you treated me, when your turn comes and you are brought down at the Scaean Gate in all your glory by Paris and Apollo."[32]

Herodotus seriously narrates an account of the Persian Cyrus' treatment of the defeated Lydian Croesus, as if miracle itself were compatible with the lawful character of nature. He describes how "Cyrus had a great pyre built, on which he set Croesus, bound in chains", and then he explains the reason for this treatment. "Learning that Croesus was a god-fearing man, he set him for this cause on the pyre, because he would fain know if any deity would save him from being burnt alive." But after "the pyre had already been kindled", Cyrus repented of what he had ordered: "He bethought him that he, being also a man, was burning alive another man who had once been as fortunate as himself; moreover, he feared the retribution . . . wherefore he gave command to quench the burning fire with all speed and bring Croesus . . . down from the Pyre.

But his servants could not for all their endeavour now master the fire."
Whereupon "Croesus was aware of Cyrus' repentance and saw all men
striving to quench the fire but no longer able to check it, he cried out
to Apollo, praying that if the god had ever been pleased with any gift
of his offering, he would now come to his aid and save him from present
destruction."

Herodotus then continues the account with a religious orientation such
as is expressed in the biblical *Book of Daniel*, when the godfearing Daniel
stood before hungry lions and was not killed. The Greek historian maintains that "suddenly in a clear and windless sky clouds gathered and a
storm burst and there was a most violent rain, so that the pyre was
quenched". This, according to Herodotus, demonstrated to Cyrus that
"Croesus was . . . one beloved of the gods".[33]

What is significant in this account is Herodotus' conviction that there
is "a divine ordering of human affairs".[34] It is this religious metaphysic
which is basic to one version of retribution both as interpreted by the
Israelites and by the Greeks. For one, such as Herodotus, who interprets
history from a religious orientation, the common distinction between
"natural" and "supranatural" or "miracle" is not cogent. The "natural"
world itself is within a divine order. Or it may be said that there is such
an order within the only world there is. The world as it is includes an
ordering factor, which as other than the relation between one physical
entity and another, orders such relations. The ordering of a physical
world by a factor which is other than physical is the same type of relation as is affirmed between the lawful ordering of the world and the
universal reality of Law. Herodotus interprets human history from the
point of view of a divine ordering within the physical world. He indicates
this type of interpretation, for instance, when he gives an account of the
Lacedaemonians' defeat of the Persians at Plataeae. He maintains that
"most of them fell near the temple in unconsecrated ground". And he
ventures the explanation for this on the basis of his religious philosophy
of history. He says: "I judge . . . that the goddess herself denied them
entry, for that they had burnt her temple."[35] His interpretation thus is a
religious version of retribution.

Herodotus attributes his same type of religious interpretation of retribution to the Persian general Mardonious who had intended to plunder
the temple at Delphi. But because he remembered that there was "an
oracle that Persians are fated to . . . perish after they have plundered the
temple at Delphi", he refused to advance against the sacred precinct and
its temple.[36]

The Chorus in Aeschylus' *The Persians* asks: "What mortal man shall escape . . . the guile of God?" "Who with agile foot can lightly leap from out its toils?"[37] And then Aeschylus interprets the defeat of the Persians as supporting his religious version of history when the Messenger announced their defeat that "at a single stroke has all your plenteous weal been shattered, and the flower of the Persians fallen and perished".[38] The mother of Xerxes thereafter acknowledged that such "affliction" was "sent of Heaven".[39] Her acknowledgment thus states Aeschylus' own religious philosophy of history with its entailed religious version of retribution.

The Chorus in *The Suppliant Maidens* declares that the subjects of King Pelasgus of Argos "had regard unto the avenging eye of Zeus, against which there is no battling".[40] Danaüs, who appealed to the Argives for sanctuary, had the same fearful respect for the inevitability of retribution assured by the gods. He affirms this religious faith when he declares: "In good time, assuredly, and on the day ordained, he who condemns the gods shall suffer punishment."[41] The king of Argos likewise acknowledged his unwillingness to deny such sanctuary, since granting refuge to any who seek protection is a moral imperative with divine sanction. He therefore admitted that "the wrath of Zeus who guardeth the suppliant compels my reverence; for supreme among mortals is the fear of him".[42]

The reason given by Pelasgus for consenting to give sanctuary is that a refusal to do so would be an act of impiety: It would be going against the obligations imposed upon human beings by the gods. Such disregard therefore of divine obligations constitutes acting for which the retribution would be far more stern than refusing sanctuary out of consideration only for fear of the displeasure or ingratitude of human beings.

Oedipus in Sophocles' *Oedipus at Colonus* declares his religious faith that "The eye of Heaven beholds the just of men, and the unjust", and then he affirms his confidence that "nor ever in this world has one sole godless sinner found escape".[43] The religious interpretation of retribution which Sophocles also affirms in both *Antigone* and in *Ajax* is for the offense of impiety. The Chorus of Elders of Thebes assures Creon that "Vengeance of the gods is swift to overtake the impenitent," when their impenitence is their deliberate refusal both to acknowledge their guilt and to appeal to divine forgiveness for their offense.[44] Tecmessa in *Ajax* responds to her husband's blasphemous denial, "I henceforward owe no duty to the gods", with fear for retribution for such impiety, and begs him to "blaspheme not".[45]

The *Old Testament's* affirmations of a religiously interpreted retribu-

290

tion for men's wrongdoing are so numerous that they alone would comprise a sizable volume. One such example is the confrontation of the god of the early Israelites with their leaders, Moses and Aaron. *Numbers* declares that "The Lord spoke to Moses and Aaron and said, 'How long must I tolerate the complaints of this wicked community?'" (14:26, 27) Such complaining against their god was the sacrilege of impiety for which they were punished by being denied entrance to the land they had been promised. They would instead die in the wilderness, "paying the penalty" for their "wanton disloyalty till the last man . . . dies there". (vs. 34) Another offense which entailed the displeasure of their god was the dishonesty of the men who had been sent by Moses to explore the territory in which they had expected to enter as their homeland: "The men whom Moses had sent to explore the land . . . died of the plague because they had made a bad report." (vs. 36,37) Thus the severity of retribution for their dishonesty was the stern penalty for the impiety of the people whose complaining against their god was brought about by the falsity of the report.

The principle of retribution on the basis of which such penalty for impiety and dishonesty was imposed is stated in *First Kings*: It is "condemning the guilty man and bringing his deeds upon his own head". (8:32) The justice of such judgment is religiously interpreted as assured by the infallible knowledge on which it is based. Such religious faith declares: "Thou alone knowest the hearts of all men", and it is by virtue of such acquaintance with the deeds of human beings, that they will receive a "reward . . . according to (their) deeds". (vs. 39)

3. *Retribution as inescapable*

The *Odyssey* makes a significant observation in pointing out that "Even bloodthirsty pirates, when they've raided a foreign coast and had the luck to carry off some loot, are haunted by the fear of retribution as they make for home with their ships full of plunder".[46] What is anthropologically significant in this observation is that notwithstanding the fact that piracy occurs external to conventional mores, even those who are engaged in its lawless practices have the same basic scruples as people who have the benefit of daily instruction in the mores of a community which prides itself on its law-abiding emphasis. It is observations of this nature which reinforce a widespread belief that conscience is innate. And such a belief persists among many people notwithstanding the arguments such as John Locke presents in his splendid philosophical critique which

291

maintains that there is no innate conscience of any specific moral obligations.

The *Odyssey* narrates a type of retribution imposed upon the Phoenicians which parallels in every respect of cosmic power the acts of retributive justice which the Israelites regarded as entailed in the ultimate sovereignty of their god. The Phoenicians had taken Odysseus into their ship under the deceptive guise of goodwill, but with the intention of selling him into slavery. Their intention, although unknown to the human Odysseus, was nevertheless known to the divine Zeus who "had their end in store for them". He brought this about by his power to bring "a dark cloud to rest above the ship" so that "the sea below it was blackened". Then he "thundered and in the same moment struck the vessel by lightning". Hence "the god took away their homecoming" as the retributive penalty entailed in the moral outrage of their dishonesty and duplicity. They thereby were denied a return to their homes which they had intended to deny to Odysseus.

In this type of interpretation, Homer affirms the same type of retribution which is affirmed in the religious philosophy of history basic to the writings of the ancient Israelites. Whereas the scope of men's knowledge is limited so that they cannot see through the deceptive plans of other human beings, such deception and hypocrisy are not unknown to a divine reality. The limits of human knowing are in no way a parallel to the scope of knowing by such a reality. The nonrestrictive character of such divine knowing therefore constitutes the basis for a religious assurance that justice is inescapable, notwithstanding the plots and schemes of men. Such inescapability is a condition for its inevitable justice. And such justice is anticipated, according to Homer, even by the pirates who defy human conventions of lawful corporate life.[47]

The *Odyssey* affirms the same basic confidence in the ultimate nature of a divine judgment, constituting a final determinant of what may and may not be done by human beings. It is this essentially religious conviction which is affirmed by Eurymachus in assuring the mother of Telemachus that he will not be harmed, but "If the gods decree his death, that is another matter and there's no escape".[48] Dishonest though he may have been in offering such consolation, he at least affirmed a philosophy of history which was cogent even for those who were not consistent in expressing piety as reverence for a divine sovereignty. What is significant, nevertheless, in Eurymachus' statement is the conventional acknowledgment of the inescapability of a divine decree. And it is such a decree which is basic to every religiously interpreted version of retribution.

The *Iliad* declares the same fundamental religious confidence in the inescapability of a divine judgment upon human wrongdoing when it affirms that "The Olympian may postpone the penalty, but he exacts it in the end, and the transgressors pay a heavy price, they pay with their lives, and with their women and their children too". The confidence characteristic of genuine religious faith in inevitable justice, although temporarily deferred, is likewise affirmed in the certitude: "All this will happen without fail."[49]

Hesiod declares the same confidence in the inevitable justice of retribution upon human wrongdoing, although he does not affirm this as a religious belief. He merely declares that "Justice" entails "mischief to men, even to such as have driven her forth".[50] Thus, notwithstanding the most vigorous efforts of human beings to curtail the justice of a judgment upon their evil doings, such just judgment nevertheless is established. It thus demonstrates the futility of human beings' attempt to achieve what *in principle* is impossible to achieve. And it is impossible by the nature of human life itself, internal to an ordered world, to dislocate its basic order. Hence attempts to do so are frustrated. And they are frustrated not by men's efforts which are motivated by a feeble sense of justice, but by the ultimate criterion of justice itself which is normative wisdom in a world under divine sovereignty. Such a religious interpretation is affirmed by Eteocles in Aeschylus' *Seven Against Thebes* when he declares: "From heaven-sent ills there's no escape."[51] The ills to which he refers are retribution for the long chain of evils which hounded his father Oedipus, and which began when his grandfather Laius defied the oracle of a god. Such "heaven-sent ills", therefore, are retribution for impiety, and are entailed in disrespect for a god.

The inescapability of retribution for moral offense is affirmed by Danaüs, who acknowledges that "not even in the realm of Hades, after death, shall he escape arraignment for outrage" against the basic moral conditions for ordered human life.[52] And Pelasgus acknowledges the same fear of such penalty for defying the basic moral obligation of granting sanctuary to those who seek defense against the wrong intended by others. He declares that he is not willing to "surrender" suppliants "from these seats of sanctuary" over which he, as king, has control within his own kingdom. And this decision expresses his acknowledged fear of the inevitable retribution which he would "bring upon ourselves" by denying sanctuary to the helpless. His acknowledgment thus takes account of the "abiding vengeance of the all-destroying god, who, even in the realm of Death, doth not set this victim free".[53]

293

Greek mythology, to which the notion of retribution is as basic as it is to reflective Greek religion, includes a belief that there are agents of the gods, who though not themselves gods, nevertheless, are in their service. Their function is to reinforce the universal order in which justice is inescapable for wrongdoing. In the event that the "all-seeing" eyes of Zeus were to be engaged with one detail while another slipped from his sight, his retributive justice would be supplemented by the Erinyes or Furies. These avenging spirits of the dead pursue all who do evil. The Erinyes of *Agamemnon*, for example, haunted Clytemnestra by coming to her in terrifying dreams. After Orestes avenged the murder of his father by killing Clytemnestra, he was pursued by her Erinyes, disordering his vision as his penalty for this outrage. Thus a retributive penalty for a moral outrage was assured by the Erinyes when it was not directly imposed by a god.

Electra in Euripides' drama describes the penalty which the Erinyes imposed upon Aegisthus for his many evils, hounding him "in his drunken fits" in which he jumped "upon the grave" of the murdered Agamemnon and pelted his monument with stones.[54]

The Chorus in *Andromache* warns the wife of Menelaus that her evil intentions to destroy her rival will not escape penalty: "Ah lady, retribution for this deed will yet visit thee."[55]

After Lycus killed the ruler of Thebes, he was reminded by Amphitryon in Euripides' *Heracles*: "Expect for thy evil deeds to find some ill thyself." And then he made the specific prediction that "soon will he be entangled in the snare of the sword, thinking to slay his neighbors", he himself will be slain.[56] As he uttered his last words, "O kingdom of Cadmus, by treachery I am perishing", the Chorus reminded him: "Thou wert thyself for making others perish." It thus gave him anything but consolation when it told him: "Endure thy retribution; 'tis only the penalty of thine own deeds thou art paying."[57]

Iris, "the handmaid of the gods", explains that until Heracles "had finished all his grievous toils, Destiny was preserving him . . . But now that he hath accomplished the labours of Eurytheus, Hera is minded to brand him with the guilt of shedding kindred blood". What is significant in this discourse by Iris is the explanation why there is such inescapable retribution. It is not only a retaliatory method of punishing human beings for their wrongdoing, but it is also a way of holding in check men's increasing threat to the sovereignty of the gods: "Otherwise, if he escape punishment, the gods will become as naught, while man's power will grow."[58]

Even though this is affirmed in a drama by Euripides, it recalls a belief which was current among the ancient Greeks in their earliest mythology of the resentment of the gods for men's intrusion into their domain. This explanation, therefore, does not defend retribution for a moral reason, as penalty for a moral offense. It rather accounts for it with an ironical reason that the pride of the gods was offended by a threat of men's pride. It is thus a contest of prides, such as was at stake in the ancient mythological accounts of the wars between the giants and the gods. Hence a pride which goes beyond the limits tolerable for a human being expresses the vestigial trait whose ancestry is as ancient as Greek mythology itself, and so the dramatist continues a thought in his dramas whose origin is long before the Epics and any other version of written literature.

The most eloquent expressions of the inescapability of retribution for infidelity to a god are affirmed in the Old Testament. *Deuteronomy* affirms such a judgment against any "man or woman, family or tribe, who is moved . . . to turn from the Lord our God and to go worshipping the gods of those nations . . . he may inwardly flatter himself and think, 'All will be well with me even if I follow the prompting of my stubborn heart'; but this will bring everything to ruin. The Lord will not be willing to forgive him . . . and . . . will blot out his name from under heaven." (29:18-21) In return for a man's dismissing the thought of god as uppermost in his mind, god will cancel all thought of him. The total abolition of all memory of him from the thought of god will, therefore, be a cancellation of the record of him in human history, and it will be as if he had never been.

First Samuel includes a moving narrative of a religious faith that God is attentive to the lives of men and will establish justice among them. This is an account of the pursuit of David by King Saul, who took with him "three thousand picked men". "He encamped beside the road . . . while David was still in the wilderness", and at night, David and his companion entered the camp "and found Saul lying asleep . . . with his spear thrust into the ground by his head." David's companion said to him: "God has put your enemy into your power today", and he appealed to David for permission to kill him. But David refused to give such permission, saying that no man has "ever lifted a finger against the Lord's anointed and gone unpunished". David thereby expressed his piety in respecting one upon whom the Lord had conferred special distinction, and he declared another aspect of his religious faith when he affirmed: "As the Lord lives . . . the Lord will strike him down; either his time will come and he will die, or he will go down to battle and meet his end,"

With this acknowledgment of his reverence for the priority of God's role in human history to anything that he himself might presume to do, he proposed to his companion that they take the spear of Saul, which was by his head, as a way to let him know that he was spared by one who revered God more than he feared the threat of Saul himself. (26:3-11)

First Kings narrates an equally moving expression of religious faith in the inescapable justice which the god of Israel dispenses in the wisdom of his sovereignty over his people. A man named Naboth owned a vineyard which was near the palace of Ahab, the king, which Ahab wanted, and offered to buy, but its owner refused to sell because it had been in his family for generations. The King was angry at this refusal, and expressed his sullenness by even refusing to eat. His wife Jezebel brushed off the refusal of Naboth to sell, assuring the King that she would see that he got the land he wanted. So she thought of a scheme of writing an order to the notables of the city, sealing it with the King's seal, and proposing that they proclaim a fast in which the seat of honour was to be given to Naboth, next to whom two scoundrels were to be placed who would accuse him of "cursing God and the king". Then Jezebel proposed that they take the innocent Naboth out "and stone him to death". When the prophet Elijah heard of what took place, he delivered the word of God's judgment to the King for this moral outrage of taking an innocent man's life in order to steal his property: "Where dogs licked the blood of Naboth, there dogs shall lick your blood", and "Jezebel shall be eaten by dogs by the rampart of Zezreel". (21:1-24) Thus both Jezebel and the King were destroyed before even enjoying one day in the possession of the property they had acquired by fraud.

Job affirms a faith in the retributive justice of God's judgments which might also have been affirmed by the prophet Elijah in his condemnation of the wickedness of the King and his wife. He declares: "Beware of the sword that points at you, the sword that sweeps away all inquity; then you will know that there is a judge." (19:29) Eliphaz, in speaking to Job, cites an example of retribution which might also apply in principle to the wrongdoing committed by Ahab and Jezebel in their plot to deprive a man of his life in order to appropriate his property. The friend of Job declares that the homes of the godless "enriched by bribery, are destroyed". (15:34)

One of the psalms affirms a principle of the inescapable judgment of God's justice which likewise might well have been declared by the prophet Elijah against the evil scheme of the King and his wife, when it declares "Though the wicked grow like grass and every evildoer prospers, they ill be destroyed for ever." (92:7) Another psalm likewise declares a religious belief in God's inescapable justice which could have been cited by the Prophet in his accusation against the two punished by God for their evil. This fifty-second psalm asks: "Why make your wickedness your boast, you man of might" who "love evil and not good, falsehood, not speaking the truth". The question is intended to bring to clear awareness the inevitable retribution that "God (will) pull you down to the ground, sweep you away, leave you ruined and . . . uprooted from the and of the living". (vs. 1-5)

Basic to the philosophy of human history affirmed throughout the *Book of Psalms* is that "The way of the wicked is doomed". (1:6) Because the Psalmist believes in the truth of this proposition of the inescapable judgment of retributive justice, he asks the question: "Why do the people hatch their futile plots?" (2-1)—plots as those invented by Jezebel. After declaring the encouraging assurance that "The Lord gives heart to the orphan and widow", the Psalmist affirms his belief in the justice of God's unfailing judgment, maintaining that "the Lord . . . turns the course of the wicked to their ruin", (146:9) "and brings evildoers to the dust". (147:6) He also affirms a contrast to such judgment, declaring: "The Lord gives new heart to the humble."

Isaiah points out a correlation between men's presumption and their ruin in retributive judgment of God upon "the cities of ruthless nations", maintaining that God "has turned them into heaps of ruin, and fortified towns into rubble; every mansion in the cities is swept away, never to be rebuilt". (25:2, 3) In spite of all that such "ruthless nations" may do to fortify their cities with the presumptuous confidence that their fortifications are their security, they are confronted with the stern reminder that "The Lord has thrown down the high defences of (their) walls; has levelled them to the earth, and brought them down to the dust". (vs. 12)

Isaiah affirms a basic premise of a theology with which he interprets history when, as a spokesman for God, he declares: "All is on record before me; I will not keep silence; I will repay your iniquities." (65:6, 7) Such iniquities, instigated by the evil schemes of men, do not include within their own nature a capacity to endure, and their incapacity to endure demonstrates the folly of those who trust in them. Such trust, therefore, is misdirected. Rather than being directed to what is worthy of being approved, it is directed to what is unworthy of men's approbation because counter to the approbation of God. The Prophet declares to those who misdirect their trust to what cannot support it: "What you conceive and bring to birth is chaff and stubble; a wind like fire shall devour you." This same stern judgment is applicable to nations as well as to individuals: "Whole nations shall be heaps of white ash, or like thorns cut down and set on fire." (33:11, 12)

The foregoing expressions of Isaiah's conviction of the inescapable justice of God's judgment is based upon his theological premise: "High God of retribution that he is, he pays in full measure." (59:18)

The prophet Ezekiel declares the same conviction of the inescapability of God's judgment of justice. Maintaining that these are "the words of the Lord God", he declares: "I will bring retribution upon him; I will cast my net over him, and he shall be caught in its meshes." (17:29)

Referring to Israel as a people corrupted by Jeroboam, their ruler, *Ecclesiasticus* maintains: "Their sins increased beyond measure, until they were driven into exile from their native land; for they had explored every kind of wickedness, until retribution came upon them." (48:24, 25) The counsel which *Ecclesiasticus* affirms in light of the inescapability of retributive justice is: "Do not enlist in the ranks of sinners; remember that retribution will not delay." (7:16)

4. *Retribution as a shadow of the past*

Rieu points out that "Homer causes two shadows to add their sombre significance to every page, that of the past and that of what is yet to come."[59] Whatever parents do which adversely affects the lives of their children and their grandchildren is an instance of the persistence of the past as a determining factor in a later time. And whatever a person has become as the conditioning of a past is his nature which conditions his future. The *Iliad* maintains that if there is a delay in confronting an individual with an expression of retribution, it will, nevertheless, eventually come about. Such retribution is not only confined to an individual who is responsible for an act that entails its eventual penalty, but it extends beyond him to his children and beyond them to their children. "If the Olympian at once has not finished this matter, late will he bring it to pass, and they must pay a great penalty, with their own heads, and with their women, and with their children."[60]

Thus according to this version of retribution, individuals who are not responsible for wrongdoing may, nevertheless, suffer from the wrongdoing of another. Hence this aspect of retribution entails a question of its justice, since moral justice is a correlation of an individual's acting with its consequences for which he himself is responsible. Such moral justice, however, is repudiated when an individual suffers for the wrongdoing of nother. But whether morally just or not, there nevertheless are such onditioning of human life by factors over which individuals themselves ave no control, and therefore of which they are morally guiltless.

The Chorus in Aeschylus' *The Seven Against Thebes* does not question he fairness or justice of the consequences entailed in the refusal of Laius o respect the warning of the Delphic oracle. After defying it, and becomng the parent of Oedipus, his attempt to dispose of his child brought bout the long disastrous sequence in which his child and grandchildren uffered the curse for his defiance of the oracle. Without commenting on ts injustice, the Chorus merely declares: "Of ancient time is the transression I recount, and swift its retribution: yet unto the third generation t abideth."[61]

Sophocles, on the other hand, in *Oedipus at Colonus,* states a profound ritique of the ancient belief that the punishment of children for the leeds of their parents is morally just. In this drama, Oedipus himself rgues that the oracle to his father occurred before his own birth and herefore he was "no willing sinner" in all that was entailed in his father's lefiance of the sacred oracle. He argues that if "it pleased the gods" to nflict the curse from which he and his children suffered, then the morality f the acting of the gods must be called into question, otherwise men's eflecting on what constitutes moral responsibility must be repudiated.[62]

Near the end of the drama, the Chorus affirms the moral philosophy f Sophocles when it declares: "Wrongfully in life oppressed."[63] And yet, n a desperate attempt of the dramatist to save the gods from an acusation of injustice, he concludes the play with a type of *deus ex machina* vhich is intended to bring about justice. The Chorus then declares: "Be e now by Justice blessed." Not clear how this came about, the Messenger ffirms that "he was taken" possibly by "a messenger from heaven, or lse some gentle painless cleaving of earth's base" engulfed him. Whatver the circumstances may have been, "He passed away—an end most narvellous."[64] If this conclusion could have satisfied some of the specators of the play, it surely could not have satisfied those who reflected n the moral problem of the sequence of events regarded as a divinely anctioned instance of justice.

If reflecting were to persist without being squelched by some theatrical rick or a cessation of thinking itself, it would be evident that much that ccurs in human life cannot be regarded as "fair" or "just" when considered within the scope of moral responsibility. Yet, since it occurs, it nust be acknowledged as a part of reality for which concepts of moral iustice are inapplicable. Much that is regarded as "retributive justice"

299

therefore has nothing whatsoever to do with justice when this is inter
preted within the scope of acting for which an individual himself i
responsible. Insofar as an individual has no means of exerting contro
over another individual whose acting nevertheless may impair his ow
life, he suffers for acting for which he is not morally responsible. Sopho
cles himself pointed this out, but then continued to create a drama i
which his critical thinking was totally suspended.

Euripides is as clear as Sophocles about the moral problem entailed i
the traditional interpretation of retribution as "just". The only retribu
tion, however, which may be regarded as just, and therefore as actuall
"retributive justice", is what takes place in an individual's own life b
what he himself has done which merits such entailment. On the othe
hand, there is so much which takes place that adversely affects individuals
lives for which they are not responsible that no serious reflecting ca
gloss over this disturbing problem. All that serious reflecting can conclud
is that much which occurs in human life is unrelated to an individual'
responsibility, although it may well be entailed in another's responsibility
But imposing a penalty upon one who is innocent of the penalized offens
is a moral injustice.

In order to save oneself from the otherwise unavoidable indignatio
of protesting against such obvious unfairness, one has to learn to restric
the use of moral categories, such as "justice" or "fairness", in taking
account of all that occurs. A part of moral maturity is acknowledging
that one himself is responsible for consequences entailed in what h
himself does. And for whatever he suffers in the sequence of acting with
whatever it entails he must have the courage to acknowledge as his responsibility. But he has every moral right to disavow responsibility for
whatever else takes place which is not conditioned by his own acting.

Fair or not fair, it is a fact that an individual himself suffers from the
wrongdoing of others. This is not limited to heredity, but to every corporate act which entails an impairment of individuals' well-being when
they themselves are not responsible for what a community has done.
Individuals without political influence do not declare war, and yet millions
of such individuals suffer as the consequences of its cruelty. Children
born into poverty so excessive that they are denied the minimum nutri-
tion for health may well suffer throughout their lives from a deficiency
of food for which they were not responsible. And their parents may have
been no more responsible for the poverty into which they were born.
But the fact that individuals do suffer for much for which they are not
responsible makes the concept of retribution all the more sobering. Its

sobering impact upon human thinking is acknowledged by Euripides in *Hippolytus*: "For this cows man, how stout of heart soe'er, to know a father's or a mother's sin."[65]

One's own courage in facing his future is weakened by his awareness that he carries a burden for which another was responsible, and yet even though he is not morally responsible for it, he nevertheless must shoulder the load. The mere awareness of this inequity when thought of in terms of moral justice or fairness is enough to embitter anyone who reflects. But such embitterment itself adds to one's load. And so an individual spares himself avoidable illness of his soul which impairs his entire attitude toward life by curtailing his own use of terms such as "fair", "just", and "right". In applying them only to his own acting, he saves himself from rebellion against so much that cannot be reconciled with any version of justice or fairness.

Heracles in Euripides' drama acknowledges: "I am the son of a man who incurred the guilt of blood before he married my mother." The guilt referred to was the murder of Heracles' mother's father, and so his grandfather. He, therefore, acknowledges "the foundation . . . badly laid at birth" from which he was "cursed with woe".[66] But he expressed a moral strength which equalled his physical strength when he also acknowledged that this "needs must . . . be". The meaning of this is clarified in another translation: "When the foundation of the race is laid in sin, needs must the issue be ill-starred".[67] This may be regarded as Euripides' realistic awareness of what actually takes place, although it does not include his appraisal of its moral justice or injustice. As a fact, it is simply one of the givens with which an individual is confronted in doing what he can to live as well as is possible within the scope of his own capacities. What he cannot change, he sensibly accepts, as Heracles did.

It may well be that the popular version of retribution imposed by gods was one of the religious notions of which Euripides progressively became more skeptical. And had he been acquainted with a statement in *Exodus*, he would certainly have rejected outright this religious interpretation of it. Speaking for the god of the Israelites, the priestly authors of *Exodus* declare: "I punish the children for the sins of the fathers to the third and fourth generations of those who hate me." (20:5) Repugnant as this version of religion may be, it, nevertheless, is reaffirmed in a most unambiguous manner for the second time in *Exodus*, when its priestly authors declare that the tutelary deity of the Israelites "punishes

301

sons and grandsons to the third and fourth generation for the iniquity of their fathers". (34:7)

Although this is morally offensive, it is, nevertheless, a fact that children are penalized for the wrongdoing of their parents. Children are born addicted to drugs because of the addiction of their mothers. This is only one of many stern facts of human life which must be acknowledged without also explaining it as the authors of *Exodus* do. But entirely apart from any proposed explanation, *Exodus* takes account of a fact. The justification, however, for attributing such a factual aspect of human life to the justice of a god is another problem, which in no way is necessarily entailed in the fact itself that there is such a sequence in human life.

First Kings points out such a sequence as a fact when it narrates the reign of Jeroboam who "did not abandon his evil ways", one of which was "appointing priests for the hill-shrines from all classes of the people", irrespective of their qualification for such an office. Democratic though his policy may have been at the time, it, nevertheless, was an offense to the tribal god: "By doing this he brought guilt upon his own house and doomed it to utter destruction." (13:33, 34) The detail in this account which confronts reflecting with a troublesome problem is the fairness or the justice of destroying members of a family for the wrongdoing of a ruler. Accepting an appointment to the priesthood for one of the many hill-shrines which dotted the land was an act for which a man himself was responsible, but the scriptural text does not correlate such a father's offense with the penalty it entailed for his children. It correlates rather the offense of the ruler for the "utter destruction" of a family of such a priest. The morally offensive character of this interpretation is even intensified by the text which declares that the tribal god will "destroy . . . every mother's son, whether still under the protection of the family or not". (14:11)

Second Samuel narrates a dialogue between David and the prophet Nathan in which David admitted: "I have sinned against the Lord." And "Nathan answered him, 'The Lord has laid on another the consequences of your sin: . . . the boy that will be born to you shall die." (12:13, 14) That there is such a sequence in human life between a parent's behavior and its consequences for another is a fact. But what is not equally factual is the soundness of explanations which may be offered for such a sequence. One of these is religious, such as Nathan offered to David. In such an explanation, what takes place in human life is regarded as an instance of divine justice. When such an interpretation, however, goes counter to an individual's own religious beliefs about the nature of divine reality, it must be rejected as indefensible. This is what the prophet Ezekiel himself did in reacting to religious interpretations of this type which were affirmed in earlier scripture. And as a prophet, he attributes his critique of this interpretation to "the words of the Lord": "What do you all mean by repeating this proverb in the land of Israel: 'The fathers have eaten sour grapes, and the children's teeth are set on edge'?" Then Ezekiel again attributes to "the Lord God" the decree: "This proverb shall never again be used in Israel. . . . The soul that sins shall die." (18:1-4) Ezekiel thus states a critique of the notion of retribution which had previously been affirmed in earlier priestly writings as having divine sanction. He maintains that it is indefensible to regard as divine justice any version of retribution which attributes an impairment of an individual's life to the wrongdoing for which another is responsible. In criticizing a previously affirmed version of retribution, the Prophet eliminates from prophetic theology a morally offensive priestly interpretation of a divine version of justice.

Although Ezekiel deliberately turns critical upon the priestly tradition for identifying divine justice with what an individual suffers as a consequence of another's wrongdoing, the *Book of Job, Proverbs,* and *Psalms* had already affirmed versions of such justice with which he himself agreed. In the *Book of Job,* Elihu declares: "Far be it from God to do evil . . . For he pays a man according to his work and sees that he gets what his conduct deserves." (34:10, 11) This is not only a remarkably sensitive religious version of theology, but it is also a remarkably sound moral philosophy. *Proverbs* likewise specifically limits divine judgment upon an individual to what he alone is responsible for either in his wrongdoing or in his morally praise-worthy acting. It declares that "The Lord's curse rests on the house of the evildoer, while be blesses the home of the righteous". (3:33) The same type of restriction is affirmed in *Psalms,* which declares: "Thou doest requite a man for his deeds." (12:63) Such morally defensible interpretations of the correlation between what an individual does for which he is responsible and its consequences entailed in his own acting are also theologically significant. They thus avoid attributing to a divine judgment occurrences in human life which do violence to a human being's sense of what is just.

Ezekiel, of course, is not the only major prophet to have been impatient with the earlier priestly version of divine justice. Although Isaiah does not state a specific critique of such a priestly version as Ezekiel does, he, nevertheless, affrms an interpretation of divine judgments as a theological premise which is compatible with critical reflecting on moral responsibility when he declares that people who suffer severe misfortunes "have earned their own disaster". (3:9) Yet this unrestricted defense of the correlation of disaster with an individual's own wrongdoing is as indefensible as is the priestly doctrine that divine justice correlates the suffering of children with the wrongdoing of their parents and their parents before them

Anyone who is aware of the extent of disasters entailed in industry and in travel would recognize the indefensibility of Isaiah's position. Children who are injured and deformed for life in accidents occurring in travel suffer from disasters for which there is no relation whatsoever to their moral guilt. The same criticism must be directed against Isaiah's flippant optimism that "All goes well with the righteous man". (3:10) His assertion, "Happy the righteous man", is a distortion of the relation between righteousness and happiness. The only relation which can defensibly be affirmed is that the righteous person does not suffer a regret for his wrongdoing, and therefore is spared the penalty of sorrow and regret which are entailed in deliberate wrongdoing.

What alone is defensible in this passage in *Isaiah* is the purely formal statement that an individual "reaps the reward that he has earned". (vs. 11) It is formal in the sense that it is not interpreted by reference to any morally significant aspect of human life, such as happiness or suffering, or any one of an almost countless number of morally censurable ways of acting or morally praiseworthy ways of acting. As stated, it is a form which can be interpreted by citing any of these morally determinate ways of acting. Such interpretations then would be subject to appraisals for their defensibility or their indefensibility as the formal statement itself cannot be so subjected.

5. *Retribution as moral judgment*

Proverbs points out a realistic understanding of a type of acting when it declares that "Bread (even when) got by fraud tastes good". The fraudulent means by which it is acquired, of course, does not affect the taste, and taste which is enjoyed in eating such a food induces an individual to take it notwithstanding the fraudulent means by which it was acquired. The appeal of food is dominant when an individual is hungry; and his hunger displaces other considerations which may more feebly assert themselves. An individual's reflective awareness that the fraud by which he acquired his food will entail a handicap to him does not effectively control his desire for such food. Desire itself is not capable of realizing the nature of a moral judgment upon such fraudulent means, as *Proverb* points out:

304

"But afterwards it fills the mouth with grit." (20:17) If it were possible under the pressure of desire to be aware of deferred consequences of acting, and if such awareness were an effective restraint for desire itself, there would be no heartaches in human life brought about by impulsively determined actions. But desire usurps the consciousness of which an individual is capable, and during its assertive dominance excludes reflective restraint.

After desire is momentarily satisfied, reflecting has its opportunity to take account of a disadvantage which for the time was ignored. But no matter how grave a handicap of acting may be, the intensity of a desire which presses for its exclusive right to be asserted ignores it. Heraclitus, therefore, was as realistic as the proverb itself when he acknowledged: "It is hard to fight desire; what it wants it buys with the soul."

Proverbs uses a figure which even the least reflective of people could understand when it points out that "The man who sows injustice reaps trouble, and the end of his work will be the rod". (22:8) The graphic way in which this relation is indicated between two activities which are separated by a time-interval takes account of the basic nature of a difficulty of making choices which do not entail regret. A consequence entailed in an act is not simultaneous with the act itself, and therefore does not have the same centrality in attention as the want which motivates the act. Sowing and reaping are not simultaneous, and this fact is the parallel of acting under the pressure of desire and the deferred consequences of such acting. "The rod" does not loom on the horizon of an attractive appeal to enjoy a good. But appeal, pleasant though it may be when it alone is dominant in attention, does not determine the nature of reality. It, therefore, so readily collides with it, and so with an intelligence which is informed of the nature of reality.

Jeremiah affirms a profound understanding basic to all efforts to preserve natural resources against the inroads of greed which is not restrained by a reflective awareness of the long-range disaster that eventually penalizes such greed. His ancient warning is as applicable today as it was centuries before the present era: "Your wrongdoing has upset nature's order, and your sins have kept from you her kindly gifts." (5:25) The shortsightedness accompanying whatever is done to get what is desired is the handicap to an acting which otherwise might have the benefit of enlightened reflecting. If such acting were not universal, moral tragedies likewise would not be.

The most direct correlation of a penalty for acting with insufficient reflective restraint is internal to an individual's own life, and such a

305

correlation is the nature of intrinsic moral judgment. One of the profoundest observations of such an intrinsic moral judgment upon a moral evil is affirmed by Eldridge Cleaver, who with insight equal to the ancient Prophets, declares: "The price of hating other human beings is loving oneself less."[68] The *Book of Job* declares the same understanding of the directness with which moral penalty is entailed in morally censurable aspects of human life: "The fool is destroyed by his own angry passions." (5:2) There is no postponement in the moral penalty entailed in this type of acting which is deprived of all reflective restraint. An uninhibited act of anger entails consequences which are themselves the most obvious indictment of such behavior. In other words, the act of unrestrained anger itself includes its own moral judgment. It is judged as an act of folly by its own total negation of reasonable restraint, and such unrestrained acting of which human beings are universally so capable account for the universality of this tragic aspect of human history.

Eliphaz affirms one of his profound comments on the tragic character of human history when he mentions to Job the pathos of the fact that "men perish outright and unheeded, die, without ever finding wisdom". (4:20, 21) Failing to live wisely is its own moral judgment, since a life without sufficient benefit of enlightened acting is denied the supreme good of living wisely. As *Psalms* points out, an individual who "scoffs at all restraint" does so because an awareness of the advantage of reflective restraint is possible only for one who has already cultivated such restraint. (10:5) And without such benefit of character, there could be no awareness internal to one's own acting of the consequences which it entails. Being "obsessed with his own desires" is, as *Psalms* points out, an individual's "own undoing", which is moral judgment intrinsic to his own way of acting and so to his own way of living. (vs. 2) It is judgment upon his own character that his desires usurp the field of his consciousness, and in so doing exclude his awareness of his own folly in so acting.

Proverbs is certainly one of the books in the Bible which indicates a clear understanding of the nature of intrinsic moral judgment. In fact, it affirms an entire moral philosophy in the greatest possible economy of words when it declares: "The wicked are brought down by their wickedness." (11:5) So stated, this is not supported by either a religious metaphysic or a theology, but is affirmed as a factual statement, summing up observations of a vast scope of human history. The same may be said of another proverb: "The wicked are choked by their own violence." (10:11) The same clarity of understanding of the nature of human life is likewise affirmed in *Proverb's* digest of centuries of reflecting, naively attributed to Solomon, as if citing their origin from him should confer upon them credentials which they do not already carry in their own wisdom. One of the most forceful declarations of the fact of intrinsic moral judgment upon an individual for what he himself is, and so does, is: "An evil man is ensnared by his sin."

If this proverb had been affirmed by Solomon, it would certainly sum up his reflecting in restrospect. It is doubtful, however, that the same king after floundering in the follies of luxury and licence should also have had clarity of understanding enough to acknowledge that "A righteous man lives and flourishes". (29:6) This, of course, might be an expression of disguised regret with which he became acquainted too late in his life to have benefitted earlier from his own wisdom. If he were the author of at least some of the proverbs, he spoke from his own experience when he maintained that "Wicked men have no future to look forward to; their embers will be put out". (24:20)

No more unencumbered digest of a way of living, with its intrinsic judgment, could be affirmed than is given in *Ecclesiastes*, attributed to "the Preacher, the son of David". He admits that "Whatever my eyes, coveted, I refused them nothing, nor did I deny myself any pleasure". Without also intending to point out a correlation of this manner of living with his own attitude toward the worth of life, he nevertheless does so when he acknowledges: "I saw that everything was emptiness and chasing the wind." (2:10, 11) The correlation between his type of living and what he himself says about it is the most eloquent indictment of its folly.

If, of course, anyone should deliberately want to live with a sense of "emptiness" and be satisfied to spend his life "chasing the wind", then he would not also regard himself as an exhibit of moral folly. But there is no evidence internal to the comment in *Ecclesiastes* that there is this dishonest gloss by its author over the folly of his own life. He must, therefore, be respected for his honesty to have stated so clearly what he himself recognized as the correlation between his unrestrained hedonistic scheme of living and the sense of emptiness which it itself entails.

One "function of tragedy", as Rieu points out, is "to mourn the wastage of virtue".[69] The insight into this aspect of literary tragedy might also be affirmed as a premise in a moral philosophy which takes account of the tragic character of much human life. Much human life is a misuse of native capacities, which if they had been used with more discipline might have yielded a life enriched with moral benefits, otherwise made impossible by a disregard for their more sensible use. The *Iliad's* version of

Helen credits her with an ability, which is the equal of moral philosophers, when she comments upon her husband Paris: "He will never change, though one day he will suffer for it."[70]

Euripides attributes to Phaedra a comparable intelligence, which also would qualify her as a moral philosopher, commenting on the nature of an inevitable moral judgment internal to an individual whose folly or villainy entails a handicap to himself, which he might have avoided had he lived with more sense than he did. She declares: "Time unmasks the villain soon or late."[71]

The Chorus in Aeschylus' *The Libation-Bearers* likewise affirms an awareness of the nature of intrinsic moral penalty entailed in what one does that is incompatible with well-being: "Calamity, racking his soul distracts the guilty man so that he is steeped in misery utter and complete."[72]

Although both Aeschylus and the author of the *Iliad* consistently express a profound religious orientation, neither, however, interprets from a religious perspective the examples which they cite of intrinsic moral penalty. Both cite such instances without comment of a metaphysic, as if they are indisputable facts of human life. And the same may be said of Euripides' *Hippolytus* in which Phaedra affirms what the dramatist himself regards as factual, that "soon or late", acting incompatible with moral well-being will entail its own impairment.

Such a correlation is affirmed in every comment made in both Greek and Israelite reflecting on the nature of retribution. Retribution is moral judgment entailed in human acting as its inescapable accompaniment.

6. *Retribution as moral penalty in kind*

If the nature of retribution as it is interpreted in both ancient Greek and Israelite reflecting were to be distinguished from any other version of moral judgment, it would be on the basis of their emphasis upon a moral penalty correlated with a moral offense in which the penalty is similar in nature to the offense. A thoroughly unambiguous version of such an interpretation of retribution is affirmed in *Genesis*: "He that sheds the blood of a man, for that man his blood shall be shed." (9:6)

This type of relation between offense and its penalty is ordinarily regarded as retaliatory. A reason for this identification is that penalty is commensurate with offense. The narrative in *Genesis* of the relation of Joseph and his brothers illustrates this principle of retribution as moral judgment. When his brothers went to Egypt to get food during the threat-

308

ened starvation among the Israelites, Joseph "kept them in prison for three days". During this time, "They said to one another, 'No doubt we deserve to be punished because of our brother, whose suffering we saw; for when he pleaded with us we refused to listen. That is why these sufferings have come upon us.' " (42:21) Their conversation among themselves thus expressed their awareness of the justice of being punished in kind for an offense for which they themselves were responsible. Reuben, the oldest son, reminded his brothers of their offense against their brother, saying: "Did I not tell you not to do the boy a wrong? But you would not listen, and his blood is on our heads, and we must pay." (vs. 22) Thus Reuben in this narrative in the first book in the Old Testament affirms a principle of retribution which is basic to the biblical version of moral penalty entailed for moral offenses.

Exodus applies this same principle in affirming the retributive penalty for offenses against the helpless, such as children without the protection of a father. The injunction it affirms as a command of the god of the Israelites is that "You shall not ill-treat any widow or fatherless child". (22:23) And it points out the inevitable penalty which their god will impose: "If you do . . . your own wives shall become widows and your children fatherless." (vs. 24)

The *Book of Judges* includes a narrative of the capture of a Canaanite king, Adoni-bezek, who was taken to Jerusalem by men of Judah where they "cut off his thumbs and great toes". Gruesome as this treatment certainly is, devoid of charity and pity, it nevertheless performed the role of confronting the captured king with retributive justice, since he acknowledged: "I once had seventy kings whose thumbs and great toes were cut off picking up the scraps from under my table." This version of retribution is accompanied by the commentary of a religious interpretation which includes a theology that interprets divine judgment in terms of retributive justice: "What I have done, God has done to me." (1:6, 7)

A narrative in *Second Samuel* of the prophet Nathan's confrontation with King David is another eloquent example of the Old Testament's version of retributive justice which is interpreted from a religious orientation that attributes it to a judgment imposed by the god of the Israelites. David wanted the wife of Uriah the Hittite, but he did no want his desires to be known by others. He therefore ordered that Uriah be put in a vulnerable position in fighting against the Ammonites. In the encounter, Uriah was killed, and David took his wife. All of what transpired may have been undetected by men, but according to the narrative, it was not unknown to their god. Nathan, the prophet of their god, therefore confronted David with the accusation :"You have struck down Uriah the Hittite with the sword; the man himself you murdered by the sword of the Ammonites, and you have stolen his wife." (12:9) Then the Prophet pronounced the judgment of the god upon the King according to the principle of retributive justice, and specifically of the retaliatory pattern: "Your family shall never again have rest from the sword." (vs. 10)

David's conscience was not entirely dead, notwithstanding all that he had done to diminish its acuity and to cancel its warnings against his wrongdoing. Hence he admitted to the Prophet: "I have sinned against the Lord." (vs. 13) Thus this acknowledgment was evidence that his moral nature was not destroyed by his evil but transcended its tyranny over his repeated inclinations to folly.

The centuries of Israelites' reflecting on human life, its folly and its wisdom, were preserved in *Proverbs,* which affirms the inescapable judgment of their god upon the injustices against the defenceless. It declares: "The Lord will take up their cause and rob him who robs them of their livelihood." (22:23)

The Prophet Isaiah does not independently come to the religious interpretation of men's accountability to their god for their offenses against others. Like *Proverbs,* he too had the benefit of centuries of profound reflecting of his people upon the inevitable penalty entailed in men's wrongdoing. He thus warned his contemporaries, who had forgotten the wisdom of their forefathers, that "When you cease to destroy, you will be destroyed, after all your betrayals, you will be betrayed yourself". (33:1) Although Isaiah does not include the religious commentary that this will be effected by a divine intervention in human life, he nevertheless is confident that its inescapability is the way God establishes justice among men, notwithstanding their futile attempts to avoid it.

The Prophet Ezekiel includes a theological explanation to reinforce the sternest of his warnings against his contemporaries for their moral offenses. As a prophet of "the Lord God", he accuses the Israelites of being "most surely guilty of blood" in their dealings with others, and he declares the retributive penalty they must expect: "And blood shall pursue you." (35:6) And then Ezekiel directs the same type of warning to the Edomites, the descendents of Esau, the older son of the patriarch Isaac. Speaking as a representative of their god, he declares: "I will do to you as you did to Israel . . . when you gloated over its desolation. O hill-country of Seir, you will be desolate, and it will be the end of Edom." This stern accusation then concludes with the reminder: "Thus men will know that I am the Lord." (vs. 15) In this narrative with its theological feature, the Prophet declares a philosophy of history which had been reaffirmed throughout previous centuries, and its impression was indelible upon the mentality out of which the Old Testament emerged as one of the great religious books of mankind.

Centuries of Greek reflecting on the morally sobering nature of human life is expressed in the tradition which begins with the Epics and continues through the great tragedies. The narrative in the *Odyssey* of Aegisthus, usurping the throne of Agamemnon and later murdering him, includes the comment that this moral outrage "brought him disaster in the shape of Orestes; for that brave youth, returning from Athens, killed Aegisthus . . . . and so the slayer was slain".[73]

The *Iliad* includes a pictorial version of prayers as "Daughters of almighty Zeus", and it interprets their relation to human beings according to the religious orientation characteristic of the Epics. It maintains that "The man who receives these Daughters of Zeus with humility when they approach him is greatly blessed by them and has his own petition granted". The warning of retribution, however, is then added: "But when a man hardens his heart and rebuffs them, they go and pray to Zeus . . . that he may himself be overtaken by Sin and punished through his fall."[74] Both ancient Greeks and Israelites were confident that human life is included in a wider domain over which men do not have final control, but are subordinate to an ultimate sovereignty which holds them accountable to moral obligations which they may not disregard without inevitable penalty.

The Chorus in Aeschylus' *Agamemnon* affirms what in every respect is repeatedly affirmed throughout the Old Testament. The difference, of course, is in the terminology by which the two cultures refer to the deities whom they revere. But other than this linguistic difference, the moral principle which is affirmed is basically the same: "While Zeus abideth on his throne, it abideth that to him who doeth, it shall be done—for it is an ordinance."[75] The formal character of this principle is likewise affirmed in the first book of the Bible, and it is basic to the many versions of retrbiutive judgment ordained by a god whom the religious Israelites revered.

Although Clytemnestra is a strange medium for affirming any moral wisdom of considerable profundity, Aeschylus nevertheless gives her the credit for acknowledging the inescapability of retributive penalty. Referring to her own moral outrage against Agamemnon, she declares: "With death dealt him by the sword he hath paid for what first began."[76] In saying this, she is, of course, referring to Agamemnon's responsibility for sacrificing her daughter on the altar to Artemis in his attempt to atone for his offense against the goddess by killing one of her sacred deer, which in turn was the reason for her antagonism to him as the commander of the forces on their way to Troy. Although the mythology is peculiarly Greek, what is not peculiar to Greek mentality is the acknowledgment of an inevitable retribution, often in kind, which is its retaliatory version. And it is on the basis of this retaliatory version of retribution that Clytemnestra defends her own acting.

Her own citing of a sound principle in defense of her moral outrage constitutes a profoundly instructive lesson: The most indisputable of moral principles can be cited for evil purposes of justifying moral offenses, as if, under such a gloss, their offense is diminished or cancelled.

The Chorus in Euripides' drama confronts Heracles, as the last in a series of usurpers to the throne of Thebes, with the accusation: "Thou wert thyself for making others perish, endure thy retribution; 'tis only the penalty of thy own deeds thou art paying."[77] Each usurper succeeded to the throne by the murder of its king, and each in turn was displaced by the same method. Thus the Chorus enunciates a principle which expresses the conclusion at which Greek reflecting arrived throughout the centuries, which in every way parallels the conclusion formulated into a comparable moral principle by the Israelites. The chorus in *The Madness of Heracles* maintains: "Thine own deeds' retribution dost thou gain."[78]

The same retaliatory version of a retributive judgment of justice is affirmed by the chorus in Euripides' *Hecuba*. In pronouncing judgment upon Polymester, it declares: "So shalt thou lose thy own life for the life thou has taken."[79] The inevitability of such retributive justice is as fundamental to the sober reflecting of the Greeks as it is to the reflecting of the Israelites. Their mythologies and theologies differ in some respects, but not their versions of what is just in the penalty imposed for wrongdoing, since both affirm the same sound insight into moral penalty as entailed in its own evil.

7. The intention to do evil to another recoils upon itself

Greek mythology includes a story of Thamyris, a Thracian singer, who boasted that he excelled the Muses in his abilities, and thereupon lost his sight and his musical talents as punishment. This is an example of the Greek version of a retribution in which an individual is requited in terms of his own offense. His offense was his arrogance in relation to the Muses from whom he had received his talents, and their punishment of him for his offense was taking away the talents they had given him.

Orestes murdered Aegisthus in the same place in which Aegisthus had murdered Orestes' father. This version of retribution, in which an evil recoils upon the one who perpetrated it, is affirmed by Orestes in reminding Aegisthus: "Where thou didst slay my father thou must die."[80]

The Theban herald points out this same version of requital for an offense of impiety when Capaneus raised a ladder against the gates of the Theban fortifications, "swearing he would sack our town, whether the god would or not".[81] For this boast, as the herald points out, he was destroyed on that very ladder by a stroke of lightning which was the punishment imposed by the god. Another interpretation of the same punishment, of course, is that his intention to destroy Thebes recoiled upon his own destruction. If this were the explanation for his death, it would not be a religious interpretation of such retribution. But if the basis for his destruction was his insolent defiance of the gods by declaring that, as one having the power of a king, he was subordinate to no other sovereignty, then the explanation would be from a religious orientation.

The literature of the ancient Israelites is rich in examples of a religious interpretation of retribution in which requital is a recoiling upon an offender of the essential nature of his own offense. In this particular rubric, *First Kings* interprets the punishment inflicted by the god of the Israelites upon King Ahab of Samaria and his queen. The prophet Elijah declared that the final judgment against both of these offenders would occur in the same context in which they had committed their offense. He declared to the King: "Where dogs licked the blood of Naboth, there dogs shall lick your blood." And to the queen, he declared the same version of retribution: "Jezebel shall be eaten by the dogs by the rampart of Jezrell", which was the very plot of ground she had schemed to steal from Naboth by having him murdered. (21:19-24)

This occurrence of the punishment which the two royal personages suffered for their offense, both against their god and against one of their citizens, made so vigorous an impression upon the Israelites that it is mentioned in considerable detail in both *First Kings* and also in *Second Kings*. The version affirmed in the latter account is the decree of the god of the Israelites that he "will take vengeance on Jezebel for the blood of (his) servants the prophets and for the blood of all the Lord's servants. All the house of Ahab shall perish." (9:7, 8) This account then refers to the death of Ahab's son, Jehoram, killed by Jehu, who ordered that his body be thrown "into the plot of land belonging to Naboth". (vs. 25)

This account specifically mentions the version of retribution in which the nature of an offense recoils upon the offender in the same terms as the offense. The plot of land which the royal family sought to steal became the plot on which its members were thrown, and in which the Queen was forbidden to be buried. (vs. 10)

The same type of retribution is pointed out in a confrontation of King Solomon with one of his officers, Shimei. The King declared: "You know in your own heart all the mischief you did to my father David; the Lord is now making that mischief recoil on your own head." (*I Kings* 2:44, 45)

One of the most dramatic of the Old Testament accounts of retribution of requital in kind is given in *Esther*. The account opens with a description of the honor King Ahasuerus conferred upon a Macedonian officer, Haman, who plotted to exterminate the Jews in Persia: "So the king took the signet-ring from his hand and gave it to Haman . . . enemy of the Jews." (3:10, 11) Haman had an especially intense antipathy for one Jew, Mordecai, who was also "in attendance at court and . . . did not rise nor defer to him". Haman "was filled with rage" and "sent for his friends and his wife Zeresh and held forth to them about the splendour of his wealth and his many sons, and how the king had promoted him and advanced him above the other officers and courtiers". (5:11) He asked them what he should do to punish Mordecai for his disrespect, and they proposed that he have "a gallows seventy-five feet high" constructed on which Mordecai was to be hanged. The account points out that "Haman thought this an excellent plan, and he set up the gallows." (5:14) Within a day, the retribution in kind occurred when Ahasuerus decreed that "the wicked plot which Haman had devised against the Jews should recoil on his own head, and that he and his sons should be hanged on the gallows". (9:26)

Eliphaz in the *Book of Job* declares that there is one thing he knows as a certitude. It is "that those who plough mischief and sow trouble reap as they have sown". (4:8) His friend Elihu, who also speaks with Job, illustrates this principle by citing that "kings on their thrones" have power to put their enemies into servitude. When, however, "they grow arrogant" in their power, "Next you may see them loaded with fetters, held fast in captives' chains". (36:7, 8)

The general principle of retribution is reaffirmed by Job when he acknowledges his agreement with the interpretations affirmed by his two friends. He declares about "the mighty" that "For a moment they rise to the heights, but are soon gone", and he affirms with the same type of certitude as his friends, that "iniquity is snapped like a stick". (24:24)

Psalms uses graphic figures of a pit and net to stress the type of recoiling of a penalty for evil when it declares that "The nations have plunged

314

into a pit of their own making; their own feet are entangled in the net which they hid". (9:15) Thus scheming to destroy others, they themselves are destroyed by the same type of destructive means they devised for others. The same version of retribution employing the same figure is again affirmed in *Psalms*: "Men . . . . have dug a pit in my path but have fallen into it themselves." (57:6)

Proverbs retains the same figure of the pit which is used in *Psalms* that connotes recoil of evil in the penalty itself by which the one who did the evil is punished. It declares: "If he digs a pit, he will fall into it." (26:27) Another specific example in *Proverbs* of such retribution is a recoil of heartlessness upon a heartless individual. It declares: "If a man shuts his ears to the cry of the helpless, he will cry for help himself and not be heard." (21:13)

This basic principle of retribution is also affirmed in *Proverbs* without citing examples of its exemplification in human life when it declares: "If a man repays evil for good, evil will never quit his house." Countless instances in human life can be cited as interpretations of the variable "evil" to which reference is made in his assertion. And according to this principle, every such instance will be correlated with a penalty in kind. Evil is entailed as a requital for evil.

Another version of this retributive relation is between an individual's refusal to benefit from reproof and what he himself becomes through his continued disregard for correction. He finally becomes incapable of ever benefitting from correction. Ignorant of his own folly, he continues to be enslaved by his folly. *Proverbs* declares: "A man who is still stubborn after much reproof will suddenly be broken past mending." (29:1) The same principle is again affirmed in declaring that "Correction is the high road to life; neglect reproof and you miss the way." (10:17) Thus the penalty for ignoring correction, which would save an individual from imperiling his life with his own stupidity, is that he continues to be too stupid to know which correction is advantageous for his own good.

A man who builds a house to exhibit his wealth subjects himself to the peril of requital for his motive. Motivated by pride, he will be taught by a penalty for his arrogance. And according to the religious background out of which this proverb arose, such a man will succumb eventually to the divine impatience with his untutored insolence: "The Lord pulls down the proud man's home." (15:25)

Isaiah declares that a human being "reaps the reward that he has earned". (3:11) As has already been acknowledged in the foregoing discussion, this certitude affirmed by Isaiah confronts reflecting with many grave questions about its defensibility, since there are so many apparent exceptions. But one who entertains the notion that there are exceptions does not have the unwavering religious faith that Isaiah had. Whether his faith is defensible or whether it is uncritical, because not sufficiently cautious in its claims, can hardly be decided by one who does not have this religious faith.

But even without a comparable faith, no one who understands the nature of intrinsic moral judgment would affirm the unqualified skepticism as is affirmed in *Ecclesiastes*: "Good man and sinner fare alike . . . the one and the same fate befalls every man." (9:3) Insofar as this is a generalization about mortality, it is certainly sound: Every living being dies irrespective of his conduct. But there is a vast difference in what the death of one human being terminates and what it terminates in another. The life of one who has endeavored to live with respect for others' rights and to do what he can to give them a helping hand does not have the same spiritual death that another has who was indifferent throughout his life to the rights of others. They indeed both die, but what is entailed in their lives before their death makes the basic difference in the significance of their death.

References

Chapter I

1. *Letter to a Child Never Born*, p. 113, Simon and Schuster, N.Y. 1975, Trans. John Shepley
2. Cf. Rieu, E.V., *The Iliad*, p. xviii, Methuen and Co., London, 1953; Lattimore, Richmond, *The Iliad of Homer*, p. 28 f., University of Chicago, Chicago, 1951.
3. Scully, Vincent, *The Earth, The Temple, and The Gods*, p. 6, revised edition, Frederick A. Praeger, N.Y., 1969.
4. *The Iliad*, p. xxi, footnote 1.
5. *Op. cit.*, p. 42.
6. *Op. cit.*, p. 54.
7. Pratt, J.B., *The Religious Consciousness*, p. 2, Macmillan Co., N.Y. 1927.
8. *Op. Cit.*, p. xx.
9. *Op. cit.*, p. 42.
10. *Iliad*, Bk. VI, 345. Trans. E. V. Rieu, p. 109-110.
11. Grant, Frederick C., *Hellenistic Religions*, p. 103, Library of Liberal Arts, Bobbs-Merrill Co. Indianapolis, 1953.
12. 1. 1226-1229, Trans. F. Storr, Loeb Classical Library, Harvard, No. 20. 1968.
13. 1. 190, Trans. E. P. Coleridge, *The Complete Greek Drama*, edited by W. J. Oates and Eugene O'Neil, Jr., Random House, N.Y., 1938.
14. 1. 196, Trans. A. S. Way, Loeb Classical Library, No. 12.
15. E. P. Coleridge, *op. cit.*, p. 767.
16. Lattimore, Richmond, *Aeschylus*, footnote 2, p. 2, Vol. I, *The Complete Greek Tragedies*, University of Chicago, 1974 (Fourth Impression)
17. 1. 100, Trans. E. P. Coleridge, *op. cit.*, p. 849.
18. 33:6, *The New English Bible*: second translation, *Revised Standard Version*.
19. 27:10, NEB. (*The New English Bible*)
20. Scully, V., *op. cit.*, p. 42.
21. Bk. XVIII, 1. 130-132, Trans. E. V. Rieu, *op. cit.*, p. 262-3.
22. Bk. VII, 203, Trans A. D. Godley, Loeb Classical Library, No. 119, p. 519.
23. *Ibid*, 519-21.

24. *Ibid. Bk.* VIII, 109, No. 120, p. 111.
25. *Ibid.*
26. 1. 470-71, Trans. H. Weir Smyth, Loeb, No. 145, p. 53.
27. 1. 275, Loeb No. 145., p. 241.
28. *Heracles* 1. 1314, Trans. E. P. Coleridge, Random House, vol. I, p. 1050.
29. 1. 381-2, Trans. Robert Potter, Random House, vol. I, p. 1136.
30. 1. 981, Trans. A. S. Way, Loeb No. 12, p. 239.
31. *Orestes* 1. 976, Trans. E. P. Coleridge, Random House, vol. II, p. 142.
32. 1. 208, Trans. E. P. Coleridge, Random House, vol. I, p. 778.
33. 1. 1240f, Trans. Gilbert Murray, Random House, vol. I, p. 1005.
34. 1. 1428, Trans. E. P. Coleridge, Random House, vol. I, p. 1053. (N.B. title in Loeb Classical Library, "Madness of Hercules", Trans. A. S. Way, No. 11)
35. Translation of A. S. Way, "Madness of Hercules."
36. *Lamentations* 1, 1; 5:15 NEB.
37. *Ibid.*, 1:7, RSV.
38. *Ibid.*, 2:1, NEB.
39. Bk. I, 178, *op. cit.* vol. I, No. 117.
40. *Ibid.*, 181.
41. *Ibid.*, 190
42. *Ibid.* III, 159.
43. *II Corinthians*, 4:18.
44. VI, 146f. Trans. Richmond Lattimore, *op. cit.*, p. 157.
45. VII, 203, *op. cit.*, Loeb No. 119, p. 519.
46. I, 207, *ibid.*, Loeb No. 117, p. 261.
47. *Ibid.*, I, 5. p. 9.
48. 1. 466, Trans. H. Weir Smyth, Loeb No. 146., p. 41.
49. *Prometheus Bound*, 1. 938, Trans. H. Weir Smyth, Loeb, No. 145, p. 301.
50. *Ibid.* 1. 958 f.
51. *Oedipus at Colonus*, 1. 612 f., Trans. F. Storr, Loeb, No. 20, p. 207.
52. 1. 295, Trans. F. Storr, Loeb, No. 21, p. 281.
53. *Philoctetes*, 1. 503, Trans. F. Storr, No. 21, p. 407.
54. *Trachiniae*, 1. 1270, *ibid.*, p. 359.
55. *Ibid.*, 1. 945, p. 333.
56. *Ibid.*, 1. 1f, p. 259.
57. *Heracleidae*, 1. 865, Trans. E. P. Coleridge, Random House, vol. I, p. 907.
58. *Ion*, 1. 969, Trans. A. S. Way, Loeb, No. 12, p. 95.
59. *Hecuba*, 1. 55f, Trans. E. P. Coleridge, Random House, vol. I, p. 808.
60. *The Trojan Women*, 1. 1204, Trans. Gilbert Murray, Random House, vol. I, p. 1003.
61. Ibid. (*The Daughters of Troy*), 1. 1203, Trans. A. S. Way, Loeb, No. 9, p. 447.
62. *The Trojan Women*, 1. 1203., Trans. Gilbert Murray, *op. cit.*, Vol. I, 1003.
63. *Helen*, 1. 1142, Trans. E. P. Coleridge, Random House, vol. II, p. 42.

54. *Hecuba,* 1. 57f, Trans. E. P. Coleridge, Random House, vol. I, p. 808.
55. 1. 478f, Trans. A. S. Way, Loeb, No. 10, p. 317.
56. *Heracles,* 1. 883, Trans. E. P. Coledridge, Random, vol. I, p. 1037.
57. 1. 340f, Trans. E. P. Coleridge, Random, vol. II, 120.
58. 1. 344, Trans. A. S. Way, Loeb, No. 10, p. 153.
59. *Hecuba* 1. 956f. Trans. A. S. Way, Loeb, No. 9, p. 321.
70. *The Phoenissae,* 1. 554f Trans. E. P. Coleridge, Random II, p. 184.
71. *Phaedo* 62 B, Trans. Harold North Fowler, *Plato,* Harvard, 1943.
72. Bk. IX, 320, Trans. Richmond Lattimore, p. 206.
73. 11, 5.
74. 1. 136, Trans. Anonymous, Random II, p. 486.
75. *Prometheus Bound,* Trans. H. Weir Smyth, Loeb, No. 145, 1. 147, p. 229.
76. *Ibid.,* 1. 188, p. 233.
77. 1. 1230f, Trans. F. Storr, Loeb No. 20, p. 263.
78. 1. 819, Trans. F. Storr, Loeb. No. 21, p. 187.
79. *Ibid.,* 1. 1008, p. 203.
80. *Oedipus the King,* 1. 1529, Trans. F. Storr, Loeb No. 20, p. 139.
81. 1. 126f, Trans. E. P. Coleridge, Random, vol. II, p. 114.
82. 1. 301, Trans. E. P. Coleridge, Random, vol. I, p. 770.
83. 1. 301, Trans. A. S. Way, Loeb No. 12, p. 185.
84. 1. 488f, Trans. E. P. Coleridge, Random, vol. I, p. 819.
85. 1. 190f, Trans. E. P. Coleridge, Random, vol. I, p. 767.
86. *Op. cit.,* p. xxiv.
87. *Prometheus Bound,* 1. 252, Trans, H. Weir Smyth, Loeb No. 145.
88. 1. 479f, Trans. E. P. Coleridge, Random, vol. I, p. 931.
89. 1. 479, Trans. A. S. Way Loeb No. 11, p. 537.
90. Bk. I, 1. 32f, Trans. E. V. Rieu, p. 2.
91. Bk. I, 1. 34, Trans. Richmond Lattimore, p. 28.
92. Bk. IX, 1. 597, Trans. E. V. Rieu, p. 161.
93. Bk. VII, 50, Trans. A. D Godley, Loeb No 119, p. 365.
94. Bk. VIII, 124, Trans. A. D. Godley, Loeb No. 120, p. 127.
95. Godley, A. D. *Herodotus,* "General Introduction", p. vii, Loeb No. 117.
96. 1. 380, Trans. E. P. Coleridge, Random Vol. I, p. 774.
97. 1. 381, Trans. A. S. Way, Loeb, No. 12, p. 195.
98. 1. 925f, Trans. E. P. Coleridge, Random, Vol. I, p. 787.
99. *Ibid.,* v. 1110f, p. 791.
00. Trans. Anonymous, Random, Vol. II, p. 762.
01. 6;26,27. NEB.
02. 6;27.RSV.
03. *Jeremiah,* 7;6. (RSV)
04. E. V. Rieu, *The Iliad,* "Introduction", p. xx.
05. VII, 184, Loeb, No. 119, p. 501.
06. *Ibid.,* 186, p. 503.
07. Bk. VIII, 24 Loeb No. 120, p. 25.
08. Bk. IX, 70, No. 120, p. 243.
09. *Ibid.,* 13, p. 171.
10. Bk. VII, 213, No. 119, p. 529-531.

111. Bk. VIII, 32, No. 120, p. 33.
112. *Ibid.*, 73, p. 71.
113. Bk. I, 87, No. 117, p. 113.
114. *Ibid.*, 166, p. 209.
115. 1. 718, Trans. H. Weir Smyth, Loeb No. 145, p. 169.
116. *Ibid.*, 1. 420-432, p. 145.
117. *Suppliant Maidens* 1. 470, Loeb No. 145, p. 53.
118. *Ibid.*, 1.475, p. 53.
119. *Ibid.*, 1. 439, p. 47.
120. *Ajax*, 1. 964, Trans. F. Storr, Loeb No. 21, p. 81.
121. *The Complete Greek Drama*, ed. by W. J. Oates and Eugene O'Nei
     Jr., Vol. I, p. 958, Random House, N.Y. 1938.
122. 1. 27, Trans. Gilbert Murray, Random, Vol. I, p. 960.
123. *Ibid.*, 1. 470, p. 977.
124. Euripides, *The Suppliants*, 1. 488f, Trans. E. P. Coleridge, Random
     Vol. I, p. 931-2.
125. *Peace*, 1. 60, Trans. Anonymous, Random, Vol. II, p. 673.
126. Bk. VII, 215, Trans. E. V. Rieu, p. 96.
127. Bk. XXII, 416, p. 323.
128. *Opt. cit.*, p. 332.
129. 1. 748, Trans. H. Weir Smyth, Loeb No. 145, p. 173.
130. 1. 489f, Trans. F. Storr, Loeb No. 21, p. 297.
131. *Hecuba*, 1. 864f, Trans. E. P. Coleridge, Random, Vol. I, p. 827.
132. 11:17, RSV.
133. *The World as Will*, Bk. 11, 27 in *The World as Will and Idea*, Vol. I
     p. 192, Routledge and Kegan Paul, London, 1948 (Ninth Impression)

Chapter II

1. *The Trojan Women*, 1. 470f, Trans. Gilbert Murray, Random, Vol. I
   p. 977.
2. *Ibid.*, 1.633, p. 984.
3. *The Daughters of Troy*, 1. 633, Trans. A. S. Way, Loeb, No. 9, p. 407.
4. *Iphigenia in Tauris*, 1. 475, Trans. Robert Potter, Random, Vol. I, p
   1073.
5. *Ibid.*, 1. 412f, p. 1072.
6. 1. 1510, Trans. Robert Potter, Random, Vol. I, p. 1181.
7. 1. 107, Trans. E. P. Coleridge, Random, Vol. I, p. 1019.
8. *The Suppliant Maidens*, 1. 150f, Trans. H. Weir Smyth, Loeb No. 145,
   p. 15.
9. *Ibid.*, 1. 666, p. 69.
10. 1. 211, p. 21.
11. 1. 925, Trans. H. Weir Smyth and H. Lloyd-Jones, Loeb No. 146, p. 77.
12. 1. 760f., p. 65.
13 1. 755f, p. 65.
14. 1. 68f, Loeb. 146, p. 165.
15. 1. 60f, *ibid.*, p. 163.
16. 1. 70f, *ibid.*, p. 165.

17. 1. 1622, Trans. Robert Potter, Random, Vol. I, p. 1185.
18. I. 1.134 9f, Trans. E. P. Coleridge, Random, Vol. II, p. 105.
19. 1. 665, Trans. Gilbert Murray, Random, Vol. II, p. 375.
20. 1. 1622, Trans. Robert Potter, Random, Vol. I, p. 1185.
21. *The Analects of Confucius*, VIII; xix, p. 77, Trans. W. E. Soothill, Oxford University Press, 1937.
22. *Ibid.*, VII, xxii, p. 65.
23. *Ibid.*, IV, viii, p. 30.
24. 1. 608, Trans. F. Storr, Loeb No. 20, p. 363.
25. *Orestes*, 1. 668, Trans. E. P. Coleridge, Random, II, p. 130.
26. 1. 84f, Trans. E. P. Coleridge, Random, Vol. II, p. 172.
27. 1. 356, Trans. E. P. Coleridge, Random, Vol. II, p. 406.
28. 1. 356, Trans. A. S. Way, Loeb No. 10, p. 555.
29. *The Trojan Women*, 1. 407f, Trans. Gilbert Murray, Random, Vol. 1, p. 977.

*hapter III

1. *Op. cit.*, p. 7.
2. *Ibid.*, p. 3.
3. Bk. XIV, 235, Trans. E. V. Rieu, p. 203.
4. Bk. XVI, 129, ibid., p. 231.
5. Bk. III, 1. 28, Trans. Richmond Lattimore, p. 52.
6. Bk. XVI, 1. 208, *ibid.*, p. 245.
7. Bk. XVI, 1. 211, Trans. E. V. Rieu, p. 234.
8. *Ibid.*, Trans. Richmond Lattimore, p. 245.
9. Bk. VI, 1. 189, Trans. E. V. Rieu, p. 85.
10. *Ibid.*, Trans. R. Lattimore, p. 107.
11. Bk. VII, 1. 165. Trans. E. V. Rieu, p. 94.
12. Bk. XVIII, 1. 328, *ibid.*, p. 340.
13. *Herodotus*, vol. I, p. xvi, Loeb Classical Library, Harvard, 1966.
14. *Ibid.*, Bk. II, 120, p. 413.
15. *Ibid.*, Bk. IX, 65, p. 237.
16. *Aeschylus*, Loeb No. 145, xxvii.
17. 1. 595f, *ibid.*, p. 63.
18. *Ibid.*, footnote 1, p. 63.
19. 1. 808, *ibid.*, p. 81.
20. 1. 305, Trans. H. Weir Smyth, Loeb No. 145, p. 243.
21. 1. 280f, Trans. F. Storr, Loeb No. 20, p. 27.
22. *Aeschylus*, p. xxviii, Loeb No. 145.
23. 1. 690f, Trans. F. Storr, Loeb No. 21, p. 179.
24. *Op. cit.*, p. xxi.
25. 1. 32, Trans. F. M. Stawell, Random, Vol. II, p. 290.
26. 1. 884f, Trans. Gilbert Murray, Random, Vol. I, p. 992.
27. 1. 887f.
28. 1. 340f, Trans. E. P. Coleridge, Random, Vol. II, p. 120.
29. Smyth, H. Weir and H. Lloyd-Jones, Loeb No. 146, footnote 1, p. 45.
30. *Odyssey*, Bk. XVI, 195, Trans. E. V. Rieu, p. 233.
31. *Ibid.*, Trans. R. Lattimore, p. 245.

32. Bk. IX, 100, Loeb No. 120, p. 277.
33. *The Seven Against Thebes*, 1. 625, Trans. H. Weir Smyth, Loeb No 145, p. 373.
34. *The Persians*, 1. 573, Trans. H. Weir Smyth, Loeb No. 145, p. 157.
35. *Ibid.*, 1. 601f, p. 159.
36. *Trachiniae*, 1. 104, Trans. F. Storr, Loeb No. 21, p. 267.
37. *Electra*, 1. 1269, ibid., p. 229.
38. *Andromache*, 1. 680, Trans. E. P. Coleridge, Random, Vol. I, p. 863.
39. 1. 580, Trans. E. P. Coleridge, Random, Vol. II, p. 128.
40. *Medea*, 1. 362f, Trans. E. P. Coleridge, Random, Vol. I, p. 731.
41. *Ibid.*, Trans. A. S. Way, Loeb No. 12, p. 313.
42. 1. 920, Trans. E. P. Coleridge, Random, Vol. 1, p. 1038. p.
43. *Ibid.*, Trans. A. S. Way, Loeb No. 11 (*The Madness of Hercules*) p. 203.
44. 1. 865, Trans. E. P. Coleridge, Random, Vol. I, p. 786.
45. *Ibid.*, Trans. A. S. Way, Loeb No. 12, p. 231.
46. *Ibid.*, Trans. David Greene, *The Complete Greek Tragedies*, Vol. III p. 199.
47. 1. 1203, Trans. E. P. Coleridge, Random, Vol. I, p. 876.
48. *Ibid.*, Trans. A. S. Way, Loeb No. 10, p. 507.
49. *Odyssey*, VII, 196, Trans. E. V. Rieu, p. 95.
50. *Iliad*, VI, 487, Trans. R. Lattimore, p. 166.
51. *Ibid.*, V, 629, Trans. E. V. Rieu, p. 91.
52. *Ibid.*, Trans. R. Lattimore, p. 145.
53. Bk. VI, 103, Loeb No. 119, p. 255.
55. *Antigone*, 1. 960f, Trans. F. Storr, Loeb. No. 20, p. 387.
56. *Oedipus at Colonus*, 1. 1720, Trans. F. Storr, No. 20, p. 299. and *Philoctetes*, 1. 331, Trans. F. Storr, Loeb. 21, p. 393.
57. *Philoctetes*, 1. 200, Trans. F. Storr, Loeb No. 21, p. 383.
58. 1. 1340, Trans. F. Storr, Loeb. 20, p. 417.
59. 1. 1338.
60. 1. 919, Trans. William Arrowsmith, Vol. III, *The Complete Greek Tragedies*, ed. Grene and Lattimore, Vol. III, p. 316.
61. *The Madness of Hercules*, 1. 919, Trans. A. S. Way, Loeb No. 11, p. 203.
62. *Heracles*, 1. 310 and 1. 282, Trans. E. P. Coleridge, Random, Vo. I, p. 1022-1023.
63 . *Ibid.*, 1. 282, Trans. William Arrowsmith, *op. cit.*, p. 292.
64. *The Heracleidae*, 1. 1350, Trans. E. P. Coleridge, Random, Vol. I, p. 1050.
65. *The Madness of Hercules*, 1. 1350, Trans. A. S. Way, Loeb No. 11, p. 239.
66. 1. 1255, Trans. E. P. Coleridge, Random, Vo. I, p. 794.
67. *Ibid.*, Trans. A. S. Way, Loeb No. 12, p. 259.
68. *Hecuba*, 1. 1293, Trans. A. S. Way, Loeb No. 9, p. 349.
69. 1. 976f. Trans. E. P. Coleridge, Random, Vol. II, p. 142.
70. *Iliad*, XVI, 441, Trans. R. Lattimore, p. 342.
71. XVIII, 1. 119, Trans. E. V. Rieu, p. 334.

72. Bk. XX, 1. 75, Trans. E. V. Rieu, p. 290.
73. *Ibid.*, Trans. R. Lattimore, p. 300.
74. *Hesiod*, Trans. H. G. Evelyn-White, Loeb No. 57, p. 21, Harvard, 1977.
75. 1. 519, Trans. H. Weir Smyth, Loeb No. 145, p. 261.
76. 1. 694, *ibid.*, p. 277.
77. 1. 694, Trans. David Grene, *op. cit.*, Vol. I, p. 336.
78. 1. 1045f, Trans. H. Weir Smyth, Loeb No. 145, p. 103.
79. 1. 295f, Trans. H. Weir Smyth and H. Lloyd-Jones, Loeb No. 146, p. 301.
80. 1. 1486, Trans. Robert Potter, Random, Vol. I, p. 1114.
81. *Ibid.*, Trans. A. S. Way, Loeb No. 10, p. 409.
82. 1. 407, Trans. E. P. Coleridge, Random, Vol. II, p. 180.
83. 1. 408, Trans. A. S. Way, Loeb No. 11, p. 377.
84. *Andromache*, 1. 1268, Trans. E. P. Coleridge, Random, Vol. I, p. 877.
85. *Ibid.*, Trans. A. S. Way, Loeb No. 10, p. 511.
86. 1. 1298, Trans. E. P. Coleridge, Random, Vol. II, p. 104.
87. 1. 391, Trans. H. Weir Smyth, Loeb No. 145, p. 251.
88. 1. 595f, *ibid.*, p. 63.
89. 1. 667, *ibid.*, p. 69.
90. 1. 1485, Trans. H. Weir Smyth and H. Lloyd-Jones, Loeb No. 146, p. 133.
91. 1. 175, *ibid.*, p. 19.
92. *Ajax*, 1.970, Trans. F. Storr, Loeb. 21, p. 81.
93. *Philoctetes*, 1.335f, ibid., p. 393.
94. 1. 175, *ibid.*, p. 139.
95. *Op. cit.*, p. 23.
96. *Antigone*, 1. 164, Trans. F. Storr, Loeb No. 20, p. 327.
97. 1. 615, Trans. E. P. Coleridge, Random, Vol. I, p. 935.
98. 1. 1160f, Trans. A. S. Way, Loeb No. 12, p. 507.
99. *Ibid.*, Trans. Richard Aldington, Random, Vol. I, p. 716.
100. 1. 611, Trans. E. P. Coleridge, Random, Vol. I, p. 935.
101. *Electra*, 1. 890, Trans. E. P. Coleridge, Vol. II, p. 93.
102. *Ibid.*, Trans. A. S. Way, Loeb No. 10, p. 81.
103. 1. 711, Trans. E. P. Coleridge, Random, Vol. II, p. 29.
104. *Ibid.*, Trans. A. S. Way, Loeb No. 9, p. 529.
105. *The Daughters of Troy*, 1, 888, *ibid.*, p. 427.
106. *Iphigenia in Tauris*, 1. 478, Trans. Robert Potter, Random, Vol. I, p. 1073.
107. *Iphigenia in Aulis*, 1. 537, Trans. F. M. Stawell, Random, Vol. II, p. 301.
108. *Heracleidae*, 1. 718, Trans. E. P. Coleridge, Random, Vol. I, p. 904.
109. *Ibid.*, 719.
110. *The Children of Hercules*, 719, Trans. A. S. Way, Loeb No. 11, p. 311.
111. 1. 380, Trans. E. P. Coleridge, Random, Vol. II, p. 179.
112. 1. 382, Trans. A. S. Way, Loeb No. 11, p. 373.
113. 1. 583f, Trans. E. P. Coleridge, Random, Vol. I, p. 820.
114. 1. 1240f, Trans. Gilbert Murray, Random, VI. I, p. 1005.

115. Bk. I, Trans. E. V. Rieu, p. 15.
116. *Op. cit.*, p. 21.
117. *Ibid.*, p. 27.
118. 1. 138, Trans. H. Weir Smyth, Loeb No. 145, p. 15.
119. *Prometheus Bound*, 1. 314-315, Trans. H. Weir Smyth, Loeb No. 145, p. 243-245.
120. 1. 499f, Trans. F. Storr, Loeb No. 20, p. 47.
121. *Hyppolytus*, 1. 885, Trans. E. P. Coleridge, Random, Vol. I, p. 787.
122. *Ibid.*, 1. 1365, p. 797.
123. *Heracles*, 1. 1125, Trans. E. P. Coleridge, Random, Vol. I, p. 1043.
124. *Hecuba*, 1.1.488f, Trans. E. P. Coleridge, Random, Vol. I, p. 818.

Chapter IV

1. Bk. III, 1. 56, Trans. E. V. Rieu, p. 45.
2. Bk. VI, 1. 70, *ibid.*, p 102.
3. Bk. VI, 1. 59, *ibid.*, p. 101.
4. *Ibid.*, Trans. R. Lattimore, p. 154.
5. Storr, F. *Sophocles*, p. 161, footnote 1, Loeb No. 21.
6. Bk. IX, 5, Loeb No. 120, p. 163.
7. 1. 612, Trans. F. Storr, Loeb No. 20, p. 207.
8. 1. 1285, Loeb, No. 21, p. 475.
9. 1090-1165, Trans. E. E. Coleridge, Random, Vol. I, p. 874-5.
10. 1. 1130f, Trans. Anonymous, Random, Vol. II, p. 854.
11. *Op. cit.*, p. 3.
12. *Ibid.*, p. 4.
13. *Ibid.*, p. 39.
14. *Ibid.*, p. 5.
15. *Ibid.*, p. 9.
16. *Ibid.*, p. 9.
17. *Ibid.*, p. 5.
18. *Odssey*, Bk. VI, 1. 229, Trans. E. V. Rieu, p. 86.
19. *Ibid.*, Bk. VIII, 1. 21, p. 100.
20. *Ibid.*, 1. 22, Trans. R. Lattimore, p. 121.
21. *Ibid.*, Bk. XVII, 1. 63, Trans. E. V. Rieu, p. 243.
22. *Ibid.*, Bk. XIII, 1. 322, Trans. E. V. Rieu, p. 193.
23. *Ibid.*, 1. 302, p. 192.
24. *Ibid.*, Trans. R. Lattimore, p. 206.
25. *Iliad*, Bk. XVII, 1. 176f, Trans. E. V. Rieu, p. 314.
26. *Ibid.*, Trans. R. Lattimore, p. 359.
27. *Ibid.*, Bk. XIX, 1. 86f, Trans. E. V. Rieu, p. 351.
28. *Ibid.*, 1.90, Trans. R. Lattimore, p. 394.
29. *Ibid.*, 1. 86, *ibid.*, p. 394.
30. *Ibid.*, Bk. XVIII, 1. 311, Trans. E. V. Rieu, p. 339.
31. *Ibid.*, Trans. R Lattimore, p. 383.
32. *Ibid.*, Bk. XVI, 1. 688, Trans. E. V. Rieu, p. 303.
33. *Ibid.*, Bk. XVII, 1. 118, Trans. E. V. Rieu, p. 312.
34. 1. 175, Trans. H Weir Smyth and H. Lloyd-Jones, Loeb No. 146, p. 19.

35. 1. 903, Trans. E. Weir Smyth, Loeb No. 145, p. 187.
36. 1. 1005, *ibid.*, p. 195.
37. 1. 608, Trans. E. P. Coleridge, Random, Vol. I, p. 899.
38. 1. 1415, Trans. E. P. Coleridge, *ibid*, p. 798.
39. *Ibid.*, Trans. A. S. Way, Loeb No. 12, p. 273.
40. 1. 975f, Trans. E. P. Coleridge, Random, Vol. I, p. 830.
41. Bk. III, 1. 308, Trans. E. V. Rieu, p. 52.
42. *Op. cit.*, p. 3.
43. *Ibid.*, p. 13.
44. 1. 885, Trans. H. Weir Smyth and H. Lloyd-Jones, Loeb No. 146, p. 73.
45. 1. 1f, Trans. E. P Coleridge, Random, Vol. I, p. 885.
46. 1. 294, Trans. E. P. Coleridge, Random, Vol. II, p. 75.
47. 1. 700, *ibid.*, p. 131.

Chapter V

1. Hesiod, *op. cit.*, p. 9.
2. *Ibid.*, p. 25.
3. *Odyssey*, Bk. I, 37, Trans. E. V. Rieu, p. 2.
4. 1. 223, Trans. H. Weir Smyth and H. Lloyd-Jones, Loeb No. 146, p. 23.
5. 1. 903, Trans. F. Storr, Loeb No. 21, p. 441.
6. 1. 437, Trans. E. P. Coleridge, Random, Vol. I, p. 733.
7. *Prometheus Bound*, 1. 455, Trans. H. Weir Smyth, Loeb No. 145, p. 257.
8. 1. 1076, Trans. Gilbert Murray, Random, Vol. I, p. 999.
9. *Op. cit.*, p. 13.
10. *Ibid.*, p. 17.
11. 1. 236f, Trans. H. Weir Smyth, Loeb No. 45, p. 266f.
12. 1. 167f, Trans. W. Weir Smyth and H. Lloyd-Jones, Loeb No. 146, p. 19.
13. *The Suppliant Maidens*, 1. 655, Trans. H. Weir Smyth, Loeb No. 145, p. 69.
14. 1. 1620, Trans. Robert Potter, Random, Vol. I, p. 1185.
15. *Hippolytus*, 1. 104 Trans. A. S. Way, Loeb 12, p. 171.
16. *Op. cit.*, p. 19.
17. *Peace*, 1. 198f, Trans. Anonymous, Random Vol. II, p. 677-8.
18. *Ibid.*, 1. 220, p. 678.
19. 1. 530, Trans. H. Weir Smyth and H. Lloyd-Jones, Loeb 146, p. 321.
20. 1. 550f, Trans. R. Lattimore, *op. cit.*, vol. I, p. 154.

Chapter VI

1. *Prometheus Bound*, 1. 1070f, Trans. H. Weir Smyth, Loeb 145, p. 145, p. 313.
2. *Philoctetes*, 1. 640, Trans. F. Storr, Loeb No. 21, p. 417.
3. *Philosophy of History*, p. 73, Trans. J. Sibree, P. F. Collier and Son, N.Y., 1900.
4. *Odyssey*, Bk. XXIII, 1. 67, Trans. E. V. Rieu, p. 328.
5. *Ibid.*, Trans. R. Lattimore, p. 337.
6. 1. 830, Trans. H. Weir Smyth, Loeb No. 145, p. 181.

7. Bk. XXIV, 1. 455f, Trans. E. V. Rieu, p. 349.
8. *Op. cit.*, p. 7.
9. *Ibid.*, p. 23.
10. *Ibid.*, p. 17.
11. *Ibid.*, p. 17.
12. *Ibid.*, p. 17.
13. *Prometheus Bound*, 1. 1076, Trans. H. Weir Smyth, Loeb No. 145, p. 313.
14. 1. 109, Trans. H. Weir Smyth, Loeb, No. 145, p. 13.
15. 1. 111, *ibid.*, p. 119.
16. *Ibid.*, 1. 716f, p. 169.
17. 1. 470, Trans. E. P. Coleridge, Random, Vol. II, p. 182.
18. 1. 1015, Trans. Elizabeth Wyckoff, *The Complete Greek Tragedies*, Vol. IV, 500.
19. 1. 200, Trans. Frank William Jones, *ibid.*, Vol. IV, p. 146.
20. Bk. VII, 102, Loeb No. 119, p. 405.
21. Bk. II, ch. 1, *op. cit.*, p. 8.
22. *Ibid.*, Bk. I, ch V, p. 2.
23. *Republic VI*, 500 D. Trans. Paul Shorey, Loeb Classical Library, Harvard, 1943, p. 69.
24. *Ibid.*, 500 C.
25. Bk. III, 89, p. 117.
26. *Hippolytus*, 1. 1448f, Trans. David Greene, Vol. III, p. 220-221.
27. *Agamemnon*, 1. 830f, Trans. H. Weir Smyth and H. Lloyd-Jones, Loeb No. 146, p. 69-70.
28. *Ethics*, note under proposition XLII, p. 280, ed. James Gutmann, Hafner Co., 1949.
29. *Op. cit.*, p. 62.
30. *Op. cit.*, p. 280.
31. *Op. cit.*, 496 B. p. 51.

Chapter VII

1. *Odyssey*, Bk. XXIV, 1. 351, Trans. E. V. Rieu, p. 346.
2. *Ibid.*, Bk. XVI, 1. 422, p. 239.
3. *Ibid.*, Trans. R. Lattimore, p. 251.
4. *Iliad*, Bk. I, 1. 59, Trans. E. V. Rieu, p. 3.
5. *Ibid.*, Bk. IV, 1. 235, p 63.
6. *Ibid.*, Bk. XVI, 1. 385, Trans. E. V. Rieu, p. 294.
7. *Ibid.*, Bk. I, 1.277, Trans. E. V. Rieu, p. 9.
8. *Op. cit.*, p. 23.
9. *Ibid.*, p. 25.
10. *Ibid.*, p. 10.
11. *Apology* 41, C-D, Trans. N. H. Fowler, *Plato*, p. 145, Loeb Classical Library, Harvard, 1943.
12. Bk. VIII, 1. 143, Trans. E. V. Rieu, p. 133.
13. Bk. VI, 1. 129, *ibid.*, p 103.
14. *Op. cit.*, p. 19.

15. 1. 60f, Trans. H. Weir Smyth and H. Lloyd-Jones, Loeb No. 146, p. 163-165.
16. 1. 595, Trans. H. Weir Smyth, Loeb No. 145, p. 63.
17. *Ibid.*, 1. 385, p. 43.
18. *Ibid.*, 1. 381, p. 43.
19. *Ibid.*, 1. 77, p. 11.
20. *Ibid.*, 1. 773, p. 79.
21. 1. 77, Trans. F. Storr, Loeb No. 20, p. 321.
22. 1. 1075, Trans. W. Weir Smyth, Loeb No. 145, p. 419.
23. *Antigone*, 1. 456, Trans. F. Storr, Loeb No. 20, p. 349.
24. *Oedipus at Colonus*, 1. 280, Trans. F. Storr, *ibid.*, p. 173.
25. *Hecuba*, 1. 800f, Trans. E. P. Coleridge, Random, Vol. I, p. 826.
26. *Ibid.*, 1. 1030, p. 832.
27. *The Suppliants*, 1. 593, Trans. E. P. Coleridge, Random, Vol. I, p. 934.
28. 1. 104, Trans. A. S. Way, Loeb No. 11, p. 263.
29. 1. 101f, Trans. E. P. Coleridge, Random, Vol. I, p. 888.
30. Bk. VI, 1. 129, Trans. E. V. Rieu, p. 103.
31. *Ibid.*, 1. 130.
32. 1. 1232, Trans. E. P. Coleridge, Random, Vol. I, p. 1047.
33. *Ibid.* Trans. A. S. Way, Loeb No. 11, p. 229.
34. 1. 798, Trans. E. P. Coleridge, Random, Vol. I, p. 826.
35. *Electra*, 1. 740, E. P. Coleridge, Random, Vol. II, p. 89.
36. 1. 400f, Trans. H. Weir Smyth, Loeb, No. 145, p. 253.
37. Bk. I, 29, p. 33.
38. *Op. cit.*, p. 13.
39. *Ibid.*, p. 29.
40. Bk. IX, 7, Loeb 120, p. 163.
41. *Odyssey*, Bk. XIV, 1. 83f, Trans. E. V. Rieu, p. 199.
42. *Ibid.*, Trans. R. Lattimore, p. 212.
43. *Ibid.*, Bk. XVIII, 1. 1414, Trans. E. P. Rieu, p. 263.
44. *Ibid.*, Bk. IV, 1. 351, Trans. E. P. Rieu, p. 52.
45. 1. 548, Trans. H. Weir Smyth, Loeb No. 145, p. 263.
46. 1. 1045f. *ibid.*, p. 103.
47. *Prometheus Bound*, 1. 77, *ibid.*, p. 223.
48. 1. 425, *ibid.*, p. 47.
49. 1. 349, *ibid.*, p. 39
50. 1. 232, *ibid.*, p. 23.
51. *Andromache*, 1. 439, Trans. E. P. Coleridge, Random, vol. I, p. 858.
52. *Ibid.*, Trans. A. S. Way, Loeb No. 10, p. 449.
53. *The Suppliants*, 1. 301f, Trans. E. P. Coleridge, Random, vol. I, p. 928.
54. *Orestes*, 1.990 and 975, Trans. E. P. Coleridge, Random, vol. II, p. 141, 142.
55. 1. 370, Trans. E. P. Coleridge, Random, vol. I, p. 773.
56. *Odyssey*, Bk. XIII, 1. 390, Trans. E. P. Rieu, p. 195.
57. *Ibid.*, Bk. II, 1. 372, *ibid*, p. 25.
58. *Ibid.*, Bk. III, 25, *ibid.*, p. 28.
59. *Ibid.*, 1. 25f, Trans. R. Lattimore, p. 52.
60. *Ibid.*, Bk. XV, 1. 245, Trans. E. P. Rieu, p. 218.

61. *Ibid.*, Trans. R Lattimore, p. 231.
62. *Iliad*, Bk. VI, 1. 183, Trans. E. P. Rieu, p. 105.
63. 1. 403, Trans. H. Weir Smyth, Loeb No. 145, p. 45.
64. *Ibid.*, 1. 381, p. 43.
65. *Ibid.*, 1. 815f, p. 81.
66. 1. 791, Trans. F. Storr, Loeb No. 20, p. 223.
67. *Oedipus the King*, 1. 1528, *ibid.*, p. 139.
68. 1. 1035, Trans. F. Storr, Loeb No. 21, p. 453.
69. *Ibid.*, 1. 315, p. 391.
70. *Ibid.*, 1. 643, p. 417.
71. *Ibid.*, 1. 179, p. 381.
72. *Ibid.*, 1. 447f, p. 403.
73. 1. 993f, *ibid.*, p. 337.
74. 1. 1266f, *ibid.*, p. 359.
75. 1. 158, Trans. E. P. Coleridge, Random, vol. I, 726.
76. *Ibid.*, Trans. A. S. Way, Loeb 12, p. 297.
77. *Ibid.*, 1. 332, p. 311.
78. *Ibid.*, 1. 1415f, p. 397.
79. 1. 501, Trans. A. S. Way, Loeb No. 11, p. 167.
80. *Ibid.*, 1. 1243, *ibid.*, p. 231.
81. *Ibid.*, 1. 857, Trans. E. P. Coleridge, Random, vol. I, p. 1036.
82. *Ibid.*, 1. 667, *ibid.*, p. 1032.
83. 1. 343, Trans. H. Weir Smyth, Loeb No. 145, p. 39.
84. Bk. VII, 104, p. 409.
85. 1. 312, Trans. E. P. Coleridge, Random, vol. I, p. 928.
86. 1. 179, Trans. F. Storr, Loeb No. 21, p. 139.

Chapter VIII

1. *Op. cit.*, p. xxii.
2. 1. 634, Trans. Gilbert Murray, Random, vol. II, p. 374.
3. Bk. XXIII, 1. 210f, Trans. E. V. Rieu, p. 331.
4. Bk. I, 32, p. 37.
5. Bk. VII, 10, p. 319.
6. *Op. cit.*, p. 61.
7. Bk. VIII, 32, p. 33.
8. *Ibid.*, 33, p. 33.
9. *Ibid.*, 37, p. 37.
10. *Ibid.*, 38, p. 37.
11. Bk. I, 105, p. 137.
12. *The Persians*, 1. 810f, Trans. H. Weir, Loeb No. 145, p. 179.
13. 1. 337, Trans. H. Weir Smyth and H. Lloyd-Jones, Loeb 146, p. 33.
14. *Ibid.*, 1. 365f, p. 35.
15. *Ibid.*, 1. 380f, p. 35.
16. 1. 190, Trans. H. Weir Smyth, Loeb. 145, p. 19.
17. *Ibid.*, 1. 225, p. 23.
18. *Ibid.*, 1. 355, p. 39.
19. 1. 15, *ibid.*, p. 323.

20. 1. 1440, Trans. F. Storr, Loeb No. 21, p. 491.
21. 1. 1329, *ibid.*, p. 479.
22. 1. 209, Trans. E. P. Coleridge, Random, vol. I, p. 727.
23. 1. 665, Trans. H. Weir Smyth, Loeb No. 145, p. 69.
24. *Ibid.*, 1. 348, p. 39.
25. *Ibid.*, 1., 385, p. 43.
26. 1. 395, Trans. H. Weir Smyth and H. Lloyd-Jones, Loeb No. 146, p. 37.
27. 1. 238, Trans. E. P. Coleridge, Random, vol. I, p. 891.
28. *Ibid.*, 1. 260, p. 892.
29. *Ibid.*, 1. 790, p. 826.
30. *Ibid.*, 1. 1087, p. 834.
31. *Odyssey*, Bk. XXIII, 1. 67, Trans. E. P. Rieu, p. 327.
32. *Iliad*, Bk. XVII, 1. 99, *ibid.*, p. 312.
33. *Ibid.*, Bk, II, 1. 195f, *ibid.*, p. 24.
34. Bk. VII, 57, p. 373.
35. *Ibid.*, 11, p. 323.
36. Bk. VIII, 69, p. 67.
37. 1. 748f, Trans. H. Weir Smyth, Loeb No. 145, p. 173f.
38. *Ibid.*, 1. 534, p. 155.
39. *Ibid.*, 1. 825f, p. 181.
40. *Ibid.*, 1. 830f, p. 181.
41. *Ibid.*, 1. 1000, p. 195.
42. 1. 370, Trans. H. Weir Smyth and H. Lloyd-Jones, Loeb No. 146, p. 35.
43. *Ibid.*, 1. 465, p. 41.
44. *Ibid.*, 1. 920, p. 77.
45. 1. 500, Trans. H. Weir Smyth, Loeb. 145, p. 363.
46. 1. 760f, Trans. F. Storr, Loeb No. 21, p. 65.
47. *Ibid.*, 1. 925, p. 77.
48. *Ibid.*, 1. 1065, p. 89.
49. *Ibid.*, 1. 1086f, p. 91.
50. *Ibid.*, 1. 130, p. 19.
51. 1. 280. Trans. F. Storr, Loeb No. 21, p. 279.
52. *Ibid.*, 1. 281, p. 279.
53. 1. 1348f, Trans. F. Storr, Loeb No. 20, p. 419.
54. 1. 388, Trans. A. S. Way, Loeb No. 11, p. 285.
55. 1. 910, Trans. E. P. Coleridge, Random, vol. I, p. 908.
56. *The Suppliants*, 1. 125, *ibid.*, p. 923.
57. *Ibid.*, 1. 463, p. 931.
58. *The Phoenissae*, 1. 186, Trans. E. P. Coleridge, Random, vol. II, p. 175.
59. *The Suppliants*, 1. 212, Trans. E. P. Coleridge, Random, vol. I, p. 926-7.
60. *Rhesus*, 1. 482, Trans. Gilbert Murray, Random, vol. II, p. 368.
61. *Hippolytus*, 1. 79f, Trans. E. P. Coleridge, Random, vol. I, p. 764.
62. 1. 910, Trans. E. P. Coleridge, Random, vol. I, p. 908.
63. *Eumenides*, 1. 525, Trans. H. Weir Smyth and H. Lloyd-Jones, Loeb No. 146, p. 321.
64. *Antigone*, 1. 615, Trans. F. Storr, Loeb No. 20, p. 363.
65. *Medea*, 1. 125, Trans. A. S. Way, No. 12, p. 295.
66. Bk. XIII, 1. 636, Trans. E. V. Rieu, p. 240.

67. Bk. VII, 16, p. 329.
68. BK. VIII, 112, p. 115.
69. 1. 195f. Trans. Anonymous, Random, vol. II, p. 1072.
70. 1. 1107f, Trans. E. P. Coleridge, Random, vol. II, p. 41.
71. *Andromache*, 1. 184, Trans. A. S. Way, Loeb No. 10, p. 431.

Chapter IX

1. Fragment 45. Nahm, M. *Selections from Early Greek Philosophy* p. 67, Appleton-Century Crofts, N.Y., 1964.
2. Fragment 2, *ibid.*, p. 68.
3. Fragment 19, *ibid.*, p. 69.
4. Fragment 29, *ibid.*, p. 70.
5. Fragment 30, *ibid.*, p. 70.
6. Fragment 65, *ibid.*, p. 72.
7. Fragment 20, *ibid.*, p. 69.
8. Fragment 2, *ibid.*, p. 68.
9. Fragment 36, *ibid.*, p. 70.
10. Fragment 61. *ibid.*, p. 72.
11. Fragment 57-58, *ibid.*, p. 71.
12. Fragment 118, *ibid.*, p. 75.
13. Fragment 69, *ibid.*, p. 72.
14. Fragment 119, *ibid.*, p. 75.
15. Fragment 35, *ibid.*, p. 70.
16. 1. 342, Trans. Gilbert Murray, Random, vol. II, p. 364.
17. *Odyssey*, Bk. XIV, 1. 283, Trans. E. V. Rieu, p. 205.
18. *Ibid.*, Trans. R. Lattimore, p. 217.
19. *Iliad*, Bk. V, 1. 407, Trans. E. V. Rieu, p. 84.
20. *Ibid.*, Bk. 1, 1. 42, Trans. E. V. Rieu, p. 2.
21. *Op. cit.*, p. 27.
22. *The Libation-Bearers*, 1. 50f, Trans. H. Weir Smyth and H. Lloyd Jones, Loeb No. 146, p. 163.
23. 1. 1075, Trans. F. Storr, Loeb No. 20, p. 397.
24. *Ibid.*, 1. 1105, p. 399.
25. 1. 339, Trans. E. P. Coleridge, Random, vol. I, p. 1033.
26. *Ibid.*, 1. 885, Trans. A. S. Way, Loeb No. 11, p. 199.
27. *Ibid.*, Trans. E. P. Coleridge, Random, vol. I, p. 1037.
28. 1. 1028, Trans. E. P. Coleridge, Random, vol. I, p. 832.
29. *Odyssey*, Bk. XVI, 1. 403, Trans. R. Lattimore, p. 250.
30. *Ibid.*, Bk. XXII, 1. 38, Trans. E. V. Rieu, p. 313.
31. Bk. XVI, 1. 385, Trans. R. Latimore, p. 340.
32. Bk. XXII, 1. 358, Trans. E. V. Rieu, p. 404.
33. Bk. I, 87, p. 113.
34. Godley, A. D. *Herodotus*, vol. 1, p. xvi.
35. Bk. IX, 65, p. 237.
36. *Ibid.*, 42, p. 211.
37. 1. 105, Trans. H. Weir Smyth, Loeb No. 145, p. 117.
38. 1. 250f., *ibid.*, p. 131.

39. 1. 290f, *ibid.*, p. 135.
40. 1. 640f., Trans. H. Weir Smyth, Loeb. No. 145, p. 67.
41. 1. 732, *ibid.*, p. 73.
42. 1. 480, *ibid.*, p. 53.
43. 1. 280f Trans. F. Storr, Loeb No. 20, p. 173.
44. *Antigone*, 1. 1105, *ibid.*, p. 399.
45. 1. 590, Trans. F. Storr, Loeb No. 21, p. 53.
46. Bk. XIV, 1. 85, Trans. E. V. Rieu, p. 199.
47. *Ibid.*, 1. 305, p. 205.
48. Bk. XVI, 1. 447, Trans. E. V. Rieu, p. 240.
49. Bk. IV, 1. 160, Trans. E. V. Rieu, p. 61.
50. *Op. cit.*, p. 19.
51. 1. 719, Trans. H. Weir Smyth, Loeb No. 145, p. 383.
52. *The Suppliant Maidens*, 1. 232, *ibid.*, p. 23.
53. 1. 415, *ibid.*, p. 45.
54. *Electra*. 1. 328, Trans. E. P. Coleridge, Random, vol. II, p. 76.
55. 1. 492, Trans. E P. Coleridge, Random, vol. I, p. 859.
56. 1. 728, Trans. E. P. Coleridge, Random, vol. I, p. 1033.
57. *Ibid.*, 1. 339, p. 1034.
58. *Ibid.*, 1. 841, p. 1035.
59. *Iliad*, "introduction", p. xii.
60. Bk. IV, 1. 160, Trans. R. Lattimore, p. 117.
61. 1. 740f, Trans. H. Weir Smyth, Loeb No. 145, p. 385.
62. 1. 964f, Trans. F. Storr, Loeb No. 20, p. 241.
63. 1. 1565f. *ibid.*, p. 289.
64. 1. 1663, *ibid.*, p. 295.
65. 1. 425, Trans. A. S. Way, Loeb No. 12, p. 197.
66. 1. 1261, Trans. E. P. Coleridge, Random, vol. I, 1049.
67. *Ibid.*, Trans. A. S. Way, Loeb No. 11, p. 233.
68. *Soul on Ice*, p. 17, Dell Publishing Co., N.Y.
69. Rieu, E. V., *Iliad*, "Introduction", p. xxiv.
70. Bk. VI, 1. 352, Trans. E. V. Rieu, p. 110.
71. *Hippolytus*, 1. 428, Trans. E. P. Coleridge, Random, vol. I, p. 774.
72. 1. 70, Trans. H. Weir Smyth and H. Lloyd-Jones, Loeb No. 146, p. 165.
73. Bk. III, 1350, Trans. E. V. Rieu, p. 36
74. Bk. IX, 1. 510, Trans. E. V. Rieu, p. 159.
75. 1. 1560, Trans. H. Weir Smyth and H. Lloyd-Jones. Loeb No. 146, p. 139.
76. *Agamemnon*, 1. 1525, *ibid.*, p. 135.
77. *Heracles*, 1. 756, Trans. E. P. Coleridge, Random, Vol. I, p. 1034.
78. *Ibid.*, Trans. A. S. Way, Loeb No. 11, p. 189.
79. 1. 1030, Trans. E. P. Coleridge, Random, vol. I, p. 832.
80. 1. 1495, Trans. F. Storr, Loeb No. 21, p. 251.
81. 1. 496, Trans. E. P. Coleridge, Random, vol. I, p. 932.